BLACK OPS, VIETNAM

BLACK OPS, VIETNAM

The Operational History of
MACVSOG

ROBERT M. GILLESPIE

Naval Institute Press
Annapolis, Maryland

Naval Institute Press
291 Wood Road
Annapolis, MD 21402

Library of Congress Cataloging-in-Publication Data
Gillespie, Robert M.
  Black ops, Vietnam : the operational history of MACVSOG / Robert M. Gillespie.
    p. cm.
  Includes bibliographical references and index.
  ISBN 978-1-59114-321-5 (hbk. : alk. paper) — ISBN 978-1-61251-064-4 (ebook)
  1. Vietnam War, 1961–1975—Regimental histories—United States. 2. United
States. Military Assistance Command. Vietnam Studies and Observations Group—
History. 3. Vietnam War, 1961–1975—Military intelligence—United States. I. Title.
II. Title: Operational history of MACVSOG.
  DS558.4.G57 2011
  959.704'38—dc23

                                                        2011018600

⊗ This paper meets the requirements of ANSI/NISO z39.48-1992
(Permanence of Paper).
Printed in the United States of America.

19 18 17 16 15 14 13 12 11 ·   9 8 7 6 5 4 3 2 1
First printing

All photos reproduced with the permission of Steve Sherman.

Contents

Abbreviations

ABCCC	Airborne Battlefield Command and Control Center
AE	Advisory Element
AHC	Assault Helicopter Company
AHEC	Armed Helicopter Escort Company
AIZ	Air Interdiction Zone
ARA	Aerial Rocket Artillery
ARVN	Army of the Republic of Vietnam
BA	Base Area
BDA	Bomb Damage Assessment
C&C	Command and Control
CAT	Civil Air Transport
CBU	cluster bomb unit
CCC	Command and Control Central
CCN	Command and Control North
CCS	Command and Control South
CIA	Central Intelligence Agency
CIDG	Civilian Irregular Defense Group
CINCPAC	Commander in Chief, Pacific
CISO	Counterinsurgency Support Office
CNO	Chief of Naval Operations
COMSEC	Communication Security
COMUSMACTHAI	Commander, United States Military Assistance Command, Thailand
COMUSMACV	Commander, United States Military Assistance Command, Vietnam
COSVN	Central Office for South Vietnam
CRF	Coastal Recovery Force

CRP	Combat Recon Platoon
CSG	Combined Studies Group
CSS	Coastal Security Service (So Phong Ve Duyen Hai)
DIA	Defense Intelligence Agency
DMZ	Demilitarized Zone
DOD	Department of Defense
DZ	drop zone
E&E	Escape and Evasion
ECM	electronic countermeasures
EEI	essential elements of information
ELINT	electronic intelligence
EWOTS	Early Warning Observation Teams
FAC	Forward Air Control
FANK	Forces Armees Nationales Khmeres (Cambodian National Army)
FLIR	forward looking infrared radar
FOB	Forward Operating Base
FWMF	Free World Military Forces
GCMA	Groupment de Commandos Mixtes Aeroportes (Composite Airborne Commando Group)
HALO	high-altitude, low-opening (parachute team)
ICC	International Control Commission
IDHS	Intelligence Data Handling System
ISSA	Interservice Support Agreement
JACK	Joint Advisory Commission, Korea
JCRC	Joint Casualty Resolution Center
JCS	Joint Chiefs of Staff
JPRC	Joint Personnel Recovery Center
JSCM	Joint Chiefs of Staff Memorandum
JTD	Joint Table of Distribution
JUSPAO	Joint U.S. Public Affairs Organization
JUWTF	Joint Unconventional Warfare Task Force
KKK	Khmer Kampuchea Krom
LLDB	Luc Luong Duc Biet (Vietnamese Special Forces)
LOC	lines of communication
LSAD	Liaison Service Advisory Detachment
LZ	landing zone
MAAG	Military Assistance Advisory Group
MACSOG, MACVSOG, or SOG	Military Assistance Command, Vietnam, Studies and Observations Group
MACV	Military Assistance Command, Vietnam

MAF	Marine Amphibious Force
MAROPS	maritime operations
MLT	Mobile Launch Team
MR	Military Region
MST	Mobile Support Team
NAD	Naval Advisory Detachment
NCO	noncommissioned officer
NLF	National Front for the Liberation of South Vietnam
NOFORN	No Foreign Dissemination
NSA	National Security Agency
NSAM	National Security Action Memorandum
OJCS	Office of Joint Chiefs of Staff
OPLAN	Operations Plan
OSS	Office of Strategic Services
PARU	Police Aerial Reinforcement Unit
PAVN	People's Army of Vietnam
PCF	Patrol Craft, Fast
PLA	People's Liberation Army (China)
POL	petroleum, oil, and lubricants
PRC	People's Republic of China
PRU	Provincial Reconnaissance Unit
PTF	Patrol Type, Fast
PSYOPS	Psychological Operations
R&D	Research and Development
RON	Remain Over Night
RPG	rocket-propelled grenade
RT	Recon Team
RTAFB	Royal Thai Air Force Base
SAAT	Safe Area Activation Team
SAC	Strategic Air Command
SACSA	Special Assistant for Counterinsurgency and Special Activities
SAM	surface-to-air missile
SAR	search and rescue
SCU	Special Commando Unit
SEACORD	Southeast Asia Coordinating Committee
SEATO	Southeast Asia Treaty Organization
SES	Strategic Exploitation Service (So Khai Thac Dia Hinh)
SFG	Special Forces Group
SIT	Strategic Intelligence Team

SLAM	search, locate, annihilate, monitor
SMAG	Special Mission Advisory Group
SMF	Special Mission Force
SMM	Saigon Military Mission
SMS	Special Mission Service
SMSAD	Special Mission Service Advisory Detachment
SOCOM	Special Operations Command
SOD	Special Operations Detachment
SOG	Studies and Observations Operations Group
SOS	Special Operations Squadron
SOW	Special Operations Wing
SPAF	Sneaky Pete Air Force
SSB	single side band (radio circuit)
SSPL	Sacred Sword of the Patriot League
ST	Spike Team
STD	Strategic Technical Directorate
STDAT	Strategic Technical Directorate Assistance Team
STRATA	Short Term Roadwatch and Target Acquisition
STS	Strategic Technical Service (So Ky Thuat)
SUPPFAC	Support Facility
SVN	South Vietnam
TACC	Tactical Air Control Center
TASS	Tactical Air Support Squadron
TCAE	Training Center Advisory Element
TDY	temporary duty
TES	Special Topographical Exploitation Service (So Khai Thac Dia Hinh)
TFAE	Task Force Advisory Element
TRADOC	Training and Doctrine Command
USARV	U.S. Army, Vietnam
USIA	United States Information Agency
UW	unconventional warfare
VIAT	Vietnamese Air Transport
VNAF	Vietnamese Air Force
VOF	Voice of Freedom
VSSPL	Voice of the Sacred Sword of the Patriot League

Reproduced by permission from Douglas Pike, John Plados, et al., *War in the Shadows* (Boston: Boston Publishing, 1988), 89.

Antecedents

Throughout the First Indochina War (1946–54), the United States provided arms, equipment, and economic aid to aid the French—first in their effort to maintain their Southeast Asian colony and then to stem the perceived spread of communism south from the new People's Republic of China (PRC). The French were ultimately stymied in their effort by the highly aggressive, determined, and popular Viet Minh. After the debacle at Dien Bien Phu, wearied by their exertions and facing political chaos at home, France granted independence to the kingdoms of Laos and Cambodia. Ho Chi Minh had already proclaimed the independence of the Democratic Republic of Vietnam (North Vietnam) while the fate of the southern half of the former colony was to be determined by international arbitration at Geneva, Switzerland.

As the United States began to replace France as the dominant Western power in Southeast Asia, the deliberations at the Geneva conference were looked upon with dismay by the American government. The United States viewed any concession to the northern communists as a blow to both democracy in Asia and to American prestige, especially in the wake of the disastrous "fall of China" to Mao Zedong's People's Liberation Army in 1949. The provisions of any agreement that would settle the fate of Vietnam were, therefore, caught in the tangled web of postwar tensions between the United States, the Soviet Union, and the PRC.

The Cold War was at its height and Vietnam was becoming one of the key storm centers of the new global rivalry. The United States was determined to prevent the fall of the new South Vietnamese government to the communists, and the center of the American effort in the mid-1950s was the Saigon Military Mission (SMM) headed by Col. Edward M. Lansdale.

The Lansdale Era

Lansdale, a U.S. Air Force officer on loan to the Central Intelligence Agency (CIA), was well known in anticommunist circles as the man who had assisted Defense Minister Ramon Magsaysay in saving the government of the Philippines during the communist Hukbalahap uprising (and in getting Magsaysay elected president). He became America's man on the scene in Asia and was dispatched to Vietnam to see what could be done to reverse what seemed to be a disaster in the making. A small outfit, the SMM was limited to a very specific mission—prevent the fall of South Vietnam and prepare stay-behind teams who would continue to harass the North.

Arriving in Vietnam on 1 June 1954 (one month before the signing of the Geneva Accords that were to temporarily divide the country), the SMM worked under severe manpower restrictions imposed by the agreement. The team began an extensive program of clandestine political and psychological warfare in southern Vietnam and psychological and paramilitary sabotage efforts in the North. The SMM utilized every means at its disposal to subvert the communists and upset their plans for a future reunification of Vietnam.

In North Vietnam, Lansdale's subordinate, Maj. Lucien Conein, carried out sabotage, paramilitary operations, and agent placement. The organization's efforts were amply assisted by the three-hundred-day regroupment period specified under the terms of the Geneva agreement. Before the French withdrawal from Hanoi, Conein located, trained, equipped, and infiltrated stay-behind teams of Vietnamese agents. Supported by the CIA proprietary airline Civil Air Transport (CAT) and by the U.S. Navy's Task Force 98, Conein was able to smuggle large amounts of weapons, ammunition, explosives, and communications equipment into North Vietnam before the northern SMM team departed on 9 October 1954. Prophetically, the operational lifetime of the agents proved short, due in large part to security leaks that led to the round-up of many agents by the North Vietnamese.

Lansdale and Conein struck pay dirt, however, by helping to spark a mass exodus of refugees from the North. The French had guaranteed transportation to any who wished to go south, expecting that perhaps 400,000 landlords and businessmen would prefer to make the move. They were soon overwhelmed, however, by the nearly 1 million people that moved toward Haiphong and other ports for transport. Food and shelter were at a premium and a humanitarian crisis seemed imminent. Great Britain, Nationalist China (Taiwan), and the United States sent in ships and supplies to alleviate the situation.

The refugees were mainly Catholics who had been spurred into their exodus by their militant anticommunism and their former collaboration with the French (it is estimated that 60 percent of North Vietnam's Catholics left the country). With the French permanently bailing out, bishops, priests, and leaders of congregations exhorted their followers to leave their homeland. Also driving them on was the none-too-subtle propaganda effort of the SMM and the United States Information Agency (USIA). This effort was aided by themes that decried "Christ has gone to the south" and "The Virgin Mary has departed from the north." The Catholics were joined by large numbers of landlords and ex-soldiers who had supported or fought for the French.

Lansdale eventually became head of the joint U.S./French Training Relations and Instruction Team, National Security Division, and was charged with coordinating all American civilian and military efforts in southern Vietnam. His work then centered on providing for the physical security of, and garnering popular support for, the new American-backed savior of South Vietnam, Ngo Dinh Diem.

Diem

While the regroupment was under way and the deliberations at Geneva were reaching completion in June, Emperor Bao Dai, seeking a more credible nationalist with which to head the government of the southern half of Vietnam, dismissed his cabinet and appointed Ngo Dinh Diem as premier. A staunch nationalist and anticommunist who had spent the entire French war outside Vietnam, Diem simply ignored the outcome in Switzerland and acted as if it had never taken place. The Americans and their new protégé were delighted with the results of the regroupment. The immigrants would help offset the North's population edge in the projected reunification elections and also provide Diem's shaky pro-Catholic regime with anticommunist support. Against long odds (and U.S. expectations) Diem survived a conflict with rival religious sects and political factions for control of South Vietnam in 1955. Later in the year Diem replaced Emperor Bao Dai as head of the government in a blatantly rigged referendum and then set about establishing an authoritarian regime that rapidly eroded the popular support he had previously garnered.

He then launched a two-year campaign against southern communists and Viet Minh of all political stripes, many of whom were working openly in anticipation of the Geneva-mandated election that was to have taken place in 1956 (and which would probably have united Vietnam under a northern-dominated coalition government). By the fall of 1957, tens of thousands of antigovernment cadres had been either killed or denounced as "dangerous to the state" and detained in political reeducation centers. President Diem then abrogated the Geneva agreement by never holding the nationwide elections. He was supported in this decision by the American government.

By the early 1960s, however, Washington found itself in a peculiar political quandary. After it had provided large amounts of military and economic aid to the government of South Vietnam, it seemed no closer to solving the problem of the growing communist insurgency within the country. Although Diem's continued assault on the southern communists had decimated their ranks, the hard core of the movement dug in deeper and began to strike back. Only in May 1959, however, did the politburo in Hanoi finally signal that armed struggle in the South had its complete support. The Saigon government continued to ignore the admonitions of its American sponsor to institute needed reforms that would have both eliminated popular support for the newly created National Front for the Liberation of South Vietnam (NLF or derogatively, Viet Cong) insurgents and curried favor among the increasingly dissatisfied Vietnamese population. President Diem proved too headstrong and nationalistic to knuckle under to American demands. The United States was thus faced with supporting an intractable client that it could neither control nor easily influence.

American military aid, however, did allow Diem to expand his military forces, and in February 1956, the First Observation Group was created. The mission of this three-hundred-man unit was to act as a stay-behind force tasked with carrying out unconventional warfare operations in the event of a conventional People's Army of Vietnam (PAVN) invasion across the 17th parallel that divided the two countries. The group operated outside the normal Vietnamese chain of command and answered directly to Diem. Modeled on the U.S. Army Special Forces, the First Observation Group was, without doubt, *the* elite unit of the Vietnamese military and became a natural magnet for possible covert operations. The unit was a section of the Presidential Liaison Office, whose other two branches were the Northern Service (also known as Bureau 45), So Bac, responsible for agent operations and intelligence gathering in North Vietnam; and the Southern Service, So Nam, which conducted similar operations within South Vietnam.

Five years after his SMM tour, Brigadier General Lansdale returned to South Vietnam as the head of a task force established by President John F. Kennedy to investigate possible solutions for the United States in South Vietnam. Lansdale discovered that the situation had deteriorated dangerously since his last visit and reported as much to the president. On 11 May 1961, Kennedy signed National Security Action Memorandum

(NSAM) 52, authorizing a series of covert operations to prevent the fall of the Saigon government to the communists. The CIA was tasked to provide the manpower and resources for a covert war against the North.

CIA Operations

Under Chief of Station William Colby, the agency began to initiate covert actions, including the infiltration of agent teams and the conduct of psychological and maritime actions. Direction and approval of these operations came from the 303 Committee in Washington, which had responsibility for all U.S. covert operations worldwide. Although still limited by the Geneva Accords, Kennedy also called for an expansion of the First Observation Group, whose mission was altered from conducting guerrilla operations to carrying out the infiltration of teams "under light civilian cover to southeast Laos to locate and attack Vietnamese communist bases and lines of communication, and to form networks of resistance, covert bases, and teams for sabotage and light harassment within North Vietnam." [1]

The new operations included the insertion of agents into North Vietnam for sabotage and intelligence-gathering operations during which they would be supplied and supported by specially modified C-47 aircraft of Vietnamese Air Transport (VIAT). This proprietary airline, created by the CIA and manned by Nationalist Chinese aircrews, provided deniability for the agency's complicity. By July there were nine CIA officers working with the First Observation Group in addition to one Military Assistance Advisory Group (MAAG) officer. Coinciding with the CIA's program was the arrival in South Vietnam of four hundred U.S. Special Forces troops, many of whom went to Nha Trang to train the Luc Luong Duc Biet (LLDB), the Vietnamese Special Forces.

A clandestine cover was provided for the First Observation Group by the creation of the Special Topographical Exploitation Service (So Khai Thac Dia Hinh), or TES, a branch of the Vietnamese Presidential Survey Office.[2] The Combined Studies Group (CSG) was in turn created by the CIA as the American counterpart organization that would monitor the operations. Thus, the CSG became the paramilitary command center of the new clandestine war. The necessity for a cover story was demonstrated in July 1961 when one of the TES units was captured near Ninh Binh (180 miles north of the 17th parallel), when its VIAT aircraft developed engine trouble.

The infiltration units, inserted by VIAT airdrops, consisted of four- to six-man teams operating "in the black" (with no identification). Between 1961 and 1963 more than thirty such teams and several single agents were inserted into North Vietnam by air, land, and sea with little appreciable result. By the end of 1963 only four teams and one agent were still operating. All of the others were either dead, in North Vietnamese custody, or operating under North Vietnamese control. William Colby believed that, unlike similar Office of Strategic Services (OSS) operations conducted in Europe during the Second World War, there was no base of popular support for the agents, and the control of the population by the communist regime was too widespread for them to survive there. Discouraged by the failure of the program, the CIA decided to drop it and to concentrate instead on propaganda and psychological operations within South Vietnam. Secretary of Defense Robert S. McNamara insisted, however, that the infiltrations continue. He believed that the CIA's lack of success was the result of a limited budget, and that the infiltration program would succeed if it was expanded and better financed.

OPERATION SWITCHBACK

By that time the point was moot. April 1961 saw the finale of the Bay of Pigs fiasco in Cuba and President Kennedy had soured on the agency's ability to conduct covert paramilitary operations. Within three months NSAMs 55, 56, and 57 had redefined responsibility for the conduct of such operations. The tide was shifting from the CIA to the Pentagon, even though the military had no real desire to support either covert or unconventional warfare operations. Kennedy's support for the new unconventional warfare concept in general, and for the Special Forces in particular, was exasperating to the Joint Chiefs, who were enamored of neither. With the JCS in the driver's seat, however, at least they could control the direction and scale of any operations that the president chose to pursue. The only question remaining was who would control the secret paramilitary war in Southeast Asia?

The answer was not clear. Lansdale, the most vocal special warfare supporter and the ideal candidate to head covert operations, enjoyed the least amount of support in Washington. Both the State Department and JCS opposed Kennedy, who sought to appoint Lansdale first as Ambassador to South Vietnam and then as chief of the newly established Military Assistance Advisory Group. When Lansdale was finally appointed assistant to the secretary of defense, a power struggle immediately erupted between him and the JCS.[3]

The Joint Chiefs responded to Kennedy's distrust of the CIA by creating the organizational machinery that would at least give the president the impression that they were embracing the unconventional warfare paradigm. On 23 February 1962 they implemented the office of Special Assistant for Counterinsurgency and Special Activities (SACSA) within the Special Operations Division of the Joint Staff. The first appointee to the position was Maj. Gen. Victor Krulak, USMC.

As for Lansdale, his fate was sealed on a fact-finding trip to Vietnam with Kennedy's chief military advisor, Gen. Maxwell D. Taylor. Lansdale made the mistake of ignoring Taylor's instruction to avoid his high-level contacts in Vietnam and to instead study the feasibility of erecting an electronic anti-infiltration barrier along the Demilitarized Zone (DMZ) that separated the two Vietnams. When Taylor climbed back into uniform to become chairman of the Joint Chiefs, Lansdale became the prime target of his ire. He was quickly reassigned to covert Cuban operations and his functions as special assistant were absorbed by SACSA. During a 1963 visit to South America, Lansdale was abruptly notified by the Pentagon that he would be retired from active duty. The generals had won.

In January 1963 the Joint Chiefs sent Army chief of staff Earle G. Wheeler and a group of high-ranking officers to South Vietnam to evaluate the progress of the conflict. As a direct result of this fact-finding trip, military planning for more covert actions against North Vietnam began. On 23 May 1963 Joint Chiefs of Staff Memorandum (JCSM) 398-63, "Military Operations in North Vietnam," advised McNamara that plans for covert hit-and-run actions should be developed for implementation by the South Vietnamese armed forces under the guidance of the United States and with the assistance of the CIA.[4]

What was different about the JCS plan was that it was a program whose operations would last over an extended period of time. It was also different because it was placed under the control of an operational U.S. command.[5] Adm. Harry Felt, commander in chief, Pacific (CINCPAC), was assigned the task of developing the plan, which, upon completion, became known as CINCPAC Operations Plan (OPLAN) 34-63. Felt sent his draft of the plan to the JCS on 17 June and it was favorably endorsed by them on 14 August.[6]

The CINCPAC OPLAN was warmly received by McNamara. He believed that North Vietnam, the perceived locus of the southern insurgency, had enjoyed relative immunity from any substantial penalty for its part in the violence in South Vietnam. The time had come for the communist leadership to understand that their nation would suffer reprisals. McNamara also desired the development of a notional (fictitious) Vietnamese national liberation movement, which would be the ostensible sponsor of the operations. That was, after all, what the North Vietnamese were doing in the South.

In the meantime, President Diem was stepping up his own operations against North Vietnam. On 1 April 1963 the TES evolved into the Special

Forces Command and continued (with CIA assistance) to carry out clandestine operations in the North and in Laos. By October, however, all CIA paramilitary operations were beginning to be turned over to the U.S. Army as part of Operation Switchback. This decision (based upon NSAMs 55, 56, and 57) stated in essence that whenever covert paramilitary operations became so large and overt that the military contribution, in terms of manpower and equipment, exceeded the resources contributed by the CIA, the operation would be turned over to the military.

OPLAN 34 ALPHA

The next major step in the creation of Special Operations Group (SOG) was taken as part of the Honolulu executive conference of 20 November 1963. McNamara and John McCone, the new director of the CIA, ordered that a combined plan be developed by the Commander, United States Military Assistance Command, Vietnam (COMUSMACV) that would provide for an intensified program of action against the North.[7] As a result, Gen. William C. Westmoreland's OPLAN 34A-64 was promulgated on 15 December. CINCPAC forwarded the plan to the JCS on 19 December and recommended approval.[8]

Operations were scheduled to commence on 1 February 1964 and four types of missions were envisioned. Intelligence collection (including expanded photo reconnaissance, communications, and electronic/signals intelligence) and an expansion of Vietnamese Air Force (VNAF) intelligence missions were to be implemented. Strategic and tactical psychological operations were to be targeted against the North Vietnamese leadership and population, including the use of leaflets, radio, and mail to help achieve maximum harassment and division among the population. The creation of a resistance movement was also considered, one designed to create pressure on the northern government through the development of organized guerrilla activity in the tribal highlands as well as unorganized resistance in the more populated lowlands. Military and paramilitary hit-and-run attacks, long-term agent team operations, and air attacks were to be launched with the objective of destroying military and economic assets.[9] American forces, however, were not to be utilized for operations within North Vietnam, its territorial waters, or its air space except as aircrew on reconnaissance missions.

On 21 December, McNamara brought OPLAN 34A-64 to the attention of President Lyndon B. Johnson and recommended that he form an interdepartmental committee with representatives from the Department of State, the Department of Defense, the JCS (including General Krulak), and the CIA to examine the plan and recommend appropriate action.

The committee report of 2 January 1964 analyzed the various proposed operations and outlined a schedule of three phases to cover a twelve-month period. The plan consisted of 72 principal actions, which, if they were carried out, would have totaled 2,062 separate operations including 13 air strikes, 3 amphibious raids by company-sized forces or larger, and 2,042 operations involving raids by forces of less than platoon size or psychological or intelligence collection missions.[10] The intensity of the operations was to increase with each successive phase with the purpose of causing a change in then-current North Vietnamese policies.[11] The group's recommendations were approved by the 303 Committee, which then advised President Johnson to adopt them.

Training had already begun (under CIA auspices) in September 1963 for Vietnamese troops destined for OPLAN 34-63, a campaign of border control and maritime harassment (including shellings, commando landings, and sabotage of North Vietnamese coastal communities), which was to have begun in 1964. The training and operations were to be carried out by specially selected members of the First Observation Group. The need for early cooperation on covert operations between the U.S. and the Saigon government was, however, counterbalanced by the growing instability of the relationship between Washington and the Diem regime. In South Vietnam, 1963 was a year of crisis as the communist insurgency gained ground and Diem's pro-Catholic and anti-Buddhist policies sparked demonstrations and resistance. This instability delayed bringing Saigon into the planning process until a U.S.-supported coup and the assassination of President Diem on 2 November paved the way for more active cooperation with the new Saigon government.

When OPLAN 34A-64 was nearing completion, the shape and form of the operational organization's implementing agency had still not been resolved. Due to exigencies of Operation Parasol/Switchback, the CIA relinquished control to MACV, but was still to retain input through the unit's staff. It was clear that the agency would have some say in planning, liaison, logistics, and training, but its responsibilities were not directly stated. The message also directed MACV to bring the government of South Vietnam into the planning on a discrete basis since its forces would actually conduct the operations. On 21 January, Ambassador Henry Cabot Lodge briefed President Duong Van Minh on 34A operations, stating that the plan had been approved at the highest levels of the U.S. government and was now ready for South Vietnamese review and, it was hoped, early agreement and execution.[12]

The covert program was formally implemented by a joint State/DOD/CIA message on 19 January 1964.[13] The recommendations of the interdepartmental committee had been approved by President Johnson for actions that were to cover the first four-month period (1 February–31 March 1964). The actions selected from the Saigon plan were those that were considered most feasible and that promised the greatest return for the least amount of risk. The American government could plausibly deny all of the approved actions.[14]

Missing from the program, however, were two of the key components of the original OPLAN. Thanks to the intervention of the State Department's representative (a protégé of W. Averell Harriman named William H. Sullivan) on the interdepartmental committee, the most controversial aspects of the plan had been toned down or eliminated. Gone was any mention of creating a resistance movement within North Vietnam, notional or otherwise. The possibility of destabilizing the communist regime in Hanoi brought nasty visions of Chinese intervention and a repeat of the Korean stalemate. Also missing was any mention of actions to be taken against the infiltration of communist troops and supplies through their rapidly expanding supply corridor in Laos.

The year 1964 proved to be a watershed year for the Vietnam War and for the role that the United States would play in it. The previous year had signaled the end of a less than auspicious beginning. Although the coup in Saigon that ended the life of Ngo Dinh Diem seemed to solve one American dilemma, it merely led to newer, more complex ones. The merry-go-round of Saigon politics swung into full gear while it became ever more frustrating for the American government to champion one group of generals after another. The assassination of President Kennedy three weeks after that of Diem overshadowed events in Southeast Asia, but it did signal a changing of the guard in Washington and in Saigon. The world was growing ever more tense. In October Soviet premier Nikita Khrushchev, whose policies were relatively liberal in comparison with those of Josef Stalin, was overthrown by Communist Party hardliners led by the more reactionary Leonid Brezhnev and Aleksai Kosygin. During the same month the People's Republic of China exploded its first atomic bomb.

Chapter One

1964: OPLAN 34A

Headquarters

The Military Assistance Command, Vietnam, Special Operations Group (MACVSOG, MACSOG, or SOG) was formally activated on 24 January 1964 by MACV General Order No. 6 as a separate staff section under the COMUSMACV.[1] The organization's purpose under OPLAN 34A was the conduct of covert operations that would convince Hanoi that its support and direction of the conflict in the South and its violation of Laotian neutrality should be reexamined and halted. Since the United States was seeking a change in the calculations of the Hanoi government, MACSOG was to provide "a broad spectrum of operations in and against North Vietnam in direct retaliation to [its] aggressive moves."[2]

The organization was to undertake a series of coercive actions that would escalate from light harassment, attrition of northern resources and punitive expeditions, to aerial attacks. North Vietnam was expected to respond by either ending its support of the NLF insurgency or by escalating its responses. Those responses could range from increasing its support to the NLF, to launching a conventional invasion of South Vietnam, all the way to asking for direct military assistance from the PRC, the Soviet Union, or both.

At its inception MACSOG was organized as a joint task force, combining the skills of unconventional warfare specialists from the U.S. Army, Navy, Air Force, and Marine Corps. The name of the unit was changed during the summer (for rather obvious reasons) to the Studies and Observations Group. The title was designed to bolster the cover of the unit, since it had to have some listing in the MACV table of organization and for the allocation of funds and equipment. It supposedly served as a branch of the MACV staff tasked with conducting studies and evaluations of the unconventional warfare effort.

COMMAND RELATIONSHIPS

Although MACSOG was established and manned by MACV, it was, in reality, virtually independent of it. MACV had been granted operational control over the new organization, but the Saigon command itself had no authority to conduct operations beyond the borders of territorial South Vietnam. The J-5 (plans) officer on the MACV staff had special cognizance of all MACSOG operations and was the main point of contact between the two organizations, but the actual supervisor of the unit was SACSA and his staff at the Pentagon. Eventually, MACSOG would become virtually a supporting command of MACV, equivalent to at least a small division, but its command relationship with MACV would not change.

The first commander of the new organization was Col. Clyde R. Russell, an Army Special Forces officer (all subsequent MACSOG commanders would also be Army Special Forces personnel). During the Second World War Russell had been a paratroop officer, making combat jumps into France during Operation Overlord and into Holland during Market/ Garden. After the war, he served in the regular infantry, including a stint as chief of staff at the Army Infantry School at Fort Benning, Georgia. It was only after this assignment that he joined the Special Forces. He later commanded the 1st Battalion of the 10th Special Forces Group (SFG) in Germany and the 7th SFG at Fort Bragg, North Carolina. Russell's choice as head of MACSOG was a perplexing one. His unconventional warfare training was limited to Europe and South America and he had not seen any service whatsoever in Asia. Regardless, after arriving in January, Russell set up MACSOG's headquarters in Saigon's Cholon district in the compound that had previously housed the MACV headquarters.

According to OPLAN 34A, MACSOG was to maintain a close relationship with the CIA. After all, the operations it was taking over had originally belonged to the agency and it was assumed that SOG would utilize its expertise and personnel to assist with any teething problems during the takeover. Colonel Russell was, in fact, to be seconded by a CIA deputy commander, who was supposedly going to be a high-ranking agency official. The CIA, however, balked at the idea of placing a member of upper management as second in command to a military officer. After all, for the past two years it had been attempting to back out of its commitment to an operation that it considered a failure. CIA director John McCone believed that eventually MACSOG's operations would lose their covert nature, and he wanted the agency distanced from them.

To demonstrate this strained relationship one need look no further than MACSOG's attempts to fill the CIA billets within its Joint Table of Distribution (JTD). In July 1964 SOG was to have thirty-one agency employees on the job. It had eighteen. By the end of September the number of spaces was reduced to thirty but it still had only fifteen CIA personnel on the books.[3] By the beginning of 1965 SOG had learned its lesson and had reduced the number of necessary CIA personnel to thirteen, but it still only managed to get seven spaces filled by the agency. The command issue was resolved by assigning MACSOG a lower-ranking CIA officer with the vague title of "special assistant."

PERSONNEL
The initial personnel allocation granted MACSOG a meager six officers and two enlisted men. By the end of the year they had been augmented by temporary duty (TDY) and permanent party personnel to sixty-two officers, two warrant officers, sixty-seven enlisted men, and fourteen civilians.[4] Manning MACSOG was problematic to say the least. Colonel Russell quickly realized that he was faced with a personnel dilemma. At the time there were no procedures within the U.S. military system by which he could search out and obtain qualified personnel with unconventional warfare backgrounds. Those men that could be found also had to pass the necessary Top Secret security review. MACSOG's operations, therefore, were manned by Special Forces troops who had little, if any, experience in unconventional warfare or covert operations. The unit was also going to be saddled with General Westmoreland's one-year personnel rotation policy, which tended to strip the organization of key men who had just become experienced enough to be effective in their duties.

The South Vietnamese also reorganized their clandestine establishment to support OPLAN 34A. On 1 April the Special Branch for Clandestine Operations of the Technical Exploitation Service, which had been tasked with covert operations and intelligence gathering, was split into two sections. The new Strategic Exploitation Service (So Khai Thac Dia Hinh), or SES, under the command of Colonel Tran Van Ho, became MACSOG's Vietnamese counterpart. One of its branches, the Coastal Security Service (So Phong Ve Duyen Hai), or CSS, would conduct the maritime portions of OPLAN 34A. The other new Vietnamese organization was the Liaison Service (So Lien Lac), which carried out intelligence collection and clandestine operations in Laos.

PERMISSION
Clearance procedures for MACSOG operations were highly centralized throughout the early history of the organization and strict limitations

never completely disappeared. The procedure in effect for OPLAN 34A in October 1964 was as follows: MACSOG sent its monthly proposals and schedule of operations to MACV in Saigon and then on to CINC-PAC in Honolulu. Next up the food chain were the JCS at the Pentagon in Washington. From there the proposals and recommendations crossed the river to Foggy Bottom and the State Department. Needless to say, the CIA also had input into the process.

If all of the above gave their approval, or at least agreed to a modification of the proposal or schedule, the proposals went to President Johnson, who made the final decision. If, at any point along this chain, disapproval was expressed, MACSOG had to start the whole process again.[5] After permission for operations had been obtained, a twenty-four-hour notice of intent had to be given prior to each mission launch. This notice had to be sent to all of the above agencies, each of whom had already authorized the mission.

Intelligence

Established in March, the Intelligence Branch was divided into three sections under the command of an Air Force lieutenant colonel. The Collections Section received aerial photo intelligence of North Vietnam from the Air Force and Navy. The Targeting Section collated both photo and maritime operations (MAROPS) intelligence and produced possible target packages for the missions. The Production and Estimates Section produced wall maps and charts of North Vietnamese and Pathet Lao orders of battle.

A new source of intelligence appeared during the year with the arrival of northern fishermen at Paradise Island. These detainees were an important information source, not just for MACSOG, but for Washington. They were, after all, one of the few sources of human intelligence coming out of North Vietnam.

Airborne Operations

By the end of 1963 the CIA's chief of the Far East Division (and chief of station, Saigon), William Colby, had informed Secretary of Defense McNamara at the Honolulu Conference that the agent operation was not working. Few of the agents survived very long in the highly controlled communist state. Colby later stated that, at the time, he believed that those agents who had survived to report back to their masters had all been turned by the communists. Colby was right; the CIA program was a disaster. By the spring of 1964 the agency believed that only four of the teams and one agent (teams Bell, Easy, Tourbillon, and Remus and agent

Ares) had not already been captured or compromised by the northern security apparatus. Yet, it is hard to determine exactly when Colby reached this conclusion. In the seven months leading up to the Honolulu Conference, the agency deployed fifteen teams into North Vietnam, almost half of the total agents sent in by the CIA during the entire three-year program.[6]

If he really did doubt the value of the teams or if he believed that the in-place agents had been doubled by the North Vietnamese, then the sheer number of teams inserted was very troublesome indeed. Was the agency merely trying to show up the military authorities before the changeover, or was it simply a matter of eliminating embarrassing assets? This question was made even more historically perplexing considering that at Honolulu, Colby never informed McNamara that he suspected the majority of the teams to be compromised by the North Vietnamese.

The South Vietnamese already had qualms (and always would) about the program.[7] Shortly after assuming command in early 1964 Colonel Ho questioned the usefulness of the teams and wanted to end long-term agent operations. It was not to be. Colonel Russell convinced him that the program should continue, and his sentiment on the situation was enlightening: "Ho was a fairly weak man . . . I found that I could get him to do anything the United States desired. . . . There were times when he wanted to disband the airborne effort . . . but again, because he was weak and we could put pressure on him he would agree."[8] Secretary McNamara's conclusions were of a different nature. He believed that the poor results obtained by the CIA effort were simply a matter of scale and cost. Under military control the operation would be enlarged and better funded. MACSOG would simply provide a "bigger bang for the buck." At the conclusion of the Honolulu Conference it was decided that the thirteen agent teams then in training (eighty agents) would be readied to go north for MACSOG.

Some of these teams had been in training for years and had mission profiles that matched their ethnic backgrounds, regions of origin, and dialects. They had been cloistered for training within seven Saigon safe houses by the CIA, had received airborne training, and had participated in field exercises near Monkey Mountain, outside Da Nang. Operation Switchback put an end to that. With MACSOG's takeover of the program under the rubric Airborne Operations, immediate and drastic changes began to take place. The agents and teams were informed that they were not necessarily going to be inserted into areas where they had been trained to operate.

It was at this point that problems began to appear at the southern end of the pipeline. The dozen or more teams in training throughout Saigon were brought together at the Army of the Republic of Vietnam (ARVN) Airborne Training Center at Camp Long Thanh. Doing so violated one of the key precepts of the program, compartmentalization, and the agents knew it. The team members were then free to intermingle and socialize with each other, and they could, from the various ethnic origins and dialects spoken by members of other teams, know the ultimate destination of each mission. This was a serious breach of security. As team member Quach Rang stated: "You cannot imagine what coming to Long Thanh did to our morale . . . it told us you didn't care about the secrecy any more . . . we began to have desertions . . . why should we have worked for you when it was obvious you didn't care about protecting us?"[9]

These conclusions may sound rather harsh, but they were backed up rather cynically by the later testimony of Colonel Russell. His opinion of the operation, and the men who were to carry it out, could be summed up by the following: "When we took over, we found we had a number of so-called agents who were not qualified for anything . . . they were not eager to go . . . we were without very high expectations . . . and we had to get rid of them; at the same time we couldn't turn them loose in South Vietnam . . . our solution was to put them in the north."[10]

And get rid of them he did. By the end of 1964 MACSOG had infiltrated half of its agents in eleven teams. Part of Colonel Russell's cynical attitude can probably be explained by the dawning realization that SOG was not going to be allowed to create any real resistance movement in North Vietnam. He had already requested that the JCS approve the creation of a tribal guerrilla resistance, since this operational concept fell under the purview of MACSOG's original JCS mission statement. Russell felt that the time was right for turning up the heat on Hanoi. To his astonishment, the request was disapproved in June.[11]

THE TEAMS

Meanwhile, six-man Team Attila was parachuted into Thanh Chuong District of North Vietnam, seven miles from the Laotian border, on 25 April. The team landed successfully and established radio contact with MACSOG via the CIA's Bugs radio relay site (located at Clark Air Force Base in the Philippines). Two days later, as North Vietnamese patrols closed in on its position, the team split up and evaded. All of its members were eventually captured, the last on 29 May. Radio Hanoi announced on 11 August that an enemy "spy commando" team had been sentenced to eight years imprisonment by a military tribunal. This was Team Attila.

On 19 May Team Lotus dropped into Nghe An Province. The mission of the six-man team was to destroy the Ham Rong bridge near Tanh

Hoa City (later infamous as the "Dragon's Jaw") and then to destroy the bridges between there and Highway 7. They were captured just after landing and the team leader was summarily executed. The remaining members were tried and convicted by a military tribunal. On 27 May seven-man Team Coots parachuted into the North near Lai Chau to reinforce in-place Team Tourbillon. North Vietnamese security forces were waiting for the team on the landing zone (LZ), taking all members immediately into custody.

Team Scorpion was parachuted into the province of Yen Bai, northwest of Hanoi, on 17 June. One man died in the drop and one went missing. The other five personnel were quickly rounded up. Two days later, Team Buffalo went into Quang Binh and all ten men were quickly captured. On 27 July the surviving members of Team Scorpion were tried and sentenced by a North Vietnamese tribunal, and on 24 October the members of Team Buffalo were sentenced to imprisonment. The six men of Team Eagle were dropped near a major rail line near Uong Bi on 29 June. They were quickly attacked and captured. On 18 July the six men of Team Pisces were parachuted in to reinforce in-place Team Easy and, six days later, seven-man Team Perseus was sent in to reinforce Team Tourbillon. All thirteen men were captured soon after landing.

The story of Team Boone was an instructive one. The nine men parachuted into Nghe An Province on 29 July and were assigned sabotage and harassment operations north of Highway 7, outside the town of Con Cuong. From there the team would also be able to monitor road traffic into neighboring Laos. During the drop, the primary radio operator's chute failed to fully deploy and he broke his neck. The team's secondary radioman was not familiar enough with the equipment to operate it. With no way to communicate with headquarters, team morale plummeted. The agents then made the decision to surrender to communist authorities. This was done on 2 August.

Two more team reinforcements took place during the latter part of the year. On 22 October four-man Team Alter was dropped into Lai Chau to reinforce Team Remus and on 14 November seven-man Team Greco dropped into Yen Bai to reinforce Team Bell. The communists captured both teams upon arrival. As if things were not bad enough, on 28 December Team Centaur was wiped out when its C-123 crashed into Monkey Mountain during a night training exercise. It seems that the MACSOG staff at Da Nang had wanted to scrub the mission due to extremely poor weather, but Saigon ordered it completed anyway. The twenty-eight members of Centaur were killed along with the aircraft's South Vietnamese crew. Also on board were MACSOG airborne instructor

Sgt. Dominick Sansone and Maj. Woodrow Vaden, USAF, an advisor on the Doppler navigational system. The remains of Sansone and Vaden were never recovered.

At year's end MACSOG had inserted eleven teams (seventy-five agents) into North Vietnam and, as far as the Americans knew, only one had not been captured or eliminated. That now left six teams and one agent in place and reporting (sixty-two total agents).[12]

Air Operations

SOG's aerial workhorse, inherited from the CIA, was the 1st Flight Detachment. This unit was utilized to insert agent teams, to resupply them, and to carry out psychological warfare operations (leaflet, gift kit, and radio drops) over North Vietnam. The unit also supplied day-to-day logistical airlift for MACSOG. Its aircraft consisted of four unmarked Fairchild C-123 Providers based at Nha Trang that were flown by seven National-ist Chinese aircrews. Most of these men were veterans of the Taiwan-ese 34th Squadron, which had flown hundreds of clandestine operations over the PRC. In testimony to their skill, in five years of operations, no 1st Flight aircraft was ever lost over North Vietnam. The Chinese were supported, for the time being, by several VNAF crews.

On 25 May a contingent of thirty-eight Chinese and eighteen South Vietnamese aircrew arrived at Hurlburt Field, Florida (the home of USAF Special Operations), for specialized low-level flight and bad weather paradrop training.[13] During the year another contingent of MACSOG-assigned VNAF pilots were training on U.S. aircraft carriers in the Gulf of Tonkin to drop mines into the harbors of the North as part of OPLAN 34A.

MACSOG worked hard during 1964 to replace the four C-123s (in-herited from the CIA) with six more-modified versions. The Providers were proving troublesome due to their relatively slow speed and lack of sufficient range. There were also problems with the deniability of the aircraft should they have gone down in North Vietnam. Eventually, six modified C-123s, given the cover name Duck Hook, were handed over to SOG from the 2nd Air Division of the USAF, which also provided maintenance personnel for the program. The aircraft were heavily modi-fied by the addition of electronic countermeasures (ECM), electronic intel-ligence (ELINT), and Doppler navigational systems. They were only slightly sanitized, however, and could in no way be considered deniable by the United States if they fell into communist hands.

The first aircraft arrived in South Vietnam in April and the last in June. During the year one C-123 crashed when both engines failed while the aircraft was enroute to Taiwan for maintenance. Another of the new aircraft was the one that crashed into Monkey Mountain during a night airdrop training exercise. The 2nd Air Division quickly replaced both aircraft. During the next few years four of the original six C-123s deployed to MACSOG were lost.

Relations between SOG and the Nationalist Chinese aircrews inherited from the CIA began to sour during the year. Part of the problem was the imposition of more military discipline, but it was probably more basic than that. The Air Operations Section began to demand that after the crews had dropped off their agent teams and/or supplies, they circle around and gather intelligence on North Vietnamese anti-aircraft artillery and radar installations and their capabilities. Needless to say, this was not a very popular request.

Another problem for the Air/Airborne Operations Sections was a seeming lack of imagination when it came to the choice of drop zones (DZs) for the agent teams. The insertions invariably took place in close proximity to one another. Granted, there were limitations upon possible DZs, but one team was never infiltrated very far away from another and replacements usually went into the same DZs as their parent teams. This allowed northern authorities too many opportunities for the capture or destruction of the teams. In response to this problem, MACSOG would seek and find alternative methods of agent insertion.

Maritime Operations

CIA MAROPS had been based since 1962 along the Tien Sha Peninsula, spread between Marble Mountain and Monkey Mountain, east of the city of Da Nang. When SOG inherited the bases and their assets from the CIA during Operation Parasol/Switchback, the agency's inventory of craft consisted of two Swift PT boats (PTs 810 and 811) that had arrived in January 1964. Built by Seward Seacraft of Burwick, Louisiana, the aluminum-hulled Swifts (designated PCFs for Patrol Craft, Fast) were of Korean Conflict vintage, weighed in at 19 tons, and were powered by two diesel engines. They carried a five-man crew and were armed with twin .50-caliber machine guns and had another .50 piggybacked with an 81-mm mortar. Although they could achieve a speed of twenty-eight nautical miles per hour, they had a range of only sixty nautical miles above the 17th parallel and they constantly broke down. The Swifts exemplified the naval aspect of the "new look" military, since the Navy lacked any more modern fast patrol boats in its inventory. Previously, the agency had utilized eight Yabuta-type junks built by exiled northern craftsmen to infiltrate operatives by sea. This state of affairs says something about U.S. preparedness for the mission that MACSOG was to implement. The

U.S. Navy did not have any more modern vessels in its inventory that could serve the program. So, in order to speed up the process by which North Vietnam would be dissuaded from its present course, Secretary McNamara ordered the Navy to procure two Norwegian-built PTFs (Patrol Type, Fast) in 1963.

Built as a joint venture by Norway and West Germany, the Tjeld (Nasty)-class PTF was an 80-foot 80-ton diesel-powered composite-hulled craft propelled by two British-made Napier/Deltic engines. It was capable of speeds up to forty knots and had a cruising range of 860 nautical miles at thirty-eight knots and 1,050 miles at twenty knots. The boats were heavily armed with an 81-mm mortar piggybacked to a .50-caliber machine gun forward; a 40-mm cannon on the afterdeck; and one 20-mm cannon on each side of the deckhouse.

It was believed that the foreign origin of the Nastys would add to their deniability. Initially, the PTFs were manned, for lack of trained Vietnamese crews, by German and Norwegian mercenaries recruited in July 1963. Due to "constant inebriation," the Germans were quickly sacked without ever going out on a mission, but the three Norwegians, familiar with the boat's capabilities and known as "the Vikings," were better suited to the operation. Their final mission took place on 27 May 1964. When the Department of Defense discovered that training, maintenance, lack of crew morale, and the weather were hampering the pace of operations, it ordered the purchase of four more Nasty boats.

THE NAD

Clyde Russell may have believed that he was inheriting a fully operational and equipped covert maritime operation from the CIA, but he was soon disabused of that view. He was rather shocked to discover that, as was the case with agent operations, SOG's takeover of maritime operations was in name only. The operation was to be run by the Naval Advisory Detachment (NAD), which, along with its South Vietnamese counterpart, the CSS, was headquartered in a building known as the "White Elephant" at 52 Bach Dang Street in downtown Da Nang. Within the NAD, an Operations/Training section was established to plan and execute all MAROPS against North Vietnam. A SEAL/Recon section (consisting of Detachment Echo of SEAL Team 1), which had served in the CIA program, was soon joined by U.S. Army and Marine Force Reconnaissance personnel to train the South Vietnamese boat crews and commando and scuba teams that were to carry out the raids.

Although maritime operations were to be a joint SES/SOG operation, all of the South Vietnamese elements were subordinated to MACSOG.

The NAD trained the crews and commandos, planned the missions, and provided all of the resources. The crews of the PTFs (Luc Luong Hai Tuan or Sea Patrol Force) were volunteers from the South Vietnamese Navy. Known to the Americans as Team Nautilus, the crews were trained by U.S. naval personnel, as was the maintenance element (Team Vega). The SES provided five fifteen-man Sea Commando teams (Lich Su cua Biet Hai) for cross-beach operations in North Vietnam (Teams Nimbus and Romulus, trained by the U.S. Marine and Army contingents, respectively). Specialized frogman teams (Lien Doi Nguoi Nhai) were trained by the SEALs for underwater missions in the rivers and estuaries of the North. The CSS also ran and controlled its own civilian agents in Team Cumulus.

During the year a U.S. Navy Mobile Support Team (MST) arrived to assist the NAD in a rather interesting manner. U.S. Navy crew that had been factory-trained in London at Napier and Son brought the new PTFs to Da Nang via Subic Bay. They were then directly assigned to the NAD. Although previously uninformed about their intended advisory task, the crews were converted into Boat Training Teams. They then proceeded to train and advise the now all-Vietnamese crews on gunnery, tactics, navigation, and maintenance of the Swift and Nasty boats. Operational control over the men and boats rested with MACSOG, but the permanent affiliation of the naval personnel was with the Naval Operations Support Group (responsible for U.S. naval forces involved in special operations in the Pacific) at Coronado, California. The second branch of the MST was the Maintenance Training Team, which was responsible for hull and engineering maintenance training.

On the down side, desertion rates among the Vietnamese were at a critical level early in the takeover. Some of this was attributed to the imposition of stricter military discipline upon the operation, but some was no doubt due to fallout from the relationship between the Vietnamese Special Forces and the Diem regime during the Buddhist crisis of the previous year. After the coup that toppled Diem, some Liaison Service officers had been shot or arrested while others were in hiding. As the MACSOG Documentation Study related, "the stigma of VNSF had rubbed off on them."[14] The Americans also complained that there was indifference on the part of the Vietnamese to damage done to the boats, and that the crews and teams were only in it for the higher rates of pay and allowances that they received. Some or all of these problems might also have been related to the changeover in control from CIA to MACSOG.

Regardless, the mission was plagued by teething troubles that slowed down operational planning and implementation. The limited operating

ranges of the Swift boats hampered the pace of early operations and besides, they were too slow and lightly armed to compete with the faster
and more heavily armed P-4 torpedo boats and Swatow gunboats of the
North Vietnamese Navy. To the dismay of the NAD, the first of the Nastys to arrive (PTFs 1 and 2) were powered by gasoline engines, were too
loud, and were hard to restart once the engines had been shut down. This
did not bode well for crews that were tasked with operating in stealth
along the Tonkin coast. Although the arrival of the Nasty boats more
than leveled the playing field between the CSS and the northern navy as
far as speed and range were concerned, there was a never-ending search
for heavier armament for the boats. During 1964 the crews experimented
with mounting extra weapons, including 57-mm cannon, 81-mm mortars, and 106-mm recoilless rifles.

FIRST MISSIONS

Regardless of the prompting of the politicians in Washington, MAROPS
got off to a very slow start. The mission statement of MACSOG's maritime
arm confirmed that the purpose of the organization was the destruction
of select military targets, interdiction of waterborne logistics, collection
of intelligence (through the capture and detention of personnel for intelligence exploitation), and psychological warfare. The operations were
authorized to extend between the 17th and 21st parallels. The earliest
missions of the program (begun under CIA auspices) were Cado cross-
beach commando and sabotage operations that were meant to punish and
harass North Vietnam and to force it into assigning more troops to defend
its coastal areas. There has been much discussion since the war as to
whether American personnel went on at least some MAROPS missions,
but no reliable testimony or documents support this contention.

Three Cado attacks were launched on the North Vietnamese naval
facility at Quang Khe, a major base for patrol vessels in Quang Binh
Province.[15] The first action took place on 13 or 16 February, when a
four-man scuba team was launched from a Swift boat to attach limpet
mines to one or more of the craft moored in the estuary. It did not go
well. Three of the frogmen were captured and one drowned. Further
attempts against the same target made on 12 and 15 March were equally
inauspicious. One was unsuccessful and in the other, all four men were
lost with no result.

Seven Sea Commandos were landed from a Swift boat on the coast
of Ha Tinh Province on 16 March in order to attack a bridge on Route
1. This operation too failed and two men were lost. The following night
nine men landed in Quang Binh Province to attack another bridge on

Route 1. This operation was also unsuccessful and two more men were lost. A twenty-six-man action team was dispatched to attack a storage area at Hai Khau on 12 June. The team destroyed the target and escaped unmolested, but the "storage area" reportedly turned out to be a factory for the manufacture of *nuoc mam* sauce. On the same night another team landed and blew up the Hang Bridge in Thanh Hoa Province.

During this early period, the NAD was also pressing forward on the psychological warfare front. On 27 May the first operation directed against the North Vietnamese fishing fleet was carried out when a PTF and a Swift boat captured a fishing vessel. The boat was towed to Cu Lao Cham Island and its crew was interrogated and indoctrinated as part of psychological operations (see below). The boat and crew were released on 2 June. Operation Lure was launched on 16 June in an effort to convince northern naval officers and crews to rally to the Saigon government along with their vessels. Leaflets were deposited in lighted buoys off the North Vietnamese coast, which promised freedom, gift kits, and a payment in gold with which to begin a new life in the South. The operation was conducted for three months with negative results.

On the evening of 26–27 June a seven-man demolition team supported by twenty-four Sea Commandos landed and blew up a bridge in Thanh Hoa Province. During the mission they killed six North Vietnamese personnel and escaped without loss. This was followed by another successful operation during the early morning hours of 1 July. Approximately thirty-two men landed and destroyed the pump house of the Dong Hai Reservoir, near the mouth of the Khien River, with a 55-mm recoilless rifle. The team managed to capture two North Vietnamese militiamen but it also lost two of its own.

A commando group landed near Ron on 15 July, but encountered security forces, suffered casualties, and was forced to withdraw. A reflection of North Vietnam's determination to respond aggressively to these coastal attacks was demonstrated on the night of 28 July, when, after attacking installations on Hon Gio Island, SOG craft were pursued for forty-five nautical miles by North Vietnamese Navy Swatow-class gunboats. On the night of 30 July four PTFs, utilizing 57-mm recoilless rifles, attacked military and radar installations on Hon Ngu Island (located off the central coast of North Vietnam) and Hon Me Island (near the port of Vinh). On their return journey to Da Nang, the PTFs passed within four miles of the U.S. destroyer *Maddox* (DD-731), which was on an intelligence-gathering mission along the North Vietnamese coast known as a Desoto patrol.[16]

THE GULF OF TONKIN INCIDENTS

Maddox was in the gulf to gather radar and communications emissions data from northern coastal installations. Capt. John J. Herrick, the on-site commander of *Maddox*, was cognizant of the 34A raids, but was not acting in tandem with them. This might sound a little contradictory since the 34A raids would produce just the type of emissions that the destroyer was intended to collect. The possibility that the Desoto Operation might be combined or "piggy-backed" with 34A had been discussed by the Joint Chiefs, the secretaries of state and defense, and Ambassador to South Vietnam Taylor, but the concept had been turned down. The two operations remained (at least to the United States) independent of one another.[17] The intelligence collected by Desoto along with other SIGINT intelligence, however, was dispatched to MACSOG under the cover name Kit Kat.

Just what the North Vietnamese were supposed to think about them was another matter altogether. Hanoi was contending not just with the coastal attacks and the nearby American destroyer. On 29 July MAC-SOG parachuted agent team Boone into the North near Route 7 in Nghe An Province. One of the team members was separated and captured that night. The rest of the team surrendered on 2 August. On 1 August, eight Laotian T-28 fighter-bombers, flown by Thai pilots, attacked targets that were, according to the U.S. Embassy in Vientiane, within two miles of the North Vietnamese frontier. Hanoi claimed that the planes crossed into their airspace and had attacked the border outpost at Nam Can, also on Route 7. It further claimed that the aircraft then flew on and attacked a second outpost at Noong De, fourteen kilometers inside North Vietnam. The following day the aircraft returned and struck again. American officials later conceded that the charges were probably accurate.[18] This escalating rash of shellings, bombings, and commando landings, combined with the presence of the destroyer, was the key to understanding Hanoi's response during the next few days.

Neither the U.S. government nor the military saw any of these actions as being provocative. National security advisor William Bundy later stated that "rational minds could not readily have foreseen that Hanoi might confuse them."[19] Rational minds? As Dr. Edwin Moise has so succinctly put it: "Had the Soviet Union stationed a vessel equipped with five-inch guns . . . off Charleston during a week when the Soviet Union was also sending Cuban gunboats to shell the South Carolina coast, it is unlikely that it could have remained there even twenty-four hours without being attacked by U.S. forces."[20] The Desoto patrol became even more provocative when the Joint Chiefs chose to move *Maddox* inshore from its usual twenty-mile cruising range to within four miles of the North Vietnamese coast (still one mile within international waters as claimed by the United States). Similar missions conducted off the coasts of the PRC, the USSR, and North Korea never approached closer than a twenty-mile limit.

The North Vietnamese Navy (being most irrational) dispatched three P-4 torpedo boats and two Swatow gunboats to defend Hon Me Island. At 1350 hours on 2 August the three P-4s set out to attack *Maddox*. Whether the boats were ordered to attack, or by whom, still remains a matter of conjecture, but come on they did.[21] *Maddox* opened fire first, firing three warning rounds at a range of ten thousand yards.[22] At most, six torpedoes were launched at the destroyer, none of which struck home. *Maddox* replied with rather ineffective gunfire. Within fifteen minutes of *Maddox*'s first salvo, four F-8E Crusader fighter-bombers from the U.S. aircraft carrier *Ticonderoga* (CV-14) attacked the North Vietnamese boats with Zuni rockets and 20-mm cannon. One P-4 was dead in the water and the other two were damaged by the time the Crusaders were recalled. The United States claimed that one vessel was sunk (in fact all three P-4s were sunk during one action in 1965), while Hanoi claimed two aircraft were shot down (only one aircraft was damaged, due to stress on the aircraft—not gunfire). Four North Vietnamese sailors were killed and eight were wounded during the action.[23]

Captain Herrick requested that his mission be terminated, but CINC-PAC turned him down. *Maddox* would instead be joined by the destroyer *Turner Joy* (DD-951) and both would "show the flag" in the Gulf of Tonkin. On the afternoon of 3 August another four-boat MACSOG raiding party set out from Da Nang, this time heading for mainland targets about seventy-five miles north of the DMZ. One of the boats had to turn back, but two managed to shell a radar installation at Vinh Son and the fourth bombarded a security post at Cua Ron. The following night, *Maddox* and *Turner Joy* were approximately sixteen miles off the coast when they were beset by the "Tonkin spooks." Bad weather, faulty radar tracking, edgy sonarmen, and raw nerves led to an all-night battle with nonexistent enemies.[24]

Robert McNamara, even in his later apologetic mode, still dissembled on the incidents and Washington's response to them. He and others believed that the attacks on the destroyers were so irrational (the word was used a lot when describing these events) that they speculated as to Hanoi's motives. Some believed that the North Vietnamese saw a direct connection between 34A and the Desoto patrols. Others, "pointing to

34A's ineffectiveness, found that explanation hard to accept."[25] McNamara's memory of the other operations against North Vietnam described above seemed to be rather faulty.

Although communications between Washington and the seat of the action were muddled and confused, President Johnson, who had refused to retaliate for the first attack, decided to reply to the second. Pierce Arrow, a preplanned air strike of sixty-four sorties against military targets in southern North Vietnam, was launched on the 5th. That same day in Washington, Johnson presented Congress with a draft resolution, one which would give him unprecedented power to take "all necessary measures to repel armed attacks against the forces of the United States and to prevent further aggression" in Southeast Asia.[26] On 7 August the "Southeast Asia Resolution" passed both houses of Congress with only two dissenting votes and became Public Law 88-408.

All of this was, however, more than a little disingenuous. Congress was not apprised of the 34A raids nor of the possibility that they might be associated with the actions of *Maddox*. Senator Wayne Morse of Oregon, who cast one of the two dissenting votes against the resolution, did so because he had been tipped off concerning the 34A raids. He was able to get no response from the State Department or the Defense Department about a possible connection (even if only in the "irrational" minds of the Hanoi leadership) between the two operations. When McNamara briefed Morse and other key senators four days after the incidents, he lied to them by stating that "our navy played absolutely no part in, was not associated with, was not aware of, any South Vietnamese actions, if there were any. I want to make that very clear to you."[27] Congress was also not apprised of the administration's growing knowledge that the 4 August incident had never occurred at all. They did not know that Johnson's draft resolution had been sitting on the shelf since May awaiting just such a set of circumstances.[28] Regardless, the overt escalation of the Vietnam War had begun and MACSOG had been in the thick of it.

BACK TO WORK

MAROPS were put on hold after the incidents due to an ongoing International Control Commission (ICC) investigation. The NAD craft were hurriedly transferred south to Cam Ranh Bay until the dust settled, but bad weather along the Vietnamese coast would have limited operations anyway. On 21 September all PTFs headed for Subic Bay to avoid Typhoon Tilda. They returned on 23 September, but the arrival of Typhoon Anita then backed up operations even further. A previously scheduled probe off Vinh Son could only be carried out on 3 October.

The NAD then rushed to complete previously scheduled missions before the onset of the northeast monsoon. On 10 October an action against a radar station at Vinh Son and a PAVN installation at Cape Mui Dao was scrubbed due to North Vietnamese activity and bad weather. This mission was finally completed on 28 October. A six-boat bombardment of Hon Gio was carried out on 26 November, and two nights later installations on Cape Ron were bombarded. On 1 December a bombardment of the North Vietnamese naval base at Quang Khe was scrubbed due to North Vietnamese activity and bad weather but, one week later, the bombardment of an unknown radar site was carried out. A bombardment of Quang Khe on the 22nd was again called off due to communist military activity and bad weather. The last mission of the year, a four-boat bombardment of a radar facility at Mach Nuoc was carried out on 27 December.[29]

By year's end ninety-two maritime missions had been conducted and ten Vietnamese crewmen, commandos, or frogmen had been killed in action.[30] Lack of operational success could be (and was) attributed to the limited time since operational activation, personnel motivation, bad weather, nonavailable major equipment, lack of intelligence, and procurement of MACSOG personnel.

Psychological Operations

The Psychological Operations (PSYOPS) Group was one of SOG's most interesting operations and offered up a glimpse of what original minds could do when offered the chance to carry out nonattributable "black" propaganda against an enemy. Playing to the paranoia of the structured communist state, these operations were also designed to cater to the traditional Vietnamese resentment toward (and fear of) the Chinese. SOG assumed control of and created PSYOPS programs that both heightened the tension of the leaders of the North and increased the strain between them and their population.

After all, MACSOG's objectives were psychological in nature. The purpose of the organization under OPLAN 34A was to convince the North Vietnamese to forego their support of the NLF, to convince them that the game was not worth the candle. Under the OPLAN mission statement, one of the purposes of psychological warfare operations was "to use all available media and practical means . . . phantom resistance movements, and psychological development of actual resistance."[31] Colonel Russell readily assumed that these methods would include the creation of either a notional or a real resistance movement within the North.[32] As we have seen, this was another assumption that turned out to be wrong. Under the PSYOPS Group, four sections were established: Radio, Printed

Media, Special Operations, and Research and Analysis. These sections were responsible for PSYOPS's main programs—the Sacred Sword of the Patriot League (SSPL), "black" and "white" radio operations, and printed materials and gift kits.

THE SSPL (MAT TRAN GUOM THIENG AI QUOC)

The CIA had already spent considerable time and effort in psychological operations aimed at North Vietnam. These operations tended to follow the "Wurlitzer" concept that had been developed by the agency in Eastern European operations in that each operation tended to complement and build on the fictions of the others. Most of them were the brainchildren of CIA officer Herbert Weisshart, who was assigned in 1964 to carry out psychological operations in Vietnam following a JCS directive to create a notional liberation front in North Vietnam.[33] This operation was expanded under MACSOG maritime operations Mint and Loki, in which North Vietnamese fishermen were kidnapped and transported to Cu Lao Cham Island (also known as Paradise Island), southeast of Da Nang. During their two-week stay, the detainees learned that they were the "guests" of the Sacred Sword of the Patriot League, a dissident communist movement within the North. The detainees were supposedly at the headquarters of the organization, located in a safe zone within North Vietnam itself. They were then fed the backstory concocted by the CIA and MACSOG.

The SSPL supposedly consisted of former Viet Minh led by Le Quoc Hung, who had fought the French but had turned against the takeover of the movement by "extremist" Vietnamese politicians who had betrayed them into becoming puppets of the communist Chinese. Due to their opposition, they had been forced to flee to Nghe An and Ha Tinh Provinces. On 17 April 1953, seven of their leaders formed the SSPL at the so-called Soldier's Conference. They took their name from the legendary magic sword with which the patriot Le Loi had expelled the Chinese from Vietnam after one thousand years of domination.

The communist land reform campaign of the 1950s, which had imposed collectivization on the northern peasants, led to unrest and an uprising in Nghe An that was brutally crushed by Hanoi. At this point the SSPL went underground. In December 1961 the organization held a national congress at which Le Quoc Hung was elected president. A second congress would be held in 1965, at which Hoang Chinh Nghia became president. By that time the SSPL supposedly had seven thousand members.

The detainees at Paradise Island were well fed and treated, but they were also subtly interrogated and indoctrinated. When their stay was over, they were returned to their homeland, but not before they had received gift packages and information from their captors. The gift kits included materials (soap, pencils, writing pads, cloth, and toys) that were hard to come by in North Vietnam and that were also emblazoned with the logo and colors of the SSPL. They were also provided with pre-tuned transistor radios with which to listen to SSPL broadcasts. To give the authorities at the northern Ministry of the Interior something to speculate upon, they were also instructed on how to make SSPL contacts on the mainland.

The SSPL gifts, indoctrination sessions, and radio broadcasts were surprisingly devoid of any political ideology. Their message was equally vociferous toward all foreign powers. The United States and the Saigon regime received the same harsh treatment as did the Soviet Union and the PRC. The SSPL called for a return to traditional Vietnamese values, which it was quick to compare to those of Hanoi and Saigon.

Of course, the entire operation was an elaborate fiction created with three purposes in mind. First, the returned detainees were sure to be interrogated by the northern security apparatus, which would be quite interested in any dissident group, especially one that might possibly be linked to the "spy commando" teams that MACSOG dropped into North Vietnam. Second, the detainees might possibly resent the heavy hand of the authorities, especially if they wanted to take away their "gifts." Third, the detainees would more than likely spread the word of this dissident movement among their fellows and might actually create a focus of unrest within the North.

Granted, this all sounds a little fantastic and the reader might find it unrealistic that the northern regime and population would actually fall for it. There were reports, however, that they not only believed it, but attributed the actions of the SSPL not to the southerners or Americans, but to the Soviet Union. According to Navy captain Bruce Dunning, a staffer at SACSA, the North Vietnamese security authorities attributed the SSPL to two PAVN lieutenant colonels who had defected to the USSR in 1964.[34]

RADIO OPERATIONS
Bolstering the fiction of internal resistance to the northern regime, MACSOG's radio office at Number 7 Hung Thap Tu Street, Saigon, produced a plethora of programming aimed at North Vietnam. Radio Red Flag was a "black" (nonattributable) station that purported to be broadcasting from within the North itself as the voice of dissident communists who were opposed to the "takeover" of their movement by those who supported the PRC.

Radio Red Flag began broadcasting on 13 April from a 750-watt transmitter (belonging to the ARVN Psychological Warfare Directorate) located at Dong Ha. SOG's other station, the Voice of Freedom (VOF), went on the air on 27 May. VOF was a "white" station whose source of origin was identified, but which broadcast straight news and entertainment. Its purpose was to inform the North Vietnamese and to compare life in the totalitarian North with that of the "free" South Vietnam. VOF was broadcast from a 20-kW shortwave and a 20-kW medium wave transmitter, both of which were located in the city of Hue. MACSOG also began the process of constructing a new facility that would house the VOF and a 200-kW transmitter at Hue.

POISON PENS

Another method of disturbing the serenity of the North was the use of printed materials. Poison-pen letters were drafted in Saigon by CIA specialists and then mailed into North Vietnam from third-party countries. These letters, addressed to prominent political and military cadres, used subtle hints and innuendoes (and sometimes, secret ink) that would arouse the curiosity and suspicion of the security personnel who routinely scrutinized and censored all mail. Psychological Operations also produced the gift kits that were air-dropped into the North Vietnam, floated ashore during MAROPS missions, or given to fishermen by the SSPL. MACSOG was also big on dropping and shooting propaganda leaflets into North Vietnam. By year's end the North had been inundated by 41 million leaflets and 20,000 gift kits.

Logistics

One can imagine the utter logistical chaos that must have reigned when MACSOG took over OPLAN 34A. Under the CIA there had been almost no supply accountability. No one had to sign for anything or track it either. An Army major, who was originally assigned the task of straightening out logistics after the takeover, could not make the system work and was quickly relieved by Navy lieutenant Terry Lingle. According to Lingle, the major had seemingly "gone native" and was living with a Vietnamese female employee within the compound. When the major left, a top sergeant then took up with the woman. Lingle complained that drinking and carousing were the order of the day and that, although most of the men tried hard, the majority of the personnel were parachute riggers, not supply specialists.[35]

One of the key issues faced by MACSOG after the takeover was providing for the budgeting and funding of a covert military operation. These problems were worked out by making the Department of Defense (DOD) responsible for all classified funding, while the individual services took over the cost of all TDY personnel assigned to MACSOG. The Navy took on MAROPS support, and Air Force funding was utilized for air assets and maintenance. The Chief of Naval Operations (CNO), JCS, MACV, and CINCPAC were made responsible for standard military items.

A financial audit was conducted in October to assist in establishing procurement procedures, accountability, and material/property control. It also helped in estimating the 1965 budget, which originally ended up (for DOD responsible items) estimated at $6,516,850. After review by higher headquarters, this figure was lowered to $5,102,000.[36] The JCS then tasked the CNO with being the executive agent for MACSOG classified funds. Annual budgets were to be forwarded to the Joint Chiefs via MACV and CINCPAC. After approval, the CNO programmed the funding and negotiated congressional approval. These funds were to be passed on quarterly by the CNO's comptroller.

Even the most hard-headed in Washington and Saigon soon realized that lack of mission success during the year was linked to nonavailability of major equipment items, unsuitability of others, modifications to existing equipment, and start-up problems. Within maritime operations, for example, CINCPAC's decision to increase the number of PTFs to eight caused a backup. SOG's logistics and personnel system was not geared to the quick reaction required, and training and readiness slipped by as much as six months.

CISO

Another hurdle at this early point in the conflict was the lack of shipping and delays in transportation. This was 1964 and the tremendous American logistical buildup of later years had yet to take place. Agreement was reached in June between DOD, CIA, and the Counterinsurgency Support Office (CISO), Second Logistical Command, Okinawa, to provide quick requirement supply for MACSOG. CISO had been created in 1962 by the 1st Special Forces Group as an equipment pipeline for the newly created, CIA-supported Civilian Irregular Defense Groups (CIDG) in South Vietnam. CISO provided standard U.S. military and other "unique" items that were necessary for paramilitary and covert operations. Under the leadership of Conrad "Ben" Baker, CISO also assisted by procuring more common items through open purchase in Japan.

One of the necessary operations carried out by the Logistics Branch was the leasing of MACSOG's Nasty-class PTFs to the South Vietnamese government. Although it was pure window dressing, the leases were thought necessary in order to provide a cover for the arrival of the new vessels and to provide American deniability in case of international repercussions. The PTFs were handed over to South Vietnam on a five-year basis. By year's end an audit of property and inventory was completed and some fiscal responsibility was established. This was an absolute necessity, since supply activity had grown to encompass about seven hundred line items of equipment. These included everything from uniforms, a wide variety of weapons and ammunition, spare parts and medical supplies, to PTFs and aircraft parts. The volume of material handled averaged about fifty tons per month.

Communications

At the beginning of 1964, MACSOG did not have a separate Communications Branch. This was probably another reflection of the tenuous and troubled relationship between MACSOG and the CIA. How much communications support was the agency supposed to provide to the new unit? Evidently, not very much, since the CIA did not hand over any of its communications facilities to MACSOG. The transfer of the agency's Four Sparks facility in Saigon, for example, would not take place until 1966.

SOG's JTD soon provided for two officers and two enlisted men to control communications, but they still had to be supported by TDY personnel provided by MACV J-2 until permanent party personnel arrived. In the end, the military provided operational and administrative circuits for MACSOG, connecting MACV to the NAD, Camp Long Thanh, the U.S. Embassy, and Tan Son Nhut Air Base. The CIA was only tasked to provide maintenance of maritime operations communications equipment and cryptographic support (in the form of one-time pads provided to agent teams). SOG/SES also utilized the CIA's Project Bugs radio relay site in the Philippines to receive and relay all agent team traffic to and from North Vietnam.

By the end of 1964 teletypewriter (TTY) circuits had been established between MACSOG's Saigon headquarters, the NAD at Da Nang, and the 1st Flight Detachment at Nha Trang. A single side band (SSB) radio circuit had also been established from the same headquarters to Camp Long Thanh, 1st Flight, and the NAD.

Comment: Training and Doctrine

The original Cold War mission of U.S. Special Forces (created in 1952) was to conduct unconventional warfare operations by seeking out, training, and supporting indigenous personnel capable of becoming effective guerrillas. This would, of course, take place behind enemy lines in the event of a conventional Soviet invasion of Western Europe or serve the same purpose in a general conflict in Asia. In the new era of decolonization and wars of national liberation, however, the mission of the Special Forces was altered in accordance with which side in a particular conflict the United States supported, the titles of freedom fighter or revolutionary guerrilla seemingly altering in every context.[37] In Vietnam, for example, the mission of the Green Berets was transformed to the opposite of its original: to seek out, engage, and neutralize guerrillas.

But what kind of conflict was the struggle in Vietnam? Was it a civil war between rival political ideologies? Was it a nationalist conflict to rid Vietnam of another colonial aggressor and determine the fate of a unified nation? Was it simply another front in the ongoing struggle between the superpowers? Or was it all of the above, tangled together in a hopelessly complex skein that the American political and military leadership never fully understood or addressed? America's original response was that the conflict was more political than military, or that the two motives were at least equally important. In a revolutionary war, the guerrilla could not exist without the active participation of at least a sizable portion of the civilian population. Therefore, there had to be enough sympathy for the cause of the guerrilla and dissatisfaction with the current regime for the problem to exist in the first place.

"Counterinsurgency" (a term utilized by the United States in order to avoid the more negative connotations of the term "counterrevolutionary") warfare became the answer. Counterinsurgency doctrine emphasized both military and psychological approaches. Nation building, propaganda, and modernization were placed on an equal footing with conventional military force as weapons that would be utilized to bolster the client regime, oppose the guerrilla enemy, and gain the support of the population. In the new counterinsurgency era, these were the weapons that would be utilized by the Special Forces. But was this the kind of conflict that MACSOG was supposed to fight? The organization was to be an unconventional warfare force, which, by definition, was to utilize military and paramilitary units consisting of indigenous forces trained, equipped, and led by an external force. It would incorporate guerrilla warfare, covert or clandestine activities, subversion, sabotage, and intelligence gathering. All well and good, except for the fact that, even with the inclusion of personnel who had participated in both Operation Hotfoot and Operation White Star in Laos, very few U.S. servicemen, Special Forces or not, had any training or experience in waging such a struggle.

A few examples might suffice to illustrate this point. The trials and tribulations of Colonel Russell upon his takeover of MACSOG have already been discussed. These problems were not going to disappear over time. Col. John Singlaub (MACSOG's third commander) stated that he received personnel "who didn't have a clue, who'd never heard the word unconventional war, had never heard of special operations."[38] Lt. Col. Edward Partain, the first commander of agent team operations, although a Special Forces officer, had no experience in unconventional warfare or agent operations. The same was true of the next two officers who commanded this section of MACSOG, Reginald Woolard and Robert McLane.[39]

Of the first four chiefs of the NAD, none had any unconventional warfare experience. Col. Charles Norton, chief of the Command and Control Detachment at Da Nang (after cross-border ground operations had commenced) encapsulated the whole problem and MACSOG's solution: "We all learned from each other . . . no one saw recon as a Special Forces mission in those days."[40] This was the supreme irony of McNamara's rationale for Operation Parasol/Switchback. The military supposedly had more personnel and resources to throw at the problem, when, in fact, it had neither.

Another problem facing MACSOG was the military's reluctance when it came to men who specialized in unconventional operations or whose careers placed them outside the bounds of the military mainstream.[41] When Don Blackburn (SOG's second commanding officer) was tasked with opening cross-border operations in Laos, his first choice as mission commander was Lt. Col. Arthur D. "Bull" Simons. Blackburn was stonewalled in his appointment, however, by General Westmoreland's dictate that all colonels assigned to a headquarters had to have attended one of the military's war or staff colleges. Simons' exemplary record, outstanding career, combat Ranger experience, Special Forces qualifications, and two tours leading Operation White Star in Laos availed him nothing. Simons was a reserve officer, not a West Pointer or mainstream officer.

The result was that the Pentagon had to process a special exception to Westmoreland's rule to allow him to join MACSOG.[42] After commanding the Son Tay raid, Simons did not make the promotion list for brigadier general in 1971, even after the prompting of Defense Secretary Melvin Laird. Westmoreland, then Army chief of staff, refused to buck the system. Simons was an excellent colonel, but "just because he was an exceptional combat leader didn't mean he'd make a good general."[43] After Simons retired in 1971 he was never asked to lecture at any of the Army's schools or staff colleges. The Air Force Academy and the Armed Forces Staff College were not so picky.

MACSOG's institutional problems could have been alleviated by closer cooperation with the one U.S. agency that did have experience in unconventional warfare, the Central Intelligence Agency. But, as we have seen, the CIA considered 34A to be a dead letter. It was also perturbed that its organizational aptitude had been challenged and found wanting by the politicians and the military. These questions of ability and the takeover of northern operations could only be seen as a slap in the face by the agency. The result was that the CIA let the military go it alone. The agency obviously lacked any interest in supporting MACSOG with any but the most meager means. The CIA limited its support of MACSOG to psychological operations, since, within the agency, psywar specialists were never considered "first string operatives."[44]

Thus the difficulties faced by MACSOG at its creation and, indeed, during the entire life span of OPLAN 34A. MACSOG's commanders had to build the organization from the ground up, waging battles with the military bureaucracy and often facing condescension or outright indifference from the CIA, their fellows, and their superiors. Officers and men had to learn on the job; thus the helter-skelter approach to building the organization.

Chapter Two

1965: SHINING BRASS

Headquarters

On 1 May 1965 Colonel Russell was replaced as chief, MACSOG, by Col. Donald D. Blackburn. A native son of Florida, Blackburn was commissioned in the Army in 1940 and was shipped out to Luzon as an advisor to a Filipino infantry battalion. When the islands fell to the Japanese in 1942, he evaded capture and took to the bush, ending up in the mountains of northern Luzon. There he took part in organizing and commanding Igorot tribesmen behind Japanese lines. Building a jungle camp and training center, Blackburn soon led his "headhunters" in anti-Japanese operations. By the time Douglas McArthur returned to the Philippines, Blackburn's force had grown to regimental size and, at the age of twenty-nine, he had been promoted to lieutenant colonel (the youngest in the U.S. Army). In 1955 these exploits were celebrated in the book *Blackburn's Headhunters,* which, in turn, was made into the film *Surrender—Hell!*

After the war Blackburn did a tour as provost marshal of Washington, went to infantry school, and learned to become a "normal" officer. In 1950 he was made an instructor of military psychology and leadership at West Point. Blackburn was sent to South Vietnam in late 1957 as senior advisor to the Vietnamese general commanding in the Mekong Delta and was then given command of the 77th SFG at Fort Bragg, North Carolina.

In 1960 he was given the task of organizing and commanding Operation White Star, the covert Special Forces advisory effort in Laos. He was serving on the SACSA staff at the Pentagon when he got the call from Clyde Russell to take over MACSOG. It is indicative of the Army's relationship with its Special Forces branch that although Blackburn had an exemplary and spotless career, he had not been promoted in ten years, lending credence to the adage that a colonelcy was the highest rank that could be attained by a Special Forces man.

MACSOG's Administrative Branch performed functions similar to G-1 and adjutant general staff organizations by carrying out personnel and administrative functions that were typical of any military or corporate organization. These included preparing administrative and personnel policies and procedures (for both U.S. personnel and civilians in the employ of SOG); records management; in/out-processing; and personnel allocation. The branch also handled the processing of personnel actions, including awards and decorations, rest and recreation leaves, tour extensions, verification and issuance of security clearances, and officer/ NCO efficiency reports. Liaison personnel came from the CIA and from the South Vietnamese SES. On 16 January the SES was reorganized and renamed the Strategic Technical Service (So Ky Thuat) or STS. The Vietnamese Special Forces Liaison Service, which had been tasked with intelligence collection and covert actions in Laos, was now made integral to the STS. The organization was still commanded by Colonel Tran Van Ho, the former commander of the SES.

In January MACSOG had a roster of 63 officers, 2 warrant officers, 14 civilians, and 67 enlisted personnel. By December the number of men assigned had increased to 89 officers, 3 warrant officers, 15 civilians, and 119 enlisted men.[1] During the year one American was killed in action, two were killed in accidents, two were wounded, and two were missing in action.[2]

CROSS-BORDER CONCEPTS

Although early in the conflict the Americans lacked detailed intelligence on communist troop and supply movements across South Vietnam's borders, ample evidence existed that Hanoi was utilizing the neutrality of Laos and Cambodia as a shield for units seeking sanctuary from offensive operations near those borders. As early as December 1963 Gen. Paul Harkins had proposed two cross-border concepts known as OPLANS 98-64 and 98A-64.[3] They envisaged intelligence collection, harassment, and hot pursuit of communist forces into Laos by ARVN and supporting American advisory personnel. The forays were to proceed no further than thirty-one miles across the border and would have been supported by VNAF assets. The United States was to exert control of the effort and coordinate the operations. Both proposals went nowhere.

On 6 August 1964 the new American commander, General Westmoreland, commented to CINCPAC and the JCS on South Vietnamese plans

ORGANIZATIONAL STRUCTURE, JANUARY 1965

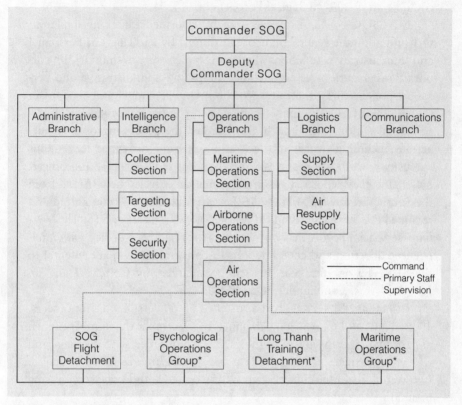

*Augmented by TDY/TDY MITs as required

for cross-border operations into Laos. The Liaison Bureau would serve as headquarters under Lieutenant Colonel Ho Tieu in Operation Anh Dung. This "three bridgehead" concept was to consist of two phases. During the first, the South Vietnamese would establish bridgeheads in Laos, one near Lao Bao, fifty kilometers wide and fifteen kilometers deep; one of similar size opposite Dak Prou; and one twenty kilometers wide and eleven deep opposite the border outpost of Dak To. The LLDB were to man the first bridgehead, I Corps personnel the second, and II Corps personnel the third.

The LLDB strike force was to consist of four Airborne Ranger companies, three recon teams from Project Delta (ARVN cross-border units), and later, an Airborne battalion. The Corps were to utilize CIDG units, plus one Ranger battalion each and such infantry as could be spared. In

Phase II of the plan, the lodgments were to be expanded to connect the bridgeheads to a depth of forty kilometers. U.S. advisors were to accompany the operations while air support was to come from the VNAF. This operational plan, however, was also frowned upon at higher levels.

MACV had also prepared contingency plans for larger-scale anti-infiltration efforts. One was a proposed manned defensive line that would have stretched below the DMZ from South Vietnam into Laos. The manpower necessary for the system was estimated at four to six American and allied divisions. Another OPLAN envisaged a three-division thrust from northern Thailand toward the PAVN logistical hub at Tchepone, Laos. The Defense Department believed that the manpower requirements, the magnitude of logistical and political problems, and the weather and terrain made both proposals impracticable.

Westmoreland did not give up. If interdiction by conventional forces was precluded, then perhaps the Special Forces could step into the breach. This was the genesis of Golden Eagle, an offshoot of a bilateral Thai/U.S. defense plan. U.S. Special Forces would penetrate the strategic Bolovens Plateau of Laos from Thailand with USAF support, and thence attack the Ho Chi Minh Trail from the west. As a fallback position, MACV proposed the smaller-scale Operation Shining Brass as an alternative.

On 12 October 1965 the Joint Chiefs sent dispatch 3924, granting authority for the commencement of cross-border operations against the North Vietnamese logistical corridor running south from North Vietnam, through the Laotian panhandle, and into the border regions of South Vietnam.[4] It had been decided that, due to increased communist infiltration, some response was necessary. Covert ground operations against the Ho Chi Minh Trail were about to begin.[5]

LAOS

Granted complete independence from France in 1953, a coalition government had been created in the Kingdom of Laos under the Geneva agreements that ended the First Indochina War the following year. The communist Pathet Lao, who had fought side by side with Viet Minh against the French, took the field again when the coalition collapsed due to events that are best described as "convoluted." Aided by the North Vietnamese and the Soviet Union, the Pathet Lao were opposed by an inept Royal Lao Army assisted by covert CIA operatives and U.S. Army Special Forces during Operations Hotfoot and White Star. The Thai government also got in on the action by building and deploying (with CIA assistance) clandestine special operations volunteers.

The powerbrokers on both sides, however, were not really interested in "winning" the Laotian conflict. The United States was beginning to realize that the landlocked kingdom was not the place for a major confrontation with Hanoi, the Soviets, or the Chinese (who were also making threatening noises). At the time, the North Vietnamese were concerned with their western neighbor only to the extent of maintaining their logistics and communications conduit through the panhandle to South Vietnam. The Soviets and Chinese were interested only because the United States was interested.

American plenipotentiary W. Averell Harriman brokered the end of the "Laotian Crisis" on 23 July 1962 with the signing of a Declaration on the Neutrality of Laos. The situation was defused by the formation of a tripartite coalition government formed under Prince Souvanna Phouma, the (supposed) removal of all foreign troops, and supervision of the agreement by the members of an International Control Commission.[6] This settlement, however, fared no better than the first and the Pathet Lao went back to war with the aid of their North Vietnamese allies. Once again the United States became the Lao government's backer as the secret war heated up. America's goal was to keep the Pathet Lao at bay and to interdict communist supplies and manpower destined for the South.

Intelligence

The Intelligence Branch was suffering under an increased workload, but things took a turn for the better when MACSOG gained increased photo interpretation capabilities and manning. During the year the branch produced its first major work, a Coastal Shipping/Inland Waterways Study for maritime operations.

In December MACV required that SOG intelligence come in line with standardized intelligence procedures by having essential elements of information (EEI) promulgated for both MAROPS and agent teams in North Vietnam. Going one step further, MACSOG developed a sanitized Spot Report so that its intelligence information could be quickly disseminated to relevant commands within MACV.

The initiation of the Spot Reports pointed out one of the trickiest aspects of MACSOG's intelligence-gathering operations, one that was compounded by the addition of intelligence gathered during its Shining Brass forays. How was the intelligence gathered going to be disseminated to other commands without compromising security? The easiest answer was to distribute the information through the joint U.S./SVN Combined Intelligence Information Center disguised as being collected by a "friendly guerrilla unit."

Operations

The Operations Branch was responsible for the control and supervision of the staff elements of MACSOG's operational groups. These staffs included the Maritime Operations, Airborne Operations 34A (agent operations in North Vietnam), Air Operations, and the new Airborne Operations Shining Brass and Medical Sections. The task of the Medical Section was to provide screening and outpatient care for indigenous agents and the mercenaries employed in the new Shining Brass program.

Airborne Operations Group

During the year Airborne Operations Section became the staff element monitoring the operations of the newly created Airborne Operations Group. The initiation of Operation Rolling Thunder in March led to a change of mission for MACSOG agent teams emplaced in North Vietnam. Small demolitions, disruption of lines of communication (LOCs), and psychological operations gave way to roadwatch activities and intelligence collection. By October the agents had also been authorized to recruit their own local assets for intelligence collection. Other incentives for the change were that the Defense Department wanted eyes on the ground in the North in order to provide target information for the bombing campaign, to assist downed and evading U.S. aircrew, and to provide early warning in the event of overt Chinese intervention.

Teams already scheduled for insertion also faced the mission changes. They were quickly retrained and renamed Early Warning Observation Teams (EWOTS), whose mission was to conduct roadwatch activities and intelligence collection. Washington was worried over possible Chinese intervention, and EWOTS would serve as a trip wire, giving warning of a possible Chinese buildup in North Vietnam.[7] EWOTS was given approval on 30 October and went into effect during November. Two new teams were infiltrated during the year and nine teams (eighty-three men) were in place at year's end.

RESISTANCE

By March of the year Operation Rolling Thunder, the sustained U.S. bombing campaign in the North, had begun, replacing SOG's covert effort as the chief method by which Washington hoped to curb Hanoi's effort in the South. With this loss of mission, Colonel Blackburn began to request that Washington allow his agent teams to build a guerrilla movement within North Vietnam. Colonel Russell had previously broached the subject with Washington, wanting to organize minority tribal elements, Catholic communities, and the Chinese population into a real resistance movement. Although the creation of an indigenous movement opposed to the northern regime had been one of the original goals of MACSOG, nothing had been done during the organization's inaugural year.

In the spring of 1965, however, things were looking up. President Johnson had approved the "Tempo and Scope Proposal," a JCS plan to arm and train the minority hill tribes of the North for resistance operations.[8] Leonard Ungar, the U.S. ambassador to Laos, the State Department, and the CIA, however, staunchly disapproved of the plan and it was shelved. The key reason for the failure to create such a movement was that the U.S. government had publicly declared that it had no intention of overthrowing the Hanoi regime. There was serious trepidation in the halls of power lest the United States should be discovered to be violating its public policies. This was not, however, going to stop the commanders of SOG from continuing to ask.[9]

Undeterred, Don Blackburn (who had already raised the ire of Washington and the Vientiane embassy by proposing the infiltration of agent teams by foot into North Vietnam from Laos) proposed that Hanoi's strengths be turned against it. He sought permission to create and sponsor a front organization within South Vietnam that would mirror that of the communist-dominated National Liberation Front.[10] The organization would serve to unify expatriate elements within the South (and could also serve as a recruitment pool), it could gain foreign recognition and assistance, and it might possibly serve as a springboard for a real resistance movement in the North.

The answer was an unequivocal no. The official policy of the United States precluded support for such a movement, real or notional. This attitude was one that would plague MACSOG throughout its existence. Washington could never seem to comprehend that it could carry out covert operations on one hand while denying them on the other. For the commanders of SOG this attitude was infuriating to say the least. They were the leaders of a covert organization fighting a clandestine war in two (later three) countries. As Col. John Singlaub (SOG's third commander) put it: "If covert was to be consistent with overt policy, why was it necessary to operate covertly at all?"[11]

AGENT TEAM ACTIVITIES

Agent team insertions began again in May when Team Remus Alpha was dropped in to reinforce Remus.[12] The five-man team landed safely and contacted headquarters. Later that month, five-man Team Horse parachuted into Son La Province to reinforce Team Tourbillon only to be captured near its landing zone.

Team Dog/Gecko, a nine-man reinforcement for Team Easy was inserted on 17 September. The drop went well and communication was established with MACSOG/STS. The team was redesignated Easy Alpha on 30 October. This communication was, however, the last one made by the agents. On 7 November another attempt was made to reinforce Team Tourbillon. The infiltration of eight-man Team Verse appeared to go well and communication was established.

One of the benefits of the mission changes was JCS authorization in September for the use of Nakhon Phanom Royal Thai Air Force Base (RTAFB), as a staging center for the helicopter insertion of agent teams. The American Embassy in Vientiane grudgingly gave approval for the use of Laotian airspace for agent team insertions into western North Vietnam. This would at least allow for a little variety in MACSOG's ability to keep teams viable in the North. On 19 November, ten-man Team Romeo went in on the first pure EWOTS mission. A transport aircraft delivered the men from Tan Son Nhut to Khe Sanh and from there the team was lifted by two H-34 helicopters piloted by South Vietnamese crews. The choppers ferried the team while a third H-34 carried their American and Vietnamese operations officers. The men were transported into Le Thuy District of Quang Binh Province, close to the Ho Chi Minh Trail. Radio contact was established and the team then headed off to its regrouping point.

The men on the ground soon realized, however, that they had been inserted on the wrong landing zone. After six weeks of roaming through harsh terrain, Romeo was informed that they had been located and to expect an airdrop of supplies. The drop did take place, but the team watched in horror as its supply bundles fell five miles away. By that time the agents were being tracked by communist security troops. The team actually captured five members of the Quang Binh Border Defense Forces, who had been scouring the countryside for them since the team had landed. Going against doctrine, the team did not kill its captives. This was a good move on its part, since any hostile actions or resistance by a team prior to its capture led to summary execution. One week later, on 14 January, Team Romeo was surrounded and taken captive. All that SOG knew was that the team radio operator had sent the coded distress signal and the short message "Romeo already captured," repeated twice. Contact was later restored, however, and the team reported that the radio operator had been mistaken.

TRAINING
The agents who made up the teams were recruited by the Liaison Service from among northern refugees. Through contacts with the Catholic

clergy and in the ARVN, the South Vietnamese could usually find men willing to volunteer for a "secret mission." When enough men with the right qualifications to fill the complement of a team were recruited, they were dispatched to Camp Quyet Thang, the ARVN Airborne Training Center at Long Thanh. Located about twenty-two kilometers northeast of Saigon in Bien Hoa Province, the camp had been built on the site of a former Japanese airstrip that had been converted to a training facility by the CIA in March 1963.

Upon arrival, the prospective agents immediately entered an isolation compound known as Ku Cham, the Forbidden City. There they would remain isolated, both from other teams and from personnel training for other MACSOG operations. Training was initially provided by the CIA with Army Special Forces instructors relegated to being jumpmasters. By 1965 the agency was phasing out its contribution, and a twelve-man Special Forces team (Detachment A-727B) was dispatched from Okinawa to take over instruction.

Three months of introductory courses on weapons, tactics, communications, medicine, and psychological operations were first up on the bill of fare. During the second training phase, the men specialized in one of those skills. This was followed by a month of field exercises, both in the vicinity of Long Thanh and at Monkey Mountain, outside Da Nang. The trainees also underwent continuous and intense parachute training during their stay.

What kind of men volunteered for the agent program? Many were idealistic youngsters who wanted to strike a blow for their nation. Others had previous experience in clandestine work, either for the French or for one of the covert South Vietnamese services. Many were veterans of the ARVN, looking for higher pay, for another way to take the war to their enemy, or just for the adventure. Many Americans derided the volunteers as opportunistic men simply looking to make more money, but this explanation quickly runs aground when one considers the risks that they were willing to take. It certainly fades into insignificance when one considers the price that they were ultimately going to pay for their activities.

Shining Brass

THE TRAIL

During the First Indochina War the Viet Minh had maintained north/ south communications through a system of paths and trails along the Laotian/Vietnamese border. When armed conflict with the Diem regime heated up during 1958, Hanoi dispatched the newly established 559th Transportation Group, under the command of the legendary Colonel (later General) Vo Bam, south in order to improve and maintain the system in its bid for a unified Vietnam. In the early days of the war the Trail was utilized by the North Vietnamese strictly for the infiltration of manpower. This was due to the fact that Hanoi could supply its southern allies by sea more efficiently than by land.[13] With the growing American commitment, the sea routes for supply infiltration were gradually choked off by naval power so the Trail was shifted to double duty.

After establishing his headquarters at Vinh Linh, North Vietnam, Vo Bam set to work on planning and taking the initial steps in modernizing the logistical system. The task was daunting. The terrain of the eastern Truong Son Mountains, through which the logistics corridor meandered, was a sparsely populated region of rugged mountains, triple-canopy jungle, and dense rainforests. The North Vietnamese called the logistical system the Truong Son Strategic Supply Route, but for the Free World Military Forces, it was named for North Vietnam's legendary leader, Ho Chi Minh.

By April 1961 the transportation hub of Tchepone, on Laotian Route 9, was taken by PAVN and Pathet Lao forces. The 559th Group then "flipped" its line of communications to the western side of the mountains. This expansion was accomplished in an effort to beat the signing of the 1962 Geneva Accord on Laos.[14] The following year the 559th had a complement of 6,000 personnel in two regiments, the 70th and 71st.[15] This figure does not include combat troops in security roles or North Vietnamese and Laotian civilian laborers, which would have effectively doubled the number. During 1961 U.S. intelligence estimated that 4,000 men had gone south on the Trail; in 1962, 5,300; and in 1963, 4,700.[16] These were "confirmed" infiltrators, counted on the basis of at least two persons or documents. During the same period, data showed that there were probably an equal number (around 12,850) of probable infiltrators.[17] The supply capacity of the Trail had reached twenty to thirty tons per day in 1964, and it was estimated by MACV intelligence that 12,000 (actually 9,000) PAVN regulars reached South Vietnam that year.

Two types of units served under the 559th Group, *binh tram* and commo-liaison units. A *binh tram* was the equivalent of a regimental logistical headquarters and was responsible for securing a particular section of the network. While separate units were tasked with security, engineer, and signal functions, the *binh tram* provided the logistical necessities. Usually located one-day's march from one another, commo-liaison stations were responsible for providing food, housing, medical care, and guides to the next way station.

The popular conception of Hanoi's logistical arrangements on the Trail sometimes bordered on the romantic (or at least harkened back to the experience of the First Indochina War). The image of barefoot hordes pushing heavily loaded bicycles, driving oxcarts, or acting as human pack animals moving hundreds of tons of supplies in this manner from North Vietnam to the South bears little relation to the reality of 1965. What most did not realize was that the truck (especially Chinese, Russian, and Eastern Bloc models) was quickly replacing the human, bicycle, and oxcart as the main method of transportation for supplies on the Trail.

As early as December 1961, the 3rd Truck Transportation Group of the General Rear Service Department became the first motor transport unit fielded by PAVN to work the Trail. Thanks to its efforts, trucks could then drive south as far as Na Bo (just northeast of Tchepone) on Route 9. During 1964 motor roads were built across Route 9 to Ta Bac and Xa Xeng. This logistical effort provided a quadrupling of supply capacity.[18] MACV estimated in 1965 that PAVN supply requirements for their southern forces amounted to 234 tons of all supplies per day. It also believed that the supplies moved south by different routes—195 tons through Laos, 25 tons through Cambodia, and 14 tons by sea.[19] Defense Intelligence Agency (DIA) analysts concluded that during the Laotian dry season the communists were moving thirty trucks per day (90 tons) over the Trail.[20]

PAVN built and maintained four major base areas in Laos, each of which served as a conduit to one of its southern military regions. Those personnel or supplies heading for the B-4 or B-5 Fronts of Military Region 5 went directly across the DMZ or through Base Area 604 along Route 9 or Base Area 611 adjacent to South Vietnam's Ashau Valley. Reaching the latter two areas required a twenty-day march from North Vietnam. Men destined for the B-1 Front headed to Base Area 614 near the Ashau Valley, while those traveling further south to the B-3 Front moved through Base Area 609, a fifty-day trip from Vinh.

Until 1965 the 559th Group's commo-liaison chain extended only as far as Base Area 609. During the year, however, it began construction of new trails (eventually known as the Sihanouk Trail) to connect the segments that ran through southern Laos into Cambodia, allowing the direct reinforcement of the Central Office for South Vietnam (COSVN) and the B-2 Front. Thanks in part to these improvements it was estimated by MACV that 24,000 to 36,000 men made the march south in 1965.[21] In fact, the amount of supplies transported during the year almost equaled the combined total for the previous five years. A 50,000-troop cadre, including seven infantry regiments and twenty battalions, made the trip south.[22]

In April 1965 command of the 559th Group devolved to General Phan Trong Tue, the former northern minister of transportation, and the unit was placed under the auspices of the People's Army General Department of Rear Services. Under Tue's guidance, the group's forces were divided into units by geographical sectors, which essentially corresponded to divisional commands. The newly created Group 665 coordinated troop movements south and the transport of the wounded to the North. The initial network, now the 70th Transport Group, was supplemented by the 71st and 72nd Groups, the former to extend the Trail into Cambodia, the latter to build connections into South Vietnam.[23]

Tue commanded 24,000 men in six truck transportation battalions, two bicycle transportation battalions, a boat transportation battalion, eight engineer battalions, and forty-five commo-liaison stations. An engineer regiment and four anti-aircraft artillery battalions were also attached to the 559th. The motto of the unit became "Build roads to advance, fight the enemy to travel."[24] Between December 1964 and May 1965, 2,294 trucks were seen moving south on the Trail and 2,492 were seen moving in the opposite direction.[25]

For the Free World Military Forces, interdiction of the Trail system had become one of the war's top priorities, but operations against it were complicated by the "neutrality" of Laos. The endless intricacies of Laotian affairs and American and North Vietnamese interference in them eventually led to a mutual policy of each ignoring the other, at least in the public eye. This did not, however, prevent both sides from violating that neutrality: the North Vietnamese by protecting and expanding their supply conduit and by supporting their Pathet Lao allies, the Americans by propping up the Royal Thai military, building and supporting a CIA-backed clandestine army to fight the communists, and by bombing the Trail incessantly.

INTERDICTION
On 14 December 1964 USAF Operation Barrel Roll had carried out the first bombing of the Trail system in Laos.[26] On 20 March 1965, after the initiation of Operation Rolling Thunder against the North, President Johnson gave approval for a corresponding escalation against the Trail. Barrel Roll would continue in northeastern Laos while the southern panhandle was bombed in Operation Steel Tiger. The first mission of the new operation was launched on 3 April. By mid-year the number of sorties being flown had grown from twenty to one thousand per month.[27]

In late January 1965, MACV requested operational control over bombing in the southern half of the panhandle directly adjacent to South Vietnam. General Westmoreland claimed that the area was an integral part of the southern battlefield. This request was granted and that area came under the auspices of MACV in Operation Tiger Hound. Bombing in the western half of the DMZ was carried out under Operation Nickel Steel. It was also in January that MACV began to actively campaign with CINCPAC and the JCS for the launching of cross-border ground operations.

Political complications were not all that hampered air and ground operations. The weather in southern Laos played a large role in operations and it posed myriad problems for any interdiction campaign. The southwest monsoon (from mid-May to mid-September) brought heavy precipitation (70 percent of 150 inches per year), with the heaviest rainfall in July and August. The skies were usually overcast and temperatures were high. The northwest monsoon (from mid-October to mid-March) was relatively drier with lower temperatures and clearer skies. This was complicated, however, by morning fog and overcast, and by the smoke and haze produced by the slash-and-burn agriculture practiced by the indigenous population. On the ground, the CIA had initially been given the task of stopping, slowing, or, at the very least, observing the communists' infiltration effort. Within Laos the agency had initiated Project Pincushion during 1962 for those very purposes. This operation later evolved into Project Hardnose, in which CIA-led reconnaissance team operations took place.

OVER THE FENCE

The South Vietnamese military had been conducting operations in Laos since 1960. This effort had been run from Nha Trang by Colonel Tran Khac Kinh, deputy commander of the LLDB, and by the following year, the CIA had assigned three paramilitary experts to work with it. The missions were carried out by Montagnard elements led by LLDB forces under the Border Surveillance Program. There were forty-one team-size and eight company-size operations conducted during this period.[28]

These operations, launched from Dak Pek and Khe Sanh, were from one week to three months in duration, were walk-ins, and received no air support. From June to August 1962, the project's most auspicious mission was a two-month overwatch of the PAVN-occupied airfield at Tchepone. These operations were halted in late 1962 due to the signing of the Geneva Accords on Laos, but they were scheduled to resume in January 1963. Due to the Buddhist crisis, however, they were delayed until August. In the interim, Special Forces personnel TDY from the 1st SFG had formed eight-man agent teams that were scheduled to carry out operations in Laos based on SOG's northern operations. This was the genesis of Operation Leaping Lena.

In July, Colonel Russell and Col. Theodore Leonard (commander, 5th Special Forces Group) were called to Saigon to meet with General Westmoreland and General Taylor, two ambassadors, Henry Cabot Lodge and Leonard Unger, and Secretary of Defense McNamara. Russell and Leonard were rather shocked when they were queried as to how long it would take the 5th SFG to begin operations in Laos. Leonard responded with his own questions. With what forces? What was the mission? The colonels stated that they could not promise any tangible results unless American troops participated in the effort. McNamara agreed with them, but then stated that the State Department did not want to risk American exposure in "neutral" Laos.

On 17 March President Johnson approved NSAM 288, authorizing the ARVN to conduct cross-border operations and opening the door for later American participation. Laotian general Phoumi Nosavan and ARVN general Nguyen Khanh met, carried out negotiations, and then signed a secret agreement providing free passage of the border to ARVN units and for information sharing between their two armies. On 5 May the 5th SFG received authorization for Project Delta (the ARVN program) and the first cross-border mission was code-named "Leaping Lena." The Americans would train and equip the reconnaissance teams, but they would not participate in the missions themselves. Leaping Lena consisted of five eight-man patrol teams of Montagnards commanded by LLDB personnel that were parachuted along Route 9 in the vicinity of Tchepone.

The first team was airdropped on 21 June, three more the following day, and the fifth on 1 July. The result was a fiasco. One team was lost and never communicated, the second was captured when it landed in a communist-occupied village, and three remained in radio contact only briefly. Of the forty personnel inserted during the operation, only six returned on foot, bringing back little if any intelligence other than to confirm the presence of communist forces in the target area. The postmortem on the operation was that in order for cross-border operations to be successful, they would have to be led by American personnel. It was at this point that the State Department stepped in to throw cold water on the operation. The specter of PAVN or the Pathet Lao displaying captured Americans to the world press haunted the men of Foggy Bottom. As a result of the State Department's foot-dragging, the initiation of the operation was delayed until the autumn.

In October MACSOG received authorization to utilize American personnel in cross-border operations into the Laotian panhandle under the cover name Shining Brass. The missions were to be run as a separate section under Airborne Operations. SOG planned to conduct the operation in three phases of steadily mounting pressure. Phase I (the only one then authorized) would consist of launching reconnaissance teams to gather intelligence on communist logistical routes and base areas. The intelligence would then be utilized by the USAF 2nd Air Division to launch air strikes. Phase II would consist of the insertion of larger exploitation forces that would take advantage of communist weaknesses by raiding targets of opportunity exposed by the recon teams. These activities would be stepped up under Phase III, which also envisioned the development of guerrilla movements in southeastern Laos.[29]

Although Westmoreland had attempted to have the Shining Brass and Tiger Hound boundaries aligned, this was refused. The operations were to be conducted in only two small areas along the border. The northern zone of operations was opposite Kham Duc, straddling Highway 165, and was 3 miles wide and 12 miles deep. The second was opposite Ben Het/Dak To, and was 7.5 miles wide by 12 deep. The recon teams were further limited by having to cross the border on foot, although evacuation or reinforcement by helicopter was authorized. Due to the nature of the terrain in eastern Laos, Westmoreland adamantly threatened to scrub the entire operation without helicopter insertions and this demand was finally granted.

THE BULL

Lt. Col. Arthur D. "Bull" Simons was the man Blackburn wanted to head the newly inaugurated cross-border missions. Simons had been commissioned during the Second World War as an artillery lieutenant out of ROTC from the University of Missouri. He first served in the 98th Field Artillery in the New Guinea campaign, and then commanded Company B, 6th Ranger Battalion, which he led in the invasion of the Philippines. During the Korean Conflict he served as an instructor of hand-to-hand combat and close-quarters shooting at the Army's Ranger Training Center. By 1958 he had been assigned to the 77th Special Forces at Fort Bragg, and while there he met Don Blackburn, who made him commander of a battalion-level "C" team.

By 1961 Simons was again serving under Blackburn as commander on the ground in Operation White Star, where he trained Kha tribesmen on the Bolovens Plateau for operations against what was going to become the Ho Chi Minh Trail. Returning from Laos, Simons commanded Special Forces in Panama and was serving as chief of staff of the Kennedy Center for Military Assistance when the call arrived from Blackburn. Simons was notorious for his stubbornness, single-mindedness, and his total lack of interest in the constraints imposed by higher authority. One of his first deeds upon taking charge of Shining Brass (and which exemplifies the man's character) was his single-handed alteration of the border between Laos and South Vietnam by simply moving the line on the map westward by ten kilometers. He later stated that he "could not live with some of the restraints put on me. . . . I got away with it only because I didn't make any mistakes . . . if I got caught they'd get some other conductor for the trolley car and throw my dead body off the track."[30] Colonel Blackburn thought the Bull was the perfect man to get Shining Brass off to a good start. After both men had served their time in Vietnam, it was to Simons that Blackburn again turned to lead Operation Kingpin, the raid on the POW camp at Son Tay, North Vietnam, in November 1970.

Now all MACSOG had to do was find the men to carry out the missions. Due to personnel shortages at the 5th SFG, recruiting for Shining Brass had to be carried out at the 1st SFG on Okinawa. The program only accepted men who had combat experience in Vietnam and who had already attained the rank of sergeant first class. The volunteers were initially trained on the island and then returned to their parent units to await pending presidential approval of Shining Brass. As that date drew closer, the two-man teams were sent TDY to South Vietnam in staggered increments. They were then taken to Camp Long Thanh to mate up with their indigenous four-man teams.

Vietnamese recruits for the program were volunteers from ARVN frontline units. The camp commander at Long Thanh, Colonel Ho Thieu, had contacts in the Airborne Branch and Ranger training programs and utilized them to gather the cream of the crop. The men were transported to Long Thanh for training, but their arrival created more chaos than order. When Colonel Russell had arrived during the previous year he had found little, if any, training going on at the camp. The facilities were inadequate (no demolition or firing ranges), communications were poor, and the barracks were overrun by rats. Nor were there enough cadre for the Montagnard strikers, ARVN rangers, agent teams, and MACSOG personnel. The camp proved to be another cross for Russell to bear in his takeover from the CIA.

Long Thanh was rapidly improved by the addition of new firing and demo ranges, modern communications equipment, refurbished trainee housing, and more cadre. Although the security personnel (made up of CIDG strikers) were still tempted to desert for higher wages in Saigon, the trainees were tasked with patrolling the area surrounding the camp as training exercises. It was quickly determined that the Special Forces training detachment at Long Thanh was not qualified to train the Shining Brass teams. Special Forces combat veterans among the volunteers, therefore, were tasked to assist in the training of the others. Although derided by some of the Americans, the South Vietnamese volunteers could be made into adequate soldiers, many felt, if leadership and teamwork could be instilled in them.

ALPHA-1

After two in-country training missions, the first Shining Brass operation was launched on 18 November against Target Area Alpha-1, a suspected truck terminus on Laotian Highway 165, fifteen kilometers inside Laos.[31] Recon Team (RT) Iowa, consisting of Sgt. Maj. Charles Petry, S1C Willie Card, and four Vietnamese, was helilifted across the border. The insertion went well and SOG had its first team on the ground. In the air above the LZ, however, tragedy had already struck. The weather had been atrocious for the previous three days. The mission would have been scrubbed again due to incessant rain and heavy overcast had an insertion helicopter not located a hole in the cloud cover through which to descend. Orbiting above was a VNAF H-34 command helicopter and an 0-1 Forward Air Control (FAC) aircraft, piloted by Air Force major Harley Pyles. In his backseat was MACSOG Air Liaison Officer captain Winfield Sisson.

Aboard the H-34 command ship was the operations officer for Shining Brass, Capt. Larry Thorne, who was already a living legend in the Special Forces community. Born in Finland, Thorne had led his own commando company during the Russo-Finnish War and had become a national hero by being awarded the Mannerheim Cross (the equivalent of the Medal of Honor) for his exploits behind Soviet lines. When Germany invaded the USSR in 1941, Finland went back to war against its old enemy and Thorne fought for four more years at the side of the Germans, who awarded him the Iron Cross First Class. After the war (and charges of being "an enemy of the people"), Thorne escaped to the West and joined the U.S. Army as a private. He was quickly commissioned and joined the Special Forces. Thorne was an expert at every form of special operations and was renowned for his open and friendly manner.

After Team Iowa radioed the command ship that it had been successfully inserted, Thorne informed Kham Duc that he was returning. He and the three-man helicopter crew then disappeared. Two years later the H-34 was found and the body of the pilot was recovered, but Thorne's remains were nowhere to be found. To make matters worse, the FAC aircraft had returned to Kham Duc, but after lifting off for the return trip to Da Nang, it too disappeared. On the first Shining Brass mission three Americans had gone MIA.

Back in Laos, RT Iowa slogged through more rain to reach its target. After three days the team was ambushed and the point man was killed. The others managed to break contact with the North Vietnamese and, propitiously, the weather improved. Iowa then struck back, calling in air strikes that caused multiple secondary explosions. Each strike, in turn, exposed more targets, and aircraft were soon scrambling to attack them. In all, RT Iowa directed fifty-one sorties against Alpha-1 before Petry decided that it was time to go. The team was extracted by helicopter, without incident, on the following day.

FACILITIES

Shining Brass was originally assigned five recon teams directed by a Command and Control (C&C) Detachment located at Da Nang. Initially, Kham Duc, in the northwestern corner of Quang Tin Province, was designated as a launch site for Shining Brass operations, but it was quickly determined that the distance from Long Thanh (where the teams were assembled and trained) was too far from Da Nang (from whence the teams headed to the launch site). Bull Simons decided that, to save wear and tear on the teams, Forward Operating Bases (FOBs), complete with barracks and airstrips, would be constructed nearer to the border area. This would eliminate the necessity of utilizing Long Thanh as a base of operations. Kham Duc was then designated FOB-1.

Dak To, in Kontum Province, was initially designated as FOB-2. Colonel Blackburn proposed an expansion of operations into the new Tiger Hound area, and that its planned installation at Dak To be moved to Kontum for better security. A third FOB was to be opened at the western end of Route 9 on the Khe Sanh Plateau in Thua Thien Province. During the remainder of the year 7 Shining Brass missions were launched and they were supported by 155 tactical air sorties.[32] The missions also generated twenty-one intelligence reports on communist activities. After each mission the teams were initially debriefed at the FOB. They were then flown to Da Nang to be thoroughly grilled by the C&C Detachment commander. Next, they were flown to Saigon and questioned personally by Bull Simons (and possibly by Don Blackburn) at headquarters. This direct intelligence-collection process continued until the move of the MACSOG headquarters to MACV 2 in 1968.

By October Bull Simons was already looking forward to the expansion of Shining Brass and the creation of exploitation forces. Hearing of the reputation for loyalty of ethnic Chinese Nungs (and of their reputation as fierce fighters), Simons decided to form experimental Nung teams for Shining Brass. An NCO who had strong connections within the Chinese community was dispatched to Bien Hoa where the III Corps Special Forces Mike Force (composed of Nungs) was located. Two teams' worth of men were quickly recruited.

Next, a recruitment center called the Liaison Bureau (not to be confused with STS Liaison Service) was opened adjacent to the Chinese neighborhood of Cholon. This effort led to the recruitment of fifty more Nungs who would form the nucleus for the intended exploitation force. The recruits were supplied, equipped, and then examined at the Seventh-day Adventist Hospital in Saigon before they were flown to Long Thanh to begin their training.

THE OTHER WAR

On 25 November 1964 President Johnson nominated William H. Sullivan as U.S. ambassador to Laos, replacing Leonard Ungar. Sullivan arrived in Vientiane in December and immediately assumed tight control over all political, economic, military, and paramilitary operations in Laos. The new ambassador had been mentored by W. Averell Harriman and had served as his assistant during the negotiations that led to the second Geneva Accords. He was considered Harriman's "handmaiden" and worked diligently to uphold the fiction that the United States was supporting the neutrality agreement. This position of control was one that he would maintain for his entire tenure as ambassador. It was also going to bring him into direct and continuous conflict with MACV, the USAF, and MACSOG.

Shining Brass was not the only game in town. The CIA was running its own clandestine war in Laos and a key part of that effort in the Laotian panhandle was Project Hardnose. Begun in May 1964, it consisted of twenty radio-equipped indigenous roadwatch teams that had been trained by the Thai Police Aerial Reinforcement Unit (PARU), an elite CIA-sponsored unconventional warfare outfit.[33] Not satisfied with a training mission, the Thais demanded (and in 1965 got) a piece of the reconnaissance operation. In Project Star, the Thais fielded four (eventually ten) six-man recon teams for roadwatch and trailwatch missions.[34] The Laotian government had little input into any of these efforts.

The quandary of Laotian neutrality, guaranteed and violated by everyone, posed unique problems. Flagrant violation by either U.S. or South Vietnamese forces might have brought international condemnation and possible expansion of the war by the Soviets and/or Chinese. It would also undoubtedly bring about the fall of the pro-American regime of Souvanna Phouma. This possibility went a long way toward explaining why the United States was reluctant to overturn the 1962 Geneva compromise that kept Souvanna's government in power. The North Vietnamese, on the other hand, could not afford to commit the manpower necessary to topple the Lao regime, which might have also brought about international condemnation or a possible expansion of hostilities. Thus, the conflict in Laos became a shadow war, covertly waged by both sides.

The decisions and actions of Ambassador Sullivan were going to come under intense attack and the ambassador himself would be vilified, especially by MACSOG, during his tenure. One must, however, consider the complex juggling act that Sullivan was going to have to maintain in the Kingdom of a Million Elephants. The Laotian regime was virtually an ally of the United States, and, during the remainder of the conflict, the Laotians were going to concede to almost every American request for action, short of outright invasion.

Air Operations

1ST FLIGHT DETACHMENT

During 1965 the Air Operations Section became the staff element overseeing the missions of the new Air Operations Group. The group's 1st Flight Detachment C-123K Providers, now named Heavy Hook, conducted twenty-two successful missions along with thirty covert psychological operations missions (delivering 60 million leaflets and gift kits) into the North.[35] In addition, 1st Flight provided logistical support to MACSOG, the C-123s flying 3,647 hours and delivering 328 tons of cargo and equipment.[36]

There were, however, continuing problems with the three VNAF crews that were assigned to fly the C-123s. One of the crews was lost due to ground fire (see below) while the separation of the Vietnamese crews from their aircraft—the pilots were stationed in Saigon but the planes were at Nha Trang—due to Vietnamese administrative and personnel policies and the air crews' increasing unreliability were causes for concern over the security of the operation. As a result, MACSOG began to work toward the total elimination of South Vietnamese aircrews from the program. Problems with the Nationalist Chinese crews that had cropped up in 1964 were solved by eliminating those pilots that had come into the program under the CIA and replacing them with a whole new contingent.

By 1965 SOG was in the pipeline for newer Lockheed C-130 transport aircraft, but, as with so many MACSOG operations, it was taking time for increased modifications and crew training. Until the aircraft arrived, SOG would have to make do with what it had. During the year one Heavy Hook C-123 was shot down by ground fire while en route from Nha Trang to Saigon. This was the only aircraft lost by the unit during the year.

83RD VNAF SPECIAL OPERATIONS GROUP

When MACSOG was handed the mandate to conduct cross-border reconnaissance missions into Laos, it had no organic air assets upon which to
draw. The clandestine nature of the operation necessitated that MAC-
SOG have a dependable unit that was on call solely for the insertion and
extraction of its recon teams, to provide liaison and forward air control,
and to provide tactical air support. Cross-border ground operations were
going to make heavy use of air assets. As they evolved, a typical recon
mission would be supported by three troop carrier helicopters, two to
four helicopter gunships, two fighter-bombers, and a FAC aircraft.

The Vietnamese Air Force responded by assigning the 83rd Special
Operations Group to handle these responsibilities. Based in Saigon, the
group provided tactical air support in the form of six A-1G Douglas
Skyraider fighter-bombers per day for the cross-border missions. Six
Sikorsky H-34 Choctaw helicopters of the unit were also tasked with recon insertions/extractions. It was a start, but six aircraft were not enough
for the expanding Shining Brass missions. FAC and liaison functions were
to be handled by the Cessna U-17 observation aircraft of the group.

SOG proposed that the H-34s of the 89th at least be reinforced,
or, better yet, replaced with new Sikorsky HH-3E Jolly Green Giants.
The HH-3E was the most advanced model under consideration, but its
acquisition was never going to take place. The vintage H-34 would serve
the unit throughout its existence. So, from the beginning of the mission,
MACSOG's South Vietnamese helicopter assets would have to be supplemented by U.S. units assigned on a temporary basis to the task.

Due to the geographic location of Shining Brass operations, those
aircraft usually consisted of U.S. Marine Corps helicopter transport and
gunship squadrons that already worked the I Corps area of operations.
Two of those Bell UH-1 Iroquois (ubiquitously known as the Huey) gunship units were VMO-6 "Klondike" and VMO-2 "Deadlock." The U.S.
Army also contributed troop-lift support in the form of the Marble Mountain–based 282nd Assault Helicopter Company (AHC) "Blackhawks"
and their attached gunships, the "Alley Cats," the 57th AHC "Gladiators" and "Cougars," and the 119th AHC "Gators" and "Crocs."

FACS

Another sign of the "new look" military was the lack of reconnaissance
aircraft appropriate for the interdiction mission in Southeast Asia. The
Air Force had been utilizing U-2 and RF-101 Voodoo jet aircraft for Trail
reconnaissance and photography, but they were too fast and too vulnerable at lower altitudes. The perfect aircraft for the mission was the propeller-

driven, low and slow Cessna 0-1 Bird Dog, a Korean Conflict–era aircraft that the Air Force had abandoned in its search for modernization. On 8 May 1964 the 2nd Air Division had activated the 20th, 21st, and 22nd Tactical Air Support Squadrons (TASS) at Da Nang, Pleiku, and Tan Son Nhut, respectively, but there still seemed to be a lack of available aircraft (even after stripping the VNAF of its 0-1s). Since the Army was the only service that still utilized the 0-1, the Air Force had to ask for its assistance as well. It must have been rather embarrassing for the men in blue to go hat in hand to their rival in the air, but it was done.

Eventually four TASS squadrons supported SOG missions: the 19th based at Bien Hoa; the 20th at Da Nang; the Pleiku-based 21st, and the 23rd at Nakhon Phanom, Thailand. These units were supported by the 0-1 aircraft of the U.S. Army's 219th Aviation Company, whose 2nd Platoon covered the Shining Brass area and whose 4th Platoon covered the Daniel Boone area when operations in Cambodia were authorized in 1967.

MACSOG was also looking for alternative methods of agent team insertions into North Vietnam. It already utilized airdrops and over-the-beach infiltrations, but one method that was untried but tempting was the use of helicopters for insertions. VNAF H-34s could fly the agents to the western border, cross into Laotian airspace, refuel at a CIA airstrip, and then land the teams in North Vietnam. MACSOG believed that the method was feasible, and to prove its point, Team Romeo was successfully inserted by the H-34s of the 89th.

Maritime Operations

In January the Maritime Operations Section was established as the staff at MACSOG headquarters for its operational arm, the NAD. As with Airborne Operations, the inception of Rolling Thunder led to a change in mission from punitive and harassment operations to intelligence collection and shipping interdiction.[37]

Six Nasty PTFs and three Swift PCFs were in the inventory at the beginning of the year. Four new PTFs were added for a total of ten. However, due to maintenance problems, six PTFs and two Swifts were normally all that were operational at any one time. During the year the number of Vietnamese Sea Commandos declined to 148. MAROPS conducted 155 missions in 1965 during which fifty North Vietnamese vessels were destroyed and nineteen were damaged, including three naval patrol craft.[38] There were 59 shore bombardment and 25 psychological harassment missions (during which 1,000 radios, 28,742 gift kits, and 1,124,600 leaflets were distributed) during the year. CSS casualties for the year were one man killed in action and eighteen wounded.[39] PTF 4 was lost on an operation and the gasoline-powered Nastys that had arrived during 1963 (PTFs 1 and 2) were stripped and sunk for target practice.

In March the Joint Chiefs authorized CINCPAC to carry out Drift operations, the distribution of gift kits and transistor radios ashore and offshore. Cado missions were also tasked with psychological deception operations (usually the firing of propaganda leaflets via 81-mm mortars) by agents infiltrated in rubber boats. They were also authorized to conduct Swallow missions in which North Vietnamese were kidnapped ashore for intelligence exploitation. Later, CINCPAC would use Cado to designate all three missions.

The NAD suffered its first casualty of the conflict on 28 October when its commander, Lt. Cdr. Robert Fay, USN, was killed in action. Fay was inspecting the camp perimeter in a jeep when the area came under mortar attack. He was struck by fragments and later died of his wounds. In his honor, the NAD renamed its main facility Camp Fay.

Psychological Operations

To bolster the fiction of the SSPL, MACSOG's radio office in Saigon produced The Voice of the SSPL (VSSPL), which began broadcasting in April. A "black" radio operation, the VSSPL claimed to be located within North Vietnam and elaborated on the fictitious organization and the betrayal of the people by the communists. MACSOG was now running three clandestine radio operations: the VSSPL, Radio Red Flag, and the VOF. The organization sought and received funding for the purchase of one thousand transistor radios per month for distribution in North Vietnam and along the Trail.

Meanwhile, at Paradise Island, three camps were established at the SSPL's "secure area." Camp Phoenix was utilized for initial delivery of detainees brought in by MACSOG MAROPS forces and for initial interrogations. Camp D-36 was used for indoctrination of those detainees who showed a willingness to join the SSPL, and, separate from the other two, Camp Dodo was a well-hidden base for a small contingent of SOG PSYOPS and communications personnel.

Plans

The Plans Branch was established during the year to develop plans for MACSOG and to coordinate them into larger MACV contingency planning. These tasks had previously been handled by the separate staff branches. The chief work produced by the branch during its inaugural year was the Combined Joint Unconventional Warfare Task Force, Southeast Asia Plan and a supporting Joint Table of Distribution. This plan would have placed MASCSOG in command of all unconventional warfare forces in Southeast Asia in the event of the outbreak of general war.

Logistics

In 1965 logistics and construction tried to keep pace with the rapid expansion of MACSOG's missions. The consolidation and construction at Camp Fay, Da Nang, was the outgrowth of the CIA's legacy. The NAD's beach camps, strewn along the peninsula on which Da Nang East was situated, were being consolidated due to security concerns, an influx of refugees into the area, and the construction of a Marine airstrip at Marble Mountain. One of the most interesting bits of information contained in the Logistics Appendix to the yearly Command History was the situation at MACSOG's supply facility at House 10 in Saigon. The branch was having difficulties due to an expiring lease on the location of its logistical headquarters. MACSOG went so far as to request that the South Vietnamese government intervene on its behalf to condemn the property so that it could stay on the premises.

It is not difficult to imagine the strains put upon the Logistics Branch during the year by the initiation of the Shining Brass program. The recon teams and exploitation forces would have to be fitted with weapons, uniforms, communications equipment, and specialized gear from CISO. Shining Brass construction was proceeding apace at Kham Duc and Dak To, while the C&C Center was moved from Da Nang East to Camp Fay.

SOG's budget submittal for the year amounted to $4,977,160. The Air Force contribution was heavy: original modifications to C-123 aircraft amounted to $1,864,000, which was paid from the secretary of defense's contingency fund; follow-on modifications to aircraft, C-123s and C-130s, amounted to $4,000,000 plus maintenance costs.[40]

Communications

During 1965 all was still not well with MACSOG communications. As with its other programs and their support mechanisms, the unit was having to build itself from scratch. The unit's single side-band radio network was being extended, connecting its headquarters in Saigon with Nha Trang and Da Nang. On 12 October it was again extended, this time to include the new C&C Detachment for Shining Brass operations at Da Nang. The C&C also needed high-frequency FM receivers and transmitters in order to stay in contact with its recon teams in the field. By November the SSB net was again extended, this time to the 1st Flight Detachment at Nha Trang and to the newly established FOB at Kham Duc. The following month saw the addition of SOG's second FOB at Dak To.

MACSOG was continuously experimenting with the ground-to-air communications of its recon teams. It initially chose the AN/PRC-92 as its field radio, but was having difficulty obtaining crystals for them. It then decided to switch to the AN/PRC-64. NAD at Da Nang was also having difficulties with the PRC-92. These radios seemed to be taking a physical beating aboard the PTFs while spare parts and repair personnel were hard to come by. It says something that after one and one-half years in operation, with communications maintenance assistance promised from various units, MACSOG had to ask MACV to step in and twist some arms to get those agreements fulfilled.

Comment: The MACSOG/MACV Relationship

The relationship between MACSOG and its superiors was a difficult one to grasp. Although William Westmoreland was COMUSMACV from 1964 until 1969, he was not chief, MACSOG's direct superior. That position was held by SACSA, on the Joint Staff at the Pentagon. It might be useful at this point to sketch out the command relationships in Southeast Asia. MACV was a subordinate unified command consisting of forces from all of the armed services, but unlike Gen. Douglas MacArthur during the Korean Conflict, Westmoreland was not a theater commander. That position was held by CINCPAC in Honolulu. COMUSMACV was in control of and responsible for only military personnel and actions within the borders of South Vietnam. He did not control Operation Rolling Thunder, U.S. Naval Task Force 77 off the coast (whose aircraft participated in Rolling Thunder), or U.S. military personnel (generally from the Air Force) deployed in Laos or Thailand.

Since MACSOG's mandate was specifically geared for out-of-country missions, it did not fall under either CINCPAC or MACV's purview. The organization carried out liaison with MACV and with CICNPAC and kept them apprised of its actions, but it did not take orders from them. Although both MACV and CINCPAC had input on MACSOG operations, it was to the Joint Chiefs and secretary of defense that the organization was responsible.

The real interface between MACV and SOG was through their intelligence staffs. Since MACSOG's real contribution to the military effort was through intelligence collection and dissemination, this was reasonable enough. It would seem that any contribution that the unit had to make to the American effort would be through intelligence requirements passed through MACV J-2 and then fulfilled by MACSOG. Intelligence briefings, therefore, would seem to be the one place where the two organizations would come together for a common purpose.

Unfortunately, the relationship between the two organizations was a rocky one at best. Both Col. Clyde Russell and Col. Donald Blackburn faced hurdles as commanders in their relationship with Westmoreland and his staff. Author Richard Shultz believed that much of this friction was related to the fact that the commanders of MACSOG were not flag-rank officers.[41] Although they commanded forces that grew to almost divisional size, the chiefs of SOG remained only colonels. This might seem a small point, but in the civil/military culture it loomed large. As general officers they would have approached MACV, the Pentagon, and Washington on more equal footing.

Another problem that reached beyond the immediate relations between the groups was the attitude that separated the mainstream military from the "unconventional warfare set." Although the U.S. military had created effective elite and unconventional forces throughout its history, it had never been comfortable with them. This was illustrated by the fact that whenever conflicts in which American elite forces had participated came to an end, the units were immediately disbanded and eliminated from the military lineup.

There were several reasons for these attitudes. One was the American military's inherent distrust of both the officers and men who served in such units. They were obviously independent and elitist thinkers who could not possibly fit within the prevailing military orthodoxy. At best they were square pegs in round holes, at worst they were undisciplined and uncontrollable "dogs of war" that the peacetime military could live without. Paradoxically, another general military attitude was that elite units attracted the best officers and NCOs and, therefore, drained them out of the mainstream.

Although the 1960s saw the ascendance of counterinsurgency warfare doctrine and practice within the American military, one should take this renaissance with a grain of salt. Vietnam was played out as the first conflict since the military had shifted from the "one war" massive nuclear retaliation doctrine of the 1950s to Maxwell Taylor's "flexible response" paradigm. The military accepted the platitudes of the new counterinsurgency doctrine only as a defensive measure, which (along with President Kennedy's support for the Green Berets) had served to put the nails into the coffin of the "one war" concept.[42] At best the high command mouthed the jargon of unconventional warfare while they dug in their heels against any attempt to convert conventional forces to unconventional roles.

This explains why U.S. forces, once committed to what had been a political war for the "hearts and minds" of the South Vietnamese, rapidly became a conventional force fighting a conventional war with a conventional strategy in Southeast Asia. This practice was extended even to Special Forces activities. One of the chief counterinsurgency success stories of the advisory period was the creation of the Civilian Irregular Defense Groups (CIDG) by the CIA/Special Forces. Unfortunately, under Switchback, the CIDG units were too quickly enlarged by MACV, converted into an *offensive* force, and then deployed, along with the Special Forces, to the South Vietnamese frontier for a program of border surveillance. Morale plummeted and the program never regained the successes of its earlier configuration.[43] Once major forces were introduced, the Pentagon decided that they were all that were necessary to achieve U.S. objectives. As far as the Pentagon was concerned, units like the Special Forces and MACSOG became both superfluous and redundant.

A prime example of these attitudes was the career of Don Blackburn, the longest-serving colonel in the U.S. Army. Although promoted for exemplary service during the Second World War (the youngest American ever promoted to lieutenant colonel), he had not been elevated in rank for ten years. Although he would eventually be promoted to brigadier general, he was one of the few exceptions to the rule that no officer who made a career of Special Forces would ever see a general's star. Blackburn's relationship with Westmoreland and MACV was lukewarm at best. During his tenure as chief, MACSOG, he briefed Westmoreland personally only once. As far as Blackburn was concerned, Westmoreland was "a conventional commander of conventional units and was not interested in an outfit like SOG."[44] He doubted if any of the intelligence that MACSOG collected was utilized by MACV, derided coordination with the MACV staff, and never felt that MACSOG was a tool that Westmoreland used effectively.[45] He also well understood that the previously described attitudes were not limited to just MACV. "It wasn't only Westmoreland. . . . It was Max Taylor . . . it was Harkins . . . it was Abrams. . . . They were all so conventionally oriented."[46] Special operations were anathema to his superiors and were never highlighted in their considerations. During his tenure Blackburn lived in the same quarters with Westmoreland's deputy for an entire year, and although the officer was cognizant of his position, he never asked Blackburn one question about SOG operations.[47]

On the other hand, Col. John Singlaub (MACSOG's third CO) got along well with both Westmoreland and the MACV staff. He would also rise to the rank of major general, not because of his unconventional warfare experience, however, but because of his more mainstream career. When Singlaub was informed by Army chief of staff Harold Johnson that he had been chosen to command MACSOG, Singlaub tried to get out of the assignment, knowing that taking command of the organization might have an adverse effect upon his career. Johnson told him not to worry and informed him that Westmoreland had specifically asked for him. Why? "He was not an iconoclast like Blackburn, a special operator that Westmoreland had little time for."[48]

Jack Singlaub's tenure, however, did not alter Westmoreland's attitudes toward the organization. COMUSMACV considered SOG "a well intended effort and it did provide us with some intelligence, but the intelligence was not great; it wasn't going to win or lose the war."[49] MACSOG's contribution was simply as an annoyance to the enemy, "a pinprick . . . in the final analysis SOG didn't amount to a damn."[50] Asked in an interview with Richard Shultz if MACSOG could have made a more significant contribution if he had been able to control it more completely, Westmoreland replied "five to ten percent . . . of the impact of it was totally coincidental."[51] In other words, there was total indifference toward any contribution that MACSOG might have made.

Col. Steven Cavanaugh, fourth commander of SOG, was also ambivalent about his relationship with COMUSMACV and his staff. He believed that "MACV didn't feel that we were contributing a great deal. . . . I felt there was a general animosity."[52] But he did manage to get along well with Gen. Creighton Abrams, Westmoreland's successor. SOG's last commander, Col. Skip Sadler, also got along well with Abrams, and that was saying something. Abrams was notorious for his ambivalent attitude toward elite units in general and the Special Forces in particular (Abrams was known throughout MACSOG as "the Hatchet Man"). This attitude was exacerbated during his tenure as COMUSMACV by the notorious "Green Beret murder case," and the role played in it by the commander of the 5th SFG, Col. Robert Rheault. Even after he and his men were exonerated by MACSOG, Abrams still saw to it that his career was destroyed.

Chapter Three

1966: MISSION EXPANSION

Headquarters

Raised in Southern California, John K. Singlaub had served in the Office of Strategic Services (OSS) in the European Theater during 1943–44. He was a member of a multinational Jedburgh agent team that parachuted into France to organize, train, and lead groups of Maquisards against the Germans. Following his promotion to captain, he was shipped out by the OSS to China where he set to work training Ho Chi Minh's forces for actions against the Japanese. Following the war he was seconded to the CIA and served as an observer during the Chinese Civil War. He had the distinction of being one of the few American military officers tried by a Chinese Revolutionary Tribunal and found guilty in absentia. He again served with distinction in Asia first as a CIA agent running covert operations into North Korea and then as an infantry officer during the grueling hill battles of the latter part of the Korean Conflict. After attending and then instructing at the Army's Command and General Staff College, Singlaub served in staff positions at the Pentagon before being assigned as the commander of MACSOG, replacing Donald Blackburn on 14 May.

MACSOG consisted of volunteers from the 5th SFG in Vietnam, the 1st SFG (Okinawa), Navy SEAL teams, and elements of the Marine Corps Force Reconnaissance Battalion. Special Forces troops arriving in South Vietnam and assigned to MACSOG were "sheep dipped" through Special Operations Augmentation (a personnel pipeline run by the 5th SFG), making it appear that the men were assigned to that unit when they were posted under classified orders to SOG.

For MACSOG veterans who had completed their tours and returned to the United States (or other personnel who "knew somebody") and wished to be reassigned to SOG, a simple phone call could do the trick. The contact was Mrs. Billy Alexander, an employee of the Special Categories/Branch in the basement of the Pentagon. The mention of voluntary duty with MACSOG was often enough to have a man back in South Vietnam within a month. Other troops who were not assigned to Special Forces, but who had served at least one combat tour in Vietnam, could volunteer through unofficial channels at Nha Trang. Those destined for cross-border operations were then sent on to a three-week course at MACSOG's new reconnaissance training facility at Kham Duc.

It seemed that Bull Simon's penchant for ignoring the dictates of higher authority and his irreverence for the rules were shared by the men of the SOG. By 1966 personnel had begun to don unit patches that had been designed by Marine Corps major Malcolm Fites, who was assigned to SOG: upon a red shield a bomb burst; superimposed upon it, a grinning skull, dripping blood from its teeth and adorned by a green beret. Below was the unit acronym on a scroll with an anchor affixed to the letter V for Vietnam. Above was a set of master aviator wings. The wings, green beret, and anchor testified to the multiservice makeup of the unit.

The problem was that due to the unit's covert nature, it was assigned no official unit crest or insignia and it never would be. Soldiers being soldiers, however, craved the pride and esprit de corps that such insignia engendered. Recon troops at the FOBs soon began to design and wear their own patches, some of which were variations on Fites' original design. Officers, from chief, MACSOG, on down, would make various efforts to eradicate the wearing of the insignias, but to no avail. Eventually, they were tolerated as long as the men did not flaunt them off their bases. The profusion of designs, the small number of patches, and the variety of their manufacture would make them treasured mementos and highly desirable as collector's items.

LAOS

During the year a Southeast Asia Coordinating Committee (SEACORD) meeting was held at Udorn, Thailand, to hash out areas of responsibility and working relationships between MACSOG, the CIA, and the American Embassy, Vientiane. By 1966 the Laotian conflict was expanding. Five hundred more U.S. military advisors arrived during the year, most of them from the USAF, to service the bombing program in the new "Project 404." The Royal Lao Army was as ineffective as ever and did not look like it was going to change any time soon, so the United States looked elsewhere for an effective ground combat force.

The agency found what it was looking for in the Hmong, a highland tribe that the agency had recruited from during the heady days of Operations Hotfoot/White Star. The Hmong had been pretty much abandoned after the signing of the second Geneva Accord, but were more than willing to take up arms again for the central government in return for aid and local autonomy. Led by General Vang Pao (one of the most warlike and talented generals outside the PAVN in Southeast Asia), the Hmong army would eventually number 30,000 men, all of whom were trained, equipped, supplied, and paid by the CIA. The cost of the secret war was not cheap. Between 1963 and 1970 the United States was paying $80 million per year in military aid to the Royal Lao Army and to its own covert paramilitary units.[1]

Also contributing were the government and military of Thailand. The Thais were very worried about the continuing conflict to their north and east. They also had aspirations of becoming a regional power and had no desire to see the advance of socialism (or of their hereditary enemies, the Cambodians and Vietnamese). Quietly but steadily, Thailand committed forces to the conflict. The Queen's Cobra Regiment had already been committed overtly in Vietnam. Covertly, the Thais had been aiding Laos for years with paramilitary "volunteers" from their elite PARU. During the year it silently committed more volunteers and aviation and artillery units to the secret war in Laos. At the beginning of the year eight CIA Hardnose roadwatch teams were working between the strategic Mu Gia Pass and Route 9, the main logistics artery from North Vietnam into Laos. The agency was also working overtime to expand its assets in order to keep pace with the interdiction campaign (and to keep MACSOG bottled up in its area of operations). By the end of October forty teams were being fielded and the goal for the end of the year was seventy.

Between the Royal Lao Army and Air Force, the Hmong army, the Thai volunteers, U.S. Army and Air Force advisors, and CIA covert operatives (not to mention the agency's proprietary airlines, Air America and Bird and Sons), the war in Laos was expanding exponentially. Yet the CIA was left in charge of conducting and controlling it. If MACSOG had been created under the umbrella of NSAM 57 to take over CIA paramilitary operations that had grown too large to remain covert, why was the "war" in Laos left in the agency's domain? Why wasn't the military placed in charge of it? The answer lay within the walls of the U.S. Embassy in Vientiane. William Sullivan rode herd over all operations within the country with the explicit support of Secretary of State Dean Rusk and the CIA. As long as the fiction of Laotian neutrality could be sustained, even by the most slender thread, Sullivan would preserve his control.

Colonel Singlaub had no more luck with Vientiane than his two predecessors. He came to loathe Sullivan, not for his defense of Laotian neutrality, but for what it cost the Americans to maintain it. Every time he approached the ambassador with a request, no matter how small, it was like pulling teeth. As far as Singlaub was concerned Sullivan was hardly better than a little warlord out to do nothing but protect his own turf, no matter what it cost.

Intelligence

In March MACSOG received confirmation from the Laotian air force that a new trail, coming up from Cambodia, was being linked to existing trails in southeastern Laos. Previously, supplies had been sent down the coast of South Vietnam in small freighters and sampans. With the closing of this supply route by American naval forces, the North Vietnamese had to find a new method. Hanoi then began to supply the southern flank of its operations by utilizing Eastern Bloc freighters, immune to American air and naval interdiction, to ship materiel through the Cambodian port of Sihanoukville. The vessels were off-loaded onto trucks, which then moved the materiel to the border areas. None of this could have been accomplished without the acquiescence of Cambodia's Prince Norodom Sihanouk.

Hanoi then obviously felt the need to supplement this new logistical artery with an overland route connecting the two border areas. Partly as a result of this information, the first B-52 Arc Light strike was launched against the Trail on 10 December. During the year Shining Brass missions generated 371 intelligence reports on communist activities in Laos. In late 1965 the Intelligence Branch had been bolstered by the addition of a Security Section, which was tasked with conducting security reviews of personnel and installations, collecting and maintaining classified documents, and maintaining liaison with the South Vietnamese security services concerning indigenous personnel.

Footboy Operations[2]

MARITIME OPERATIONS

MAROPS began the year with nine PTFs and three Swift PCFs in its inventory. Three new PTFs were acquired, leading to a total of eleven Nastys and three Swifts. There were 134 sea commando team members split into five teams, but by December that number had been reduced to 104 men in four teams. The CSS conducted 126 primary and 56 secondary missions, resulting in 13 South Vietnamese killed in action, 31 wounded, and 6 missing.[3]

This was the worst year in CSS history as far as operational losses were concerned. Five PTFs were sunk on operations, but none were sunk due to enemy action. PTF 14 was grounded on a reef on 22 May. On the following day PTF 15 attempted to tow out her sister and became grounded. Both vessels were then destroyed to keep them from falling into communist hands. PTF 16 was lost after a collision with a friendly craft during a storm on 19 August. During the year two more vessels were sent to the bottom to prevent capture: PTF 9 was grounded on a reef and sunk by an American aircraft on 7 March, and PTF 8 was similarly grounded and sunk by another Nasty boat on 17 June.

In July CINCPAC established mission categories and assigned numerical series for MAROPS. These included Mint (Maritime Interdiction) missions—the interdiction of small-tonnage shipping off the North Vietnamese coast with an operational limit of 20° north. All vessels encountered were stopped and searched. If they were found to be carrying military cargo, the boats were sunk. The crews were removed for SSPL PSYOPS indoctrination. Loki missions were carried out in a manner similar to Mint, but in areas prohibited to them. They were primarily for prisoner detention and intelligence collection. Cado cross-beach action team operations were carried out against shore targets within the North.

During 1966, 353 prisoners were captured and transported to Cu Lao Cham (Paradise Island) for SSPL indoctrination. Later, 352 were returned to North Vietnam. A total of 86 enemy craft of all types were destroyed and 16 were damaged. Intelligence reports made numbered 37, along with 117 intelligence spot reports.[4] On the propaganda front, 2,000,600 leaflets and 60,000 gift kits were distributed by various methods in North Vietnam. Also, 2,600 pre-tuned "Peanuts" PSYOPS radios, produced by CISO, were delivered into communist territory.[5]

Maritime operations also played a role in the interdiction of enemy maritime supply lines by serving as a trip wire for the much larger Operation Sea Dragon, run by the U.S. Navy and Coast Guard. Sea Dragon began sweeping North Vietnam's coastal waters during the year, searching for vessels carrying war supplies destined for the NLF and PAVN in the South.

Air Operations

BLACKBIRDS

The Heavy Hook C-123Ks of the 1st Flight Detachment were coming to the end of their operational lives for MACSOG (at least for operations over North Vietnam). During the course of the year 1st Flight completed 110 missions, but the skies over the North were becoming steadily more dangerous for agent team insertions and resupply missions. Thanks to the Soviets and Chinese, Hanoi was steadily improving its anti-aircraft artillery defenses, including the deployment of Soviet-built surface-to-air (SAM) missiles, which had begun in 1965.

SOG had been requesting the deployment of C-130 Hercules transport aircraft since the previous year, but the Defense Department was reluctant to provide them, probably due to MACSOG's poor record with the C-123K. Any comparison between the C-123 Provider and the C-130 Hercules was striking. The Hercules had twice the speed (345 mph versus 165 mph) and three times the range (2,530–4,900 miles versus 500 miles) of the Provider. The C-130s would be useful in the not-so-friendly skies over North Vietnam.

Finally, the DOD acquiesced. In the spring of 1966, a detachment of pilots and airmen was dispatched to Pope Air Force Base, North Carolina, to familiarize them with their new mission. That summer, four heavily modified MC-130Es joined them. In October the four (later six) aircraft and their crews arrived at Ching Chuan Kang Air Base, Taiwan, where they were designated Detachment 1 of the 314th Troop Carrier Squadron. Prior to December the planes and crews flew in and out of Nha Trang on a TDY basis. After December they were redesignated the 15th Air Commando Squadron, opconned to MACSOG, and stationed with the 1st Flight Detachment at Nha Trang Air Base. The Air Operations Logistics Section conducted 442 missions during the year, transporting 4,891,228 pounds of cargo and 13,893 passengers.[6]

The MC-130Es (now designated Combat Spear) were heavily modified with Fulton Skyhook recovery yokes, electronic countermeasures, electronic intelligence devices, and Doppler navigational systems.[7] They were also the first transport aircraft equipped with forward looking infrared radar (FLIR). The aircraft were distinctive due to their midnight-black and forest-green camouflage paint jobs and removable insignia panels that led to their nickname, "Blackbirds."

LOW- AND HIGH-PERFORMANCE AERIAL DELIVERY
Two key problems faced during air operations over North Vietnam were the weather and the increasing anti-aircraft artillery threat. Resupplying agent teams was becoming more problematic, especially those that were located near urban areas, where the danger of anti-aircraft fire was greatest. At this point Prime Minister (and nominal head of the VNAF) Nguyen Cao Ky stepped forward and offered the use of the A-1G Skyraiders of his 83rd Special Operations Group. In April the first test run, a resupply of Team Romeo, was conducted. The aircraft successfully dropped to the team two modified napalm canisters stuffed with clothing, equipment, and ammunition. The VNAF completed four similar aerial deliveries of supplies during the year.

Seeing the success of the Vietnamese, the USAF decided to get into the act. If a propeller-driven A-1G could complete the mission, then why not a fast-moving jet? F-4 Phantoms of the 366th Tactical Fighter Wing, stationed at Da Nang, gave it a try. The first mission was a resupply for Team Eagle. Arriving over the target area and receiving the recognition signal, the Phantom went in at a speed of 350 knots and at an altitude of 16 meters. The supply canisters landed right on target.

PONY EXPRESS

MACSOG believed that one of the problems plaguing its agent team operations was its dependency upon parachute insertions. It was believed that the dearth of adequate drop zones in the portions of North Vietnam into which insertions were made contributed to the number of agents eliminated. Overuse had become a real problem. Several attempts had already been made to press the case with the Joint Chiefs for the utilization of helicopter insertions before MACSOG gained approval in November. Team Romeo had been successfully inserted by H-34s flown from the VNAF 83rd Special Operations Group, so the concept had been proven feasible.

SOG's claims were made even more valid with the arrival in Southeast Asia of the USAF 20th Helicopter Squadron "Pony Express." On 8 October 1965 the unit was activated at Tan Son Nhut Air Base and assigned to the 14th Air Commando Squadron in March 1966. Three months later eleven of the unit's fourteen HH-3E helicopters were dispatched to Udorn, Thailand, ostensibly to assist in the CIA's covert effort in Laos. The HH-3E was just what SOG was looking for. It had twice the range and speed of the H-34 and, from Udorn, it could range deep into North Vietnam without refueling.

KINGBEES

The only Vietnamese air force unit tasked with the insertion and extraction of MACSOG recon teams were the "Kingbees" of the 83rd Special Operations Group. They flew unmarked Korean Conflict–vintage H-34 Choctaw helicopters and were based at Da Nang. The Sikorsky H-34 was a sturdy old warhorse with a relatively slow speed (97–122 mph) and limited range (247 miles). But what it lacked in both it made up in sheer toughness. Its front-mounted reciprocal engine provided the crew with extra protection and the aircraft could take a lot of damage and keep right on flying. It also operated better at higher elevations than the UH-1, a real plus when working in the Truong Son Mountains.

The Kingbees flew recon team insertions, search and rescue (SAR) missions, and some agent team insertions. The helicopters were commanded and crewed by fearless Vietnamese aviators, some of whom became living legends. The Kingbees were renowned for flying impossible missions into the hottest LZs to extract a team in trouble. USMC aviation units, which already supported Shining Brass missions, began to support operations from the new FOB at Khe Sanh during the year. These missions were flown by the aviators of HMM-165 White Knights, VMO-2 Deadlock, VMO-3 Scarface, and the Knights of VMO-6.

TAC AIR

Close air support for recon team operations was usually provided by the A-1Gs attached to the 83rd Special Operations Group. The slower, propeller-driven Douglas Skyraiders (nicknamed "Spads") were another Korean Conflict–era holdover that got a new lease on life in Southeast Asia. It was ironic that the USAF had been on the verge of disbanding all of its Skyraider units on the eve of the Vietnam War. The men in blue had wanted to create an "all jet" service for the age of massive retaliation. The new doctrine of flexible response and the nature of the conflict in Vietnam, however, played to the A-1's strengths.

The aircraft became a favorite of all Free World Military Forces (FWMF) troops due to their heavy ordnance loads, long loiter times, and the precision of their bombing attacks. Many a recon team breathed easier when informed by a FAC that the Spads were on the way. USAF A-1E squadrons that often supported cross-border missions were the Da Nang/Nakhon Phanom–based 602nd Special Operations Squadron (SOS) Sandys, the Pleiku-based 6th SOS Spads, and the Nakhon Phanom–based 1st SOS Hobos and 22nd SOS Zorros.

No mention of tactical air operations would be complete without mentioning the courageous efforts of the Air Force, Navy, and Marine Corps aircrews that flew in support of the interdiction effort. From the bombs, rockets, and guns of the AC-47 Spookys, AC-130 Spectres, F-105 Thuds, F-100 Huns, F-4 Phantoms, and A-4 Skyhawks, MACSOG recon teams counted on and received life-saving support and dealt the communists heavy blows.

INNOVATION

The temporary bombing halt of North Vietnam, dictated by President Johnson at the end of the previous year in order to induce the North Vietnamese to negotiate, freed up additional aircraft for the interdiction mission in Laos. From 3,023 Air Force and Navy sorties flown in December, the total rose in January to 8,000, mainly against targets in the central and southern panhandle of Laos.[8] But, due to the weather, terrain, and lack of substantive visual confirmation, it was difficult to determine if the bombing was effective. The Air Force was determined to up the ante by fielding its latest generation of technological advances in order to improve its detection and bombing of the communists. The expansion of night missions (when the North Vietnamese moved the bulk of their supplies) during the year led to Operation Shed Light, an attempt by the Air Force to improve and modernize its capabilities.

Shed Light had four subordinate projects. Tropic Moon fielded four TV-equipped A-1Es while Project Lonesome Tiger saw B-26K bombers equipped with forward-looking infrared radar. Operation Black Spot utilized C-123s equipped with two radar systems, TV, infrared, and armed with cluster-bomb dispensers. Gunboat, a proposal to provide gunship capabilities for the C-130 Hercules, was also looked into. Once again the Air Force was caught behind the times. Night vision devices (even the monocular version) had not been an Air Force priority, but they were an absolute necessity for reconning the Trail at night. The Air Force was again forced to go to the Army with requests for vital equipment.

Evaluation of the effectiveness of B-52 Superfortress strikes on the Trail system was always an unknown quantity. MACV often quoted the fear of rallied or captured communist soldiers as incentive for continuation of the program, but others were not convinced. Col. Francis R. Cappelletti (chief of Targets Division, 7th Air Force) was doubtful since there was no statistical basis for MACV's claims. Capelletti felt that the huge expenditure of bombs that were dropped in area saturation missions could be better utilized by tactical aircraft for pinpoint strikes.[9] Bomb Damage Assessments (BDAs) simply did not support MACV's claims for destruction of communist personnel or logistics. Gen. William Momyer (commander, 7th Air Force) was even more skeptical, concluding that B-52s had been "relatively ineffective."[10]

One of the reasons for this ineffectiveness was the early warning system developed by the communists. Ever-present Soviet trawlers waited for the B-52s to take off from Guam and tracked them by radar until they were handed over to the North Vietnamese system. Similarly, PAVN ground observers and radar covered the B-52 base at U-Tapao, Thailand, and advised their southern headquarters, COSVN, on the course of the approaching bombers.

Control of the bombing campaign was problematic from the first. Formed in 1962, the 2nd Air Division, USAF, controlled air operations in South Vietnam until 1 April 1966, when the 7th Air Force was established. To control the bombing of Laos and North Vietnam from Thai bases, the 13th Air Force was set up at Udorn, Thailand, on 6 January 1966. The 7th/13th Air Force shared a joint command at Udorn, but the commander of the 13th reported on operational matters to the 7th and on logistical and administrative matters to the 13th (located in the Philippines). The Strategic Air Command (SAC) retained direct control over its B-52s.

MACV controlled the bombing within South Vietnam and in the Tiger Hound area of Laos, and ran Rolling Thunder through the 7th Air Force and Naval Forces, Vietnam. Command and control for Laotian air operations was run through CINCPAC, who issued orders to the 7th Air Force, which in turn issued operational orders to the 7th/13th Air Force at Udorn. Targeting requests for all of the operations came from CINCPAC, MACV, the CIA, and the American Embassy, Vientiane. This command schizophrenia was never resolved and, needless to say, did not permit close coordination of the air effort.[11]

Psychological Operations

In 1965 MACSOG psychological operations continued at an ever more rapid tempo. Notional concepts for the SSPL and its radio counterparts, the Voice of the Sacred Sword of the Patriot League (VSSPL) and Radio Red Flag, and the Voice of Freedom continued while MACSOG propaganda teams churned out leaflets, gift kits, and poison-pen letters for the North. CISO kicked in its contribution, the production of "Peanuts" radios that could only be tuned in to MACSOG radio broadcasts. In November the 20-kW transmitter for the VSSPL was transferred to Thu Duc, outside Saigon, and, in December, it was joined there by Radio Red Flag.

Due to the buildup of American forces in and around Da Nang, it became imperative that the cover of the SSPL not be blown at Cu Lao Cham Island. The threat posed to the cover story of the operation by the possibility of a boatload of U.S. personnel on a sight-seeing trip off the coast was a real one. One rather humorous solution was for MACSOG personnel to "spread the word" that Paradise Island was, in fact, the notorious "Black Syph" or "Black Clap" Island.

This military version of an urban myth had been created by old sergeants as far back as the First World War and had persisted in U.S. military lore ever since. New troops were warned by the old salts that sexual relations with the natives (regardless of geographic location) could lead to an incurable form of venereal disease (the Black Syph or Black Clap). Infection would lead to the incarceration of the individual on an island for the rest of his life. This drastic measure was taken so that the folks back home would be protected from the disease. Although this story might sound preposterous, the author can attest that he heard it during his military service in the mid-1970s and it no doubt persists to this day.

Airborne Operations

Three new long-term agent teams were infiltrated during 1966 and teams inside North Vietnam were resupplied twenty-eight times by air. One team and two subteams (twenty-two men) were lost. Eleven agents were killed in action, three died of wounds, and six died of other causes, leaving eleven in-place teams (seventy-nine agents) at the close of the year.[12] The first insertion of the year saw the nine men of Team Kern helicoptered into the North on 5 March to an area near the strategic Mu Gia Pass. The team continued to broadcast until 5 September and it was written off in December.

Team Hector took a transport aircraft to Nakhon Phanom and was then helilifted by HH-3Es of the 20th Helicopter Squadron into western Quang Binh Province on 22 June. The team sent a message stating that it had landed successfully. Eleven-man reinforcement team Hector Bravo parachuted into North Vietnam on 23 September. Less than five minutes after insertion the landing zone erupted into a firefight and four agents were killed outright. The rest took to the bush and eventually linked up with Hector.

Team Samson helicoptered in on 5 October. The eight men were landed at an LZ in Laos and were then to proceed across the border into North Vietnam on foot toward the Tay Trang Pass. From there they would be able to observe Route 4, a major supply conduit. The team continued to broadcast until 2 December. Reinforcement team Tourbillon Bravo parachuted into North Vietnam on Christmas Eve and was the first agent team insertion from a C-130 Combat Spear aircraft.[13]

Under Colonel Blackburn, MACSOG had begun to take a rather cynical tack in the treatment of financial contracts signed by its agents at the time of their recruitment. The contracts stipulated that the dependents of the agents would continue to receive their pay and benefits, even if they were captured. Blackburn wanted the budget amount reduced by paying a one-time death benefit. So, without regard to the contracts and knowing that many of its agents were serving time in North Vietnamese prisons, MACSOG reduced the number of agents by declaring so many of them dead each month until it had written them all off. The STS was convinced to go along with the cutoff since it could not afford to cover the costs itself. According to author Sedgwick Tourison, the money paid to dependents dried up long before MACSOG stopped payments to the STS. "Like the covert operation itself, those who had custody of the money that never reached the families would prefer that the subject be left closed."[14]

SAAT

Due to the increasing number of aircrews being lost to anti-aircraft artillery fire over North Vietnam (and the creation of the Joint Personnel Recovery Center), MACSOG felt called upon to create a ground force that could enter North Vietnam and assist in the rescue of downed airmen. These forces, known as Safe Area Activation Teams (SAAT), would be inserted into the North, search remote crash sites, and neutralize any ground opposition to a rescue attempt. The program had just been established when a call arrived at the Joint Personnel Recovery Center [JPRC]. On 12 October a Navy A-1, piloted by Lt. Robert Woods, was shot down over northern Thanh Hoa Province. Navy SAR helicopters were unable to lower a penetrator through the triple canopy to pull the pilot to safety. The arrival of North Vietnamese ground forces in the area then drove off the SAR attempt. On 14 October, after several more tries, the JPRC was called in. Since the SAAT teams were not yet available, the best available Shining Brass team was tapped for the mission.

Spike Team Ohio consisted of three Green Berets and eight Nung troopers commanded by Sgt. Dick Meadows.[15] The team was pulled out of Laos and transported to the aircraft carrier *Intrepid* (CV-11) for a briefing. At sunup on the 15th the team was ready to go but the weather closed in over Thanh Hoa and the mission was postponed. The next morning dawned clear and sunny and the team was lifted in to Lieutenant Woods' last known location. Ohio had only been on the ground for fifteen minutes when it encountered a PAVN patrol. The team then killed four of the North Vietnamese, but it had also given away its position and was then surrounded by many more PAVN troops. Although the team carried out a loud and hurried search, there was no sign of the pilot.

Ohio had been on the ground in North Vietnam for four hours, and the rescuers were in need of rescue. The team headed for its insertion point and called *Intrepid* for extraction. Two HH-3 SAR helicopters dropped in jungle penetrators and pulled the team out. As the helicopters lifted away, however, the ground erupted in small arms fire and one of the ships was badly damaged. It managed to remain airborne and kept flying toward the coast. With the carrier in sight the chopper finally gave out and dropped into the sea. All of the passengers and crew jumped free and were picked up by a boat from the destroyer *Henley* (DD-762).

Cross-Border Ground Operations

Despite the best aerial anti-infiltration efforts of the USAF, the total estimated for all PAVN infiltration during 1966 was between 58,000 and 90,000, including at least five full regiments.[16] North Vietnamese *binh tram* labor forces were busy building new roadways and it was estimated that a total of 415 miles were added during the year. A June DIA estimate credited PAVN with 600 miles of roads passable by trucks within the corridor, at least 200 miles of which were good enough for year-round use.[17]

New additions included opening the Ban Karai Pass from North Vietnam into Laos and drivable roads all the way to the Sihanouk Trail and the Cambodian frontier. CINCPAC intelligence studies showed that the North Vietnamese had about 1,200 trucks working the infiltration routes while reports from CIA roadwatch teams suggested that 600 trucks were operating in Laos, 400 of which were in the southern panhandle and half of which were operational at any one time. In actuality 3,570 trucks were working the logistics system in both northern and southern Laos.[18]

It was estimated by the CIA that 39 PAVN engineering battalions and 24,800 laborers (16,000 of whom were assigned to maintaining the Trail) were in Laos. In April, Joseph McChristian, chief of MACV Intelligence, put infiltration at 7,000 men per month (about 11.5 battalions). He believed the North Vietnamese could move 308 tons of supplies per day: 269 tons on the Trail, 25 tons through Cambodia, and 14 tons by sea.[19] To cover the construction and maintenance of its new Cambodian supply routes, Hanoi had established the 470th Transportation Group, which had its own *binh trams*, way stations, and security units.

North Vietnamese infiltration highlights for the year included the movement of the 52nd PAVN Infantry Regiment 2,000 miles from North Vietnam south to eastern Cochin China. This first movement of so large a force at one time took six months to complete. Of the 52nd's original complement of 2,800 men, 1,200 arrived at their final destination, most of the rest having been felled by disease or accidents on the Trail. During the last six months of 1966 Hanoi infiltrated 2 infantry divisions, 2 artillery regiments, and 4 battalions of anti-aircraft troops. Compared to the 103 infiltrated battalions of the previous year, 1966 saw an increase in communist forces within the South to 136 battalions.[20]

RUNNING RECON

For the reconnaissance teams of MACSOG, this increase in communist activity meant an increase in the number and tempo of missions. After the Intelligence Branch had compiled and collated information gathered from aerial reconnaissance, MACV J-2, and its own teams, a target package was put together by the Ground Studies staff. After approval by higher authority, the package was sent to the C&C Center at Da Nang. A recon team stationed at one of the FOBs was then assigned the mission and sometimes spent up to a week planning and training for it. One unusual aspect of SOG's recon operation was that each team volunteered for each mission. If, for whatever reason, a team refused the mission, team members were not penalized, either by their superiors or by their fellow recon men. If a man decided that "running in the woods" was not for him, he could step off his team and take a job at the camp without fear of dishonor or repercussion, since "one was believed to have as much courage for being able to quit as keep running."[21]

The team of three Americans and nine indigenous troops (or some combination of the above) would then be helilifted over the border from a launch site and inserted into a pre-chosen landing zone. From it the team would move as stealthily as possible to carry out its assigned mission. The goal was to stay on the ground, undetected, as long as possible (the optimal mission length being five days). Once contact was made with communist forces or the mission was completed, helicopters moved in to extract the team as quickly as possible. Recon teams were expected to run one five-day operation per month, but this limit was normally exceeded. These missions could include one or more of the following: area and point reconnaissance, road- and riverwatches, wiretapping of communication lines, bomb damage assessment, planting electronic beacons and sensors, and prisoner snatches.

For team members a premium was placed on combat experience. The Americans were usually noncommissioned officers, veterans of the Special Forces A-Teams, CIDG, or the Mike Forces. Team leaders were chosen for experience in the field, not by rank. The indigenous troops (indigs) were mercenaries, usually ethnic Chinese Nungs or Montagnards—totally loyal and tough hill tribesmen hardened by years of hunting and fighting in some of the most demanding terrain in Asia. In case of necessity, recon teams on the ground could call in air support by radioing an orbiting FAC. The most immediate support usually arrived in the form of helicopter gunships or A-1 Spads that had been tasked to that particular mission. Strikes on targets of opportunity by tactical air forces were a little more complicated.

To illustrate just how complex and vital the communications system could be, let's look at the commo linkage between a reconnaissance team calling for an air strike on a target in Laos. The team would notify its launch site (via the FAC), which, in turn, would relay the message to Da Nang (the C&C/Tactical Air Control Center [TACC]). The TACC would then relay the request to the TACC at Udorn, Thailand (which sought to obtain Vientiane embassy approval—this usually took about twenty minutes). Upon receiving approval, Udorn would authorize the FAC to send in tactical aircraft. Later, after another battle with the embassy in Vientiane, Airborne Battlefield Command and Control Centers (ABCCC) were authorized. The ABCCC (a specially configured C-130) would then route aircraft to the FAC, which led them to the target. This procedure was also simplified by allowing the teams to directly contact the ABCCC.

Once the sun went down, however, the FAC returned to base and the team was on its own. The team members withdrew to a preselected area and circled themselves back-to-back for a Remain Over Night (RON). In the morning, the team contacted the FAC, got itself together, and continued the mission. Team members had to be constantly aware of any sign that they were under observation or being tracked by the communists. They tried to pick routes to the target that their enemy would not expect them to use and went to great lengths to cover their trail. The highest compliment a recon man could make about another was that he was "good in the woods."

Each man was fully cognizant that, in case of capture, his commanders and government would disavow any knowledge of his existence or actions and deny any ties to the United States. This state of affairs explained the great lengths to which recon teams would go to ensure that a comrade was truly dead and not just wounded. It also explained the pacts that the members of teams (both U.S. and indigenous) made with each other that no one would be left behind. Considering the treatment that wounded or captured team members could expect at the hands of the communists (usually torture and summary execution), the recon men preferred to fight to the death.

EXPLOITATION FORCES

Looking to expand the cross-border effort, General Westmoreland pushed for the initialization of Phase II of the Shining Brass concept by seeking authorization for the use of exploitation forces. Ambassador Sullivan demurred. He saw the interdiction and ground reconnaissance programs as inherently incompatible (once again irrationality creeps in). In his opinion the two were competing concepts that prompted interservice rivalry. He observed that one Shining Brass representative complained to him about giving their target to the Air Force, thus "depriving Shining Brass personnel of their "'brownie points'."[22] Regardless of the ambassador's objections, three exploitation battalions (Haymaker Forces) were authorized on 20 June, each of which would consist of three companies (Havoc Forces) of four platoons (Hornet Forces) each.[23]

Helicopter insertions for all Shining Brass operations were also approved during the year, but their depth of penetration into Laos could not exceed five kilometers.[24] Exploitation forces were limited to a depth of no more than ten kilometers and no more than one platoon could participate in any operation. An incongruity in SOG's operational boundary was adjusted when authority came through for insertions into an area five kilometers in depth from the DMZ south along the border to the original Shining Brass boundary.

SHINING BRASS

The C&C Detachment had begun its life in 1965 in a squad tent, equipped with a 26-D radio van parked across the runway from the hanger that housed the 219th VNAF Squadron's H-34s at Da Nang Airfield. For various reasons (security being one of them) the detachment was moved to SOG's safe house at 22 Le Loi Street in Da Nang proper in 1966. This solution too was fraught with security problems, so the hunt began for a new location for the headquarters.

During 1966 Shining Brass forces were authorized to expand to twenty reconnaissance teams (which on 3 October were redesignated Spike Teams [STs]) of three Americans and nine indigenous personnel each. The C&C controlled FOB-1 Kham Duc, but it was closed out in July when it became apparent that weather conditions at the site were not conducive to constant operations and due to constant North Vietnamese harassment. It would, however, be utilized as MACSOG's reconnaissance training center and as an alternate launch site until 1968. A new FOB-1 was opened at Phu Bai next to an ARVN training camp and airstrip that was utilized to launch the teams. Its associated launch site was located at Khe Sanh in I Corps. The teams working the northern sector of the Shining Brass area took the names of U.S. states while its exploitation forces took the names of American cities. The FOB's exploitation and security force personnel consisted of Cambodian Khmer Kampuchea Krom (KKK) mercenaries, ethnic Cambodians from the Mekong Delta region who originally opposed the governments of both South Vietnam and Cambodia.

FOB-2 was located at Kontum, in the Central Highlands, and its associated launch site was at Dak To (opened as Kham Duc was being phased out). The Spike Teams working the southern portion of the Shining Brass area also took the names of U.S. states. The FOB's exploitation and security forces consisted of Nungs and South Vietnamese (who could avoid the ARVN draft and be paid higher wages by SOG). The first platoon-size exploitation force operation was launched from FOB-2 on 26 June.

During the year 105 recon missions were launched into Laos, including 12 platoon-size Hornet Force operations. They were supported by 405 tactical air and 130 helicopter gunship sorties. Communist prisoners captured in Laos totaled 12, intelligence reports generated totaled 371.[25] American casualties amounted to 3 killed and 5 missing in action. Indigenous casualties were 16 killed and 25 missing in action.[26]

MISSIONS

One important intelligence revelation during the year was a newly discovered east–west infiltration road in the tri-border region (where the borders of Cambodia, Laos, and South Vietnam met) that was designated Route 110. A MACSOG recon team went in on 26 May to evaluate the situation and to mine the road. The logistics pileup that they discovered in the area led to the launching of the Search, Locate, Annihilate, Monitor (SLAM) concept in October.

By mid-July COMUSMACV feared the advent of a communist "monsoon offensive" that would probably be spearheaded by the PAVN 324-B Division in the I Corps Tactical Zone. This led to an increase in Shining Brass operations in the FOB-1 area. Nine teams probed the Trail between 11 and 30 July and twelve more were sent into the same area in September. MACSOG also supported Operation Prairie, a III Marine Amphibious Force search and destroy operation in Quang Tri Province. Between 18 September and 15 October, SOG launched nine in-country missions and eight into Laos near the DMZ to support the Marines.

Continuing reconnaissance activities along Route 110 were responsible for the launching of the first two SLAM missions.[27] A ground probe and wiretap operation in the area by Spike Team Colorado from 3 to 7 October came upon large concentrations of North Vietnamese troops and provided the intelligence necessary for the first mission. The target chosen for SLAM I was a sector on Route 110 two miles in diameter that was immediately struck by B-52s and followed by 7th Air Force tactical strikes and propaganda leaflet drops.

On 13 October SLAM II was carried out close to Route 110 where other teams had discovered the bivouac areas of two North Vietnamese battalions. After the strikes, SOG had its first opportunity to launch a platoon-size BDA of a B-52 strike area in Laos. Hornet Force platoons proceeded to carry out several BDAs in the SLAM II area, but the results were not heartening. There was little evidence that the airstrikes had killed either any humans or animals. Many of the bombs had left craters less than a foot in diameter on the ground, since most of the explosive force of the ordnance had been spent in the overhead canopy. One platoon BDA went into an area that had been saturated by BLU-3 CBU (cluster bomb units). The munitions did manage to penetrate the canopy and exploded on the ground, but, once again, there was no evidence of casualties.

Joint Personnel Recovery Center

In May Gen. Hunter Harris, commander, Pacific Air Force, approached legendary Air Force colonel Harry "Heine" Aderholt and proposed that he develop a post-SAR operation for Southeast Asia. General Harris was seeking solutions to the problems of what to do for downed or evading airmen after immediate SAR attempts had failed and how to coordinate efforts for the liberation of prisoners of war. Aderholt had made his reputation in special operations and was intrigued by the opportunity. After examining the situation, he decided that MACSOG should undertake the mission, since it already possessed the assets and authority to operate anywhere in Southeast Asia. The Joint Chiefs agreed and Aderholt became the first chief of the newly created JPRC in September.[28]

The organization did not get off to an auspicious beginning. Bloody interservice turf battles raged for eight months before control and authorization procedures were finally ironed out. Victory was declared when it was determined that an Air Force officer would always be at the helm and that, due to the interservice nature of the organization, all credit would be shared equally.[29]

The mission of the JPRC staff was to serve as a clearinghouse for the flow of intelligence on American prisoners or evadees, to determine the validity of that information, and to organize rescue attempts utilizing MACSOG forces or local troops. The mission also included the tracking of MIAs, locating and liberating prisoners and prison camps, and offering bribes and other incentives for information concerning the liberation of Free World Military Forces' POWs.

LITTLE DACHAU

A successful raid on a communist POW camp had already occurred during the month of the JPRC's inception.[30] The 1st Battalion, 327th Infantry of the 101st Airborne Division had just completed participation in Operation Hawthorne and was protecting the rice harvest in the Tuy Hoa Valley of Phu Yen Province. Its Tiger Force (an all-volunteer recon unit) was approached by two South Vietnamese who claimed to be escapees from a prison camp located in the mountains bordering the valley. The battalion commander interviewed the two men, threw together a plan, and alerted the Tiger Force for a quick raid. Coordination with two other platoons was slowed after they became bogged down in an old French minefield. With the force finally united, they moved out for the camp, but they had lost time. Dawn was already breaking when gunfire erupted. The Tiger Force swept into the camp and the guards fled.

They had left behind thirty-five South Vietnamese prisoners, both ARVN and civilian. The camp had originally held ninety prisoners, including a Republic of Korea Marine, but they had been starved, beaten, and worked to death in what the American soldiers came to call "little Dachau." The success of the operation was attributed to timely intelligence and rapid reaction to it. The time interval from the arrival of the escapees until the launching of the raid was only one day. This success, however, was followed by two failures that threatened to destroy the new JPRC. On 1 October 1966, the first Bright Light mission launched into North Vietnam took place. The team found the pilot of a downed aircraft already dead, but it did recover his remains.

CRIMSON TIDE

On 12 October an NLF defector emerged from the Mekong Delta and informed his captors that he knew the location of a camp holding a black American NCO (who could have been either Edward Johnson or Carl Jackson, both of whom had been captured in the Delta). Six weeks later, and after the approval and input of the entire IV Corps and MACV staffs, the JPRC was ready to launch a SOG Hatchet Company for the rescue in Operation Crimson Tide. Capt. Frank Jaks, the MACSOG force commander, was worried. There was no real briefing, no real intelligence, and six weeks had passed since the NLF soldier had defected. To Jaks "it seemed that everybody and his brother knew about the mission."[31] As the twelve helicopters roared into the LZ, four of the ships carrying one platoon shifted east and were separated from the rest of the company. Then all hell broke loose. Intersecting communist heavy machine-gun fire opened up, followed by mortars and intense small arms fire. When air support arrived it came from F-100 jets that dropped their bombs on the Hatchet Force. The JPRC had requested that prop-driven A-1E Skyraiders provide the air support, but this was turned down by 7th Air Force, who better understood what kind of air support would be necessary. And then the sun began to go down.

By the next morning the communists had abandoned the area and Jaks found what was left of his lost platoon. The two Green Berets who commanded the unit had been killed, and of their forty Nungs, all were dead or seriously wounded.[32] It was later determined that the company had landed between two communist battalions, approximately two thousand men supported by heavy machine guns and mortars. Crimson Tide put the fear of God into MACV, the JPRC, and American field commanders, who became wary of expending too many lives to save a few. After all, a disaster of such proportions went into one's personnel jacket.

LANGUAGE SKILLS
During the middle of December a traveling tinker walked into an ARVN outpost to report that he had seen two American personnel being held in a hamlet near Ba Tu, Cambodia. The hamlet, which was also purported to contain several weapons-manufacturing shops and caches, was in an area defended by an NLF battalion and was bordered on three sides by minefields. SOG decided to launch a prisoner rescue operation utilizing elements of the 25th Infantry Division; Lt. Fred Caristo, who was fluent in Vietnamese and Cambodian, was to accompany Operation Cobra Tail, the first JPRC cross-border mission.[33]

At 1200 hours on 30 December the lead helicopter of the SOG force touched down on the wrong side of a minefield and Lieutenant Caristo leapt off. The pilot, recognizing his error, lifted off and attempted to land at the correct LZ. Caristo, the only American soldier on the ground, dashed fifty meters through the minefield and the intense fire that the communists were laying down once they realized what was occurring. Caristo smashed through the back wall of the hut that had been designated as the location of the prisoners and questioned the two civilians inside who related to him that the prisoners had been moved out of the camp the previous evening. The assaulting U.S. forces had, in the meantime, become bogged down by intense communist fire in another minefield.

Caristo went to their assistance and was leading them through the mines when he was knocked down by the blast of a Bangalore torpedo. After leading the force through, he spotted an NLF trooper manning a .57-mm recoilless rifle and wounded the man with his rifle. Assaulting U.S. force began to grenade and then overrun a series of bunkers. Caristo, realizing that women and children had taken refuge in the complex, entered the bunkers and convinced their occupants to surrender. His language skills also allowed him to recognize thirty-four communists who were attempting to blend in with the civilians and his immediate translation of captured documents led to the discovery of two arms caches. Caristo blamed the failure of the operation on the two-week delay in getting approval, planning, and then launching the raid. For his actions on this mission Fred Caristo was awarded the Distinguished Service Cross.

Logistics

No sooner did MACSOG Logistics get a handle on its equipment and materials than it was tasked with another round of expansion. The enlargement of the Shining Brass program (from ten to twenty Spike Teams and three battalion-size exploitation forces) meant that those forces would have to be equipped, armed, and maintained in a relatively short period of time. This the Logistics Branch managed to do.

To reflect this expansion of mission and responsibilities, the branch's Supply and Aerial Resupply Sections were joined by a new Transportation Section. The logistics finance officer was bolstered during the year by a comptroller, a budget analyst, a transportation officer, a civil engineer, and a R&D officer. The expansion of logistics was a reflection of the big buildup in American forces in South Vietnam. MACSOG was no longer one of a few U.S. units in Southeast Asia. This new condition alleviated some problems, notably dependence on CISO for common items of supply, but it created others, such as the continuation of the inflation of the Vietnamese piaster (currency) that strained MACSOG's budget.

One improvement made during the year was the institution of the Clothing and Equipment Review Panel. Its mission was to evaluate the utility of issue items of equipment and that of new or unconventional items that were being tested in the field by the operational units. Construction, of course, continued apace. Shining Brass FOBs at Phu Bai and Dak To and the recon school at Kham Duc were either built or expanded. The growth of the program also necessitated the construction of a new C&C headquarters at Camp Fay, while the NAD continued the consolidation of its units in the Camp Black Rock area.

As a reflection of the expanded size of SOG's operations and the increased responsibility of logistics, the CNO launched an audit of the branch during July and August. This occurred just in time to put the new comptroller and budget analyst to work. The proposed 1967 budget amounted to $19,742,600 (excluding support provided by individual services/agencies).[34] This effectively doubled the combined budgets of the previous two years.

Plans

With the inception of Shining Brass, MACSOG (and General Westmoreland) envisioned the reconnaissance missions as paving the way for more conventional American operations to cut the Ho Chi Minh Trail. As far as MACV was concerned, this was now MACSOG's raison d'être. In November, Col. Harry Kinnard and Lt. Col. Bull Simons developed OPLAN Full Cry. In this plan, the 1st Air Cavalry Division would leap the

Laotian border and create an airhead at Attopeu. It would then head for Saravane and finally Savannakhet. The 3rd Marine Division would simultaneously attack west from the DMZ, crossing Route 9 through Tchepone to Savannakhet. ARVN forces would push up through the Ashau Valley, and the U.S. 4th Infantry Division would attack west from Pleiku/Kontum. Thus, Laotian neutrality would be violated by a full-blown American/South Vietnamese invasion. What the outcome of such an operation would have been, at the tactical, strategic, and political levels, is unknown.

Comment: SACSA

The position of Special Assistant for Counterinsurgency and Special Activities at the Pentagon was held by the following general officers:

MAJ. GEN. VICTOR H. "BRUTE" KRULAK, USMC (02/1962–01/1964)

A 1934 graduate of Annapolis, Brute Krulak commanded the 2nd Marine Parachute Battalion and saw his first action at Vella Lavella in the Pacific during the Second World War. In 1943 he was awarded the Navy Cross on Choiseul Island when he led a weeklong diversionary raid to cover the invasion of Bougainville. He also took part in the savage fighting on Okinawa. During the Korean Conflict Krulak served as chief of staff of the 1st Marine Division.

General Krulak was the first officer to hold the position of SACSA on the Joint Staff at the Pentagon and was chiefly responsible (for good or ill) for the development of U.S. counterinsurgency doctrine and policy in the early 1960s. After his service as SACSA, he was promoted to lieutenant general and commanded the Fleet Marine Force, Pacific until his retirement in 1968. Long an opponent of the "search and destroy" doctrine in Vietnam, he championed a policy of pacification in the villages as the path to victory.

MAJ. GEN. ROLLEN H. "BUCK" ANTHIS, USAF (02/1964–01/1966)

Rollen Anthis served during the Second World War in various U.S. Army Air Force transport commands. After the war he served as commander of the 1603rd Air Transport Wing, USAF, Europe. Anthis was then assigned to Headquarters, USAF, as deputy chief of the Operations and Control Division and later as chief of the Manpower Division in the office of the deputy chief of staff for operations.

He was assigned to South Vietnam in 1961 with the dual role of commander, 2nd Advanced Echelon (later 2nd Air Division) and chief of staff to the Air Force section of MACV's predecessor, the Military Assistance Advisory Group (MAAG). He was promoted to major general in 1963 and then assigned to the Pentagon as SACSA. He later assumed leadership of Headquarters Command, USAF, and then commanded the 17th Air Force in Germany. Anthis rounded out his career as chief of staff, Combined Planning Staff, CENTO, in 1969 and, in 1971, as assistant commander, USAF Logistics Command. He retired on 1 May 1973 and died on 19 August 1995.

MAJ. GEN. WILLIAM R. "RAY" PEERS,
USA (02/1966–01/1967)

Ray Peers began his career as a second lieutenant during the Second World War, when he was assigned to Detachment 101 of the OSS in the China-Burma-India Theater. He was promoted to lieutenant colonel while performing duties that included supervising more than ten thousand U.S.-led Burmese Kachin tribesmen against the Japanese. From 1949 to 1951, he was seconded to the CIA for anticommunist operations against the newly established PRC. He later served as chief of Special Projects on the Army general staff and as director of Security, Mapping, and Combat Intelligence for the Department of the Army from 1961 to 1962. He was then assigned to the Pentagon as SACSA.

From 1967 to 1968 he served as the commanding general of the 4th Infantry Division in South Vietnam. His later assignments included stints as commanding general, First Field Force, Vietnam, and as commanding general of the Eighth Army in Korea from 1971 to 1973. Ray Peers is best remembered today as the officer who headed the Army's official investigation into the events at My Lai 4 that led to the massacre of between three hundred and four hundred Vietnamese civilians in 1968. He retired as a lieutenant general and died in 1984.

MAJ. GEN. WILLIAM E. "BILL" DEPUY,
USA (03/1967–03/1969)

William Depuy began his career during the Second World War in the 357th Infantry Regiment of the 90th Infantry Division. He eventually became a battalion commander and served throughout the European Campaign. In 1950 he was seconded to the CIA where he headed China operations. In May 1962, after several European assignments, Depuy served as director of Special Warfare in the office of the deputy chief of staff for Military Operations. He was later director, Plans and Programs, office of the assistant chief of staff for Force Development.

In May 1964 he was assigned to South Vietnam as assistant chief of staff of Operations, MACV. In this capacity he devised and helped implement the "search and destroy" strategy followed by the majority of U.S. troops. Depuy then became the commanding general of the 1st Infantry Division in South Vietnam in March 1966. After returning to the United States in 1967, he was assigned to the Pentagon and became SACSA.

Depuy later served as assistant vice chief of staff of the Army, as deputy commanding general, Continental Army Command, and later as the first commander of the new Training and Doctrine Command (TRADOC). As such, he was instrumental in the reorganization of the Army in the post-Vietnam period and was considered the father of the "Airland Battle" doctrine. He retired from active duty in 1977 and died in September 1992.

MAJ. GEN. JOHN F. "FRITZ" FREUND,
USA (03/1969–03/1970)
Although a graduate of the U.S. Naval Academy, an eye condition kept Fritz Freund out of the Navy at the beginning of the Second World War. He took a commission from the Army instead. He served as an artillery officer in North Africa, Italy, and France and later became one of the Army's earliest proponents of guided missiles and nuclear weapons. He arrived in South Vietnam in 1964 as senior military advisor in II Corps, served as director of training for MACV, and as commanding general of the 199th Light Infantry Brigade. In 1968 he was assigned as chief of staff of the VII Corps in Germany.

Freund was then assigned to the Pentagon as SACSA in 1969 and later served as assistant chief of staff for Intelligence. He later commanded the First Region of the Army Air Defense Command until his retirement in 1972. He rounded out his military career as head of the Connecticut National Guard from 1972 until 1983. He died on 22 March 2001.

BRIG. GEN. DONALD D. "DON" BLACKBURN,
USA (03/1970–02/1971)
Don Blackburn was commissioned in the U.S. Army in 1940. Stationed in the Philippines in 1942, he evaded capture by the Japanese and ended up in the mountains of northern Luzon, where he organized and commanded Igorot tribesmen behind Japanese lines. By the time Douglas MacArthur returned, Blackburn's force had grown to 20,000 men and he had been promoted to lieutenant colonel. After the war he served as provost marshal of Washington and did a tour as a staff officer at the Pentagon. He

then taught military psychology and leadership at West Point. He was sent to South Vietnam in late 1957 as senior advisor to the ARVN general commanding in the Mekong Delta.

Blackburn was then given command of the 77th Special Forces Group at Fort Bragg, North Carolina. In 1960 he headed Operation White Star, the covert military advisory group in Laos. On 14 May 1965, Colonel Blackburn was appointed as chief, MACSOG, where he served until May 1966. It was under his leadership (and with the tutelage of his protégé, Lt. Col. Arthur D. "Bull" Simons) that Operation Shining Brass was inaugurated.

Returning from Vietnam, Blackburn was assigned to the NATO Military Committee and then as assistant deputy director of Intelligence and Evaluation, for the Defense Communications Planning Group. There he was instrumental in the development of electronic sensors for Operation Igloo White. He was promoted brigadier general and assigned as SACSA in 1969. In his new position, General Blackburn was instrumental in the design and implementation of Operation Kingpin, the Son Tay POW raid, in November 1970. In the post-raid political fallout, he was reassigned to an R&D post on the Army general staff, but soon retired after thirty-three years of service.

BRIG. GEN. LEROY J. "ROY" MANOR,
USAF (02/1971–02/1973)

Leroy Manor joined the Army Air Force during the Second World War and flew seventy-two combat missions as a P-47 pilot with the 358th Fighter Group in Europe. In the postwar period he attended staff college and had several U.S. and European assignments. He then went to Headquarters, USAF, as chief, Tactical Evaluation Division. He then served four years in the office of the deputy chief of staff for Plans and Operations. He was then assigned as chief, Plans and Capabilities Branch; chief, Analysis of Southeast Asia Operations Study Group; and as chief, Operations Review Group.

In May 1968 Manor assumed command of the 37th Tactical Fighter Wing and flew 275 combat missions over North and South Vietnam. Returning from Southeast Asia, he commanded the 835th Air Division. He then took command of the USAF Special Operations Force at Eglin Air Force Base, Florida, in February 1970. While assigned there, Brigadier General Manor also became the overall commander of the task force that conducted the Son Tay POW raid. He was moved to the Pentagon and replaced Don Blackburn as SACSA in February 1971. Manor later served as vice commander and then commander of the 13th Air Force in the

Philippines. He was promoted to major general and then served as chief of staff, Pacific Command. He retired from the Air Force in June 1978.

THE SOG–SACSA RELATIONSHIP
It might be instructive at this point to discuss the attitudes of MACSOG's superiors and the staff members at SACSA as to what they thought about the contributions made by SOG toward the military effort in Southeast Asia. We have already seen that the opinion of COMUSMACV (both General Westmoreland and General Abrams) was not very positive toward the contributions made by SOG. The relationship between MACSOG and its superiors at the Pentagon was not much better. The position of SACSA had, after all, been created in 1962 to slow down the Kennedy administration's special warfare policies, not to embrace them. At the time of MACSOG's establishment, SACSA served as a watchdog in the creation, modification, and especially in the limitation of its missions. General Krulak and his staff performed their functions well, tailoring MACSOG to meet the political expectations of the White House.

At its establishment, SACSA consisted of only three (later four) action officers, each of whom oversaw the staff's divisions: Plans, Doctrine, and Resources; Programs and Review; Special Plans; and Operations. In its later incarnations, the organizational layout of SACSA is not known, except that in the latter 1960s the Special Operations Division was the main center of activity. One must also consider, however, that SACSA did not deal with only the conflict in Southeast Asia; it had cognizance and control of all covert and clandestine military activities worldwide.

What one must also keep in mind about MACSOG is that the organization was a political, not a military, creation. As far as the Joint Chiefs were concerned, SOG was peripheral and unrelated to the main military effort. The Joint Chiefs tolerated the organization only because the White House had foisted it on the Pentagon, but that was all that they were willing to do. The views of two members of the SACSA staff support this view. Navy commander William Murray believed that the JCS went along with MACSOG only as long as it wasn't "going to get the corporate military into any trouble."[35] When then Lt. Col. Robert Rheault joined SACSA staff in July 1966, he saw firsthand that "the conventional military guys were in control in Washington and they opposed Special Forces."[36]

During the tenures of three generals—Anthis, Peers, and Depuy—the temperament at SACSA changed from that of being a watchdog to open advocacy of SOG operations. This was reasonable considering that all three men had backgrounds in special operations and/or unconventional warfare. It did not help much, however. General Peers became notorious for his stormy confrontations with the denizens of Foggy Bottom over what he saw as their foot-dragging over Laotian operations. Robert Rheault remembered a terse conversation with Peers after one foray to the State Department. Peers claimed that there were "nothing over there but a bunch of shoves"; when Rheault asked him what a "shove" was, Peers replied, "a cross between a shit and a dove."[37]

In the spring of 1967 Peers was replaced by Depuy, who had just finished a tour as commanding general of the 1st Infantry Division in South Vietnam. Initially, Depuy was an advocate for MACSOG, but by 1968 he had soured on the operation. Author Richard Shultz believed that, as a protégé of Chairman of the JCS Earle Wheeler, he may have contributed to General Wheeler's growing enmity toward the organization.

One reflection of this change in attitude (and reflecting the disengagement sensibility of the military at the time) was the downgrading of the rank of SACSA. The position had been a three-star slot, but was reduced to a brigadier general's position. By the time MACSOG's former commander, Don Blackburn, became SACSA, priorities were changing and the conflict was winding down. Blackburn was offered a unique perspective on the position. As the commanding officer of SOG he had complained that SACSA "didn't do anything, we didn't need him . . . we never needed him."[38] Yet while he held the position himself he claimed that he "did not recall signing one paper on SOG the whole time. . . . You're being blocked by MACV and CINCPAC . . . but you're not making end runs to go around them."[39]

The action officers themselves had another perspective on both MACSOG operations and their supervisors' attitudes toward them. Key to this understanding was the knowledge that the officers believed that the JCS tolerated SOG operations only because of pressure from the White House and understood that the Joint Chiefs were skeptical that covert operations contributed much to the effort in South Vietnam. It was also interesting that few, if any, of the action officers assigned to SACSA had any experience in covert or unconventional operations. As to the role that SOG had to play in Southeast Asia, one officer's attitude toward SOG was that the people assigned were, in general, "undisciplined, wild-eyed Army Special Forces people . . . who believed that the whole of Southeast Asia could be conquered by a handful of Green Berets."[40] This was essentially the same perspective that existed at MACV, where Westmoreland and Abrams saw little value in SOG.[41]

Chapter Four

1967: DANIEL BOONE

Headquarters

Col. John Singlaub retained his command as chief, MACSOG, for another year. For the first time, a commander of the unit had evaded General Westmoreland's one-year rotation policy. This said a great deal about the working relationship between COMUSMACV and the chief of MACSOG. During October Singlaub requested a boost in the organization's JTD, the official allocation of manpower and resources deemed by higher authority to be necessary for the fulfillment of the unit's missions. As of October, SOG's headquarters was allocated 275 men (108 officers, 3 warrant officers, 149 enlisted men, and 15 civilians). Due to increased mission tasking during the year, the organization was seeking more manpower (152 officers, 3 warrant officers, 251 enlisted men, and 10 civilians for a total of 416) and a change in its organizational arrangement, which had not altered significantly since 1965.[1]

Organizationally, the Saigon headquarters was divided into six branches: Administration, Plans, Intelligence, Operations (joined to Training Studies during the year), Logistics, and Communications, each of which was subdivided into various sections that served as staff elements. The Joint Personnel Recovery Center served as a separate element within the unit. Suffice it to say that with the exception of the headquarters staff, all U.S. members of SOG were volunteers. One can quickly deduce that MACSOG was a small operation in terms of American personnel, but the size of the unit could be (and was) deceiving. The JTD also included 7,615 South Vietnamese personnel within all of its operations.

During the year Jack Singlaub butted heads with the commander of the 5th SFG, Col. Francis J. Kelly. Kelly had created two programs utilizing his Mike Forces in Blackjack Operations that coincided with and were similar to MACSOG's Hornet and Havoc missions, some of which took place within South Vietnam. This led to increasing tensions and turf jealousy between the 5th SFG and SOG.

By the time of Singlaub's tenure as chief of SOG, in-house complaints over the unit's organization, which had begun at its inception, were rife. The original bone of contention was that the unit's building-block structure was naval in nature. It consisted of divisions and groups, not the Army's typical staff structure. This was understandable during the first two years of SOG's life, when the NAD's contribution was paramount. As the Army's commitment to the unit increased, however, the basic structure did not change. As time passed, SOG's senior officers were continually vexed by the complexity of the increasing number and types of missions with which they were saddled. As new mission tasking took place every year, according to a JCS study of SOG, the unit "grew like topsy" and chief, MACSOG's responsibilities grew apace.[2] SOG was (and is) usually referred to as a Joint Unconventional Warfare Task Force, but like so many aspects of the unit, that was in name only. Instead of being an integrated command, in which service command relationships, prerogatives, and parochialism were surrendered, SOG was made up of building blocks that were based upon service, not functional lines.

EVALUATIONS
General Westmoreland was never quite satisfied with MACSOG and especially with its northern operations. In October he requested that CINCPAC carry out a thorough review of the operations and propose any changes that might be necessary. The committee that conducted the review, made up of representatives from the armed services, the CIA, and DIA personnel, ended up suggesting only minor mission changes. Their conclusions concerning northern operations, however, were not what MACV or the politicians in Washington wanted to hear. The SSPL, SOG's fictitious northern resistance movement, the committee concluded, should be expanded and made more viable.[3]

Westmoreland was not satisfied. No sooner had he received the CINCPAC evaluation than he commissioned an ad hoc advisory group chaired by Brig. Gen. A. R. Brownfield to look into and evaluate MACSOG. Chief among General Westmoreland's questions was whether the expense incurred by the unit was commensurate with its operational returns. The Brownfield Committee's report would not be finished or released until February 1968.

It was determined during the year that SOG's branches had been operating long enough under their none-too-subtle titles. On 3 February new cover names and numerical designations were handed out. Footboy was the overall title given to all operations conducted against North Vietnam. These included maritime operations (Plowman), psychological operations (Humidor), airborne operations (Timberwork), and air operations (Midriff). Due to a media leak during the year, cross-border ground operations (Shining Brass) received the new title Prairie Fire. On 1 November, MACSOG's Vietnamese counterpart, the Strategic Technical Service (STS), was reorganized and renamed the Strategic Technical Directorate (STD).

Intelligence

Considering all of the data that were collected by MACSOG operations, the Intelligence Branch had to have been one of the organization's busiest. With intelligence reports flowing in from Shining Brass/Prairie Fire, Plowman, and Timberwork, and with the addition of the new Daniel Boone and Muscle Shoals programs during the year, the division proudly claimed that even with the trebling of intelligence product it was handling the situation. During the year, cross-border operations in Laos produced 277 intelligence information reports on communist activities. The new Daniel Boone program generated 155 reports on Cambodia while Plowman maritime operations generated 463.[4]

SOURCES

Intelligence was MACSOG's bread and butter since the unit had to collect, collate, and disseminate it. The collection process was rather straightforward. Recon teams collected evidence and firsthand information on the ground and MAROPS personnel either interrogated prisoners on the spot or transferred them to Paradise Island where they could be more thoroughly debriefed. CSS personnel also collected data on North Vietnamese coastal defenses and environmental conditions. Timberwork collected information either from its agents or from resupply missions to those agents while air operations collected data on North Vietnam's anti-aircraft defenses and radar installations.

The pertinent information was then collated and analyzed by the cognizant geographic "study groups." The North Vietnam Study Group maintained intelligence on the North, the Laos Study Group managed intelligence relative to Laos and the DMZ, and the newly inaugurated Cambodian Study Group kept up with intelligence collected in the Daniel Boone area of operations.

Dissemination of the intelligence collected was rather more problematic. Since MACSOG was a covert operation, its intelligence had to be processed through MACV J-2 so that its original source was hidden. This was handled through the Joint Translation Center and the Combined Intelligence Information Center, both MACV clearinghouses for communist intelligence, which removed any indications of MACSOG involvement and shared the information out to relevant MACV units.

The real question was how higher headquarters and other allied units responded to the intelligence so gathered. Information concerning communist troop movements, logistical stockpiles, and transportation centers was passed on to higher headquarters, but tactical intelligence was extremely perishable. Whether it was responded to in a timely manner, if at all, became largely a matter of luck. This problem was compounded by the rather byzantine procedures that had to be followed by the 7th/13th Air Force in the process of gaining approval to strike out-of-country targets.

Another aspect of the problem was the inability of some branches within the system to accept the intelligence information that they received from MACSOG. Navy captain Bruce Dunning (a staff officer and division chief for SACSA from 1966 to 1969) stated that when confronted by intelligence collected from Project Humidor, he and the SACSA staff simply dismissed it. They believed that SOG/STS was simply giving them what they wanted to hear (e.g., dissatisfaction with the cadre and blaming Hanoi, not America, for the bombing campaign). It all seemed "too good to be true."[5] It was not until confirmation was obtained by debriefing Spanish émigrés repatriated from North Vietnam that SACSA, SOG's direct superiors, began to believe it.

THE COMPUTER GOES TO WAR

The correlation and collation of the massive amount of information, both on paper and photographs, was simplified by the use of automatic data-processing systems. These computers stored and collated information and were the cutting edge of data technology during the Vietnam Era. The first computer in the field in Vietnam was a Univac 1005 located at the headquarters of the 25th Infantry Division at Cu Chi in 1966. It was fed information from intelligence and operations reports broken down by region. The computer stored the information and correlated it upon request.

The Combined Intelligence Center at MACV headquarters acquired its first computer, an IBM 1400, soon afterward. Others with more power were soon added, including an IBM 360 and a 1311, which were mainly used for map overprints. By 1966 MACSOG had obtained an Intelligence Data Handling System (IDHS) in the form of an IBM 360 computer and an FMA Filesearch system.

Computers also greatly enhanced the painstaking work of aerial photo interpretation. The state-of-the-art AR 85-Viewer computer could interpret ground positions, distances, elevations, and other data. Computer-aided photo processes made Vietnam the first conflict to utilize pictomaps—photo mosaics that eliminated distortion and overlaid geographical (e.g., topographical lines) and tactical symbols on the maps.

SLEEPING WITH THE ENEMY

The real problem for MACSOG was its collaboration with, and dependence on, its South Vietnamese counterparts. All of SOG's Timberwork long-term agents and its civilian employees were hired and vetted by the South Vietnamese National Police Force, known as one of the most corrupt components of one of the most corrupt regimes on earth. U.S. intelligence agencies had long known that the South Vietnamese government and military were riddled with communist *dich van* agents, the numbers of which were estimated to range anywhere from 5,000 to 30,000.[6]

Of course, most of these agents were low-level sources, but many had served for years under false covers, during which time they could have risen to prominent and trusted positions within the political, economic, and military structure of South Vietnam. One did not have to go that far, however. The nature of the American disposition in South Vietnam (with its gargantuan logistics bases and plethora of amenities) provided ample opportunity for the communists to infiltrate agents in the guise of cooks, laundresses, clerks, secretaries, interpreters, and so forth. It was, therefore, more than probable that most MACSOG and STD programs were compromised, at some level, from their inception.

That MACSOG was prey to these agents is amply documented. For example, Lieutenant Hong Tran, a MACSOG STRATA team leader, was captured by the communists in southern Laos in 1971. When he was interrogated by North Vietnamese authorities, he was shown photographs taken from the water tower inside the main SOG compound at Da Nang.[7] While Maj. Pat Lang, intelligence officer with the STD advisory team, was going through counterintelligence investigation files, he noticed that there were severe discrepancies in the polygraph examinations given to Vietnamese civilians who provided support activities for MACSOG in Saigon. Two of these individuals (whom Lang had very serious doubts about) were the driver of Colonel Singlaub and the bartender at House 10, the transient billet within SOG's headquarters itself.[8]

Attempts to include the South Vietnamese authorities in the embrace of the American effort in order to enhance their confidence and cooperation were rife and probably self-defeating. As an example, Gen. Joseph

McChristian, chief of MACV intelligence, advanced a policy of releasing classified information to the South Vietnamese up to and including those bearing the NOFORN (No Foreign Dissemination) classification. After a review by the DIA, most of this material was released by MACV on a need-to-know basis.[9]

Two examples should suffice to describe the detrimental effects of such policies. Colonel Singlaub reported in his memoirs that he held briefings and discussed all of his operations with Colonel Ho, head of the STS/STD. Only later did he learn that Ho then briefed President Thieu on agent team operations in North Vietnam. Only later did he discover that there was a communist spy present at every briefing.[10]

Almost two decades after the end of the war, intelligence analyst Sedge-wick Tourison reported to ex-SOG major George Gaspard that North Vietnamese newspapers and television had hailed agent "Francois," who had helped the Ministry of Security to thwart many U.S. spy operations; he was cited as a senior South Vietnamese officer working at MACSOG headquarters. After comparing the agent's face to Gaspard's extensive photo collection, Tourison recognized the man as a major who had run the long-term agent program.[11]

Agent Francois was the alias of Do Van Tien, who had worked with MACSOG since its creation. After the fall of the southern regime, Tien was sentenced to three years (1975–78) in a political reeducation camp. According to his fellow prisoners, Tien's sentence was reduced in return for his cooperation in providing to the Vietnamese security apparatus a complete inside account of STS/STD and MACSOG methods and ac-tivities. According to authors Kenneth Conboy and Dale Andrade, who conducted interviews with the agents who had been captured in North Vietnam and had been incarcerated with Tien, the man had not been a spy during the war. Such are the vicissitudes of the intelligence business.[12] Perhaps even more problematic was CIA and U.S. military intelligence penetration of the entourages of both President Thieu and Prime Minis-ter Ky. They were both probably well bugged as well. American interests may have best been served by avoiding security investigations of the top South Vietnamese leaders.

Footboy Operations

MARITIME OPERATIONS (PLOWMAN)

MACSOG's maritime operations have generated a lot of criticism since they first became public knowledge. The operations have been accused of being a waste of effort, being poorly conceived, and being run willy-nilly by directives from a bureaucracy in Washington that did not know what to do with them. There is some truth to these accusations. When MACSOG took over the operation from the CIA, Maritime Operations' mission was to serve as a lever to deter North Vietnamese support for the NLF insurgency. With the initiation of Rolling Thunder, however, the program became redundant. At this point, MAROPS evolved into an interdiction, intelligence collection, and psychological operations campaign.[13]

Although the North Vietnamese went to great lengths to protect their coastline by the employment of much-needed personnel, artillery batteries, and radar installations, it is unknown whether these actions were done as a response to MAROPS, Rolling Thunder, Sea Dragon, or all of the above. The reduction of coastal traffic, interdiction of supplies, and virtual elimination of the North Vietnamese fishing fleet below the 19th parallel were testimony to the effect that this small force had on Hanoi's capabilities and also reflected poor coordination between MACSOG's branches. Since detainees "taken" by the SSPL for indoctrination were seized by the same PTFs that were destroying coastal traffic, the projects worked at cross-purposes. The connection between the two operations must also have been rather obvious to the North Vietnamese authorities. At the same time, the U.S. Navy's interdiction effort was having a detrimental effect on the ability of the PTFs to capture detainees. Regardless, during the year 328 prisoners were taken for psychological indoctrination at Paradise Island and 102 North Vietnamese craft were destroyed and 3 damaged. South Vietnamese CSS casualties were 1 man killed, 3 wounded, and 1 missing in action.[14]

AIR OPERATIONS (MIDRIFF)
There was some friction going on during the year between MACSOG and the USAF over the control, use, manning, and maintenance of SOG air assets. On 1 September an interservice agreement was hammered out between MACSOG and the 7th Air Force, creating the position of deputy commander for Special Air Operations (DCSO), who would be directly responsible to the commander of the 14th Special Operations Wing. At SOG, he was known as director of the newly formed Air Studies Group. His task was to provide liaison, direct supervision, and operational control of Air Force assets supporting SOG.

Three operational air units, the 1st Flight Detachment (Heavy Hook), the 15th Air Commando Squadron (Combat Spear), and the 20th Helicopter Squadron (see below) were officially dedicated to supporting MACSOG operations. These aircraft were utilized to carry out agent team infiltration and resupply (for Timberwork); provide infiltration, exfiltration, and close air support for cross-border ground operations; to drop psychological materials (for Humidor); and to carry out routine airlift functions for MACSOG. In December, two new Combat Spear MC-130s were received by the unit. The other two aircraft were due for replacement in early 1968. Logistical airlift for the two fixed-wing units during the year included the transportation of 10,738,580 pounds of cargo and equipment and 25,016 passengers.[15]

MACSOG also enjoyed the dedicated support of the VNAF 83rd Special Operations Group, headquartered in Saigon. The 83rd provided H-34 support for Timberwork agent team operations in North Vietnam and H-34, A-1, and U-17 support for the cross-border program. On 15 February, however, the elements of the group were transferred and reassigned. The group's A-1Gs were transferred to the 516th VNAF Squadron. The Saigon-based H-34 "Kingbees" were reinforced and formed the nucleus of a new squadron, the 219th. The U-17s were organized into the 110th Liaison Squadron, and both it and the 219th formed the backbone of a new outfit, the 41st Tactical Wing, stationed at Da Nang.

Typical mission tasking for Laotian operations from FOB-1 at Phu Bai would include two "Covey" FACs from the 20th TASS at Da Nang, two UH-1 gunships from USMC HML-367 "Scarface" at Phu Bai, and three 219th Kingbees. A-1 support came from a variety of USAF and VNAF units. Other Army aviation assistance would be tasked from I and II Field Force assets as necessary. A mission launch from Nakhon Phanom RTAFB would include two FACs from the 23rd SOS "Nails," three H-3 (later, H-53) helicopters of the 21st SOS "Knives," and four A-1s from the squadrons of the 56th Special Operations Wing in rotation. It is easy to determine that on any given day approximately one hundred aircraft were being flown in support of MACSOG missions.

Blackbirds
Only two 15th Air Commando Squadron MC-130Es were ever lost by MACSOG, and both losses occurred during 1967. The first was destroyed on the ground during a mortar attack on Nha Trang Air Base on 25 November. The other vanished on a mission to drop a false resupply to Project Oodles phantom team Mikado. This aircraft disappeared over northwestern North Vietnam, approximately twelve miles south of Yunnan Province, China, on 29 December.

MACSOG continued to utilize high-performance aircraft (usually F-4C Phantom jets) for some agent team resupply missions. They were employed when the agent or team was located within the surface-to-air missile ring that defended key areas within the North. The larger and slower C-123s and MC-130s would have been much easier targets than the fast-moving jets. On 3 February air operations in support of agent team missions and psychological operations were given the cover name "Midriff."

Mustacio and Cowboy

While coming into a very hot LZ for a team extraction in 1965, Nguyen Van Hoang, the pilot of a VNAF Kingbee, was hovering about one foot off the ground. His copilot was quickly shot in the chest and died instantly. The door gunner was then seriously wounded (and later died on the way to the launch site). The pilot himself took a round in the face, but he calmly continued to hold the aircraft steady while the recon team scrambled aboard. He then lifted the ship off the LZ through a hail of machine-gun and rocket-propelled grenade (RPG) fire while the team leader held a field dressing to the pilot's wound to keep him from bleeding to death.

After the H-34 landed at the launch site, the pilot finally passed out at the controls. The aircraft itself had been struck by more than fifty rounds. While recuperating from his wound in the hospital the pilot grew a mustache to hide the scarring of his face. When he returned to duty, he was affectionately nicknamed "Mustacio." As if the mustache were not enough, Hoang took to wearing a long, white silk scarf and aviator sunglasses that made him resemble (at least in the eyes of the recon men) former air marshall Nguyen Cao Ky.

While returning Spike Team Nevada to Kontum after a mission on 3 July 1966, the tail of Mustacio's Kingbee (which was designed to pivot for storage on an aircraft carrier) swung loose and struck the forward fuselage. The H-34 disintegrated at five thousand feet and crashed. Killed in the accident were Nguyen Van Hoang and his copilot, SOG captain Edwin McNamara, MSgt. Ralph Reno, SSgt. Donald Fawcett, and several Nungs.[16] It was a tragic day for MACSOG.

On 12 July 1967 a Spike Team was in trouble in Laos. While carrying out an area reconnaissance mission in Savanakhet Province, the team was ambushed by a superior North Vietnamese force. A fierce four-hour firefight ensued, during which two of the three American team members were killed. The remainder of the team split up and evaded, but they did manage to call for an extraction. An H-34 of the 219th Helicopter Squadron, piloted by Captain "Cowboy" Loc, made one attempt at an extraction but took serious ground fire. Running low on fuel, Cowboy returned to Khe Sanh, topped off his tanks, and tried it again. During the extremely difficult but successful exfiltration, Cowboy was shot through the neck and was bleeding profusely, but he still managed to fly the aircraft back to Khe Sanh while he plugged the hole in his neck with the fingers of one hand.[17]

It was not difficult to understand how Captain Loc received his moniker. He perpetually wore tailored, camouflaged flight suits and a yellow bandanna like his hero, John Wayne, and he sported a .38 pistol in a low-slung, western-style holster. He was notorious for asking anyone in earshot about his favorite film genre (guess which one). If the listener did not know the details of the plot of a film, Cowboy would launch into a detailed description of the movie.

During a conflict in which the majority of American personnel derided the courage or fighting spirit of their South Vietnamese allies, MACSOG recon men who placed their lives in the hands of the pilots of the 219th knew better.[18] Although Mustacio and Cowboy were idiosyncratic (to say the least) the MACSOG men loved them all the more for it. They are well remembered because of their quirks, but they are representative of all the other fearless aviators of the 219th whose names are now forgotten. These were the kind of pilots who routinely carried MACSOG agents, recon, and Bright Light teams into and out of Laos and North Vietnam.

Green Hornets

During the year the USAF's 20th Helicopter Squadron ("Green Hornets") began flying dedicated support for MACSOG recon missions in the new Daniel Boone area of operations. Originally, the unit had flown HH-3Es from Nakhon Phanom RTAFB, but in June the unit received fifteen new UH-1 helicopters and relocated to Ban Me Thuot to support the Cambodian operations. Half of the squadron flew UH-1F troopships while the other half was equipped with UH-1P gunships.

The 20th was the only Air Force unit in Southeast Asia that flew Hueys. The gunships were equipped with side-firing Vulcan miniguns and its F- and P-models were equipped with a more powerful turbine engine than the B- and C-models that were the mainstays of U.S. Army aviation units. It was readily admitted that the engines were a maintenance nightmare, but they generated more lift power and speed than the Army's versions and that was what mattered. The Green Hornets suffered their first casualty supporting SOG operations on 31 March. Maj. Robert Baldwin was killed as his slick lowered ammo to a Project Omega recon team in the tri-border area of Laos. He was struck in the chest by a 12.7 machine-gun round and died instantly.

Heavy Hook

D Flight of the same 20th Helicopter Squadron ("Pony Express") was transferred from Nakhon Phanom to Udorn RTAFB, and was equipped with nine HH-3E helicopters. D Flight initially supported CIA Trail interdiction and Search and Rescue efforts in Laos. It was joined at Udorn in December by the HH-3Es of the 21st Helicopter Squadron ("Dust Devils"). Initially the 21st was assigned to support the Dyemarker/Muscle Shoals program by emplacing sensors on the Ho Chi Minh Trail. It was only logical that both units would support MACSOG missions, since they had been assigned covert duties in the same operational area.

The Sikorsky Aircraft HH-3E was a twin-engine helicopter with a three- (later four-) man crew that had originally been built for the Navy as an amphibious SAR platform. After conversion for the Air Force, it was equipped with self-sealing fuel tanks, heavy armor, retractable landing gear, a refueling probe, and a door-mounted lifting winch. With a range of 779 miles, the large and ungainly helicopter was affectionately known to its crews as the "big ugly fat fellow" or Buff (not to be confused with the same acronym applied to the B-52 bomber). No one really knows who first applied the nickname Jolly Green Giant, by which the HH-3 was commonly known, but it was probably so named because of its large size and camouflage paint scheme. Although only two missions were launched from Nakhon Phanom in January, MACSOG obtained JCS authority to maintain a thirteen-man support facility (SUPPFAC) there, which was code-named "Heavy Hook."[19] When SOG began STRATA operations in the panhandle of North Vietnam in September (see below), the HH-3s of the 20th Helicopter Squadron were fingered for the infiltration and exfiltration of the teams.

Jenny, Popeye, and Commando Lava

Another new augmentation to MACSOG air operations in 1967 was the addition of a U.S. Navy Lockheed EC-121, code-named "Blue Eagle One," for Project Jenny. This project, part of Humidor, utilized the aircraft as an airborne broadcasting platform for psychological operations radio programs. Based at Nha Trang, the mission of Blue Eagle One was to orbit above the Gulf of Tonkin in a fixed track and to beam its radio signals into North Vietnam.[20] The first operational mission was flown on 1 June.

Two 7th/13th Air Force anti-infiltration programs were going through their test and evaluation stages during the year in MACSOG's Laotian area of operations. Project Popeye was an attempt to indefinitely extend rainy monsoon weather over the Trail by cloud seeding. Testing on the project began on 7 September above the Kong River watershed that ran through the Tiger Hound and Steel Tiger bombing zones. Clouds were seeded by air with silver iodide smoke and then activated by launching a "fuse" fired from a flare pistol. Fifty-six tests were conducted by 27 October and 85 percent were judged to be successful. Despite Secretary of State Dean Rusk's deep reservations, President Johnson gave the go-ahead for a weather modification program in Laos that continued until 5 July 1972.[21]

Testing on Project Commando Lava began on 17 May. Scientists from the Dow Chemical Company had created a chemical concoction (trade name Calgon) that, when mixed with rainwater, destabilized the materials that made up soil and created mud. There was a great deal of enthusiasm among the military and civilian participants in the program, who claimed that they were there to "make mud, not war." Unfortunately, experiments in Laos were disheartening. In some areas it worked very well, while in others it did not, the results depending on the makeup of the soil. The tests were discontinued on 21 October.[22]

Psychological Operations (Humidor)

By the latter part of the year it was becoming ever more obvious that Timberwork agent teams operating in North Vietnam had been compromised by the northern security apparatus and some, if not all, of them were being doubled. CINCPAC and SACSA made the decision to reorient all agent team assets toward psychological operations and to ensure the "integration of all operations around the central theme provided by the existence of the notional agent and increased use of deceptive operations."[23] This decision was made permanent by the issuance of a CINCPAC operations order.[24]

The diversionary operations created as a response to the CINCPAC order were given the cover name "Forae." In November MACSOG began Project Oodles, the first of a series of notional programs that were meant to bolster both Plowman psychological operations (prisoner snatches and indoctrination in support of the SSPL concept) and Timberwork operations. As a result, eighteen nonexistent, phantom agent teams were created. Ice blocks attached to parachutes were dumped out of aircraft over North Vietnam in order to simulate the landing of agents. These "teams" would then receive radio communications by the same method as the real ones. Resupply bundles (empty of course) were parachuted into the North to reinforce the impression that actual teams were on the ground. Battery-operated radios were then dropped into North Vietnam that broadcast back to MACSOG, completing the impression of a much larger and sophisticated agent net. These phantom radio teams were also fed information concerning the activities of the SSPL.

Meanwhile, the actual in-place agent teams would be fed information concerning the phantom agents. The communist security apparatus would then have to contend not only with keeping up with real "spy commando" teams, but also with chasing their phantoms. Forae also served a more sinister purpose, that of misleading the STS/STD. It was a common belief within MACSOG that its Vietnamese counterpart had been penetrated by communist agents and that information concerning its agent team program was making its way to Hanoi. Therefore, Forae was designed to convince the South Vietnamese that agent operations were doing well. This was highly ironic, since MACSOG's counterparts had opposed the agent team operations since their inception, believing that the returns were not worth the cost.

RADIO OPERATIONS
MACSOG maintained two radio transmitter sites. At Dong Ha, Humidor broadcast from a 750-watt shortwave transmitter, while from Hue it broadcast from one 20-kW shortwave and one 20-kW medium wave transmitter. It also had its own version of Radio Hanoi, inserted scripted material directly into the broadcasts of the real Radio Hanoi (via Jenny), and supported the Voice of Freedom (VOF). During the year a new facility for the VOF's 200-kW transmitter was under construction at Hue, but completion was taking time. The North Vietnamese could receive these broadcasts on pretuned "Peanuts" radios that were given away as gifts to Humidor detainees or floated ashore, left on the Ho Chi Minh Trail by recon teams, or airdropped by Midriff aircraft. In 1967 alone, eight thousand of these radios were inserted into North Vietnam.

BLACK OPS
"Soap Chips" was the cover name of a program that placed forged letters on the bodies of PAVN soldiers in Laos and Cambodia. Knowing that their comrades would search the bodies, Soap Chips inserted slanted information about the home front into the letters, hoping that this would lower the morale of troops in the field. Another use of enemy dead was Benson Silk, in which large amounts of counterfeited PAVN occupation scrip was placed on the deceased, knowing that this would cause consternation among his fellows and superiors and suspicion among PAVN intelligence personnel. Where had the individual gotten so much money? How could the other members of his three-man cell and/or his officers not know about it?

Perhaps the most insidious psywar program carried out by MACSOG was Eldest Son, begun in August. Captured communist AK-47 rifle ammunition and 60-mm mortar rounds were modified by CISO at Camp Chinen, Okinawa, so that they would detonate upon firing. This ammunition was then salted into ammunition caches discovered on MACSOG recon missions. The success of the program was established when American and ARVN units began to receive reports of dead communist troops either clutching exploded AKs or surrounding split mortar tubes.

The program was bolstered by forged documents and leaflets, left on the trail or on dead PAVN troops. They claimed to be from higher headquarters and stated that the ammunition problem was only temporary and simply one of poor (Chinese) quality control—there was nothing to worry about. MACSOG also dropped millions of leaflets from Midriff aircraft during the year over the Trail and into North Vietnam, supporting all of its psychological operations programs.

One of MACSOG's least publicized PSYOPS operations was its secret funding of South Vietnamese anticommunist and pro-American front groups. In 1967 the organization spent $241,000 on these activities in order to "promote speaking tours for enemy defectors and massacre victims; subsidizing conventions; underwriting and printing of publications; and financing everything from rent to phone bills so useful organizations could disseminate their message."[25]

The effect that all of this had on the North Vietnamese authorities and population is rather difficult to determine. MACSOG's intelligence and psywar specialists believed that the coastal population of North Vietnam would have been responsive to the possibility of a real, indigenous SSPL.[26] Without doubt Hanoi knew that this was all an elaborate charade created by the Americans, but if the aim of the campaign was to provoke a reaction by the regime against its own people, it succeeded. This reaction was also slowly, but steadily, increasing. Diatribes against the "foul psychological plots of the American imperialists" and articles in security and psychological warfare organs revealed that the issue was being taken quite seriously.

The North Vietnamese, masters of the art of psychological warfare, seemed to be having some problems dealing with their response to these efforts; when it came, it was often clumsy and heavy-handed. Final confirmation of the effectiveness of Humidor arrived in the form of a decree from the Central Committee of the Lao Dong Party in October. It listed twenty-one death penalty offenses against the state, nineteen of which could have been tied directly to agent team operations (real or imagined) in North Vietnam.[27]

Airborne Operations (Timberwork)

The agent operations conducted by MACSOG were the darkest chapter in the history of the organization. The roots of the problem were located deep within the anticommunist effort. One of them was MACSOG's total dependence on its Vietnamese counterparts, especially the STS/STD, which was the only source of its agents. This problem was exacerbated (as it was throughout the American effort) by the language barrier that separated the Americans from the Vietnamese. Every message to and from the agent teams had to pass through the STS for translation. Where else they might have gone was a matter of conjecture.

Since taking over the operation in 1964, MACSOG's commanders had repeated their pleas for the authority to launch a resistance program, since its creation was approved by MACSOG's original operations order.[28] Evidently the JCS were tiring of the repeated requests. In May they changed the operations order to officially eliminate the concept.[29] Colonel Singlaub was infuriated. He could not comprehend the inability of the powers that be to understand that there was a difference between overt statements of national policy and deniable covert operations that could have an impact on the communists. It was a sad revelation that, after three years of effort in Vietnam, the American government could not make this logical leap when its enemy was notorious for doing so.

NEW BLOOD

Project Timberwork opened 1967 with eight in-place agent teams (seventy-five men) and one Singleton agent (Ares). These included teams Hector, Verse, Eagle, Easy, Easy Alpha, Remus, Tourbillon, and Romeo. During the year four new teams and two Singleton agents were infiltrated.[30]

On 22 April seventeen-man team Nansen was helicoptered into Laos from Nakhon Phanom for a walk across the border, but apparently it never reached North Vietnam. Four days later the eleven men of Team Hadley were also helilifted into Laos for foot infiltration into Ha Tinh Province. Their mission was a roadwatch on Route 8, a major thoroughfare through the Nape Pass and into the Laotian panhandle. An adjunct to the mission was the emplacement of a seismic intrusion device. On 2 December Radio Hanoi announced that a "spy commando" team had been caught near the Nape Pass. But was it Team Hadley? Eighteen days later the Bugs radio relay site picked up a transmission, utilizing the correct security code. The radio operator of Hadley stated that the team had been attacked by the North Vietnamese, but that it was evading.

On 21 August two agents were parachuted in to reinforce Team Remus. Two Singleton agents, Goldfish and Pergola (two Plowman detainees), were returned to North Vietnam by sea on 13 September. Eight days later, the seven men of Team Red Dragon were parachuted into Ha Giang Province. None of the eleven men were ever heard from again.

On 18 October four-man Team Voi parachuted into the same area as had Team Hadley, ostensibly for an EWOT mission. They were, in fact, sent in to check up on Hadley. The team was to observe the stated position of Hadley with binoculars, wait for a resupply airdrop to the team, and then take photographs of whoever came out to claim the supplies. The men were parachuted in from a Combat Spear MC-130 and disappeared. Team Voi would be the last full agent team sent north by MACSOG.

Four teams were lost during the year (Nansen, Voi, Hector, and Verse), seven agents were killed, one died of wounds, five died from nonhostile injuries, and three died of disease. The operational teams were resupplied twenty-eight times (fifty-five attempts were unsuccessful) and the year ended with eleven in-place teams and one Singleton agent, for a total of seventy-one men.[31]

SUSPICIOUS MINDS

There were already suspicions within MACSOG concerning the reason for the low success rate of the agent program. Jack Singlaub was very skeptical and under no illusion that the communists had penetrated the STS/STD and, most probably, MACSOG itself. On 16 October he established a Joint Survey Team and called for a comprehensive in-house review of the entire agent program. All aspects of the operation were scrutinized including intelligence gathered, communications, and operations and a review was conducted of the case officers and their files. Also in October, the DIA carried out an evaluation of the value of the intelligence collected by the agent teams and concluded that little of value had been obtained.

CINCPAC got into the action by carrying out a year-end evaluation of the impact of Timberwork and concluded that a reorientation of 34A operations was necessary and that there would be a de-emphasis of the infiltration of new teams. In December the new SACSA, Army general William E. Depuy, requested that the DIA evaluate all Footboy operations as part of a general review and reorientation of the program. Suspicions were piling up, and with good reason.

STRATA

April 1967 saw the cancellation of the Safe Area Activation Teams and the initiation of their replacement, the Short Term Roadwatch and Target Acquisition (STRATA) program. In order to obtain more intelligence in North Vietnam that would be beneficial to the bombing campaign, all-indigenous STRATA teams were to be inserted by helicopter near vital North Vietnamese lines of communication for target acquisition and to pinpoint select installations. Unlike the agent operation, the missions were to be of short duration, usually no longer than a week, and every effort would be made to extract the teams. The team members would be dressed and equipped as PAVN troops, but also equipped with PRC-74 radios, which would (unlike the radios of the long-term agent teams) allow instantaneous voice communication with a FAC. CINCPAC issued the STRATA team authority in April and specifically spelled out that he would approve or disapprove missions for execution. The JCS and CINCPAC were to be the information addressees on coordination, intent, launch, recovery messages, and incident reports.[32]

After one training mission in Laos, the seven men of Team 111 were inserted into North Vietnam by HH-3Es of the 20th Helicopter Squadron on 24 September. Their target area was Route 101 in Quang Binh Province and their mission was to observe the intersection with Route 12 that fed the Mu Gia Pass into Laos. Four days later the team called for extraction. Due to the difficulty of the terrain and a lack of water, it had never reached its target area and two of the team members had become ill. Two HH-3Es and a flight of USAF T-28 fighter-bombers flew through atrocious weather and took ground fire to pull the team out. Although the men had not carried out their mission, MACSOG was ecstatic that it had, for the first time, recovered an agent team from North Vietnam.[33]

On 23 October the ten men of STRATA Team 112 were parachuted into Quang Binh Province. This time the mission was to observe the intersections of Routes 15 and 12, also feeders for the Mu Gia Pass. Although the team managed to assemble on the ground, they soon realized that they had been dropped far off target. The team was soon being tracked and, on 31 October, ambushed. The men split up and evaded but they were eventually captured or killed. The last man surrendered on 17 November.

With the change in emphasis in the agent program coming down from SACSA and CINCPAC, Midriff was tasked with supporting the new Operation Forae. Diversionary operations were begun on 29 November with the objective of diverting communist resources to internal security roles. This was accomplished by the establishment of Oodles agents who would be "resupplied" by Midriff aircraft and be broadcast to, in concert with false information being radioed to in-place teams considered to be under North Vietnamese control. The purpose of these "phantom teams" was to reinforce Hanoi's paranoia about infiltration by spies and commandos. The JCS mandated that eighteen such teams were to be "operational" by 1968.

CAMP LONG THANH

MACSOG's training center at Camp Long Thanh (whose Vietnamese designation was the Airborne Operations Training Center, Camp Quyet Thang) was located thirty-five miles northeast of Saigon. The cover story maintained by MACSOG was that the camp trained Vietnamese personnel in counterinsurgency techniques. At the camp MACSOG cross-border personnel, Timberwork agents and STRATA team members, and CSS commandos were trained for their various operations.

Until 1967 MACSOG had very experienced U.S. personnel (for its reconnaissance operations) upon whom to draw for its mission requirements. During the year it became obvious that the small size of the pre-conflict Special Forces was working against it. There was already a shortage of qualified personnel within the Special Forces community, and the burgeoning numbers of less experienced men entering the organization required that they receive more training for their missions (SOG often complained that the reconnaissance training provided Green Berets at Fort Bragg was inadequate). That training was provided at Long Thanh by Special Forces cadre assigned from 1st SFG. The camp was manned and defended by a CIDG battalion, which also carried out combat missions (utilizing camp trainees) in the surrounding areas.

All was not well, however, at Camp Long Thanh. Operational security all but vanished at the camp, where team members from the various programs mixed freely. The Vietnamese training cadre often allowed students to leave and go unsupervised into Saigon.[34] The agent teams were isolated prior to mission launch, but if the mission was scrubbed, they remained isolated, often for weeks. This had a corrosive effect on morale. As the pace of Timberwork operations slowed, discipline eroded, lethargy set in, and the AWOL rate ran high.

Cross-Border Ground Operations

Cross-border ground operations (still a separate section of the Airborne Operations Group) remained MACSOG's most lucrative program and contributed more to the American effort than any other. Due to exposure of the cover name Shining Brass in an article in *Ramparts* magazine, the cover name for MACSOG cross-border operations in Laos was altered to Prairie Fire on 1 March. Although the operation was authorized twenty Spike Teams and three exploitation battalions, manpower shortages tended to reduce the number of available personnel. With the addition of tasking for the Muscle Shoals program during the year (see below), SOG was authorized to raise thirty-four new reconnaissance teams.[35]

Although SOG Spike Teams labored under geographic constraints and sometimes bizarre rules of engagement, they soon realized that some limitations on their operations bordered on the ludicrous. The teams often uncovered large caches of communist rice, stockpiles so large that they could not be easily removed or destroyed. Colonel Singlaub sought permission from MACV and CINCPAC to spray the rice with Bitrex, an odorless food contaminant that simply made the rice too bitter to eat. Although MACV and CINCPAC approved, permission was denied by the Joint Chiefs on the grounds that the North Vietnamese might charge the Americans with waging chemical warfare.[36]

One of the recon team's most dangerous missions was to snatch prisoners off the Trail for extraction and interrogation. This was usually done by shooting the target with a silenced, low-powered handgun or by concussing with a small explosive charge. The problem was that the usual screams of the abductee or the noise of the explosion gave away the team's position. When permission was sought to experiment with the use of tranquilizer darts to incapacitate communist prisoners, this too was disallowed. Colonel Singlaub was amazed to learn that the reasoning behind the refusal was that the use of tranquilizer darts might be considered inhumane.

THE TRAIL

Interdicting the Trail system proved to be more easily said than done. In 1967, for example, it was estimated that 90,000 PAVN troops made the trip down from the North. Senior Colonel Dong Sy Nguyen took over command of the 559th Transportation Group during the year and established a new forward headquarters for the unit in Laos, across from South Vietnam's Ashau Valley. According to U.S. intelligence, there were 5,372 trucks working the logistics network in northern and southern Laos.[37]

If the goal of the air and ground interdiction effort was to reduce the flow of men and supplies to a trickle it did not seem to be working. There was no single "Trail" but rather a complex system of hundreds of miles or fair-weather drivable roads, a maze of smaller roads, trails, paths, bridges, supply sites, truck parks, rest areas, and overnight shelters complete with alternate routes and bypasses to complicate the work of MACV analysts. By 1967 the North Vietnamese had built 2,959 kilometers of drivable roads, including 275 kilometers of main roads, 822 kilometers of connectors, 576 kilometers of bypasses, and 450 entry roads and storage areas.[38] During the year it was also discovered that PAVN engineers

were building a link between Routes 110 and 96 and that the PAVN was
utilizing the Kong and Bang Fai Rivers to facilitate rice shipments. The
559th combated the aerial interdiction effort by utilizing night travel,
camouflage, road building and repairing, and the emplacement of anti-
aircraft defenses at key infiltration points.[39]

U.S. Air Force claims for the destruction of North Vietnamese trucks
on the Trail reached new heights during the latter part of the year. Between
November 1967 and January 1968 pilots located 15,441 trucks, attacked
7,014, and claimed to have destroyed or damaged 1,646.[40] Ambassador
Sullivan accepted these figures and believed that the communists were
losing all of their dry-season cargo before it got as far south as Route 9.
COMUSMACV and DOD were more skeptical. Secretary of Defense Mc-
Namara estimated that only 10 percent of PAVN manpower and supplies
entering the pipeline in the North was lost on the way to South Vietnam,
and that only 2 percent was lost to airstrikes.[41] By year's end, however,
optimism was growing in Washington that the effort was finally paying
off. North Vietnamese manpower infiltration was estimated at 5,500 to
6,000 per month, down from about 7,000 per month in 1966.[42]

Unknown to the Americans, however, the North Vietnamese had begun to transport and store more then 81,000 tons of supplies that had
been specially authorized by the Central Committee in Hanoi. These supplies were to be "utilized in a future offensive."[43] Since MACSOG recon
teams were the only U.S. ground forces authorized to operate in the infiltration areas, they served as eyes and ears on the ground for 7th/13th Air
Force bombing missions and intelligence collection. The Ho Chi Minh
Trail was the target and Steel Tiger/Nickel Steel/Tiger Hound aircraft the
heavy ordnance in the clandestine war to choke the supply line from the
North.

PRAIRIE FIRE

Due to security concerns the C&C Detachment in downtown Da Nang
had begun looking for another location from which to conduct its operations in early 1966. During the summer of 1967 it was decided to move
the detachment to the NAD's new facility at the base of Monkey Mountain
known as Camp Fay. By September 1967, the move was complete.

FOB-1 at Phu Bai consisted of 7 American officers and 70 enlisted
men along with approximately 135 indigenous personnel divided into 7
Spike Teams, each of which was named for a U.S. state. The FOB maintained a mission launch site at an abandoned French fort in the Montagnard village of Khe Sanh and carried out missions in Laos from the

DMZ south to the Ashau Valley. In August, the launch site was relocated outside the perimeter of the U.S. Marine's Khe Sanh Combat Base. It was redesignated FOB-3 in October and was manned by 6 U.S. officers and 73 enlisted men plus 153 indig in eight recon teams, which were given animal names, usually jungle cats. They conducted missions in the northern Prairie Fire area and the western DMZ (Nickel Steel).

FOB-2 at Kontum was similarly allotted 7 American officers and 70 enlisted men, and 135 indigs in 7 recon teams. During late 1966, the 5th SFG's Project Omega (see below) forces moved into the compound, bringing with them their own headquarters and recon teams named for tools and inanimate objects. The FOB's launch site was located near the border outpost of Dak To and launched operations into the tri-border region and Zone Alpha of Cambodia with the inception of Operation Daniel Boone.

To back up the teams at each FOB (in case of necessity or opportunity), exploitation forces had been created during the previous year. These included 2 exploitation battalions (Haymaker Forces) each of which consisted of 4 companies (Hatchet Force). Each 127-man company was formed of 3 platoons (Hornet Forces) consisting of 42 indigs and 4 Green Berets, under the command of an American lieutenant. Each FOB was also assigned a separate rifle company as a security force. At FOB-1 the exploitation force (designated companies A through C) was composed of Chinese Nungs. FOB-2's exploitation forces consisted of Nungs and South Vietnamese, while those at FOB-3 (designated by U.S. city names) consisted of Montagnards of the Bru tribe. Due to political restrictions, however, no Haymaker Force operations were ever conducted, and because of constraints on the number of troop-lift helicopters, Havoc Force operations were limited to only a few per year.

During 1966–67 both MACSOG and the 5th SFG were feeling a manpower pinch. To find enough qualified men to command and run its exploitation forces, MACSOG once again reached out to the 1st SFG on Okinawa. The 1st responded by assigning entire twelve-man "A" teams on a six-month TDY basis in what were called "Snakebite Teams." This arrangement would be continued until 1969.

During 1967 there were 187 recon missions into Laos and 71 platoon-size operations. They were supported by 329 helicopter gunship and 1,157 tactical air sorties. Ten communist prisoners were captured and the program generated 774 intelligence reports. American casualties for the year in the Shining Brass/Prairie Fire area were 13 killed in action, 2 killed in accidents, and 3 missing in action.[44]

SLAM

Both MACSOG and MACV were searching for alternative methods of interdicting the Trail. In late 1966 MACV, 7th Air Force, and SOG gained approval for a "find and pile on" concept that was designated SLAM. The first mission had gotten off the ground on 7 October 1966, when Spike Team Colorado discovered a communist base area in Laos. SLAM II began on 13 October near newly discovered Route 110. Both missions utilized large-scale tactical air and B-52 strikes to attack the communist rear.

The SLAM concept, as it had developed by 1967, had three phases. First came intelligence collection utilizing aircraft equipped with infrared, airborne radar, and FLIR plus visual reconnaissance from FACs and ground reconnaissance teams. Next, more reconnaissance was carried out, possibly followed by air strikes. Finally, large-scale tactical and B-52 strikes were followed by aerial and ground recon units. If possible, exploitation elements would be inserted to assault enemy forces on the ground.[45]

On 21 January, the U.S. Embassy in Saigon informed Ambassador Sullivan that an estimated seven thousand PAVN troops had entered South Vietnam during the month, mainly through Laos. This served to lessen the ambassador's disapproval of ground-supported aerial interdiction efforts and led to the initiation of SLAM III. By 25 January reconnaissance had decisively proven that the North Vietnamese were once again utilizing east–west Route 110 as a major supply artery, and Adm. U. S. Grant Sharp (CINCPAC) sought and gained approval for the operation. He also gave the go-ahead for Shock missions, which duplicated the SLAM concept but which employed CIA Hardnose roadwatch teams.

SLAM III was launched on 30 January against a target complex near Route 110, about 15 miles west of South Vietnam's Kontum Province. Prestrike photo-reconnaissance was followed by two fifteen-aircraft B-52 missions and massive strikes by tactical aircraft. Meanwhile, three separate Hornet platoons were helilifted into the target, one on the 30th and two on the 31st for bomb-damage assessment missions. Once on the ground, the platoons reported a plethora of other targets for air strikes.

On 2 February, Spike Team Maine was inserted and reported more North Vietnamese activity. Between 3 and 5 February, FOB-2's Hornet platoons Delta and Echo entered the area for BDAs, found an ammunition cache, and called in air support, which resulted in 35 secondary explosions. By 7 February pilots had observed more than 180 secondary explosions, and more Hornet platoons were inserted during the next two days. SLAM III officially ended on 13 February, but air-supported Hornet forces kept up the pressure. Between 10 and 27 February, eight more platoons entered the area.

SLAM IV, the largest effort so far, was launched farther north in Laos along the eastern end of Route 922, a major supply conduit that ran into South Vietnam's Ashau Valley. The Ashau was a notorious PAVN haven that had been relatively untouched thus far by Free World Military Forces. During the operation 7th/13th Air Force launched 1,526 tactical sorties and 256 B-52 strikes. As a result of the above operations, on 22 February, COMUSMACV and CINCPAC requested approval for an overall extension of the two Shining Brass operational areas to twelve miles in depth.[46] Even Ambassador Sullivan, convinced of the efficacy of SLAM missions, supported the MACV request.[47] The administration, however, was reluctant to grant it.

That attitude changed when Air Force reconnaissance revealed that the communists had taken advantage of the four-day February Tet truce in order to move two hundred trucks full of supplies per day over the Trail. President Johnson then extended the depth of penetration in Laos to a uniform twenty kilometers throughout the operational area. He also authorized helicopter insertions to the full depth of the operational zone and the use of multiplatoon exploitation forces in a single operation.[48] Colonel Singlaub also managed to secure blanket approval for cross-border missions from the JCS. Instead of having each mission approved individually, any number of teams could operate in the Shining Brass area per month as long as the embassy in Vientiane was notified.

Due to the success of SLAMs I–IV, the JCS expanded MACSOG's size and responsibilities. The number of recon teams was increased, more helicopter assets were made available, and the number of missions rose proportionally.[49] One change of former restrictions was the extension of the Nickel Steel boundary to a depth of twenty kilometers, making it uniform with the Shining Brass/Prairie Fire area. In September the JCS granted MACSOG authority to launch Prairie Fire missions from Nakhon Phanom RTAFB. The use of this launch facility would assist the organization in reaching targets in the northern area of operations. The new launch site, designated FOB-4 (code-named Heavy Hook), was completed and occupied by December.

SLAM V was launched against targets in the tri-border region and lasted from 17 June to 16 August. Fifty-three B-52 sorties were carried out during the operation. SLAM VI was about to commence in late August when Sullivan lowered the boom. The target area was spread across Base Areas 607 and 611, and MACSOG and MACV had followed all of the preplanning that had accompanied the previous SLAM missions and nothing seemed amiss. When Westmoreland requested blanket approval for the launch, Sullivan dug in his heels.

The crux of the problem, as usual, was who had ultimate authority. Sullivan's excuse was that he did not accept MACV's claim that there were no civilians in the strike zone and he demanded more aerial photography. Westmoreland was furious. After the reconnaissance was completed, the operation was launched. During SLAM VI the Air Force carried out seven B-52 missions totaling fifty-seven sorties. This was, however, the last of the large-scale SLAM operations. With the arrival of October and drier weather on the Trail, MACSOG's operational pace picked up. During one seven-day period, six Spike Teams and five Hornet units entered the Trail. Their targeting resulted in seventy more tactical and B-52 sorties.

THE FIELD MARSHAL

The interference of Ambassador Sullivan in the military operations of MACSOG, MACV, and the 7th/13th Air Forces was a long-standing one. Although North Vietnamese violation of Laotian "neutrality" was well documented and although the CIA's paramilitary war in Laos was the largest operation it ever ran, Sullivan was resolute in maintaining a tight grip on any operations that might broach his authority within his domain. Granted, Sullivan had a hard time juggling the conflicting demands of the Air Force, CIA, and MACV. He also had to keep a lid on the bombing to protect the fiction of neutrality demanded by Washington and deal with the Laotian government, no mean feat in itself.

A tough bureaucratic infighter who had no trouble saying his piece, Sullivan only managed to keep the "turf jealousy" of the competing commands and operations in Southeast Asia at a high boil. The reasoning for his negative response to pleas for expansion of Prairie Fire in Laos was that he believed the real problem lay with MACSOG: "a gung ho group who, by their very nature, are always attempting to exceed the political limitations of more reasonable men everywhere."[50] When apprised of the opinion that MACV and SOG held of him, Sullivan's response was that "this is largely a problem of morale for overgrown adolescents."[51]

MACV, the Air Force, and the commanders and troops of MACSOG responded in kind by despising the "Field Marshall" and what they saw as his gratuitous and amateur advice and what Colonel Singlaub described as his "Napoleonic ambitions."[52] It was mainly Sullivan, and through him the State Department, that imposed the territorial limits and rules of engagement in Laos that continuously hampered MACSOG and Air Force operations. And woe be it unto any Spike Team that violated any of Sullivan's rules. The American Embassy Vientiane went so far as to request that aircraft from the International Control Commission fly around team locations (which had been reported to the embassy). This was done in an attempt to discover if any of the teams were violating the terms of their defined operating areas. All that this tended to do was arouse the curiosity of the North Vietnamese, who sent troops into the area to see what was up.[53]

Over time it had become more than obvious to the North Vietnamese that the limitations and restrictions imposed by Vientiane existed, and they took full advantage of them. Sullivan drew artificial "bomb lines" around PAVN/NLF/Pathet Lao–occupied towns in the Laotian panhandle, which was done to prevent the bombing of nonexistent civilian populations. This simply made the towns safe logistical havens for the communists. With penetration of its supply lines limited in size, time, and space, PAVN simply concentrated its security forces within the zones in which MACSOG was allowed to operate. This, in turn, led to higher casualties.

By 1967 the CIA anti-infiltration effort in Laos had been in operation for four years. Armed with the new Hark-1 radio system, Lao hill tribesmen (Project Hardnose was now renamed Project Hark) in CIA employ and Thai PARU commandos (Project Star) performed operations similar to MACSOG in the Lao panhandle on the Trail. Like MACSOG recon teams, they were also supported by D Flight of the USAF 20th Helicopter Squadron and by the 21st Helicopter Squadron operating out of Nakhon Phanom.

OSCAR-8

Havoc and Hornet Force operations were usually quick reaction raids on targets of opportunity that had been uncovered by the recon teams. Such was the case when a platoon landed on a Laotian hilltop near Highway 110 and discovered 250 tons of rice. Not so successful was the first combined Hatchet Force raid and BDA mission to Target Area Oscar-8, near the intersection of Routes 92 and 922, about twenty-three miles south of Khe Sanh.[54] NSA radio intercepts indicated that not only was the area the headquarters of the PAVN 559th Transportation Group, but that North Vietnamese defense minister Vo Nguyen Giap was in the area. After an Arc Light strike by nine aircraft on the morning of 4 May, a FAC carrying SOG MSgt. Billy Waugh observed many North Vietnamese troops, who were supposed to have been pulverized and demoralized by the strike, coming out from cover and putting out fires. Waugh tried frantically to radio the assault force and call off the insertion, but the transmission was blocked by the surrounding terrain.

Right on schedule, nine H-34s and three Marine Corps CH-46 Sea
Knights rolled in to land the Hatchet Force while four Marine Corps
Huey gunships covered the insertion. As the landing took place, two of
the gunships and a SAR Kingbee were shot down. No sooner was the
force on the ground than it was surrounded by infuriated PAVN troops,
who pinned the MACSOG men down in two bomb craters in which they
had sought cover. As a C-46 extracted one of the downed Huey's crew,
tactical air support was called in and heavy communist anti-aircraft fire
opened up to greet it. During the following air strikes an A-1 Skyraider had its tail blown off and plunged into the ground. Surrounded in
their craters, the Hatchet Force was in a Mexican standoff. It could not
advance, but neither could the North Vietnamese overrun it. As daylight
ebbed, the men hunkered down and waited for a possible extraction at
first light.

After a tactical airstrike at dawn on 3 June, the extraction effort began. Two Huey gunships strafing the LZ were both damaged and pulled
out. Next, an Air Force F-4 Phantom took hits and exploded. While this
was occurring three CH-46s came in to pick up the force in the bomb
craters. The first managed to lift out eight Nungs, but the aircraft lost
an engine on the way out, crashing about 150 feet from the Hatchet
Force. The occupants then formed a defensive perimeter and dug in. The
second ship picked up almost a platoon of indigs and made it out of the
area. The last C-46 managed to extract three American personnel (SOG
NCOs Charles Wicklow, Ron Dexter, and Billy Ray Laney) and twelve
more Nungs.

As the chopper lifted off, North Vietnamese fire concentrated on it.
The craft veered out of control, hit some trees, and broke in half about
one hundred feet above the LZ. Sergeant First Class Wicklow awoke in
the midst of carnage. Laney and most of the Nungs were either dead or
dying and he could not find Dexter. Out of ammunition and shot in the
leg, Wicklow crawled away from the wreckage and passed out. Unknown
to the wounded man, Dexter, the helicopter's door gunner (Marine LCpl.
Frank Cius), and nine of the Nungs had formed a perimeter about two
hundred meters from the downed aircraft.

From the next morning (4 June) till late in the afternoon, Oscar-8
was pummeled by gunships and fixed-wing aircraft in preparation for
another extraction attempt. At 1500 hours six C-46s, nine H-34s, nine
Huey gunships, two Skyraiders, and two FACs lifted off for Oscar-8. The
first H-34 dropped off water and ammo for the men surrounding the
first C-46 crash site and managed to pick up five wounded Nungs while

the second aircraft got into and out of the bomb craters with a load of men. The third ship was shot down, but Waugh, who had returned to Khe Sanh, boarded Mustacio's Kingbee for a rescue attempt. The aircraft bulled through ground fire and picked up the crew of the downed aircraft. The next H-34 into the fire zone was so badly shot up it had to vacate the area. The last helicopter managed to extract some of the men, but, at the end of the effort, twelve Nungs still remained in a crater.

Recon overflights the next day failed to reveal any survivors at Oscar-8. Any further extraction efforts were then called off. On the previous day, Dexter, Cius, and their Nungs had been forced away from the area and the group evaded all day without encountering any North Vietnamese. The following day (the 5th) the group was separated in a Montagnard hamlet. Dexter, Cius, and a remaining Nung were then captured and returned to the hamlet, where they were reunited with the others. Dexter and Cius were then separated for the trip to a detention facility. Cius never saw Dexter again. His captors later stated that Ron Dexter's health had failed and that he had died on the way to the camp. Frank Cius was released by the North Vietnamese during Operation Homecoming in 1973.

When he awoke after escaping the downed C-46, Charles Wicklow found the North Vietnamese all around him, but they did not kill him. Neither did they tend his wounds or give him any food or water, basically ignoring him. He passed out again, and when he awoke he realized why the North Vietnamese had kept him alive. They had dragged him into the open and placed an orange rescue panel next to his body, hoping to lure in a rescue helicopter.

On the second day of his ordeal Wicklow saw two Caucasians escorted by PAVN soldiers and surmised that they must be Soviet advisors. He probably would have died of dehydration that day had he not lapped up muddy water from a puddle. On the third day it rained and he felt his energy begin to slip away in the cold. On the night of the fourth day, with maggots crawling on his leg wound, Wicklow began to crawl away. He passed out several times, but the pain also kept him going. He later believed that he had crawled about two miles that night. The next morning a face appeared before him—the black face of MACSOG staff sergeant Lester Pace, who had rappelled into the jungle to rescue him in a one-man Bright Light mission. The raid on Oscar-8 had been a disaster for MACSOG. Seven aircraft had been shot down. Twenty-three Americans—SOG team members, USAF pilots, and Marine helicopter crewmen—were lost, along with about fifty of the Nung raiders.

MEDAL OF HONOR

On 7 February an FOB-2 Hornet platoon on a BDA mission landed in eastern Laos. The force consisted of forty Montagnards and three U.S. members led by Sfc. George Tilley. Along for the ride was 1st Lt. George K. Sisler, who had volunteered to go along on the mission. After insertion the platoon was almost immediately assaulted by more than one hundred PAVN troops. After evading and setting up a defensive perimeter, Sisler realized that two of the indigs had been wounded and left behind. He advanced into intense PAVN fire and was recovering one of the men when the North Vietnamese launched an assault. Sisler counterattacked with grenades and his CAR-15, killing three North Vietnamese and knocking out a machine gun. After bringing back the second wounded man he attacked again.

By now all the American personnel were either dead or wounded. Sisler called in air strikes and rallied the rest of the team while he radioed for an extraction. The only problem was that there was no place for the helicopters to land. As the team crawled to a new position for the extraction, Sisler covered them. As he stood alone to oppose the North Vietnamese, he was killed by a sniper. Sergeant Tilley, severely wounded, led his men to two Kingbees that had managed to land. He then twice went back for wounded indigs, once charging single-handedly to halt the communists. For his effort, he was awarded the Distinguished Service Cross. 1st Lt. George Sisler was posthumously awarded MACSOG's first Medal of Honor.[55]

GERALD YOUNG

Target Area Oscar-8 again turned into a deathtrap for SOG on 8 November. RT Massachusetts, including MSgt. Bruce Baxter, SSgt. Homer Wilson, S4C Joe Kusick, and five Montagnards, was cornered on a grass-covered hilltop by hundreds of PAVN troops. The team was about to be overrun when Huey gunships and Kingbees arrived for the extraction. Wilson and several Yards made it into the first Kingbee, but the next one in was riddled by gunfire and crashed. A third came in and picked up a few men, but it was then driven off by automatic weapons fire. A fourth Kingbee came in and Baxter managed to get the rest of the team aboard and was wounded in the process. The chopper, however, never got off the LZ.

The North Vietnamese then launched an assault during which Baxter and Kusick were killed. PAVN fire scored more on the extraction ship, which burst into flames. The remaining men gathered around Baxter and Kusick's bodies as night fell, but the North Vietnamese did not move in to finish them off, hoping to lure in more rescue forces in the morning. Two HH-3 Jolly Green Giants of the 37th Aerospace Rescue and Recovery Squadron were dispatched for an attempted night extraction. The first helicopter was heavily damaged by ground fire and pulled out. The second was piloted by Capt. Gerald O. Young, flying his sixtieth combat mission. When queried over the radio as to whether he and his crew were prepared to attempt the pickup, Young answered "Hell, we're airborne and hot to trot!"[56] Young bulled into the LZ and loaded up the survivors, but during the pull-up a rocket-propelled grenade struck the right engine, setting the aircraft on fire and turning it upside down. Young was burned and fell through the smashed canopy, but he hit the ground running until he came to a wounded airman to whom he administered first aid.

When a rescue chopper came in at dawn and picked up some more of the men, Captain Young saw PAVN troops setting up machine-gun positions, hoping to use him and the wounded airmen as bait. After hiding his companion, Young yelled and waved at the North Vietnamese and then led them away on a daylong chase into the jungle. When he was certain that he had lost them he utilized his emergency radio and called for an extraction. The bodies of Baxter and Kusick were never recovered. Baxter received the Distinguished Service Cross for his exploits on the LZ. Cpt. Gerald O. Young received the only Medal of Honor bestowed on a non-SOG man for heroism while supporting a MACSOG operation.[57]

ROBERT HOWARD

While screening a Hornet Force mission operating out of Kontum on 16 November, Sfc. Robert L. Howard carried out actions that led to his being recommended for his nation's highest honor. While the Hornet Force destroyed an enemy cache, Howard's team came upon four North Vietnamese soldiers, whom he shot. The team was then pinned down by heavy machine-gun fire. Howard first eliminated a sniper and then charged the machine-gun position, killing its occupants. When a second machine gun opened up, he crawled forward to within point-blank range and threw a hand grenade, disabling that gun.

When more North Vietnamese troops took over the same gun, Howard stood in the open and fired a light anti-tank weapon, knocking it out again. The team was then successfully extracted. Though recommended for the Medal of Honor, Howard's award was downgraded to the Distinguished Service Cross. This would be the first of three recommendations within thirteen months for the Medal of Honor for Robert Howard.

DECORATIONS

The American participants of the initial three Shining Brass missions had all been awarded Silver Stars for their exploits in Laos, but the conferring of decorations (with the exception of the Purple Heart) then dried up. It was probably felt that the continuation of such a policy would draw undue attention to the program. This did not seem to bother the men of SOG, who generally felt that personal awards, other than the recognition of their comrades, were unnecessary. To the men of the recon teams the most coveted award was the Combat Infantryman's Badge (CIB); refusals of other decorations were not uncommon.

This dry spell was broken by the award of the Medal of Honor to George Sisler (whose award was posthumous), but it was tempered by the downgrading of decorations (as in the case of Howard). It also illustrated the difficulties faced when special operations personnel exhibited extraordinary bravery in denied areas. Recommendations and citations for decorations always stipulated the location and circumstances of the action, and since the award of decorations became public knowledge, citations would have to be altered to place the cited action within territorial South Vietnam. Congress and the president were loath to create any sense of falsehood about the actions of the nation's most highly decorated military personnel, so, in many instances, awards were downgraded to keep the recipient out of the limelight.

The recon men were themselves divided on the benefits of decorations. Many believed that it was deleterious to the unit because it would provide undue incentives for joining it. The idea of serving on a team with a self-aggrandizing "medal chaser" probably caused more than a few cases of night sweats. When recon man Harve Saal was preparing to leave SOG in 1970 (after three tours) he had been awarded only a CIB and a Navy Presidential Unit Citation for his participation in the siege of Khe Sanh. He had refused all other awards. While being outprocessed, he was asked by his commanding officer what award he would accept for his service in South Vietnam. Saal replied that he had never received a service award from the Army. He accepted a simple Bronze Star and was satisfied.

BIGGER PLANS

MACSOG Spike Teams and exploitation forces were finding it more and more difficult to operate in the border areas due to large numbers of well-trained communist troops and precautions by those troops against the cross-border forays. The North Vietnamese were learning. Due to these increased security operations against the recon teams, General Westmoreland planned to launch much larger ground-oriented, anti-infiltration pushes into Southern Laos.

MACV headquarters had already developed two plans for 1967–68, Prairie Fire III and Southpaw (an extension of which was called High Port). Prairie Fire III was a proposal to recruit, train, and equip Kha tribesmen on both sides of the Laotian/South Vietnamese border for anti-infiltration activities. Southpaw envisioned helilifting an ARVN battalion-sized Airborne or Ranger unit into Laos, supported by helicopter gunships, Tiger Hound aircraft, and B-52s. Phase II (High Port) of the plan would be the deployment of a division-size unit that would concentrate on destroying PAVN troop and supply centers in SLAM designated sections of the Trail.[58]

Vientiane adamantly opposed all three plans. Since CINCPAC had previously criticized the waste of manpower in SEA, Sullivan saw an opening and opposed Prairie Fire III because of "current personnel shortages in MACSOG." He went so far as to demand that current exploitation forces be disbanded and converted to Spike Teams. There was a lot of wrestling among MACV, CINCPAC, Vientiane, and Washington before all three concepts were abandoned. As far as Lyndon Johnson was concerned, any large-scale Laotian incursion had "the mark of the devil" upon it.[59]

Although Westmoreland failed in his bid for larger anti-infiltration programs, he had succeeded in extending the boundary of the Prairie Fire area to a uniform twenty-mile limit. President Johnson also redelegated authority from the State and Defense Departments jointly to CINCPAC and the U.S. Embassy in Vientiane for launching air-supported cross-border missions and gave a tentative go-ahead for Project Popeye. As a result Shining Brass Recon Teams grew from twenty to thirty to sustain up to forty missions per month. The VNAF 219th Helicopter Squadron was also beefed up from eighteen to twenty-four aircraft to support the increased number of missions.

DANIEL BOONE

The North Vietnamese supplied their forces in the extreme south by two methods. The first was to extend the Ho Chi Minh Trail southward into the tri-border region of Laos/Cambodia/South Vietnam. The second was to unload supplies directly from communist-flagged ships in the port of Sihanoukville, where Cambodian neutrality guaranteed delivery. The supplies were then transferred to trucks and transported to the frontier zones that served as NLF/PAVN Base Areas (BAs). These BAs also served as sanctuaries for communist troops, who simply crossed the border from South Vietnam and then rested, reinforced and refitted for their next campaign in safety. These logistical operations had been directed since 1966 by the PAVN K-20 Unit in Phnom Penh, which worked under the guise of a commercial company owned by local ethnic Vietnamese.[60] Although MACV, CINCPAC, and Washington were well aware of this arrangement, they had declined to interfere due to the political ramifications of conducting military operations against the wishes of Cambodia's ruler, the mercurial Prince Norodom Sihanouk.

The long-sought authorization for cross-border operations into Cambodia—Operation Daniel Boone—came through in April.[61] The purpose of the operation was to "reduce infiltration of personnel and material and to collect intelligence" and to gain proof positive (as if anyone needed any) that the NLF and PAVN forces were indeed utilizing the territory of "neutral" Cambodia for military operations against South Vietnam.[62]

GENESIS
The intraservice struggle for control over the Cambodian operations was interesting. It had begun back in 1966 when MACV first considered intelligence-gathering missions into Cambodia to protect its southern flank. During the summer, the 5th SFG was ordered by the JCS to begin the construction of recon groups modeled on MACSOG's Laotian effort.[63] Project Sigma (Detachment B-56) was formed on 20 June 1966 at Ho Ngoc Tau, near Tu Duc, in Gia Dinh Province. It consisted of eight recon teams (given numerical designations, not names) composed of ethnic Cambodian and Nung personnel. It also possessed three reaction force companies and a base defense company. Project Omega (Detachment B-50) was established in August and was composed of four Roadrunner Teams, eight recon teams, three exploitation/reaction companies and one base security company. The two units' complements included 9 officers, 65 enlisted men, and 660 indigenous troops each. MACV stepped in and assumed control of Sigma and Omega, while operational control of the units was turned over to the Field Force commanders.[64] Both were to perform long-range reconnaissance operations for them until authority came down from the JCS for the commencement of Cambodian operations.

The battle for control of the operation then began in earnest between MACSOG and the 5th SFG (under the authority of MACV) over which unit had both the means and the authority for the mission. With the Office of the Secretary of Defense, the JCS, and the State Department acting as judges, each organization made its pitch in the "battle over Cambodia." MACSOG, however, had an edge, claiming that MACV did not have authorization for out-of-country operations and that JCS/OSD/

State were not about to "give up *their* jurisdiction or controls" over such operations.[65] SOG backed up its attack by stressing its covert nature and previous authorization for cross-border operations (and success at carrying them out), and by pointing out that it already possessed standing assets for the mission. Much to the chagrin of their parent organization, operational control of Sigma and Omega was handed over to MACSOG on 3 September.

The missions were to be conducted in two operational areas within Cambodia: Zone Alpha, from the tri-border region south to the town of Snoul, and Zone Bravo, from Snoul south to the Gulf of Siam (but which had to be approved on a case-by-case basis by the JCS due to the population density of the area). Operational depth in both zones was not to exceed twenty kilometers.[66] There were, however, restrictions placed upon these operations that did not limit those in Prairie Fire. They were limited to five helicopter insertions per month, which meant that the majority of teams would have to cross the border on foot, and no exploitation forces were to be allowed in Cambodia. Helicopter gunships were permitted into Cambodian airspace for close air support (only in case of emergency), but not tactical aircraft, including FACs. Initially there were only to be ten missions allowed per month, as opposed to an unlimited number for Laos.

With onset of Operation Daniel Boone, Omega was transferred from Nha Trang to Kontum while Sigma remained at its original base at Ho Ngoc Tao. The missions were to be initiated from launch sites at Dak To and Duc Co, both in Kontum Province, and Song Be, in Phuoc Long Province, for insertions into Zone Alpha. Operations in Zone Bravo were to be launched from Song Be and Tay Ninh.[67] During the remainder of 1967, ninety-nine recon missions were launched into Cambodia. They were supported by sixty-seven helicopter gunship and thirty-four tactical air sorties (against targets in South Vietnam or Laos contiguous to Cambodia). Two communist prisoners were captured and the program generated 297 intelligence reports.[68] Construction began during second half of the year on new FOBs that would support Daniel Boone. These included FOB-5 at Ban Me Thuot (which, upon completion, would control the operations) and FOB-6 at the Sigma base at Ho Ngoc Tao.

MUSCLE SHOALS

Since the inception of the American military effort in Vietnam, the thinkers at the Pentagon (and especially Secretary of Defense McNamara) believed that the most advanced American technology should be applied to the problem of slowing or stopping the infiltration of North Vietnamese personnel and supplies across the DMZ and on the Trail. Since the beginning of the American effort, American pilots had bombarded the Trail system, but although the bombing exacted a price and had forced the communists to move their supplies by night, it did little to stop the infiltration. In September 1966 McNamara had approved the formation of the Defense Communications Planning Group, a top-secret conclave of scientists that spent the next five years advancing military technology. The best known of their creations was that of a physical and electronic barrier to infiltration that would use computers to launch attacks on an automated battlefield.[69]

By late 1967, air and ground anti-infiltration operations were augmented by a sensor-oriented system originally known as Illinois City. On 15 July it was renamed Muscle Shoals/Dyemarker after the program was divided into two major components. Dyemarker (also known as McNamara's Fence) signified that part of the barrier being built in South Vietnam's Quang Tri Province, which included fixed defensive positions, sensors, and minefields to prevent infiltration across the DMZ. It was estimated that three full divisions would be required to man the barrier and that 271 battalion-hours of engineering work and 206,000 tons of construction materials would be needed for the physical barrier itself.[70]

Muscle Shoals referred to an air-supported system that was being built up in southern Laos. It was subdivided into the Mud River anti-vehicular system and the Dump Truck anti-personnel system. Battery-operated sensors, placed by hand or air-dropped, would pick up data (seismic, infrared, or magnetic) and relay them to an orbiting Air Force EC-121 aircraft. The plane then relayed the information to a control center equipped with two IBM 360-65 computers, which analyzed the data and correlated them to its extensive memory of the Trail system. The computers provided real-time receipt, processing, and display of sensor activities and then produced targeting information that was then relayed to tactical aircraft or B-52s orbiting the Trail, waiting for targets to bomb.

The operation was to be run by the 7th/13th Air Force from Nakhon Phanom at its Infiltration Surveillance Center, also known as Task Force Alpha.[71] Cover was provided for the operation under the rubric "Communications Data Management Center." Construction was begun on the facility on 6 July and it was completed three months later. Since Prairie Fire teams already combed some of the geographic sectors in which the sensors were to be emplaced (the southern Laotian panhandle and the Nickel Steel bombing area), they were well suited to take part in the Dump Truck program. The teams would emplace sensors and mines and pinpoint targets for tactical and B-52 strikes. They would be launched from Lang Vei (near Khe Sanh) and from Nakhon Phanom. There were reservations from Ambassador Sullivan that the Laotian government would object to the proposed project, but once again Souvanna Phouma not only condoned the operation but also took a hand in attaining maximum effect.

RADIO RELAY SITES
As was proven by the debacle at Oscar-8, radio contact between the recon teams and exploitation forces, FACs, and the launch site were essential to survival. The mountainous terrain of southeastern Laos often interfered with radio communications, on many occasions by blocking the line-of-sight signals of FM radios. SOG attempted to alleviate this problem by establishing forward radio relay sites.

On 15 January a recon team led by Lt. George Sisler discovered and occupied a mountain precipice twenty-five miles across the border in southeastern Laos. The peak was also strategically located north of Route 110 near Target Area Golf-5. Towering one thousand feet above the surrounding terrain, the peak was virtually unassailable and was named the Eagle's Nest by the team, but it was officially designated Golf-5 by MACSOG.[72] The five-year occupation of this peak contributed to MAC-SOG's effort by allowing continuous radio communications between both the recon teams and their airborne FACs, and the teams and their launch sites. Realizing that the site could receive radio communications from throughout southeastern Laos and southern North Vietnam, the National Security Agency (NSA) would eventually install a Polaris III radio-monitoring station at Golf-5 and begin a program of listening in on communist broadcasts.

In March a second radio relay site was occupied and went into operation. This was Sledgehammer, located eighteen miles north-northwest of Plei Djering, on a 4,717-foot peak (Cu Grock) overlooking the Plei Trap Valley in Pleiku Province. Sledgehammer was continuously manned by four SOG communications personnel and twenty-five indigenous troops assigned from FOB-2. It remained in operation until March 1969.

Joint Personnel Recovery Center
By 1967 the JPRC was in turmoil. Colonel Aderholt, exhausted by endless wrangling with 7th/13th Air Force, departed in December 1966 and was replaced by Col. Allan Sampson. The two men could not have been more different. The fast pace of operations under Aderholt slowed down appreciably under the new management and the fallout from Crimson Tide was tangible. This was evidenced by an almost complete lack of

operations during the first half of the year. The small JPRC staff was also overwhelmed by the influx of intelligence, both real and bogus. This prompted MACSOG to request a boost in the organization's JTD in November.

In June, Sampson was replaced by Lt. Col. Horace J. Reisner, who, like Aderholt, was an escape and evasion (E&E) specialist. Reisner had also worked with the NSA from 1956 to 1960 and was well versed in Air Force intelligence matters, experience that would serve him well in the JPRC. No sooner was Reisner in command than he was ordered by the MACV staff to brief General Westmoreland on the failures of the previous year and on the slowdown of operations under Colonel Sampson. It was well known that CINCPAC, MACV, and the Air Force wanted to disband the organization and take over its responsibilities themselves. At the briefing, Reisner single-handedly convinced Westmoreland of the worth of the JPRC and gained his support.[73] MACSOG's participation in the JPRC included an in-house post-SAR capability that was on loan to MACV in denied areas. Insertions of MACSOG SAR (Bright Light) teams became commonplace. MACSOG recon team members were rotated through a one-week strip alert, fully equipped and ready to go, twenty-four hours a day.

During 1967 the JPRC launched sixteen prisoner recovery operations with only one success. This mission resulted in the freeing of twenty ARVN POWs but no Americans. Thirteen more operations were planned but were later canceled because intelligence could not be sufficiently developed. In March the JPRC, in cooperation with the Pacific Air Force, produced the film *Here There Be Tigers*, demonstrating the latest E&E techniques and the JPRC's role in them.

PROBLEMS

Considering the highly perishable nature of the intelligence on POWs, camps, or escapees, the process by which the intelligence was received, validated, and applied was too complicated and time consuming. In many cases camps or locations of prisoners were uncovered by Bright Light teams only hours or minutes after the communists had departed. Of course, this is reckoning without the possibility of a mole within MACSOG itself, communicating the information, possibly in real time, to his or her cohorts. It is an interesting fact that, during the entire life span of the JPRC, hundreds of ARVN prisoners would be freed, but only one American. Although many considered this fact to be proof positive of communist penetration of MACSOG, it may simply reflect differing NLF and PAVN procedures when dealing with ARVN and American prisoners.

During the year, the JPRC sought to develop specific intelligence on three Americans: Cpt. Humberto "Rocky" Versache, Lt. James "Nick" Rowe, and medic Sgt. Daniel Pitzer, all of whom were Special Forces men captured on 29 October 1963 when their CIDG company was overrun. These three were later joined in captivity by Leonard Tadios, and intelligence indicated that the group was held in a series of camps in the Ca Mau Peninsula and the U Minh Forest, both in III Corps.

Two U.S. personnel, James Jackson and Edward Johnson (along with Pitzer), were released by the NLF in Phnom Penh, Cambodia, in November as a goodwill gesture during a visit by Jackie Kennedy to the Cambodian capital. All three were later interrogated by JPRC as to the identity of fellow prisoners, locations of camps, and conditions. These interrogations set the stage for the dramatic rescue of Lieutenant Rowe in 1969.

LOGISTICS

MACSOG Logistics Branch functions included forecasting, procurement, storage, issue, and delivery of a wide variety of equipment and supplies; construction and maintenance of facilities; and research and procurement of unconventional weapons and equipment. With the addition of Daniel Boone and Muscle Shoals to its already varied operations during 1967, the Logistics Branch saw a large expansion of its responsibilities. Maj. John "Scotty" Crerar, the executive officer of C&C, described just how the hectic pace of MACSOG's expansion could lead to supply shortages, which could have a detrimental effect in the field: "We had to take ammunition away from teams coming out of Laos and give it to teams going into Laos . . . SOG was expanding quickly and logistics had not caught up with the demand."[74]

Approximately five hundred U.S. and eight thousand South Vietnamese personnel had to be supplied by the branch, and although occasional requirements were generated involving special handling and quick reaction procurement, the organization struggled to develop procedures similar to more conventional military requisitioning, procurement, and distribution. One can only imagine the logistic confusions and contradictions inherent in trying to supply a countrywide, multiservice, multimission organization while maintaining the necessary security covers.

The quantity of material processed during the year increased from 70,000 to 100,000 pounds per week, with the number of requisitions averaging 500 per week. Interservice Support Agreements were signed to provide spare parts, expendables, and general supplies. These ISSAs (previously connected to the Army and Navy) were now extended to also include the Air Force.

The greatest boon to logistics was the approval of a move of its Supply Section (located at House 240, 240 Nguyen Minh Chieu, Saigon) to a new property, which would provide a larger, centralized location for the storage of clothing, construction materials, and other bulk items. The Air Operations Logistics Section was tasked with 867 support missions including 30 completed agent resupply missions. Logistics also printed and prepared for launch more than 2,750,000 propaganda leaflets and prepared for delivery 21,538 gift kits. In coordination with CISO, 11,700 "Peanuts" radios were also received and delivered.

Of the information contained in the proposed 1968 budget ($26,894,900), the most interesting facts are those concerning the funding of Operation Daniel Boone. Since MACSOG only maintained operational control of Sigma and Omega, the administrative costs of the projects were covered by the 5th SFG. The 5th established a funding target of $2.7 million, including necessary construction. This was a real bargain, considering that the proposed budget for Prairie Fire, less construction, was $7,437,800.[75]

PLANS

The Plans Branch oversaw the creation of proposals for various military and political contingencies and MACSOG's role in them. They included appendices to MACV plans and contributions to Joint Unconventional Warfare Task Force (JUWTF) contingency plans for an expanded conflict in Southeast Asia. The Footboy 1968 Program was the first revision of agent team operations since 1966. This reflected continuing problems over the purpose of the missions and dissatisfaction by everyone, from MACSOG to Washington. The new plan proposed the redirection of the program from agent team insertion to intelligence collection and psychological operations.

OPLANs High Port/Firebreak were reduced versions of the Full Cry ARVN Laotian invasion plan, which provided for a parachute drop and heliborne assault plus a corridor across Route 9. MACSOG OPLAN 37B-67 Phase III Prairie Fire was SOG's response to General Westmoreland's plan for recruiting three thousand Kha tribesmen in the Laotian panhandle for anti-infiltration operations. This plan would have entailed an expansion in MACSOG's authority and increased personnel to carry out the operation.

The Manila Conference (24–25 October 1966) was attended by representatives from all of the Southeast Asia Treaty Organization (SEATO) nations. Included among the participants were President Lyndon Johnson and Prime Minister Ky. Almost as an afterthought, the final communiqué of the conference stated that U.S. forces would be withdrawn no later than six months after Hanoi withdrew its forces from South Vietnam, Laos, and Cambodia and ceased its infiltration.[76] MACV OPLAN 1-67 was the contingency plan for the withdrawal of U.S. and Free World Military Forces within the six-month time frame in accordance with the provisions of the communiqué.

COMMUNICATIONS

There were two things that MACSOG operations could not survive without—air support and radio communications: communications between recon teams, FACs, and launch sites; from launch sites to FOBs and the C&C; from the C&C to headquarters; and from headquarters to MACV, all of which had to be conducted on secure radio, teletypewriter, or telephone networks. This was the mission of MACSOG's Communications Branch.

Not only did the above units have to communicate, they had to be able to communicate securely. The communists were notorious for going to great lengths to monitor U.S. radio communications and to obtain and break radio codes. In the absence of built-in encryption within the radios themselves, codes that could be categorized had to be furnished; these were provided by the NSA. Agent team communications for Timberwork were received by the CIA's Bugs radio relay site, located in the Philippine Islands. They were then relayed to the STD, translated, and sent on to MACSOG. Due to questions of security, many were not happy with this arrangement.

Comment: Maritime Operations

Maritime Operations, the second of MACSOG's initial missions inherited from the CIA, held little promise of any real success. Carried out by SOG under orders from the JCS with the mission of halting Hanoi's support of the southern insurgency by showing U.S. resolve, it was also an abject failure. The missions served as little more than a pinprick to the North and, in retrospect, it is difficult to understand how American authorities ever expected the program to work. Those with a penchant for conspiracy theories have postulated that 34A maritime operations, folded in with the Desoto patrols, were merely a convenient method of forcing Hanoi to react, providing a fait accompli for the escalation of the conflict. The historical record, however, does not support this view.

As a platform for the support of psychological operations (á la the SSPL), MAROPS served a useful function, but one which eventually became self-defeating. The same boats that conducted the PSYOPS missions were utilized in shore raids and interdiction operations that provided obvious links to the southern regime. The contrary relationships between the arms of the American effort in South Vietnam were once again in evidence during naval operations when Sea Dragon warships denuded large areas of North Vietnam's coast of the vessels that MACSOG needed to feed its PSYOPS programs.

After the November 1968 stand-down in northern operations, SOG's maritime assets had clearly become redundant, but the JCS demanded that the program continue on the off chance that they would, once again, be ordered north. Why? What evidence was there in past operations that would have convinced the JCS that the result would be worth the effort and expense?

AIR OPERATIONS
Although aerial operations over North Vietnam were absolutely necessary to support agent team and PSYOPS missions, they also illustrated the schizophrenic nature of some of MACSOG's operations. The aerial missions were supposedly covert and deniable, yet they were conducted by aircraft that could have been quite readily linked to the American effort in South Vietnam. The Combat Spear and Heavy Hook aircraft were loaded with so much state-of-the-art electronic gear that had the North Vietnamese been able to scavenge enough wreckage, it would have been child's play to prove that they were American in origin. Luckily for MACSOG, the unit lost only one Combat Spear aircraft over North Vietnam and it went down so near the Chinese frontier that it actually managed to fit the cover story that SOG had concocted to fit the operation (that it was an out-of-theater mission that had become lost due to a navigational error).

The pilots and crews that flew the missions over North Vietnam, Laos, and Cambodia (Americans, Taiwanese, and South Vietnamese) were in a class by themselves and, as such, have entered aviation lore along with other special aviation operators like those of Civil Air Transport and Air America. They were skilled men who routinely flew deniable missions deep in enemy territory with little hope of salvation if anything happened to go wrong. As for the American and South Vietnamese helicopter crews that flew day after day behind communist lines in support of SOG's agent team and reconnaissance efforts, little more need be said than to apply the appellation that the Emperor Napoleon laid upon Marshal Michel Ney: they were *le plus brave de brave*—the bravest of the brave.

Chapter Five

1968: SUSPICIONS AND STAND-DOWN

Headquarters

Col. Steven E. "Rusty" Cavanaugh Jr. replaced Col. John Singlaub as chief, MACSOG, on 3 August. Cavanaugh had begun his career as a junior officer in the 11th Airborne Division during the Second World War. He made two combat jumps in New Guinea and the Philippines, the second of which was into a Luzon jump zone held by Donald Blackburn's Igorot headhunters. After the war, he attended UCLA as a classmate of John Singlaub. His first tour in South Vietnam was in 1961, when he served as the senior U.S. Army training officer in-country. He then headed the Special Warfare Development Branch at Fort Bragg, North Carolina, before taking over command of the 10th SFG in Germany. He was serving as chief of staff of the 8th Infantry Division when he got the call from Blackburn tasking him with taking over MACSOG.

During the period July through August, the SOG headquarters at 606 Tran Hung Dao Street was moved to the abandoned MACV headquarters at 137 Rue Pasteur in east-central Saigon (MACV having moved out to its new digs at Bien Hoa known as "Pentagon East"). This new SOG facility, known as the MACV-1 compound, would remain its headquarters for the duration of its participation in the conflict. On 9 September another SEACORD meeting was held at Udorn, Thailand, to hammer out rules of engagement for Laos.

REORGANIZATION

During 1968 MACSOG went through an organizational realignment. The administrative branches were redesignated as divisions whose subsections were transformed from sections into branches. The Operations Branch absorbed the Long Thanh Training Detachment, taking over training to support Timberwork, Prairie Fire, and Daniel Boone requirements and becoming the Operations and Training Division.

In November MACSOG compounded the reorganization by giving numerical designations to its operational elements and renaming the separate staff components at the Saigon headquarters as "studies" branches. These included the Maritime Studies (Op-31), Air Studies (Op-32), Psychological Operations Studies (Op-33), and Ground Studies (Op-34) Branches—all of which were subordinated to the Operations and Training Division. Designations of the operational arms now included the newly organized Ground Studies Group (Op-35), and the Airborne Studies (Op-36), Maritime Studies (Op-37), and PSYOPS Studies (Op-39) Groups. The Saigon headquarters began the year with 125 officers, 251 enlisted men, and 10 civilians for a total of 386 U.S. personnel on its roster. At the end of the year, this number had been reduced to 125 officers, 226 enlisted men, and 10 civilians—a total of 361.[1] Part of the reduction was due to an ISSA with the 7th/13th Air Force that was signed in 1967. On 15 August, 44 men of the 1st Flight Detachment were transferred back to the Air Force.

STAND-DOWN

On 31 October the new COMUSMACV, Gen. Creighton Abrams, was summoned to Washington for a meeting with President Johnson, the Joint Chiefs, and other luminaries. His subordinate commanders in Vietnam were in general agreement that, after the undeniable allied military victory during Tet, *the* strategic moment had arrived. The communists should be pushed to the wall by increasing the bombing campaign, striking the Laotian and Cambodian sanctuaries, and perhaps even threatening North Vietnam itself with ground forces. Abrams understood that the administration had been considering the implementation of a bombing halt in North Vietnam in return for a guarantee from Hanoi to seriously negotiate. He was not aware, however, of how badly the communist offensive had shocked the nation's leaders and citizens. The fallout from Tet had already been fast and furious, with General Westmoreland being replaced on 1 July. Although Abrams felt that the United States was dealing from a position of strength, he agreed with Johnson that the bombing halt was the right thing to do.[2]

When he returned to Saigon and informed his subordinate commanders of the decision, there was consternation to say the least. Colonel Cavanaugh was stunned to learn that MACSOG's northern operations were also going to be terminated as part of the bargain. Even though Footboy had been run as a covert operation since 1964, the stand-down was going to end all agent, air, and maritime operations in or near North Vietnam. Worse, with the end of the operations, the link between the Americans and the SSPL would become blatantly obvious, handing Hanoi a propaganda coup. Although Hanoi had not been fooled by MACSOG's antics in the North, many in PAVN and within the population were convinced that the SSPL was a reality. The communists could now claim that all "resistance activities," real or imagined, had been eliminated.

EVALUATIONS

Coinciding with the stand-down was a plethora of evaluations of MAC-SOG's activities and especially of the Footboy program. Key questions included what the operation had accomplished and what was to be done with the agents and operations that were subsidiary to it. Not satisfied with an evaluation of MACSOG operations by CINCPAC in the fall of 1967, COMUSMACV had commissioned another evaluation under the guidance of Brig. Gen. Albert Brownfield. Westmoreland had wanted to know if MACSOG's operations were worth the cost and effort. On 14 February 1968 the Brownfield Report was released to MACV. Once again, COMUSMACV had not been pleased with the result.

The report took apart MACSOG's operations and evaluated each one, with Footboy undergoing the most intense scrutiny. It was taken for granted that the agent teams were compromised and that little of intelligence value was gained from them, but, the report went on to state, it was difficult to gauge the thoughts and beliefs of the Hanoi regime. Humidor and Plowman were considered viable programs since they provided the only real human intelligence that came out of North Vietnam. The report concluded with what neither Westmoreland nor Washington wanted to hear: "the SSPL should have, for an ultimate planning goal, the overthrow of the Hanoi regime."[3]

In May SACSA carried out an evaluation of North Vietnamese media and public responses to the northern operations and proposed some more minor changes. The committee that conducted the evaluation did have one succinct observation to pass on to their superiors: "Hanoi is seriously concerned over the presence of agents in their country and particularly over the possible links between those agents and 'reactionary elements' within the population."[4]

In October Maj. Gen. William Depuy, then serving as SACSA, recommended to the Joint Chiefs that a detailed documentary history of MAC-SOG be prepared for use in planning for future conflicts. The study would be of sufficient depth that a detailed analysis of the lessons learned from each operation could be made. This was the origin of the MACSOG *Documentation Study*, which was completed in July 1970.

Intelligence

During the year, the Intelligence Division had been reorganized into four branches: Operations, Photo Analysis, Security, and Administration. By 1968 the Operations Branch had specialized itself into geographic sections: Laos, Cambodia, Vietnam (handling agent and maritime operations), and an Exploitation Section that dealt with prisoners and detainees taken in MACSOG operations. The Photo Analysis Branch was also expanded by the addition of a Photo Lab Section.

In May a Memorandum of Agreement between MACV J-2 and MACSOG was signed in an effort to better coordinate intelligence requirements. There had been friction for some time among MACV J-2, the Field Forces, and MACSOG over the timely dissemination of collected intelligence. The agreed-upon solution was to consolidate intelligence from all sources into a single J-2 priority target list. This "wish list" then went to chief, MACSOG. Another solution was the creation of weekly target conferences to be held at MACV J-2. Both Prairie Fire and Daniel Boone areas of operations also had target panels initiated in October that were to coordinate between MACV and MACSOG on identification, selection, and priority of intelligence targets for MACSOG missions.

In the Prairie Fire area, 410 intelligence information reports were generated during the year. In the Daniel Boone area, there were a total of 418 reports.[5] In January the Vesuvius Committee was formed with MACV J-2.[6] Its purpose was the gathering of hard intelligence in Cambodia on NLF/PAVN use of that country, which would then be presented as evidence to Prince Sihanouk. During the year maritime Plowman operations generated 352 reports and Timberwork agent operations produced 11 before the operational stand-down.[7]

As part of the continuing collation of intelligence information into the computer system, Plowman converted from the Automatic Data Processing (ADP) system to an Intelligence Data Handling System (IDHS) that utilized magnetic tape. The Cambodian Study Group also provided input into the ADP for mission planning. During the continuing effort in Air Intelligence Operations, MACSOG continued to collect and collate intelligence on the air defense capabilities of North Vietnam, Laos, and Cambodia. The Intelligence Division came under very close scrutiny during 1968 due to the evaluations that were being conducted of Timberwork operations. The closing out of the operation in November, however, meant that a shift of assets from North Vietnam to Laos and Cambodia could take place.

During the year the Security Branch began to collect and collate counterpart organization biographic files. All MACSOG detachment commanders were ordered to begin maintaining personnel files on their counterparts. Background security investigations of indigenous personnel were also begun (they were previously handled by the South Vietnamese Liaison Service), but security checks were completed on only 2,800 men during the year, leaving 5,000 more to go. This was hardly reassuring for a covert organization that had been in operation for four years.

Footboy Operations

MARITIME OPERATIONS (PLOWMAN)

Maritime operations continued at an increased tempo over those of 1967, and the NAD received four new Osprey PTFs. These craft were aluminum-hulled copies of the Norwegian Nastys built under license by Sewart Seacraft of Berwick, Louisiana. With eleven PTFs operational, missions could be conducted around the clock, seven days a week. This goal was attained during August, but the point was moot since all missions were halted by the 1 November stand-down of northern operations ordained by President Johnson. This was disastrous for those maritime operations linked to the SSPL portion of Humidor, since vessels supposedly belonging to the insurgent operation were removed from the scene along with the aircraft and vessels of the Free World Military Forces. Loki prisoner detentions had already been prohibited by the Joint Chiefs on 3 April and the last detainee was returned in October.

One of the results of the stand-down was that MAROPS assets could be shifted to in-country missions known as Dong Tam Operations. These utilized PTFs and action teams that were rotated for riverine operations in I Corps in cooperation with the U.S. Navy's Task Force 112. Bifrost Operations saw boats and action teams operating in cooperation with the III Marine Amphibious Force in I Corps. With the onset of the northeast monsoon, Dewey Rifle cross-beach operations in I Corps were no longer feasible due to weather and surf conditions. Two PTFs and action teams were then transferred south to III Corps and based at Phan Thiet, in Binh Thuan Province, southwest of Cam Ranh Bay. The two teams worked in cooperation with the 3rd Battalion, 506th Infantry of the 101st Airborne Division. Throughout the year 160 MAROPS missions were launched. Before the closeout, 185 detainees were taken to Cu Lao Cham Island, while 40 North Vietnamese craft were destroyed and one damaged. The CSS sustained 6 men killed in action, 10 wounded, and 4 missing.[8]

Air Operations (Midriff)

MACSOG's dedicated air assets to support Footboy operations over North Vietnam (Timberwork, Humidor, and Plowman) included the 1st Flight Detachment, which consisted of two C-123K Heavy Hook aircraft and two UC-123 Heavy Mow aircraft (on loan from the Republic of China) stationed at Nha Trang Air Base. These aircraft were also utilized for PSYOPS missions in Laos and for logistical airlift.

The 15th Air Commando Squadron (redesignated the 15th Special Operations Squadron during the year) consisted of four MC-130E Combat Spear aircraft, which were also stationed at Nha Trang. The 15th carried out agent team resupply, diversionary, and PSYOPS missions over North Vietnam and logistical airlift missions for MACSOG. For the year, 706 Midriff missions were planned, and 427 were completed.[9] The majority of scrubbed missions were cancelled due to adverse weather conditions. These mission figures also include flights by Blue Eagle One, the Project Jenny EC-121 assigned for Humidor PSYOPS broadcasts. Logistical airlift operations by SOG aircraft totaled 2,205 Heavy Hook and 2,690 Commando Spear sorties, during which 8,888,447 pounds of cargo and 34,915 passengers were transported.[10]

Psychological Operations (Humidor)

By the end of the year it was obvious, even to the true believers, that there was a serious lack of judgment back in Washington. The 1 November bombing halt was one thing, but to also call a halt to all other activities in North Vietnam, covert or otherwise, was absurd. No more Plowman missions meant that no new detainees would be taken to Paradise Island. If there were no detainees, gift kits, or propaganda leaflets after the stand-down, it would become obvious to all concerned that the SSPL had been the creation of the Americans. That meant that Project Humidor was effectively canceled, ending the fiction of the SSPL.

During the Tet Offensive MACSOG's Voice of Freedom radio transmitter at Hue was attacked and rendered temporarily inoperable. This in itself may give some insight into the communists' attitude toward the effectiveness of the propaganda effort. If more evidence of the effectiveness of the radio broadcasts was necessary it came from Dr. Le Vinh Can, a PAVN medical officer who rallied to the Saigon government at Dak To on 9 February. Dr. Le stated during interrogation that he and other members of his unit listened regularly to Radio Red Flag, Radio Saigon, and the Voice of the SSPL on their unit's radio. The men were evenly divided on whether the Red Flag and VSSPL broadcasts were genuine or not. He personally believed that the VSSPL was run by Colonel Ly Van Quoc, a PAVN officer who had defected to the USSR, and that the Soviets provided the broadcast facilities.[11]

Airborne Operations (Timberwork)

In January there were seven in-place teams (Hadley, Tourbillon, Romeo, Eagle, and Red Dragon) and one Singleton agent (Ares) inside North Vietnam. During the year two of the teams (Easy and Remus) were surfaced by the communists. As far as everyone with a need to know was concerned Operation Timberwork was in serious trouble. Colonel Singlaub, having already concluded by 1967 that the program was compromised, ordered that agent case officers prepare historical studies of their respective agents/teams. Included in these studies were to be security reviews of the operation. The conclusions reached were not good, but unfortunately they were also too late. By April the restriction on air operations north of the 20th parallel reduced the opportunity to insert any new agent teams.

In June Colonel Singlaub had requested that the CIA and MACV intelligence conduct an independent study of the agent team situation. Their conclusion was that all of the teams had been turned by the communists. It was then decided to surface the remaining teams by ordering them to exfiltrate. Once again, it was too late. Even if any of the teams had been legitimate, the 1 November halt of air activities north of the 17th parallel canceled the operation altogether.

It may be instructive at this point to take a look at the true fates of the teams and agents that so concerned MACSOG in mid- to late 1968: Singleton agent Ares, Pham Chuyen, had been infiltrated by sea in February 1961 and was either quickly captured or turned himself in. He was then played back by the North Vietnamese authorities as a double agent. Team Remus was airdropped southeast of Dien Bien Phu on 16 April 1962, captured, and turned.

Team Tourbillon was airdropped in Son La Province on 16 May 1962. All team members were captured and turned within two days of landing.

Team Easy parachuted into Son La Province on 9 August 1963. They were captured and turned upon insertion. Team Eagle was airdropped near Hon Gai on 27 June 1964. They were also captured and turned upon landing. Team Romeo infiltrated southwest of Dong Hoi on 19 November 1965. All of the members were captured and turned on 14 January after a failed resupply mission.[12] Team Hadley was infiltrated by helicopter on 26 January 1967 and captured and turned within days.

Team Red Dragon was parachuted into Ha Giang Province on 21 September 1967, captured, and turned upon insertion.[13]

SECURITY

The security apparatus of North Vietnam was extensive and redundant, as it was in all communist states because, in a totalitarian society, security and vigilance were ever the watchwords. The first line of North Vietnam's defense was the People's Police Force, whose duty it was (beyond carrying out the prevention of criminal activities) to discover, prevent, and repress all sabotage and subversive activities. Next came the People's Armed Public Security Force, which protected all key facilities against sabotage and controlled the borders. It was also tasked to prevent counterrevolutionary activities by ethnic peoples in the border regions. Overseeing the others, but also participating directly, was the Ministry of Public Security, whose functions included combating subversion, sabotage, and espionage by foreign spies and commandos.

Unknown to MACSOG, all of its agent teams had either been captured upon insertion or shortly thereafter. In most cases security forces (in some combination of the above) were waiting in the general area of the insertion and scooped up the teams without much of a problem. The North Vietnamese then offered the radio operators of the teams a choice, either to continue to operate their radios on schedule and transmit back what they were told, or be shot. The communists were also very well informed about the signals arrangements of the radio operators.[14]

If a team could be captured intact (or at least its commander and radio operator) within twenty-four hours of its insertion, the communists had a chance of convincing MACSOG and its South Vietnamese counterparts that all was well. Each of the two men had one part of a prearranged code group that went into their initial transmission. The absence of either part of the code group notified their handlers that the team was broadcasting under duress. North Vietnamese signals intelligence officers immediately went to work to get their prisoners to surrender their code groups to prevent this notification, thereby allowing them to play back the team as a double.

The Ministry of Public Security always sent officers to recruit captured radio operators to work for the Counterespionage Directorate of the State Security General Directorate. Team Romeo's radio operator agreed to transmit for them only as long as no reinforcements were requested. It was when he learned that MACSOG was sending reinforcements that he broadcasted the message "Romeo already captured" and then repeated the phrase. He was pulled off the radio and beaten, but he was not killed. The ministry rectified the problem by transmitting the next day that the last broadcast had been incorrect. The "team" then continued to broadcast as if nothing had happened.[15]

By utilizing these methods, North Vietnamese authorities had the opportunity to begin an elaborate radio charade. Supplies and reinforcements would be demanded by the doubled teams and they would be sent in, allowing the North Vietnamese to capture more agents and further study MACSOG's methods and capabilities. This effort was, without doubt, one of the most successful military counterintelligence efforts of the Cold War period.

STRATA OPERATIONS (OP-34B)

Only two STRATA operations had been conducted in 1967 and although they were a far cry from successful, MACSOG believed that the program had promise. The number of planned missions, however, was reduced due to poor weather conditions in the operational area and poor team training and morale. During 1968 a revival of the operation began. The first step was to increase the number of teams to ten and to recruit the men from only among ARVN personnel. After completing their training at Camp Long Thanh, the teams were moved to a new site at Da Nang (created from the old C&C Detachment at Camp Fay and Camp Black Rock), designated Monkey Mountain Forward Operations Base (MMFOB), to locate them closer to their area of operations. It was also decided that all missions would be launched from Nakhon Phanom by USAF HH-3E helicopters and that the size of the teams would be reduced from ten men to no more than eight and sometimes as few as four.

After these improvements, twenty-four missions were launched into North Vietnam and they were, in general, successful, although fifteen agents were declared missing during the year.[16] Although the intelligence gathered by the teams was not significant, they were definitely showing increased aptitude. Unfortunately, the 1 November operational restriction ended the missions and the men and assets were then transferred to Prairie Fire for operations in Laos. During the early months of the year Strategic Intelligence Teams (SIT) were created as a sort of urban version of STRATA. The initial nine agents in the program began training at Long Thanh during the summer. When the word came down the pipeline that northern operations were to be terminated, the program was scrubbed and the agents were shifted to the STRATA program in early 1969.

FORAE (OP-34C)

For the fourth time in as many years, the mission of MACSOG's agents within North Vietnam changed. By 1967 it had become more than obvious that agent team operations in the North were in serious trouble. In December the Airborne Operations Group was redesignated as the Airborne Studies Group, but it continued agent team and diversionary operations. Due to the conclusions of the Brownfield Report, it had already been decided to reorient Footboy toward psychological diversionary operations programs. To make the SSPL more credible, the front organization concept was to be revitalized. Due to the exigencies of the bombing halt and the negotiations in Paris, however, the concept was once again shelved.

It had been decided by the JCS and CINCPAC to utilize what was left of the agent teams as a part of a diversionary series of operations meant to play on the paranoia for internal security within North Vietnam. Approval was sought in November 1967 to develop diversionary operations to confuse and annoy the communists. MACV authorization came on 14 March 1968.[17] Thus, Operation Forae was born. It was subdivided into three projects: Urgency, Oodles, and Borden.

Project Oodles was a diversionary or false agent team concept. Phantom agent and resupply drops were conducted in North Vietnam to reinforce the notional concept. Radio transmissions then went out from the Bugs radio site as though to an actual agent or team on the ground in North Vietnam and by broadcasts to those false agents by "family members" via the Voice of Freedom.

Project Urgency was operated in conjunction with Humidor and the most zealous communists among the detainees at Paradise Island were chosen as its target. They were released along with the other detainees, but upon search and debriefing ashore, they would be incriminated by money, secret ink chemicals, and false messages surreptitiously hidden in their clothing. The difficulty in explaining the items to the northern security forces could only be imagined.

Project Borden was run as part of the Timberwork program. MACSOG would recruit NLF/PAVN prisoners of war as agents for "special missions" in the North. Allowed access to "classified information" during their training, the agents were inserted into North Vietnam with the expectation that they would be captured or turn themselves in. Undergoing interrogation by counterintelligence personnel, they were expected to divulge the "information" that MACSOG wanted them to, mainly concerning larger, nonexistent resistance and agent networks.

Another Forae operation was Project Sanitaries, in which MACSOG printed up thousands of SSPL scrip "Redemption Coupons," leaflets that were airdropped into North Vietnam, carried by Humidor detainees, or carried in by STRATA teams. The coupons were meant to convince the North Vietnamese that the SSPL was real, viable, and growing. Prior to the 1 November stand-down, eighteen missions were conducted; fourteen by STRATA teams, two by airdrop, and two by returned detainees.

Project Pollack dealt with poison-pen letters cooked up by the Printed Media Department, which were mailed into North Vietnam from third-party countries. The letters were sent to high-ranking Hanoi cadres in order to incriminate them. To confuse the communists even more, Project Uranolite was to drop a variety of "Rube Goldberg" mechanical devices into North Vietnam, supposedly to be utilized by agent teams, but in fact inserted only to baffle communist technical personnel. Also dropped, sometimes at random, were gift kits, empty boxes, and so forth that were meant to convince the Hanoi authorities that the resistance movement was nationwide and growing.

One of the most insidious planned operations was Yellow Jacket, which proposed that communist zealots among the Humidor fishermen detainees be drugged and then airdropped into the border region between Laos and North Vietnam to bolster the image of the SSPL. This proposal was, however, turned down. Due to media leakage concerning Eldest Son (the booby-trapped munitions program), its cover name was changed to Italian Green in November.

The Radio Studies Group was separated from the Psychological Operations Group at the end of the year. Radio Studies then had responsibility for the operation of the Voice of Freedom radio station and broadcasts while the PSYOPS Group retained its operation of all other "black" radio broadcasts.

CAMP LONG THANH

The fall of Kham Duc (see below) resulted in the loss of MACSOG's reconnaissance training center. As a consequence, SOG relocated the facility to Camp Long Thanh. This meant that Long Thanh would have to expand both its training operations and facilities. This expansion was reflected by the reorganization of the Operations Division into the Operations and Training Division. Another result was the reorganization of the Special Forces TDY training detachment at Camp Long Thanh into Detachment B-53. The camp thus became the training center for reconnaissance teams and exploitation forces, agent operations (including STRATA and diversionary operations), and CSS action teams.

Cross-Border Ground Operations

THE TRAIL

By January 1968 the North Vietnamese were again showing signs of modernizing their logistical effort. The number of PAVN supply and maintenance personnel on the Trail had fallen by 11,500 mainly due to an increased shift to motor/river transportation and growing use of mechanized construction equipment. The CIA estimated during the year that the 559th Group was utilizing twenty bulldozers, eleven road graders, three rock crushers, and two steamrollers.[18] This was a far cry from the early days when human porters pushing bicycles were the main mode of transport (although they were still utilized for the border crossing into South Vietnam). This increased mechanization still left as many as 43,000 Vietnamese and Laotians engaged in operating, improving, or modernizing the Trail system. It was later estimated by MACV that from October 1967 through January 1968, 44,000 PAVN troops had been infiltrated south through the Trail system to take part in the Tet Offensive.[19]

On 28 October PAVN Headquarters 500 was established as the result of a logistical crisis created by American bombing and shelling in and north of the DMZ (Operation Turnpike). The new headquarters consisted of two regiments and thirty-five engineering battalions, one infantry division, three regiments, and twenty-three battalions of anti-aircraft troops, eighteen truck transportation battalions, and two petroleum pipeline battalions—a total of 33,384 personnel.[20] As a comparison, and to indicate the depth of the crisis, the 559th Transportation Group, responsible for all of southern Laos, had only 35,108 personnel.

PRAIRIE FIRE

During the year construction continued at newly designated FOB-4, which was located at the base of Marble Mountain, southeast of Da Nang. Men were assembled and organized, but beginning in February, the FOB was tasked with providing replacements for FOB-3 at Khe Sanh. This tended to slow organization, and this was exacerbated on 10 April by a helicopter crash that claimed the lives of four team leaders. The teams assembling at the FOB took the names of deadly snakes while its exploitation forces were given letter designations (A through C).

With the closeout of FOB-3 (see below), the Bru Montagnards, who constituted the backbone of its recon teams and exploitation force, were relocated to Mai Loc in Quang Tri Province. On 24 June SF Detachment A-101 (formerly at Lang Vei) opened up shop at Mai Loc and the site was utilized for mission launches for Shining Brass and Nickel Steel operations.

It was redesignated FOB-3 until November, when its personnel were transferred to FOB-4.

FOB-1 (Phu Bai) consisted of fifteen Spike Teams, each having three U.S. personnel and nine indigenous mercenaries (redesignated as Special Commando Units [SCU—pronounced "Sue"] during the year). There were also several Vietnamese-led teams commanded by LLDB sergeants. Due to manpower shortages, however, the four exploitation companies at the FOB were reduced to three, the last having been converted into a security force. These forces were beefed up by relocating Bru Montagnard personnel from the Mai Loc area (Company B) and the hiring of Khmer Serai (a strongly anticommunist and anti-Sihanouk ethnic Cambodian paramilitary group within South Vietnam that was supported by the United States) to reinforce Company A.

Due to the addition of Operations Daniel Boone and Muscle Shoals, an operational expansion and command reorganization of cross-border operations took place on 21 November. With the closeout of the Khe Sanh base, the FOB-3 teams were divided between FOBs 1 and 2. FOB-1 was then closed down and its teams were divided between Kontum and Da Nang. The Da Nang C&C base was then designated Command and Control North (CCN), co-located with FOB-4 at Marble Mountain. Under the command of a lieutenant colonel, CCN launched Prairie Fire, Nickel Steel, Muscle Shoals, and JPRC missions into the Laotian panhandle and the DMZ.

After the reorganization, CCN was organized along battalion lines with a headquarters element, two exploitation battalions comprising four companies each, four independent rifle companies (used in security roles), and four reconnaissance companies consisting of sixty-eight recon teams (three U.S. and nine SCUs each). In addition, 567 U.S. personnel were assigned to CCN along with 3,052 Vietnamese. FOB-2 at Kontum was initially reinforced by troops from the 5th SFG's Project Omega, but this was not going to last.

As a result of the Tet Offensive, for the first nine months of the year MACSOG's cross-border operations were suspended and its teams supported the Field Force units with 236 in-country reconnaissance operations. During the remainder of the year, 310 additional recon missions and 56 platoon-size operations were conducted in the Prairie Fire area. The teams were supported by 287 helicopter gunship and 635 tactical air sorties. Only 1 prisoner was taken during the year and 410 intelligence reports were generated.[21] U.S. casualties incurred by Prairie Fire teams during both in- and out-of-country missions were 39 killed, 179 wounded, and 24 missing in action. Indigenous casualties during the same operations were 61 killed, 271 wounded, and 50 missing.[22]

SLAM VII was launched from late November through early December against Base Area 613, some thirty miles northeast of Attopeau, Laos. Thirteen recon teams, four independent platoons, and four companies were utilized in this operation and 112 tactical air strikes and 42 helicopter gunship sorties were launched in its support. The teams reported almost 400 secondary explosions and 64 large fires.[23] During the operation, teams reported on increased North Vietnamese security precautions on the Trail, and increased anti-aircraft defenses were encountered. This was made possible, in part, due to the freeing of anti-aircraft units that had been utilized in the defense of North Vietnam. President Johnson's bombing halt had allowed them to move south to defend the Trail.

LANG VEI

During the siege of the Khe Sanh Combat Base, the nearby Special Forces camp at Lang Vei was assaulted by PAVN forces. Defended by twenty-four Special Forces troops of Detachment A-101 and several companies of Bru CIDGs, Lang Vei was attacked on the night of 7 February by twelve PT-76 tanks of the PAVN 202nd Armored Regiment and elements of the 304th Division. After a determined defense, the base was overrun.

Although forewarned by MACSOG about the appearance of North Vietnamese armor in the area, MACV and III MAF (Marine Amphibious Force) ignored the intelligence as being tactically impossible. Also ignored was the responsibility of the Khe Sanh Base commander, Marine colonel David Lownds, to aid in the defense of Lang Vei. Lownds feared that any relief force would be advancing into an ambush. He was probably right. The following day, after Lownds again refused to go, SOG major George Quamo put together a scratch force of 14 Special Forces and 40 Bru from FOB-3 and helilifted into Lang Vei to extract any survivors. There was no opposition from the communists as the force recovered 14 U.S. survivors; 10 Americans had died and 13 were wounded in defense of the camp while almost 300 of the 487 CIDGs were killed.[24]

FOB-3's commander, Maj. Lucius Campbell, was then ordered to report to MACV headquarters in Saigon for a tongue-lashing. Westmoreland told Campbell to "be more responsive to the Marines."[25] He then congratulated him on the successful rescue mission. For Colonel Lownds, the real problem of Lang Vei arose over what to do with the six thousand survivors (including the survivors of Laotian camp BV-33, who had crossed the border after also being overrun by PAVN) and refugees from Lang Vei camp and the nearby village. Lownds refused to admit them into the base, since communist cadre might have been intermingled among them. After being disarmed and threatened by the Marines, most of the survivors and refugees ended up walking east down Highway 9 to safety. Eventually, the Laotian survivors of BV-33 were removed from Vietnam by Royal Lao Air Force C-47s. The episode left a bitter taste in the mouths of the Laotians. The general commanding the Laotian military region stated that he had to consider the Americans and South Vietnamese enemies because of their conduct.[26]

Although the men of FOB-3 had shared the same dangers and fought the same battle as the Marines, tensions between the two groups at Khe Sanh had already been strained and only became worse after the Lang Vei debacle. Bru CIDGs who had fought for the camp and managed to escape were stripped of their weapons at the main gate of Khe Sanh and pushed back. As one Green Beret put it, "they couldn't trust any damn gooks in their camp," even ones that had been run over by nonexistent tanks on the previous evening.[27] One Marine, Sgt. John Balanco, who worked with the Special Forces men at Lang Vei and Khe Sanh, stated that his Bru SCUs were not even allowed on the base.[28]

On 7 and 8 April, a series of meetings at the Marine headquarters at Khe Sanh set the stage for one of MACSOG's greatest mysteries. On the 14th Major Quamo boarded a SOG U-17 aircraft bearing two documents from Lieutenant Colonel Bahr (new commander of FOB-3) to CCN at Da Nang. The documents posed a series of questions pertaining to FOB-3's future in relation to the imminent abandonment of Khe Sanh by the Marines. Twenty minutes into the flight, all communication with the aircraft ceased. The aircraft, its passenger, and its crew disappeared.

Due to the sensitive nature of the documents, a thorough and continuing search effort was launched. MACSOG intelligence evidently was suspicious of Major Quamo and there were rumors that the Intelligence Branch believed that there was a possibility that he had defected to the communists. These innuendoes were not ended until 26 June 1974 when the wreckage of the aircraft and three bodies (one of which was positively identified as Cuomo) were discovered.

By the end of the siege of Khe Sanh and the subsequent pullout of Marine forces, MACSOG had lost both its FOB there and its launch site at Lang Vei. That left only one Special Forces border camp within the boundaries of I Corps. Kham Duc, located seventy-five miles to the south of Lang Vei, had served as MACSOG's first launch site and as its reconnaissance training center since 1965. It was now the only camp within range of Base Area 614 and two Laotian highways, 966 and 165.

FRED ZABITOSKY

On 19 February Spike Team Maine member Fred Zabitosky was about to participate in the last mission of his tour. (It was indicative of the combat experience of SOG's recon men that Zabitosky was at the end of his *third* combat tour in South Vietnam.) Launching from FOB-2's Dak To Launch Site, the team was inserted into Target Area Quebec-1 near Laotian Route 110, where it was attacked by a PAVN platoon. Ordering the rest of the men to return to the LZ, Zabitosky held off the communists single-handedly for half an hour. Because three other teams were also in heavy contact, Spike Team Maine would have to wait for rescue.

Before the extraction ships could come in, however, the team was swarmed by an estimated one hundred North Vietnamese troops. Only later was it revealed that the team had landed near a PAVN divisional headquarters. With air strikes pummeling the communists, the team was ordered to move down a streambed to another LZ. The first chopper in pulled out one of the Americans and three Montagnards. The second ship came in and picked up the rest of the team, including Zabitosky, when, after they were about seventy-five feet up, a rocket-propelled grenade struck the helicopter, splitting it in two. Zabitosky was thrown clear while the ship crashed on its side and began to burn.

When he regained consciousness he found that his uniform was on fire. He was badly burned, had some shrapnel wounds, and several of his vertebrae and ribs had been crushed in the fall from the chopper. Disregarding those injuries, Zabitosky stumbled to the burning helicopter and pulled out the pilots, 1st Lt. Richard Griffith and WO John Cook. The 130-pound Zabitosky threw the 6-foot, 250-pound Cook over his shoulder and carried him to another chopper that had just landed. For his heroism and selfless actions, SSgt. Fred Zabitosky was awarded the Medal of Honor.[29]

HARD TIMES

Spring of 1968 was a bleak period for the men of FOB-1. General Westmoreland had ordered an intelligence collection effort in the Ashau Valley code-named "Grand Canyon" and FOB-1 responded by inserting teams that were promptly chewed up by PAVN. On 3 March, Maj. Robert Lopez arrived at Phu Bai as the new FOB commander. He was quickly irritated by the number of failed and aborted missions in the Ashau and was infuriated when team leaders refused operations in what had come to be called the "Valley of Death." In an effort to motivate his men, Lopez accompanied a team into the Ashau on 4 March. Two days after the insertion he was killed in action. He had been the FOB commander for three days.

On the same day as Lopez's insertion, Spike Team Alaska, consisting of SSgt. John Allen, SP5 Kenneth Cryan, Pfc. Paul King, and nine SCUs, was on a recon mission in Target Area Whiskey-7 in the Ashau. The team was assaulted by a superior force, fell back to a bomb crater, and was surrounded. During a two-day period, all of the team members were killed with the exception of Sergeant Allen.[30] On the 20th a Hatchet Force company was dispatched to recover the bodies of Team Alaska. In the fierce fighting that followed, ten SCUs were killed, forty were wounded, and five went missing in action before the force was extracted. Three days later Spike Team Idaho, consisting of Sfc. Glen Lane, SSgt. Robert Owen, and nine Nung SCUs, was inserted on another recon mission into Laos. The last radio message from the team was at 1024 that day. After that, ST Idaho disappeared.

On the 24th, twelve-man Spike Team Oregon was inserted into Idaho's LZ to search for the remains of the team members. They were promptly attacked by an estimated PAVN company and suffered one SCU killed and seven wounded before they could be extracted. The decimation of the FOB's Nung element in the Ashau led to a mutiny of the Cambodian KKK members of the exploitation force in June. The men refused en masse to return to the Ashau and threatened their officers. The Cambodians were then forcibly removed from the FOB at gunpoint.

KHAM DUC

During the early morning hours of 10 May a reinforced battalion of the 1st NLF Regiment, 2nd PAVN Division, launched a mortar-supported attack on the temporary Special Forces outpost of Ngok Tavak, five miles south of Kham Duc. The outpost was defended by a 113-man Nung company of the 11th Mike Force, commanded by an Australian captain, three Australian advisors, and eight U.S. Special Forces sergeants. Also stationed at the outpost were the forty-four artillerymen of D Battery, 2nd Battalion, 13th Marines and their two 105-mm howitzers. The ground attacks were followed by savage close-quarters fighting that lasted until the following evening, when the battered camp was abandoned. Fifteen Americans and Australians had been killed, twenty-three were wounded, and two were missing. Of the approximately one hundred CIDG troops, sixty-four were missing or had deserted and thirty were killed or wounded.[31]

Kham Duc, fifteen miles east of the Laotian border, was situated on Provincial Route 14, the only north–south road in western Quang Tin Province. It too had been pounded by a mortar attack on the evening of the 10th. Defending the base and airstrip were Special Forces Detachment A-105 (9 U.S. NCOs, 12 Nungs, and a 20-man CIDG recon platoon) and 3 poorly trained CIDG companies that were permanently stationed at the camp. They were supported by FOB-4's Recon School Detachment (a lieutenant and 4 NCOs); a 45-man Hatchet Force in training (commanded by a U.S. second lieutenant and 4 NCOs); and 4 recon teams in training (20 Montagnards and 12 SOG NCOs). A MACSOG captain from headquarters was also on site with 2 roadrunner teams (one of which had launched just before the attack began). These forces were reinforced on 10 May by a 750-man task force of the U.S. 23rd Infantry Division (Americal), which consisted of the 2nd Battalion, First Infantry, 196th Light Infantry Brigade; Company A, 1st Battalion, 46th Infantry, 198th Light Infantry Brigade; and Battery A, 3rd Battalion, 82nd Artillery with five 105-mm howitzers. These personnel were spread out in company-size units around the airstrip.

After overrunning two of the three hilltop outposts of the camp on the 11th, two regiments of the 2nd PAVN Division launched company-size assaults on three sides of the main perimeter. Colonel Ladd, commander of the 5th SFG, first went to Marine Corps general Robert Cushman, the U.S. commander in I Corps, to ask for reinforcement for Kham Duc. Cushman refused, having few uncommitted troops with which to feed the battle. Ladd then went to a meeting with Marine major general Samuel Koster (who had assumed operational control of the battle) and Creighton Abrams, Westmoreland's deputy commander. With the communist "Mini-Tet" offensive looming—and in order to prevent a repeat of the situation at Khe Sanh in much less advantageous terrain—they made the decision not to reinforce Kham Duc and to launch an aerial evacuation of the base. Westmoreland concurred.[32]

Although the communist assaults against the perimeter were driven back, the Americal troops had had enough. The artillerymen of Battery A, 3rd Battalion, 82nd Artillery, began destroying their five 105-mm howitzers. A massive North Vietnamese assault, launched around noon, was smashed only by the timely arrival of aircraft dropping napalm and cluster bomb units on the communist advance. The officers of the 196th then demanded an immediate evacuation, but any form of orderly withdrawal was stymied by panicked troops (U.S. and indigenous). Americal troopers shoved Vietnamese dependents out of the way in a stampede to be first in line for the evacuation helicopters. The enraged Special Forces advisors managed to convince the Air Force to load civilians aboard a C-130 aircraft, only to watch in horror as the plane went down in flames, the victim of intense anti-aircraft fire. Nine other aircraft and helicopters were destroyed during the course of the evacuation. The members of the Special Forces command group were the last men out of the camp at 1633 on 12 May.

The United States had suffered one of its most serious defeats of the war. U.S. forces would not return to the area in force for another two years. The communists dominated Provincial Route 14, the Special Forces lost another border surveillance camp on the northwestern frontier of South Vietnam, and SOG lost another launch site.[33] MACSOG could now recon Highways 966 and 165 only by launching from the Heavy Hook facility at Nakhon Phanom. In mid-December recon team launches from Heavy Hook began in earnest and four missions were launched before the end of the year.

JOHN KEDENBURG

On 13 June FOB-2's Spike Team Nevada was evading from an entire PAVN battalion after a firefight near Highway 110 in Laos. During the running gun battle the team was surrounded several times but managed to shoot its way out. Somewhere along the line, however, one of their Montagnard SCUs went missing. Finding a hole in the canopy, team leader SP5 John Kedenburg called for an extraction utilizing dropped ropes and McGuire rigs, and four men were lifted out by the first helicopter.[34] As the second chopper appeared and the last four men were hooking into their rigs, the missing Montagnard ran into the area. Although it meant certain death, Kedenburg unsnapped himself from the rig, hooked up the SCU, and turned to face the North Vietnamese. Witnesses saw him drop six of them before he fell. An airstrike was then called in on his position.

For his selfless act of sacrifice and devotion to duty, Kedenburg was awarded the Medal of Honor.[35] Much more than that, he had paid the ultimate price to uphold the ethic of the recon team leader, who was always the first man in and was always the last man out. For this he was awarded much more than a piece of metal hanging from a colored ribbon; he gained the undying love and admiration of his comrades.

SAPPER ATTACK

On 23 August a one-hundred-man NLF sapper company waded through the surf from Da Nang and, with assistance from inside the compound, attacked CCN from the rear. After an intense ground battle, thirty-eight of the sappers were killed and nine others were wounded and captured. Sixteen Green Berets, however, had died in the assault, the largest number killed in one engagement in Special Forces history. It could have been worse. A map of the camp found on one of the sappers misrepresented the layout of CCN. The officers' quarters had been mislabeled as those of the enlisted men, most of whom were out on operations and, therefore, spared destruction in their billets. According to NLF general Dham Duc Nam, this attack was "calculated to disrupt SOG operations and release pressure on the Ho Chi Minh Trail."[36]

ROBERT HOWARD, AGAIN

In mid-November Sfc. Robert Howard accompanied an FOB-2 Hatchet platoon into Laos. After four days in the area, on 19 November, the force was ambushed by North Vietnamese troops, including a PT-76 tank. Braving intense fire, Howard crept forward and knocked out the PT-76 with an anti-tank rocket. After a medevac helicopter was shot down, Howard, already wounded, charged forward three hundred yards through PAVN fire to lead the two pilots and a wounded door gunner to safety. He was again wounded, this time by fourteen pieces of shrapnel, but all that this seemed to do was aggravate him.

He charged the communists, killed two, and dragged back a third as a prisoner. PAVN anti-aircraft fire halted the extraction until the following morning, when Howard, already wounded several times, moved forward and silenced a 37-mm anti-aircraft gun, allowing the extraction to be completed. For the second time, Robert Howard was recommended for the Medal of Honor, but his award was again downgraded, this time to a Silver Star.

On 30 December newly promoted First Lieutenant Howard was serving as a member of a forty-man Bright Light mission into Laos. The unit was in search of MACSOG private first class. Robert Scherdin, who had been separated from his team. Bypassing a PAVN company, Howard was leading his men up a hill when he and Lt. Jim Jerson were wounded by a mine. While administering first aid to Jerson, a bullet struck one of the wounded man's ammunition pouches, detonating several magazines. Howard's fingers in shreds, he was dragging Jerson off the hill when he was shot in the foot.

The remaining twenty men were organized by Howard, who administered first aid, directed their fire, and encouraged them to resist. After three and one-half hours under attack, Howard prepared for a fight to the death. The team was saved from that fate, however, when an emergency night extraction took them off without any further casualties. As badly wounded as he was, Howard was the last man to board a helicopter. After his third recommendation in thirteen months, Robert Howard was finally awarded a well-deserved Medal of Honor.[37] Besides the deco-

Col. Clyde R. Russell,
Chief, SOG, Jan.
1964–May 1965

Col. Donald D.
Blackburn, Chief, SOG,
Apr. 1965–May 1966

Col. John K. Singlaub,
Chief, SOG, May
1966–Aug. 1968

Col. Stephen E.
Cavanaugh, Chief, SOG,
Aug. 1968–Jul. 1970

Col. John F. Sadler,
Chief, SOG, Jul.
1970–Apr. 1972

Col. David R. Presson,
Chief, SOG, Apr. 1972–
May 1972; Sr. Advisor,
STDAT-158, May 1972–
Nov. 1972

Col. Robert W. Hill Sr., Advisor,
STDAT-158, Dec. 1972–Mar. 1973

rations previously mentioned, he had been awarded eight Purple Hearts for being wounded fourteen times in fifty-four months of combat.

Perhaps no man better represented the quandary of the political and moral dilemma of the Vietnam War in the heart and mind of America than Howard. He had become arguably the most highly decorated combat soldier in U.S. history, yet few of his countrymen even knew who he was.[38] Unlike Alvin York or Audie Murphy before him, Howard was not touted as a national hero by the media, he was given no tickertape parade, and no Hollywood movie was made depicting his extraordinary exploits. His treatment by the nation he had so courageously served was nothing short of a disgrace. Of course, none of this bothered the quiet, unassuming Howard. He remained in the Army and retired in September 1992 as a full colonel after twenty-six years of active service. He passed away on 23 December 2009.

DANIEL BOONE

Simultaneous with the reorganization of CCN, Command and Control South (CCS) was established at Ban Me Thuot to take over control of operations in the Daniel Boone area. By March, all Project Omega troops had been relocated from Kontum to newly established FOB-5 at Ban Me Thuot. FOB-6 (opened in November 1967 for Sigma operations in war zones C and D) was closed and those men also made the move to Ban Me Thuot, where they were merged with Omega at CCS. CCS maintained launch sites at Duc Co, Duc Lap, Quan Loi, and Song Be.

Commanded by a major, CCS was organized along battalion lines with four reaction companies, a security company, and a reconnaissance company consisting of 24 recon teams. The CCS teams took the names of carpenter's implements. A total of 158 U.S. personnel were assigned to CCS along with 1,070 Vietnamese mercenaries. The targets of its operations were zones Alpha, Bravo, and the newly opened Zone Charlie (Zone Alpha was divided north of the Fishhook, creating the new operational area).[39] Concomitant with the creation of the new zone in September, authorization was given for helicopter inserts to the full depth of the operational area (twenty kilometers) in zones Alpha and Bravo.[40] There was a plan under consideration early in the year to create reconnaissance teams composed of PAVN ralliers that would be dressed and equipped as communist troops. Three teams of 3 men each were created under the code name "Thundercloud." By mid-year, however, these teams were disbanded and the men were transferred to regular reconnaissance teams.[41]

In the Daniel Boone area of operations there were 287 recon missions launched into Cambodia during 1968. As with Prairie Fire, the

Daniel Boone teams were also deployed in-country for an additional 439 missions. They were supported by 359 helicopter gunship and 48 tactical air sorties (only outside Cambodia); three prisoners were taken and 373 intelligence reports were generated. U.S. casualties incurred (in both in-country and Cambodian missions) included seventeen killed in action, thirty-five wounded, and three missing. Indigenous casualties were twelve killed, forty-six wounded, and one missing in action.[42]

Within the Daniel Boone area, Project Vesuvius was undertaken by the recon teams for the Intelligence Branch. Target packages were put together and missions conducted in order to gather evidence that would then be presented to Prince Sihanouk in the hope of convincing him of the extent of North Vietnam's infiltration and utilization of his country.

ROY BENEVIDEZ

On 2 May SSgt. Roy Benevidez was at Daniel Boone's Quan Loi Launch Site listening to the radio transmissions of a recon team in deep trouble. The three Americans and nine Nungs were in the Fishhook area of Cambodia when they were attacked by communist troops. The U.S. team leader (a personal friend of Benevidez) was already dead and the other two Americans had been wounded. All of the Nung team members were also either dead or wounded.

Back at Quan Loi, the helicopters that had carried out the team's insertion began to take off for an extraction. Benevidez (who served in a staff position at the launch site and was not a recon man) was in such a hurry to aid his comrades that he jumped on one of the choppers without even thinking to grab a weapon, armed with only a combat knife. Reaching the scene of the action, he jumped from the hovering helicopter and ran seventy-five yards to the team, taking an AK-47 round in the left leg and grenade fragments to the face and head on the way. After administering first aid to the wounded and distributing ammunition, he directed the remaining men in fighting off the communists.

While an extraction ship came in, Benevidez was collecting classified documents from the dead team leader. As he did so he was shot in the abdomen and took more grenade fragments in his back. The pilot of the helicopter was then mortally wounded and the ship plowed into the LZ. Benevidez managed to get the wounded out of the aircraft, and as he was applying first aid to one of them, he was shot in the right thigh. Ignoring his wounds, he rallied the survivors and called in air strikes danger close.

When a second helicopter landed and he began loading the wounded aboard, Benevidez was knocked to the ground, shot through one lung. As he continued to cover the loading of the helicopter he was attacked by an enemy soldier who clubbed him over the head with his rifle and then ran his bayonet along the American's forearm. Benevidez reacted by pulling out his combat knife and shoving it into the chest of the communist trooper with such force that it could not be extracted. When two more North Vietnamese appeared around the rear of the helicopter, he dispatched them with the dead man's weapon. As he was finally collapsing from his wounds, he was hauled aboard the chopper. He had saved the lives of eight men.

Sergeant Benevidez spent a year recuperating from seven gunshot wounds, twenty-eight shrapnel holes, and a bayonet wound. The bravery of this human tank was written up, but, unbelievably, the paperwork was lost. Thirteen years later he was finally rewarded for his fearless personal leadership, tenacious devotion to duty, and valorous actions in the face of the enemy when the U.S. Congress awarded him the Medal of Honor.[43]

COMMANDO HUNT

Taking advantage of the November bombing halt imposed by President Johnson, the North Vietnamese dispatched more men, weapons, and supplies down the Trail than ever before. U.S. intelligence also showed that the communists were beginning construction of a petroleum, oil, and lubricants (POL) pipeline from North Vietnam into the Laotian panhandle. The bombing halt also had the effect, however, of freeing up an additional 480 aircraft to attack the Trail, raising the average daily sortie rate to 620.[44] Allied air commanders, "not wanting their planes to rust," then launched massive, coordinated bombing in the Steel Tiger/Tiger Hound/Nickel Steel areas. Beginning on 15 November approval was granted to the 7th/13th Air Force for the launching of Operation Commando Hunt, with the objectives of halting or limiting infiltration and further testing the Muscle Shoals sensor system. This initial phase of the operation lasted until May 1969. The communists responded as the aerial threat to North Vietnam diminished. The number of PAVN antiaircraft weapons defending the Trail rose from 166 in November 1968 to a reported 621 by April 1969.[45]

The Igloo White system (the cover name Muscle Shoals was superseded in June) had received its baptism of fire during the siege of Khe Sanh when General Westmoreland ordered that Task Force Alpha concentrate its effort on defending the beleaguered Marine outpost.[46] During the ensuing Operation Niagara, the deployment of strings of sensors (which basically took the place of manned outposts) detected communist movements and brought down a deluge of bombs in what was described as "the most concentrated application of firepower in military history."[47]

Westmoreland credited the system with helping to break the back of the PAVN siege. In this instance the system seemingly worked well, since North Vietnamese forces were massed in a limited geographic area and moving toward a fixed objective.

How well the electronic system would function along a concealed route with its targets moving toward a distant battlefield remained to be seen. Igloo White already had some problems. The anti-personnel subsystem had already failed. The wide-area Gravel mines that had been designed to alert acoustic sensors to the location of troop movements rapidly deteriorated in the heat and humidity of Laos. For the time being, the hunt for and the destruction of communist trucks would take precedence.

Commando Hunt saw continuous round-the-clock bombing of the Trail on an unprecedented scale. This sensor-directed interdiction effort utilized daytime strikes by propeller-driven and jet aircraft, nighttime missions by fixed-wing gunships, and B-52 strikes. From October to November 1968 the number of fighter-bomber sorties flown over Laos jumped from 4,700 to 12,800.[48] B-52 strikes climbed from 273 to 600 during the same time period. The 7th/13th Air Force estimated that operations during this first phase destroyed 7,322 PAVN trucks and that 20,723 communist troops had been killed by aerial attack.[49]

Air Operations Studies (Midriff)

The Air Operations Studies Group was created during the year in response to the ISSA signed between the 7th Air Force and MACSOG. The purpose of the group was to serve as a staff section to coordinate air support and logistical airlift for SOG and to support planning for operations utilizing air assets other than those that supported Footboy operations.

The group was divided into three sections: the Airlift Section planned and coordinated logistical and personnel transportation utilizing the Combat Spear and Heavy Hook aircraft. SOG was also supported by a China Airlines Tradewind (a modified Beech C-45) utilized for VIP and personnel transportation. The Helicopter Section coordinated and assigned support for Prairie Fire and Daniel Boone missions, both from assets assigned to SOG and from other MACV units. The High Performance Section coordinated air assets (both USAF and VNAF) for delivery of agent resupply in North Vietnam and E&E kits for evading U.S. personnel shot down over communist-controlled territory.

HELICOPTERS

The USAF 20th SOS "Green Hornets" flew UH-1F and P models out of Ban Me Thuot and provided lift and gun support for Daniel Boone cross-border operations. Mechanical difficulties, however, detracted from operational effectiveness during the year. Dust intake led to engine failures and crashes, including one that led to the death of the unit's commanding officer, Col. Donald Lepard. The USAF 21st Helicopter Squadron "Dust Devils" arrived at Nakhon Phanom RTAFB in November and December 1967. This unit flew HH-3Es and was tasked with supporting MACSOG, CIA, SAR, and Muscle Shoals/Dye Marker operations. On 1 August, D Flight, 20th Helicopter Squadron "Pony Express" was absorbed by the 21st, which was then redesignated the 21st SOS.

U.S. helicopter assistance for CCN operations had originally come from VNAF H-34s supplemented by Marine Corps aviation units, but the spring of 1968 saw a decrease in USMC aerial assistance for MAC-SOG. The timely arrival of elements of the 101st Airborne Division in I Corps during the summer alleviated any necessity for a large Marine contribution. Support then came from the 158th Assault Helicopter Battalion ("Ghost Riders," "Lancers," and "Phoenix") and the 101st Assault Helicopter Company (AHC) "Comancheros," "Kingsmen," and "Black Widows."

Additional assistance came from the 188th AHC "Dragons" and its gunship component, the "Redskins." Primary gunship support for recon operations came in the form of AH-1G Cobras from the 101st Airborne Division's C Battery, 4/77th Aerial Rocket Artillery (ARA) "Griffins." On occasion the 77th's A Battery "Dragons" and B Battery "Toros" also leant a hand. To support other operations, SOG teams counted on the slicks and guns of the 189th ("Avengers"), 240th ("Greyhounds"/"Mad Dogs"), 334th ("Sabres"), 361st, and 195th AHCs.

The first part of 1968 saw PAVN 85-mm and 100-mm anti-aircraft weapons arrive on the Laotian front. As the year progressed, the quantity and quality of North Vietnamese air defenses improved dramatically, a situation that was only exacerbated by the November bombing halt, which freed many more PAVN units for service along the Trail in Laos and, eventually, Cambodia. This state of affairs upped the ante for both helicopter and fixed-wing tactical air units flying missions over the Trail.

COWBOY

On 4 May the VNAF and MACSOG lost a true comrade when Captain "Cowboy" Loc died in the crash of his H-34. Cowboy had volunteered to extract a recon team in Laos after all other pilots refused to go. He flew into Laos in atrocious weather, extracted the entire team, and then dropped them at FOB-2 at Kontum. As he was attempting to return to

Da Nang he became lost in heavy overcast and crashed into the side of a mountain. He and his entire crew were killed. Perhaps the supreme irony was that Mustacio and Cowboy, both fearless men who had cheated death on the battlefield innumerable times, were killed not by their enemies, but in accidents.

Cowboy Loc had been supporting cross-border operations since the ARVN's Delta and Leaping Lena days and had been carrying out MAC-SOG missions since their inception, including the one in which Larry Thorne met his fate. During the ensuing years he and his camouflage fatigues and six-gun had become a legend among SOG recon personnel, who considered him an old-school seat-of-the-pants flyboy who would brave any amount of ground fire or the most atrocious weather to pull men from the jaws of death. What more could be asked from a brother-in-arms?

JIM FLEMING

On the afternoon of 26 November, Air Force first lieutenant Jim Fleming and his copilot had participated in the insertion of Spike Team Chisel on a riverwatch mission in Cambodia. As the three troopships and two gunships of the Green Hornets were returning to Du Co they received an emergency extraction request from the team. The three Americans and three SCUs were trapped with their backs to the river and were surrounded by communists. Along with a FAC, the five Hueys raced to pull the team out, even though all of the ships were almost out of fuel.

Arriving on the scene, one of the gunships was downed by intense ground fire, but its crew was pulled out by one of the slicks and returned to Du Co. A second troopship then turned back for lack of fuel. Only two ships then remained, Fleming's slick and the gunship of Maj. Leonard Gonzales. The two Hueys flew through a hail of gunfire to reach the team, but the communists had simultaneously launched an all-out ground assault that forced the two helicopters off. With the gunship leading, the two choppers roared in on fumes, with guns blazing, for a final attempt. Fleming moved his ship in and hovered next to the riverbank with his tail boom extended over the water. He then held his ship steady in this exposed position despite intense ground fire for the pickup of the team members. The Montagnards and Americans of Chisel broke cover, raced for the helicopter, and all made it aboard safely. For selfless gallantry and extraordinary flying skill, Lt. Jim Fleming was awarded the Medal of Honor, the only Air Force recipient assigned to an aviation unit organic to SOG.[50] For his part in the action Major Gonzales was awarded the Air Force Cross.

Recovery Studies

During 1968 the JPRC was reorganized within MACSOG as the Recovery Studies Division. After a review conducted by Colonel Reisner, the JPRC pressed MACV to allow local commanders more flexibility in conducting POW raids. In April MACV responded by sending a message to all field commanders granting permission for them to act on their own. Previously all authorization for POW rescue operations had to go through the JPRC. During the year 32 prisoner recovery operations were launched with 8 successes freeing a total of 155 South Vietnamese military and civilian prisoners.[51]

On 14 January an electronic surveillance plane was shot down over North Vietnam near the Laotian border and seven of its crew members ejected from the aircraft. An SAR helicopter crashed en route to the site and the Air Force requested that the JPRC take over the effort. To do so meant utilizing Lima Sites (covert CIA airstrips) in Laos for refueling and that meant approval had to be obtained from Ambassador Sullivan. Colonel Reisner tried to contact Vientiane, but when communications failed, he launched the mission on his own authority.

During the next two days, the helicopter crew and three of the original seven-man crew were rescued. Regardless, Sullivan was furious that the operation had been carried out without his permission. Reisner recalled one message from the field marshal in particular: "I don't work for MACV, CINCPAC, or the JCS, I work for the President and I want you all to remember that."[52] It was typical Sullivanese.

TEXAS CREST

Although this incident passed with little more than a gripe, it may have later led to the death of an American airman. On 27 February a Navy OP-2 Neptune was shot down over southern Laos. Seven of the nine-man crew bailed out and were rescued by SAR helicopters. One of the crewmen who had remained aboard the aircraft was badly wounded and presumably died in the crash. The fate of the pilot was unknown until SAR forces picked up the signal of a survival beeper. They then requested a Bright Light mission and a team was put together at Nakhon Phanom. The standard request was put through to Sullivan on the evening of the 27th for approval of the mission.

And the team waited. On the 29th permission was finally granted and the team inserted to find only the communists waiting. General Westmoreland was incensed. He demanded that Sullivan explain the one-day wait. Sullivan replied that the delay was caused by MACSOG's "failure to follow procedures ... SAR rescue forces are USAF personnel ... JPRC forces are Vietnamese," therefore it was "not possible to permit them *carte blanche* to operate in Laos where a crash occurs."[53] Sullivan had his revenge.

BLOOD, BENGE, AND OLSEN

For ten months MACSOG ran Bright Light missions along the Cambodian frontier seeking to liberate three American civilians captured by the communists during the Tet Offensive.[54] Henry Blood was a Bible translator, Mike Benge was the head of the U.S. Agency for International Development (USAID) in Ban Me Thuot, and Betty Ann Olsen was a nurse who worked with lepers. The three were captured by communist forces near Ban Me Thuot and were then led away into the jungle.

The first attempted rescue came two weeks after the three were captured. Three companies of the 173rd Airborne Brigade and five MAC-SOG teams searched the jungle, but only one of the teams made contact with the communists. One of the team members, Larry White, managed to capture PAVN documents that revealed that the three prisoners were still alive. The three were actually close enough to the Bright Light team that they heard sounds of gunfire.

On 3 April one of the Montagnard prisoners who worked for Benge escaped and notified nearby ARVN forces. On 7 April a CIA-affiliated Provincial Reconnaissance Unit (PRU) platoon found an abandoned camp containing evidence that the Americans had been there only two days previously. In mid-May intelligence led another PRU platoon into a fight with a communist company and two more MACSOG teams were sent in. Once again the prisoners had been moved. Meanwhile Benge developed cerebral malaria and became delirious for five weeks. Henry Blood was moved to another camp, contracted pneumonia, and died.

Two more Montagnard prisoners escaped on 3 May and brought word of the Americans. On 25 May two American-led CIDG teams were inserted in Operation Rayburn Cane but, once again, the civilians were gone. That summer Benge and Olsen developed scurvy and became much weaker. In late November, a MACSOG team found another recently abandoned camp that had housed the two Americans. Betty Ann Olsen, already weakened by disease and malnutrition, began to falter and slowed the column. She was then beaten by her captors and finally died. Michael Benge was first taken deeper into Cambodia and then moved north up the Ho Chi Minh Trail to North Vietnam. He was finally released in 1973.

Picking up the narrative of Operation Rayburn Cane, on the night of 30–31 August a raiding party consisting of the local PRU advisor (a Navy SEAL), the two escapees, and a nine-man PRU team set out to locate and attack the POW camp. After crossing a river, the team killed two guards and, supported by a sixty-man PRU reaction force, liberated the camp. In it they found forty-nine Vietnamese prisoners, mostly ARVN troops, shackled in a ditch full of chest-high water.[55]

AZALEA CREEK

On 17 September a female South Vietnamese prisoner escaped from a camp in An Xuyen Province at the southernmost tip of the country. She informed JPRC debriefers that the camp held one hundred prisoners and she was willing to lead a force in to get them. On 21 September a regional force company, led by its American advisors, landed and discovered an empty camp. Before disappointment could really set in, a search of near-by elephant grass revealed twenty-five prisoners guarded by a lone female NLF guerrilla. An interrogation revealed that the NLF had forewarning of the raid, had split the prisoners up, and moved a larger group out the previous midnight. They had last been seen moving toward the Ca Mau Peninsula. On 23 December there was another successful POW raid. Elements of the ARVN 32nd Regiment, while searching for a reported POW camp, launched an assault on an NLF position north of Ca Mau in An Xuyen Province. During the operation, the South Vietnamese troops overran the camp and freed eighty-three ARVN prisoners.

MUSICAL CHAIRS

With the departure of Colonel Reisner on 29 June, the JPRC began to go through rapid command changes. Lt. Col. F. K. Sloan was next in charge, but he suffered an eye injury in mid-August. He was replaced by the JPRC's Navy officer, Cdr. Dickenson Prentiss, who rotated out on 30 November. Next up was MACSOG lieutenant colonel Irving McDonald, whose tenure lasted only one month. In January 1969 the SOG deputy commander, Col. Robert Gleason, moved McDonald to intelligence and replaced him with Lt. Col. Robert Bradshaw. Gleason and Bradshaw evidently did not work well together and Bradshaw requested a transfer in late February. The senior ranking man at the JPRC, Lt. Col. John Firth, then became de facto head of the organization.[56]

IT WORKS

Through debriefings of freed and liberated prisoners that had occurred over the previous two years, the JPRC formed a good picture of the POW situation in the IV Corps region of South Vietnam. On the last day of 1968 a force was put together to find and liberate Lt. John "Nick" Rowe, who had been held by the NLF since 1963. The assault force consisted of a CIA PRU company and two platoons of the 47th Mike Force Company.[57] Three landing zones would be simultaneously occupied and then the units would sweep in on the location of the suspected camp. The operation went like clockwork. The NLF troops and their civilian dependents came out of their bunkers and attempted to flee and/or surrender, which caused some confusion. Thirty NLF members were rounded up from what was later revealed to be a hospital complex. Twenty South Vietnamese prisoners were located and freed, but there was no American. Then there was a problem: the PRU had moved off their landing zone in the wrong direction and left a hole in the cordon.

Nick Rowe had actually been in a bunker under the feet of the landing Mike Force. When they moved off the LZ, the guards grabbed Rowe and fled. He convinced them to split up, lest they become the prey of orbiting gunships and they fell for it. A single guard led Rowe away and, when his back was turned, Rowe struck him with a piece of wood. He then ran to a clearing and waved down a slick. After five years, Nick Rowe was a free man.

POST-SAR

Three attempts were made to recover American personnel in post-SAR operations in 1968, all in December and all of which were failures. A USAF RF-4C recon plane was shot down on 11 December. The pilot ejected and was recovered on the following day. The rear-seater, Russell D. Galbraith, was not recovered, but the pilot was certain that he had ejected. A MACSOG Bright Light team was standing by at Nakhon Phanom to begin the operation, but the JPRC was informed by the U.S. Embassy, Vientiane, that a CIA roadwatch team was in the area and would conduct the search. Although the team managed to locate Galbraith's chute and radio, he was nowhere to be found. Permission for the use of the MACSOG team was denied.

The following week a Navy A-6A Intruder was shot down. Once again, the pilot ejected but he could not locate his backseater, Michael L. Bouchard. The pilot was recovered but the Udorn-based Bright Light team, supplemented by two others, could not locate Bouchard. On Christmas Eve an F-105D piloted by Cpt. Charles Brownlee was shot down over Laos. SAR forces located Brownlee's inert form hanging in a tree. Parajumper Charles King was lowered down to get him when he was wounded by ground fire. As the helicopter tried to winch up both men simultaneously, the cable broke. The chopper was driven off and a request went out to the JPRC. Once again, due to the heavy presence of the enemy in the target area, Ambassador Sullivan refused permission for another try.

Liaison

Due to the Tet Offensive it became necessary for MACSOG to improve its liaison and coordination with the STD and with the Field Forces. SOG recon teams were working extensively (for the first time) with American ground forces and improved communications became essential. The 1 November stand-down on operations within North Vietnam freed MAC-SOG air, land, and sea forces for utilization in South Vietnam, and this too called for closer relationships with the Tactical Corps Zone commanders and the units under their control.

Two SOG liaison officers were assigned as assistant operations officers on the Field Force staffs to keep their commanders abreast of the capabilities and employment of MACSOG assets within their areas of operation. The headquarters of the Field Forces were located at Nha Trang (I Field Force) and at Long Binh (II Field Force). The liaison officers, carried on the rolls of CCS, also served to keep the Field Force commanders abreast of JPRC recovery operations.

Operations in I Corps under III MAF utilized Prairie Fire assets, while Bifrost operations coordinated the NAD with III MAF and the U.S. Navy's First Coastal Security Group. Dewey Rifle operations coordinated NAD with the headquarters of II Corps and the Navy's Task Force South (Task Force 115), while Dong Tam operations coordinated NAD and the Maritime Studies Branch with the U.S. Army's 9th Infantry Division Riverine Force and Naval Task Force 116 (Game Warden).

Logistics

The year 1967 brought a reorganization of logistic functions as comptroller and headquarters commandant functions separated from the division and became directly responsible to chief, MACSOG. With the changes wrought by the northern stand-down, the Air Resupply Branch was assigned to Director, Logistics.

On 1 September, the supply facility previously located at House 240 was relocated to House 50 at 50 Nguyen Van Thoai (Plantation Road), near Tan Son Nhut Air Base. The move took place without any reduction in supply or maintenance operations. A physical examination center was built, equipped, and staffed in Saigon for the MACSOG surgeon. This provided a complete medical screening facility for newly recruited mercenary personnel before they were deployed to the field. Control of all unit medical supplies was also transferred to the surgeon.

The Operations Support Branch was established in mid-March. Staffed by three officers, the branch eyeballed the logistical usage of the subordinate field commands, guaranteeing efficiency and cutting lead times for supply. The branch also carried out liaison with staff agencies and logistic activities of adjacent and higher headquarters, both within and outside MACSOG.

Comptroller

Separated from the Logistics Division on 21 October, the Comptroller Branch provided economic and financial advice to chief, MACSOG. Greater control over financial expenditures was deemed necessary due to changes in allocated fund distribution by MACV. Previously, unclassified funds had been allocated by CINCPAC and did not have to be justified. Under MACV, greater controls were instituted. The 1969 budget for classified funds came to $26,612,000.[58]

Plans

For the first time there was a de-emphasis on planning for increasing the tempo or scope of MACSOG operations and concentration on plans dealing with a possible cease-fire and/or disengagement. One could deduce from plans conceived before September that MACSOG had been planning for expanded operations, especially in Cambodia. The arrival of CINCPAC Message 102022Z and COMUSMACV 240815Z put an end to that.[59]

President Johnson, reeling from the public relations debacle of Tet, was intent on giving the North Vietnamese a strong signal that he wished to open negotiations. The bombing halt and cancellation of northern operations were to be that signal, regardless of the consequences to MACSOG's (or MACV's) operations. SOG's part in the peace process was small, but important. The Intelligence Division created fact sheets of information gleaned from operations and presented them to MACV J-2. MACV, in turn, provided the information to the senior military negotiator in Paris. The year 1968 was one of scrutiny and questioning for MACSOG, both from within and without. This is reflected in the Plans Division by a staff follow-up to the JCS/CINCPAC Joint Survey Team Report of January.

Communications

In November, Hill 950, a Marine Corps observation post abandoned after the siege of Khe Sanh, was occupied by MACSOG as radio relay site Hickory. This served as a useful communications adjunct to the Golf-5 and Sledgehammer sites occupied in 1967. During the next four years, SOG would continue to expand the number of its radio relay sites. For teams operating out of CCN, Hickory would be joined by another site located at Fire Support Base "Berchtesgaden," located in the Ashau Valley. CCC support continued from Golf-5 and Sledgehammer and was later joined by Klondike (in Kontum Province). CCS operations were aided by a site known as "the Hill" at Nui Ba Ra, located in the III Corps Tactical Zone northeast of Tay Ninh.

Comment: Airborne Operations

The CIA had never really been interested in covert operations in North Vietnam. Previous attempts at such operations in "denied area" countries (Eastern Europe, the Soviet Union, North Korea, and the PRC) had always ended in disaster. North Vietnam was considered by the agency to be an even tougher nut to crack. There were several reasons for this attitude: There was no embryonic or developed resistance movement within the North, and—even after a disastrous land reform campaign in the 1950s—there was still popular support for the Hanoi regime; control over personal movement was closely guarded and there was no outward flow of disgruntled refugees or minorities for recruitment purposes; and last, but not least, the Saigon regime offered little in the way of an alternative.[60]

CIA agent operations in the North also suffered from constant mission changes. In 1961 their main purpose had been intelligence collection; in 1962 this was altered to sabotage and harassment operations; finally, in 1963, it was again changed to psychological warfare missions. Another aspect of the agency's mission failure was that the CIA neither recruited nor vetted its own agents. This was always handled by the South Vietnamese, which prompted questions over security.

The agents inserted into North Vietnam were spread out all over the country, always in remote areas from which they did not maneuver. They did not concentrate or cooperate with one another, all were resupplied only by air, and they were forbidden (most of the time) to make contact with the local population. Perhaps the most dangerous aspect of the operation was that the agents were provided little in the way of false documentation or identification and had no background cover whatsoever. Ironically MACSOG Airborne Operations would go through the same three phases of mission change. Pressure from Washington to speed up the quantity of operatives and demands for different mission results played a large part in this. So, MACSOG simply followed the CIA formula, at a higher rate of speed.

As for the long-sought-after creation of a resistance movement within North Vietnam, just what was it supposed to accomplish? Was its goal to be the toppling of the northern regime? If the agents could theoretically build a resistance movement that truly threatened Hanoi, what then? While serving as President Kennedy's special assistant, Edward Lansdale had wanted to create just such a resistance movement in the North. It was supposed to "create a situation akin to Hungary."[61] Akin to Hungary? The painful memory of the disastrous Hungarian revolt against Soviet domination and its bloody repression (about which the United States could do nothing) was a poor example for emulation.

Contributing in no small way to the failure of the agent operation was the North Vietnamese reaction to it and the superb counterintelligence work of its security apparatus. One of the key problem areas of the program, over which SOG had no control, was the lack of instantaneous communication between headquarters and the teams. This allowed a time lapse to occur between insertion and first communication. This lapse provided a window of opportunity that the communists took full advantage of to capture and turn the teams back on their masters. By the end of Operation Timberwork, the communists were actually calling the shots, having captured radio operators' request reinforcement, capturing those men on the LZs, and then turning more radio operators. It was absolutely brilliant.

There has been much post mortem debate as to the root cause of the failure of agent operations. Although almost every American officer cognizant of the program believed that it had been infiltrated by communist agents, it was not until 1967 that any steps were taken to alter the program in response to those suspicions. In three years of operations, little about the program was changed except mission profiles and the scale of the operation. Whether or not MACSOG, the STD (or its predecessors), or both were infiltrated by agents was irrelevant, since the North Vietnamese had already been provided with too much time and operational experience in countering it. MACSOG had been encumbered with a program that it neither initiated nor over which it exhibited much control and its cardinal sin was that it did not make necessary changes over time that would have made the program more viable.

As seemed rather common among Americans during the Vietnam War, SOG made the mistake of underestimating its enemy. The North Vietnamese already had plenty of experience in running down groups of military and intelligence operatives in the same geographical areas in which the MACSOG teams performed their missions. French GCMA (Groupment de Commandos Mixtes Aeroportes [Composite Airborne Commando Group]) commandos, which conducted operations behind Viet Minh lines during the First Indochina War, were at least more successful in their operations, that is, until they were abandoned by their government and wiped out. If those experiences were not enough, Hanoi could also fall back on the expertise of their Soviet and Chinese patrons for information on how similar U.S. operations were defeated in those nations' spheres of influence.

The simple fact that in five years of operations (including the CIA's) the teams had never provided viable intelligence or operational aptitude should have warned MACSOG that the program was flawed. Yet, according to the records, it was only with the tenure of Colonel Singlaub that questions began to arise over operational security. How could a program that had lasted so long produce so little in the way of results and not arouse suspicion? And when those suspicions came to the fore, it was not operational ineptitude or the enemy's competency that was discussed, but internal security at the other end of the pipeline.

Whatever the long-term historical outcome of the "internal spies" versus "operational ineptitude" debate (which will not be settled until the opening of the Vietnamese archives), there is little doubt that the North Vietnamese security apparatus played the game with a talent rarely matched by any former enemy of the United States. It surely equaled in deception and skill the activities of the two most successful counterintelligence operations of former years, Feliks Dzerzhinski's "Trust" and the Cambridge spies.

Chapter Six

1969: COMMANDO HUNT

Headquarters

During the year, Colonel Cavanaugh remained at the helm as chief, MACSOG. He was only the second commanding officer of the organization to avoid MACV's one-year rotation policy. The year also saw the close and continued scrutiny of the organization by the Joint Chiefs. In October 1968 SACSA had ordered that a thoroughly documented study of MACSOG's history be prepared for use in future operations. From 16 to 27 July the MACSOG Documentation Team of the Office of the Joint Chiefs of Staff arrived in Saigon and proceeded to reproduce thousands of pages of documents for transfer to Washington for use in completion of the project. MACSOG also received a three-day visit from then SACSA, Army major general John Freund.

William Sullivan, nemesis of MACV and MACSOG, who had served since November 1964 as ambassador to the Kingdom of Laos, was replaced in March by G. McMurtrie "Mac" Godley, who would serve until 1973. Sullivan continued his illustrious career by moving on to become ambassador to the Philippines when that country was still under the rule of Ferdinand Marcos. He then became ambassador to Iran just as the Ayatollah Khomeini's revolution was rocking that nation. After the shah had left the country, but before the Islamic fundamentalists had seized the U.S. Embassy, Sullivan was asked by a reporter, "When the histories are written, the question is going to be asked: 'Who lost Iran?' Aren't you going to be a principal candidate?" His answer was a terse "I've lost a hell of a lot better countries than this one."[1]

Regardless of the changeover, things remained pretty much the same in Laos (with the exception of the escalating conflict). Godley still depended on the CIA for intelligence assessments and ran their covert effort. He also continued to maintain tight control over the bombing campaigns while keeping MACV and MACSOG at bay. As author George Veith has pointed out, the impact of men like Sullivan and Godley could be seen in their legacy: "a fragmented and overtly political approach to the war that helped to hasten the defeat of the United States."[2]

MANPOWER SHORTAGES
As has already been described in previous years, personnel shortages affected both the 5th SFG and MACSOG. These shortages, and the necessity to fill them, led to reductions in the qualifications for men who now donned the Green Beret. In August 1967 the Army had gone so far as to request that the 5th SFG substitute non–Special Forces qualified personnel wherever possible. The demand for more men, recruiting shortfalls, and a declining retention rate were the main causes of the changes.

By 1968, 80 percent of Special Forces qualified personnel worldwide had already served in Vietnam, but only 30 percent of all Special Forces enlisted men reporting to Nha Trang were volunteers for Vietnam duty. The 5th then allowed grade substitutions of up to three levels and the direct recruitment of non–Special Forces arrivals.[3] These measures had been intended as a stopgap measure, but they continued. Another of the reasons for the personnel shortages was the requirement of the 5th SFG to maintain special operational units (like MACSOG) at 100 percent strength, a directive that was reconfirmed by the Pentagon on 27 and 31 December 1967. By early 1969 only 10 percent of replacements reporting at Nha Trang had battlefield experience and almost 25 percent were not Special Forces qualified.[4]

Intelligence
During the year intelligence continued to pour into the division from the Ground Studies Group. The Prairie Fire program alone generated 766 intelligence reports while the total for Salem House was 607.[5] Task Force Alpha at Nakhon Phanom began producing ten-kilometer readouts from its extensive database of approved targets. The maps contained terrain features, landing zones, communist activities, and so forth. Copies of these readouts were also distributed to the C&C detachments.

Never lacking in initiative, MACSOG intelligence organized Project Ford Drum, a program of hand-held photographic reconnaissance carried out from low-flying FAC aircraft over Cambodia. The program was inaugurated in July, but it would not be formalized until 21 October 1970. The program collected intelligence in the Salem House area for MACSOG, MACV J-2, III Corps, and 7th/13th Air Force.

ORGANIZATIONAL STRUCTURE, DECEMBER 1969

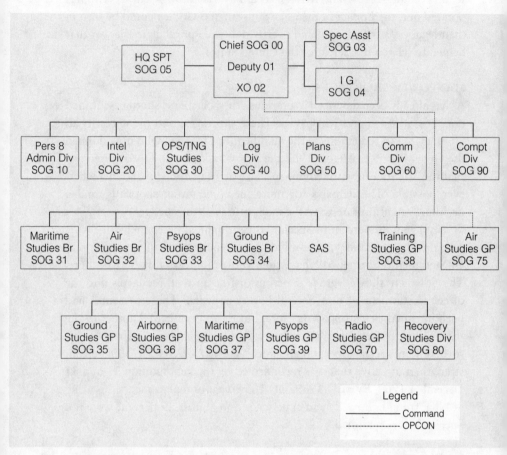

Operations and Training

AIR STUDIES BRANCH (OP-32)

The Air Operations cover name Midriff was compromised during the year and replaced in December by Shedder.

GROUND STUDIES BRANCH (OP-34)

Due to exposure of the nickname in a *Newsweek* article during the spring, Operation Daniel Boone was redesignated Salem House. In December 1968 the Ground Studies Branch had become the staff element responsible for the supervision of its three subordinate commands: the Airborne Studies Group (Op-34), the Ground Studies Group (Op-35), and the Training Studies Group (Op-36). Timberwork agent operations and Italian Green, the contaminated munitions program formerly known as Eldest Son (and which was redesignated Pole Bean in February) were placed under the control of the Special Studies Section of the Ground Studies Branch. This section was also responsible for Forae diversionary programs, STRATA, and, as of February, the new Earth Angel program. The new Training Studies Group was divided into two sections. The Field Studies Section conducted training for Prairie Fire and Salem House, while the Training Studies Section conducted training for all other programs.

MARITIME OPERATIONS: PLOWMAN (OP-37)

For the first time MACSOG's annual Command History did not contain a separate Maritime Studies Group appendix, lumping it instead into the Operations and Training Division's section concerning its staff element, the Maritime Studies Branch (Op-31). This might have been a reflection of how far down on the totem pole MAROPS had fallen. Operation Plowman was redesignated Parboil during the year. Although no operations were authorized north of the 17th parallel, the Joint Chiefs required that the NAD retain the capability of reinitiating the program of northern operations at any time. As a result, PTFs and cross-beach action teams were only utilized for southern operations.

The NAD fielded seven Nasty PTFs and four Ospreys in 1969. The three Swift PCFs in the inventory had by then been relegated to harbor defense and logistical support. Unfortunately the Ospreys were not working out. The vessels rode higher than the Nastys and tended to slam down in heavy seas, weakening the welding and sometimes cracking hulls. All four of the boats had to be replaced during the year by wooden-hulled copies of the Nasty, built under license by John Trumpy and Sons of Annapolis, Maryland. These vessels had formerly been held at Subic Bay as replacements. This left seven operational PTFs available at the end of the year.

In June, Operation Bifrost was redesignated Operation Dodge Mark at the request of CINCPAC. These cross-beach operations, conducted to maintain operational readiness for resumption of Parboil, were run in the I and II Corps Tactical Zones at the request of the Field Force commanders. During late 1968 (due the onset of the northeast monsoon) two action teams had been dispatched to an FOB at Phan Thiet in II Corps to conduct Dewey Rifle operations there. These missions continued into February 1969. In February and April, two teams went to work for Naval Forces, Vietnam along the Cambodian/South Vietnamese border to conduct Tran Hung Dao operations. In October two action teams, two PTFs, and a PCF were dispatched to an FOB at Cam Ranh Bay to conduct Dewey Rifle II missions in II Corps. At the end of December, these teams and PTFs were dispatched to the Market Time base at Qui Nhon to conduct Dewey Rifle II operations from there.

The CSS began the phaseout of its ARVN and civilian personnel during the year. This move to make the organization an all-Vietnamese navy operation was going to take some time, however, since the components to be eliminated made up over 40 percent of CSS' manpower. A target date of 1 July 1971 was set for completion of the reorganization.

Ground Studies Group (Op-35)

The rain of bombs on eastern and southeastern Laos peaked in 1969 when more than 433,000 tons fell on the country.[6] This deluge had been made possible by the end of Operation Rolling Thunder and the commencement of Operation Commando Hunt in November 1968. U.S. aircraft were now freed for interdiction missions and as many as five hundred aircraft per day were flying the crowded skies over Laos. Before the end of the conflict, U.S. and South Vietnamese aviation units would drop over three million tons of bombs on Laos, three times the tonnage that had been directed against North Vietnam.[7]

Operation Commando Hunt II began in mid-May and lasted through September. Hard on its heels came Commando Hunt III, running from 1 November until 30 April 1970. Among 7th/13th Air Force claims were that 6,428 vehicles were destroyed and that another 3,604 had been damaged.[8] During the year the Air Force estimated that PAVN started 66,196 tons of supplies down the Trail from North Vietnam, that it lost 31,954 tons to air attack, and that it consumed another 15,266 tons. That left only 28.6 percent of the cargo reaching the other end of the logistical network in South Vietnam.[9] The Defense Intelligence Agency and CIA took a more realistic approach in estimating the effect of the bombing by discounting 75 percent of pilot claims for truck destruction, to derive a more accurate figure. Their computer model, however, reached zero—where the North Vietnamese were supposed to be out of trucks—no fewer than fourteen times.[10] It seemed as if Secretary McNamara's penchant for computer models, game theory, and bean counting was moving south from the Pentagon to Langley.

But was the campaign having the desired effect upon the logistical system? The terrain, weather, and triple-canopy jungle made any correct estimation of communist losses impossible, yet claims for the destructive capability of the campaign continued to reach new heights. At the rate of truck attrition on the Trail claimed for December 1968, for example, the PAVN supply network should have been eliminated in only a month and a half.[11] Yet Commando Hunt operations had been four times that long (and claimed a 50 percent increase in effectiveness), but had no observable effect on communist operations.

Evaluation of the Igloo White–supported campaign was difficult, even for those assigned to carry out the missions. The Air Force was also quick to state that electronic monitoring merely confirmed what it already knew and that Igloo White served merely as a corollary to the work of FACs and photo interpreters. One sign of the increasing centralization of the system was the absorption of the Tiger Hound bombing program by Task Force Alpha during the summer.

THE TRAIL

On the other side of the fence, the official North Vietnamese history claimed that 3,000 trucks moved 70,000 tons of supplies with a net loss rate of 13.5 percent. During the same time frame, approximately 80,000 troops made the move south.[12] During the year the North Vietnamese logistical apparatus in southeastern Laos had become complex and efficient. Binh Tram 1 was located in the area of the strategic Mu Gia Pass, the main conduit from North Vietnam into Laos. It was maintained and defended by two transportation battalions, the 25th Engineer Battalion and a rifle battalion. In keeping with its necessity as a logistics hub, the pass was defended by somewhere between ninety and three hundred antiaircraft artillery sites.

Binh Tram 32, located at Tchepone, consisted of two transportation battalions. A few miles to the east at the village of Ban Dong, PAVN's easternmost outpost on Route 9 supported another transportation battalion, three security battalions, and two engineer units. The engineers maintained the Trail and were intent on pushing it forward into the DMZ and Khe Sanh areas. It was also the only *binh tram* in the 559th Group to have its own signal battalion. The Tchepone/Ban Dong complex was known to MACV as Base Area 604. It was defended by fourteen antiaircraft positions, while troop strength was estimated at six security battalions plus two regiments of PAVN regulars. Behind Co Roc Ridge and feeding the Ashau Valley were Base Areas 611 and 607, another logistical complex worked by two *binh trams*. Between them they controlled a transport battalion, two engineer battalions, two security battalions, and a regular infantry battalion.

In the tri-border region and opposite the Central Highlands was Binh Tram 37 (Base Areas 609 and 613) with one battalion each of engineers, transportation specialists, security troops, and regular infantry. To cover Cambodia and the NLF, the 559th (and later the 470th) Transportation Group had its own *binh trams*, way stations, and support troops.

From north to south along the Cambodian frontier were Base Areas 702 (northwest of Pleiku), 701 (southwest of Pleiku), 740 (southwest of Kontum), and 350, 352, and 353 (in and near the Fishhook region). MACV intelligence estimated that 43,000 PAVN troops and impressed Laotian civilians were engaged in operating, improving, and expanding the road net and its satellite installations.[13] The emergency situation in Military Region 4 having ended, PAVN Headquarters 500 was placed under the command of the 559th Group.

Beginning in 1966 and 1967 PAVN had begun utilizing the Kong River to transport materiel by floating it downstream in partially submerged 50-gallon steel drums and watertight bags. The supplies were gathered at launch sites behind dams at intersecting streams and then launched into the current by breaching the dam. PAVN engineers utilized several methods to direct the current and maintain deep channels, while the floating supplies (which could travel ten miles every twenty-four hours) were captured downstream by systems of jettys, booms, and nets.[14] Flowing from the South Vietnamese border, the Kong River traveled south past Ban Bak and into Cambodia. Near Ban Bak supplies could be extracted from the river and moved to roads and trails that led east to the Ashau Valley. During 1969 the North Vietnamese added the Kaman River to the system and began to improve their operations on the Banghiang River (known as Waterway VII to PAVN). The river ran past the supply centers at Muong Phine and Tchepone and became an important and integral part of the Trail complex. By mid-1971 these riverine operations were running so smoothly that PAVN supply officers could requisition specific items and amounts and have them delivered to a particular destination.[15]

A shocking development uncovered by U.S. intelligence analysts late in the year was the discovery of a petroleum, oil, and lubricants (POL) pipeline running southwest from the North Vietnamese port of Vinh. By early 1969 the pipeline had crossed the Laotian frontier and by summer it had reached Muong Nong and the approaches to the Ashau Valley. In September recon aircraft also photographed a POL area at Ban Na, twenty-two miles northwest of Tchepone.[16] The plastic pipeline, assisted by numerous small pumping stations, managed to transfer diesel fuel, gasoline, and kerosene all in the same pipe. Thanks to the efforts of the PAVN 592nd Pipelaying Regiment, the number of pipelines entering Laos was going to increase to six by 1970.

COUNTERRECONNAISSANCE

During the early days of cross-border operations, MACSOG recon teams faced no specialist PAVN forces during their forays into what was known as Indian Country. After a team was compromised, the communists threw together whatever scratch forces they could rapidly organize against the teams. PAVN troops were also assisted by Laotian trackers pressed into service, who hunted for the teams, but whom recon man John Plaster derided as "demonstrating such poor tactical sense that it seemed almost unsporting to ambush them."[17]

Often the communists utilized the "driving method": sending groups of men out beating bamboo together or against their weapons to create noise in an effort to either drive the teams into ambushes or simply to drive them off. By late 1966 PAVN had begun deploying radio-equipped teams to the Laotian frontier along the flight paths taken by insertion helicopters from the launch sites. Whenever missions flew out over the border, these teams contacted higher headquarters to provide warning.

As operations continued the North Vietnamese became more aware of the geographic and operational limitations of SOG missions, and these improvised tactics began to be organized into a system. One- or two-man LZ watching teams were deployed on or near the most promising LZs in the area, or they manned platforms in trees to watch a general area. Any sight or sound of an approaching helicopter brought immediate reaction. A series of predetermined signals (rifle shots, metallic gongs, or landline communications) forewarned communist troops in the area that a team had landed, been sighted, or was on the way. Patrols were then beefed up along trails and roads, and the communists began to sweep the jungle beside their lines of communication, searching for the team. They also posted trailwatchers, and, just before sundown, guards were posted for the night at 100- to 300-yard intervals along the roads.

In 1967 the North Vietnamese began to layer their defenses, deploying rear security units whose only function was to patrol the Trail for MACSOG forces and to react to them. A key response was the creation of specialized forces for a counterreconnaissance mission. Elements of the PAVN 305th Airborne Brigade were converted into "hunter-killer" forces that usually operated as one-hundred-man companies assigned to the *binh trams*. After the general area of a recon team was established, the counterrecon force split into platoons, which then swept toward the location of the team. When the exact position was fixed, the platoons contacted one another by radio and closed in for action.

During the year, the communists also began to deploy tracker dogs against recon teams. They were not bloodhounds, but normal Asian dogs trained to follow a scent. Although they didn't look like much, the dogs were effective and recon teams began to take their own countermeasures against them. One of these was the spreading of CS tear gas crystals along the back trail, hoping that the dog would get a noseful of the powder and destroy its ability to follow scent. The method of last resort was simply to kill the dog and its handler, but this tended to fix a team's location for other communist forces.

PAVN's search for responses to the incursions of MACSOG recon teams had reached fruition by 1969. By that time the North Vietnamese had developed a layered system that no longer merely acted defensively. The force of LZ and trail watchers had been greatly expanded, so much so that almost every usable LZ in southeastern Laos was covered. After spotting a helicopter or observing an insertion, the watchers immediately called in teams of trackers. These were no longer impressed Laotians, but specially trained PAVN regulars. Local commanders also immediately dispatched as many men as possible to patrol roads and trails.

After notification, the nearest *binh tram* commander would also order in a counterrecon company, usually accompanied by dog teams. The company split into platoons and then began to sweep for the team. Whatever local forces were available acted as blocking units or served as beaters to drive the team toward the counterrecon units. The communists were also known to set fire to elephant grass or underbrush in order to either fix a team in position or to drive it toward an ambush.

Knowledge of the local area provided PAVN forces with an edge. Troops could be sped along trails and roads faster than the teams could travel through the bush. For example, the communists could rush to pre-position anti-aircraft machine guns at the suspected location of any extraction. The North Vietnamese also began to deploy radio direction-finding equipment and specialists to the team areas. As incentive for the killing of the members of a recon team, bounties and financial rewards were offered. This resulted in a vicious, no-holds-barred, give-no-quarter form of warfare. It also resulted in higher casualties for MACSOG and it became ominously less rare for an entire team to be wiped out on a mission.

PRAIRIE FIRE

MACSOG had long complained that its launch sites (from whence recon teams were launched and which were always located near the border areas) had become "rusty." Communist observers could locate themselves along the familiar flight paths leading to the border and serve as an early warning system. It was hoped that by establishing new sites, this predicament could be alleviated. As a result, the mobile launch site concept was introduced in January (quickly renamed Mobile Launch Teams [MLTs], since it became obvious that teams were mobile and sites were not). Each of the new MLTs was to be supported by a forward radio relay site. Patrol bases served the same purpose as the MLTs. A larger unit, either conventional or belonging to MACSOG, operating near the border, was used as cover for the launching of recon teams on foot into communist-controlled territory. There was also a concerted effort during the year by the group to train and field all-Vietnamese reconnaissance teams. The total number of recon missions for the year was 404, while 48 exploitation force operations were launched. The missions were supported by 1,106 tactical air and 689 helicopter gunship sorties. Intelligence reports of various enemy activities numbered 748, generated as a result of these efforts.[18]

Located at Da Nang, Command and Control North (CCN) was commanded by a lieutenant colonel and consisted of a headquarters element and an exploitation battalion of three Hatchet companies (Company A: Cambodians, B: Bru Montagnards, C: Vietnamese) of three Hornet platoons (six U.S./42 SCU) each. The detachment was defended by a security company and possessed a reconnaissance company of thirty recon teams (three U.S./nine SCU). The new mobile launch sites were located at Quang Tri (MLT-1), Phu Bai (MLT-2), and the SUPPFAC at Nakhon Phanom (MLT-3). Some operations were also launched from the old Mai Loc Launch Site. Missions launched from CCN were supported by the Golf-5 radio relay site and a new facility, Hickory, located on Hill 950 about four kilometers north of the abandoned Marine combat base Khe Sanh. The site was occupied in November and, like Golf-5, also served as a NSA radio monitoring station. This site remained operational until it was overrun by North Vietnamese forces in 1971.

To reflect expanded missions and to standardize operational elements during year, Command and Control Central (CCC) was established at Kontum. Under the command of a lieutenant colonel, it had responsibility for operations in the southern Prairie Fire area (from the Ashau Valley south to the Cambodian border). Teams also launched Daniel Boone operations into the Zone Alpha portion of northern Cambodia. CCC maintained a headquarters, an exploitation battalion of four Hatchet companies divided into three Hornet platoons each, a security company, and a reconnaissance company of thirty teams (three U.S./nine SCUs each). Launch sites for team missions were located at Dak Pek and Dak To. In January authority was granted for utilization of Ubon RTAFB as a launch site (the Duck Hook facility) for operations in the southern portion of the Prairie Fire area and northern Cambodia when weather precluded launches from South Vietnam.[19]

CCS missions launched into the tri-border region were supported by the Sledgehammer radio relay site until it was closed in March. Sledgehammer's personnel and assets were then transferred to a new facility, Klondike, located nine miles south-southeast of Kontum on Hill 1152. The growing number of operations required still more manpower to fulfill them. The absorption of Omega and Sigma were still not enough of an addition to the manpower pool. As a result the 1st SFG on Okinawa continued to provide "Snakebite" teams on a six-month TDY basis to provide additional bodies for SOG's exploitation forces. During 1969 American casualties in the Prairie Fire area included 20 killed in action, 199 wounded, and 9 missing. Casualties among indigenous troops amounted to 57 killed, 270 wounded, and 31 missing.[20]

OPERATION SPINDOWN

During the year the North Vietnamese continued their efforts to close down the Special Forces border camps in an effort to push their logistical network further into South Vietnam. As part of this effort PAVN prepared to launch sieges against Bu Prang and Duc Lap in III Corps and to eliminate the camp at Ben Het, only three miles from the Laotian border in the Central Highlands. Arrayed against the camp were the 28th and 66th PAVN infantry regiments, several artillery battalions, and a company of PT-76 tanks.

Opposing this onslaught were about a dozen Green Berets, 1,500 Montagnards, a company of Montagnards from the Mike Forces, four tanks, and an artillery battery of 8-inch howitzers and 175-mm guns. The only road to the outpost had been cut when, on the evening of 3 March, the North Vietnamese launched their attack. Since March was the height of the dry season, PAVN would have little trouble moving up more men and supplies to keep the pressure on Ben Het. Or so they thought.

On the morning of 4 March an aerial armada swooped across the border and deposited a MACSOG exploitation force on a hilltop overlooking Highway 110, directly astride the communist's supply route into the Ben Het area.[21] Hatchet Force Company A from Kontum, under the command of Cpt. Robert Evans, had been sent in to stick a cork into a logistical bottle in Operation Spindown. The company quickly dug into the hilltop with the expectation that North Vietnamese would not be long in reacting to their presence. They were not disappointed. That afternoon, a mortar attack signaled the beginning of the communists' attempts to dislodge them.

That night a PAVN convoy tried to sneak trucks past the Hatchet Force position, but infrared starlight scopes revealed their location and

AC-119 and AC-130 gunships made them pay. On the afternoon of the second day tragedy struck when an F-4 Phantom accidentally dropped a napalm canister on the Hatchet Force position, killing six Montagnards. That night the communists again tried to sneak a convoy past the position and took a pounding for their trouble.

This action continued for six days, closing the most important Laotian highway during the peak of the dry season and squeezing the logistics of the attack on Ben Het. The bottleneck created by the Hatchet Force also stacked up the logistical stream and allowed American tactical air support to have a field day. Secondary explosions rocked the area and the smoke from burning diesel fuel poured from the jungle. Operation Spindown was considered a complete success. The six Montagnards killed by friendly fire were the only fatalities among the force while twenty other indigenous troops and four Americans were wounded. Ben Het survived its ordeal, thanks to the guns of the Hatchet Force and the bombs of the 7th/13th Air Force.

As was common during the Vietnam War, success bred official sanctions. MACSOG battalion-size exploitation forces (officially sanctioned but never authorized for usage) were then forbidden. Company-size units were restricted by the Joint Chiefs to no more than three platoons each for the Prairie Fire area. Needless to say, some very large platoons began operating in Laos.

During 1969 I Corps launched several large border-clearing operations adjacent to and in the Prairie Fire area of operations. In late January the 4th Marine Regiment conducted clearing operations in the Khe Sanh region while the 9th Marines began Operation Dewey Canyon in the Da Krong and Ashau Valleys. After initial moves across the border by elements of the 9th Marines on 21 February, General Abrams gave approval for further cross-border operations. The logistical haul seized from the North Vietnamese was impressive. Over 525 tons of weapons and ammunition were captured, along with 12 122-mm artillery pieces.[22] These operations ended on 18 March.

To support Dewey Canyon and to check out the lower end of the Ashau Valley, the Army's 101st Airborne Division (Airmobile) moved in on 1 March during Operation Massachusetts Striker. Inclement weather and communist opposition slowed the arrival of the division's elements, so a MACSOG Hornet Company from CCN was lifted in to assist the operation on the 7th. When they too became bogged down by North Vietnamese opposition, a scratch unit was formed to assist them. Task Force Meadows (led by MACSOG legend Lt. Dick Meadows) was lifted into the Laotian border area to relieve the pressure. In the meantime, the

Hornet Company had been extracted, so Meadows and his men headed on foot for U.S. Marine positions in the upper valley for resupply. It was a hard and hungry slog, but they managed to get extracted on 15 March.

PINBALL WIZARDS

By 1969 Operation Igloo White was in full swing. Its 20,000-square-foot operations center (Task Force Alpha) at Nakhon Phanom had been supplemented by a communications facility of 5,000 square feet. The men assigned to Task Force Alpha concentrated upon such arcane topics as pathway prediction, delay intervals, route segments, and choke points. Communist movements on the Trail system would trip a series of hand-emplaced or air-dropped sensors. The sensor system, ever shifting to match North Vietnamese changes in their road and trail network, fed the information to an ABCCC which then relayed the information to Task Force Alpha.

The computers collated the cumulative data and then made predictions as to where and when a particular convoy would be geographically located at a specific time. This information was fed to the ABCCC, which then relayed it to orbiting strike aircraft. According to John Prados, author of the only Western history of the Trail system, Igloo White functioned "exactly like a pinball machine . . . in truth the mavens of the electronic battlefield became pinball wizards."[23]

By late 1967 the Second World War–vintage AC-47 "Spooky" gunships that patrolled the Trail at night had become too vulnerable to communist anti-aircraft fire and had to be replaced. From September through November of that year the Air Force tested some converted AC-130As for a possible night gunship role. The Spectre, as the plane was nicknamed, was armed with four 7.62-mm machine guns and four 20-mm cannon. There was, however, reluctance on the part of the Air Force to convert the new transports and this led to the conversion of other aircraft to supplement the gunship mission.

The AC-119G Shadow and AC-119K Stinger were converted and modified versions of the venerable Fairchild C-119 Flying Boxcar transport aircraft. After initial trials, they made their appearance over the Trail in late 1969 and early 1970, respectively. During the same time period the Air Force equipped the AC-130A with a "Surprise Package" that included a low-light level television (LLLT) system, several infrared detectors, "Black Crow" truck ignition detectors, and a computerized fire control system. The aircraft was then rechristened the AC-130E Pave Spectre and was armed with four 7.62-mm machine guns, two 20-mm and two 40-mm Bofors cannon. The last modification to the C-130 was

Pave Aegis, which sported radar-jamming equipment and replaced one of the 40-mm guns with a 105-mm howitzer. This model arrived in-theater in early 1972.

BDA

One of the missions that MACSOG team members grew to despise and even fear was that of Bomb Damage Assessment (BDA). The powers that be always seemed to want to investigate the effect of airstrikes in communist-controlled areas, especially the results of B-52 strikes. The lessons of Oscar-8 never seemed to sink in. Although the damage inflicted by a cell of B-52s could be visually impressive from the air, they could also be deceiving. Teams launched into the bombed areas sometimes found little evidence of destruction, but on other occasions they were greeted by scenes of total devastation, that is, if they could see anything at all. The effect of the strike was usually to create a chain of craters surrounded by trees blown down upon one another like a giant abatis. The only way to maneuver through was to move from crater to crater, which limited both movement and visibility. If communist troops had been caught in the open by the strike, the sight of their remains could be unnerving. Pieces of human flesh, body parts, and blood would be scattered through the trees and landscape in a grotesque manner. If the communists were in any way prepared and within their bunkers, however, the results for the team could be disaster.

On 18 March CCC launched a BDA for Operation Breakfast, the first Operation Menu B-52 strike in Cambodia.[24] The team consisted of team leader Cpt. Bill Orthman, radio operator Barry Murphy, and eleven SCUs. The target, across the border from Tay Ninh Province, was the suspected location of Central Office for South Vietnam (COSVN), the highly elusive command center for communist forces in the southern half of South Vietnam. After B-52 crewmen had observed seventy-three secondary explosions on the ground the recon team moved in within minutes of the end of the strike. As the team ran from the helicopters toward a tree line, they came under intense attack as North Vietnamese troops seemed to boil out of the ground like angry ants. Captain Orthman was shot twice in the stomach while the rest of the team was annihilated before it could reach bomb craters in which to seek shelter. After calling for an immediate extraction, two of the SCUs scrambled onto a helicopter while one of the helicopters' crewmen dragged Orthman aboard. Murphy and the nine other team members were left on the LZ.

That did not mean that the mission was over. Cpt. Randolph Harrison, Orthman's superior at Ban Me Thuot, was ordered to try again. When Harrison and his team leaders discussed the proposed operation into the

same LZ as Orthman's team, they refused to comply. Three men were
arrested for failure to obey orders, but no formal charges were brought
against them since the unavoidable publicity would have shed too much
light on the clandestine operation and the bombing campaign.[25]

SALEM HOUSE
Command and Control South (CCS) had been established during late
1968 and was located at Ban Me Thuot. It consisted of a headquarters,
four reaction companies of three platoons each, a security company, and
a reconnaissance company of thirty recon teams (two U.S./four SCUs
each). During the year CCS opened two Mobile Launch Sites: MLS
North (MLSN) at Duc Lap and MLS South (MLSS) at Quan Loi. It also
launched missions from Bu Prang, Loc Ninh, Song Be, Bu Dop, Tay Ninh,
Ban Don, and Gia Ngia.

The operational areas of Salem House had been altered in 1968 and
were revised again in 1969. In Zone Alpha, which extended from the
tri-border area south to the Fishhook region, the operational depth was
increased from twenty to thirty kilometers. Zone Bravo, extending from
the Fishhook to the town of Snoul, retained its twenty-kilometer depth
of penetration. Zone Charlie also retained the twenty-kilometer limit
and (due to the population density of the area) every mission had to be
cleared with the Joint Chiefs.

There were 454 recon missions launched into Cambodia during the
year. They were supported by 398 tactical air sorties and 454 helicopter
gunship sorties.[26] In addition, 4 communist troops were taken prisoner
and 607 intelligence reports were generated. Exploitation forces were
still not authorized for the Salem House area, so its companies and platoons (made up of Montagnards) worked in-country and secured launch
sites and patrol bases for cross-border teams.

DOUG MILLER
While searching for communist activity in Base Area 609 in Ratanakiri
Province, Cambodia, CCC's Spike Team Vermont tripped a booby-trap,
seriously wounding four of the team members. The team leader, SSgt.
Franklin "Doug" Miller, applied what first aid he could in the short time
he knew he had available. The communists had surely been alerted to
their presence, so Miller told his second in command to move the wounded to a nearby defensible hilltop while he stayed in position to cover
them. A PAVN platoon soon arrived and Miller held his ground, driving
back several assaults. Each time the North Vietnamese retreated, Miller
would fall back to another position and repeat the process.

After rejoining his comrades, he moved the team 175 yards to the only available LZ, a bomb crater in which the team formed a perimeter. A Huey came in for the extraction, but it was quickly driven off by intense ground fire. The communists then launched a concerted effort to overrun the position. By then all of the team members, including Miller, had been wounded. It was then that Miller single-handedly went on the attack, twice driving back the North Vietnamese. A Bright Light team then landed and evacuated the wounded men. For his courage, leadership, and fortitude, Sgt. Doug Miller was awarded the Medal of Honor.[27] Remarkably, after receiving the big medal, Miller did not return to the United States. He remained with MACSOG and continued to run missions. He finally came home in November 1972 after an amazing five and one-half years in Southeast Asia.[28]

THE COSVN RAID

On the morning of 24 April a one-hundred-man MACSOG raiding force set out for Cambodia following a B-52 strike on that most elusive of targets, COSVN. Authority to attack this headquarters, which supposedly controlled the communist's entire war effort in Cochin, China, had been sought by Free World Military Forces for years. It was probably no more than a group of radios and officers that served as a mobile communications hub, constantly on the move to avoid air strikes, but it was considered to be one of the most lucrative targets of the allied forces. Radio intercepts and a PAVN deserter had pinpointed its location as being about fourteen miles southeast of Memot, in the Fishhook region of Cambodia.

The Hatchet Force, under the command of Cpt. Bill O'Rourke, launched from Quan Loi, but problems plagued the operation from the beginning.[29] Only three HH-3 Green Hornet helicopters were available that morning, so only two of the three platoons could be transported in the first lift. Making matters worse, the lead ship, carrying O'Rourke, had to turn back due to mechanical difficulties. Command then passed to an operations officer who had come along for the ride, Cpt. Paul Cahill.

As soon as the airstrike was over, the platoon landed, only to be met by a hail of communist fire. The men immediately rolled into bomb craters or got behind whatever cover they could find. Cahill was badly wounded and command devolved to 1st Lt. Greg Harrigan, who called in support from helicopter gunships until he was killed. Also killed in the first minutes was Sgt. Ernest Jamison, shot down as he attempted to aid a wounded comrade.

MACSOG's greatest loss that day was Sgt. Jerry Shriver. He had arrived in-country in late 1966 and was assigned to Project Omega at

Kontum. When that project was absorbed by MACSOG he moved to
FOB-5 at Ban Me Thuot. During his three back-to-back tours, he had
been nicknamed "the Mad Dog." Shriver was a soldier's soldier who had
seemingly gone native. He lived not in the barracks with the other Americans, but with his Montagnard teammates. He ate their food, spoke their
language, and observed their customs. He was also constantly in action.
He took no recreational leaves and when his team went on stand-down
after a mission, Shriver would join another team and head back out
again. As author John Plaster related, Mad Dog Shriver had also spoken
the most famous rejoinder in SOG history. His team surrounded and facing the possibility of being overrun, he informed a worried FAC, "No,
no. I've got 'em right where I want 'em—*surrounded from the inside.*"[30]
He was renowned throughout Op-35 for his abilities—he was "good in
the woods."

Shriver and several of his Yards had been pinned down behind a log
by several machine guns early in the action, but he was not one to remain in a safe position. Seeing the predicament of his fellows, Mad Dog
Shriver and his men, who followed him without hesitation, leapt up and
advanced into enemy fire and into legend. They were never seen again.
After two hours of desperate fighting, three Hueys managed to land and
pick up fifteen of the wounded.

Even though the operation had fallen apart before the first boot hit
the ground, SOG and MACV were shocked by the losses. As a result,
General Abrams had MACV analyze SOG casualties during the first two
months of 1969. A total of 15 U.S. personnel had been killed or were
missing, 68 had been wounded, and 10 helicopters had been destroyed.
But those losses were small when compared to those inflicted on the communists. MACSOG recon team members had accounted for 1,400 PAVN
killed, while air strikes during missions had killed many more. They had
also touched off 455 secondary explosions. At least 100 of the enemy had
been killed for every SOG man lost, a figure that was much higher than
the kill ratio of conventional units, which ran at about 15:1.

GAMMA

One of the covert operations run by the 5th SFG in South Vietnam was
Project Gamma, an intelligence collection operation assigned to Detachment B-57, whose mission in 1969 was to confirm the cooperation between Prince Sihanouk and the North Vietnamese. One of the agents run
by Gamma in the Central Highlands was Thai Khac Chuyen. On 10 May
1969, Chuyen was recognized by his handlers in a captured photograph
of NLF officers that had been taken in 1964.

After initial questioning, Chuyen was drugged and flown to Nha Trang where he was further interrogated and polygraphed. Convinced that he was indeed a double agent, American intelligence officers sought advice from the CIA as to how to dispose of him. Their reply was that "the most effective course of action might well be to get rid of him."[31] Following that advice, three Green Berets loaded Chuyen into a whale-boat, took him out to sea, and shot him in the head near Hon Tre Island on the evening of 20 June. Eventually (thanks to the CIA in a paroxysm of CYA [Cover Your Ass]), these events came to light.

Accused of first-degree murder were Col. Robert Rheault, the commander of the 5th SFG; Maj. Thomas Middleton, his chief of intelligence; Maj. David Crew, the commander of the B-57 Detachment; Cpt. Leland Brumley and WO2 Edward Boyle, both counterintelligence officers; Cpt. Robert Marasco, the B-57 regional commander; and Cpt. Budge Williams, B-57's operations officer.

After an inquiry by Army criminal investigators, the men were charged and then transferred to the notorious stockade at Long Binh to await trial.[32] The case created a huge stink in the American media. The "Green Beret Murder Case" also brought relations between Special Forces and General Abrams to a nadir, and that is saying something. Abrams was a regular Army tanker whose negative opinions on elite units in general, and the Special Forces in particular, were notorious (Abrams was known throughout MACSOG as "the Hatchet Man").

The dénouement of this case came on 26 August as CCC's Spike Team Florida was on an uneventful mission in northern Cambodia. The calm was broken, however, when two PAVN trackers walked up to the team's position and were killed. The team was on the run, but the men managed to elude their pursuers. After spending their RON in a gully, first light brought two more communist troops who were also killed. One of the dead men seemed unusual and a search of his body turned up a satchel of documents. The team went on the run again and called for extraction. SSgt. Kenneth Worthley was killed on the LZ but the rest of the team made it out.

In a bizarre turn of events, the dead PAVN with the documents turned out to be a colonel in the Chinese Intelligence Service and the documents themselves contained the names of double agents in South Vietnam. Sure enough, one of the named agents was Thai Khac Chuyen, the very man executed by the Green Beret counterintelligence officers. The charges against the men were quickly dropped (the CIA agents who had originally blown the whistle to cover their complicity were not going to be allowed to testify anyway) and they were released from custody.

The career of Robert Rheault, a fine officer who had only tried to cover the men under his command after the fact, was destroyed.

On 23 December CCS' Spike Team Auger made the first static-line parachute jump from a helicopter into the Fishhook area of Cambodia. A Green Hornet helicopter dropped the team of two U.S. and four Nung personnel with no difficulties. One of the Nungs broke his ankle in the jump, however, and the team called for extraction. An alternate method to daytime helicopter insertions had been found.

Airborne Operations: Timberwork (Op-36)

A reflection of the collapse of Timberwork agent operations program in North Vietnam was a reorganization of the operation. The group was also subdivided into two programs. Op-36A was the title given to Forae diversionary operations, which utilized the remaining teams in the Oodles program. Radio communication was utilized to convey information to the teams (and through them to the North Vietnamese), bolstering the idea that the agent network was a much larger and successful entity. Now that northern operations by MACSOG were forbidden by presidential order, however, the tissue of lies was growing pretty thin.

Although Operation Timberwork had been a fiasco, the remaining five teams that the operation still carried on its books were still being played in a diversionary role. It had been decided by headquarters, however, to surface the teams by ordering them to move to other locations in preparation for extraction. Team Tourbillon was the first to go under. It made excuses for not moving and finally went off the air. Its members were declared killed in action on 24 June. It was quickly followed by Team Hadley on 19 August. The members of Team Red Dragon met the same fate on 6 December. Team Eagle and Singleton agent Ares had refused to move and MACSOG ceased radio contact with them at the end of November. Although the Joint Chiefs required that MACSOG be prepared to reinitiate agent operations at a later date, for all intents and purposes Timberwork was over.

Strata missions (Op-36B), once launched into the panhandle of North Vietnam, were shifted to the Prairie Fire area due to the stand-down on northern operations. The teams initially consisted of all-indigenous civilian agents utilizing communist gear and sterile weapons. By November 1969 all of the civilian members of the STRATA program had been replaced by volunteers from the ARVN, which led to better discipline and unit proficiency. Once they were transferred to the Prairie Fire program, it did not take long for the teams to become indistinguishable from MACSOG's recon teams. On 12 January, the first American-led STRATA team headed into Laos. Op-36B teams ran sixty-three missions during 1969, the majority of them in the Salem House area.[33] The high number of missions in Cambodia reflected the phaseout of operations by American-led teams in July and their takeover by Vietnamese assets.

EARTH ANGELS

In early 1968 Airborne Operations had pioneered plans for an operation utilizing Hoi Chanhs to infiltrate the Prairie Fire area for reconnaissance work.[34] Three teams of three men each had been formed under the designation Thundercloud. Within a few months, however, the project was canceled and the men were incorporated into regular teams. Thanks to the success of Project Borden, however, the project was resurrected in early 1969 as Earth Angel.[35] It was given the green light by CINCPAC in March and the first mission of the program was launched on 8 April. A total of nineteen missions were launched under the operation during the year.[36] After a shaky start the operation scored some successes.

During the sieges of Bu Prang and Duc Lap Special Forces Camps in the Central Highlands, MACSOG was tasked with locating PAVN artillery positions located in Cambodia. A two-man Earth Angel team was sent in to find them. On the second day of their mission the two agents were captured and taken to a PAVN camp where they were shackled and thrown into a pit. Nearby were six ARVN and two American prisoners. When the PAVN troops discovered that the two men were ralliers, they beat them severely and made it known that they were intent on their execution. When the two prisoners were taken into the jungle by a single guard, supposedly to face their deaths, they managed to jump him and escape. Twenty-four hours later the two men showed up at an ARVN outpost. After contacting their handlers, one of the men volunteered to lead a Bright Light team back to the camp. Before the mission could be launched, the two Americans, WO Michael Peterson and Sgt. Vernon Shepard, were released by the North Vietnamese.

Strategic Technical Directorate

Although from its inception MACSOG was to be in an advisory role to its Vietnamese counterparts, this had never really been the case. The U.S. military funded, planned, equipped, trained, and led the forces that carried out the missions. The only exceptions to this were CSS maritime operations and the agent teams of Airborne Operations. The STD (and its predecessors) had mainly served as a source of manpower and as liaison with the various ethnic groups that made up MACSOG strike forces.

By 1968 and 1969 things had begun to change. U.S. policy was gearing for withdrawal and MACSOG, like every other unit in Vietnam, had to take seriously the challenge of training the South Vietnamese to take over their operations. Even the South Vietnamese were taking it seriously. On 1 February 1968, the STD was transferred from the South Vietnamese Special Forces Command to the Joint General Staff in Saigon. This signaled the beginning of the dissolution of the Vietnamese Special Forces and their absorption into the STD. It was a little late in coming, but who could have ever considered that the Americans were going to pull out short of either outright victory or a negotiated settlement advantageous to Saigon?

At this point it might be reasonable to illustrate the relationship between MACSOG and its South Vietnamese counterpart with some examples drawn from the previous history of the organization. That relationship could be described as ambivalent at best. Col. Charles Norton, commander of C&C Da Nang, had this to say about the STS liaison officer at the headquarters: "We kept him (a captain) out of the operational loop, because I don't think we ever trusted him. . . . I think I went over to the STS headquarters once, and that's when they gave me a medal."[37] George Gaspard believed that the relative success of the STRATA operation was attributable to the fact that he never informed his Vietnamese counterpart of location of intended insertions in North Vietnam.

By the time the STS had evolved into the STD, things had not changed much. Col. Lawrence Trapp, operations officer, Op-35 in 1967–68, held the same position in 1970. Once again the South Vietnamese liaison officers were never allowed into the Operations Center. If they came into Op-35 "they never went down the hall unless the maps were covered."[38] Some recon team missions were aborted in the briefing room by the arrival of an officer from one of the counterpart organizations. It was one thing for the South Vietnamese officer to be authorized to attend a pre-infiltration briefing, but "risking one's life for the gratification of bureaucratical [sic] protocol was quite another issue."[39] The reasoning behind the mistrust was the consistent belief that the South Vietnamese organizations had been compromised by the communists. What else could explain MACSOG's constant mission failures? This opinion was shared by all ranks and stretched from the operational elements to their headquarters. Col. Skip Sadler himself believed that "the STD headquarters . . . was totally riddled (by enemy agents)."[40]

Psychological Operations: Humidor (Op-39)

In the fall of 1968 the PSYOPS Branch became a staff element in control of the Psychological Studies Group (Op-39) and a separate Radio Studies Group (Op-70). By 1969 Project Humidor had been gutted. The Voice of

Freedom had been detached from Psychological Studies and had a separate group created for it. Although MACSOG maintained liaison with the Voice of Freedom over content (through "family messages" as part of Forae), the program was basically turned over to the Joint U.S. Public Affairs Organization (JUSPAO), the public information branch of MACV.

The Voice of the Sacred Sword of the Patriot League and Radio Red Flag were still broadcasting, but the fiction of the SSPL or an opposition communist front were wearing thin with nothing else to back them up. With the 1 November 1968 stand-down of northern operations, there were no more detainees to interrogate or to provide with gift kits or radios. There were no more overflights of North Vietnam from which to distribute propaganda leaflets.

Leaflet production and distribution then centered on the rewards programs of the JPRC. Trilingual leaflets were produced by the millions and dropped into Laos, Cambodia, and South Vietnam, promising cash rewards for the return of downed, escaped, or evading U.S. personnel. The poison-pen letters of Operation Pollack continued to flow to the North, but the wind was just going out of the sails of psychological operations.

Recovery Studies (Op-80)

During 1969 the Recovery Studies Division, known outside MACSOG as the JPRC, was designated Op-80. By late February the musical chairs had ended and Lt. Col. John Firth held the newly titled position of director, Recovery Studies Division. He held the position until July. Although Ambassador Sullivan's tenure was growing short, he had not lost his touch. When the first USAF all-weather F-111 fighter-bomber went down over Laos, MACSOG sought permission to search for the wreckage in order to sanitize it. Sullivan refused permission. After Radio Hanoi reported on the loss of the aircraft and its recovery by PAVN, Sullivan sent the following communiqué to the State Department, which is worth quoting: "When the first F-111 aircraft was reported missing, I received a message from my instant correspondents, MACSOG, indicating they would like to send one of their Batman teams into south Laos to look for the wreckage."[41] Although protecting the security of America's newest military hardware was not high on Sullivan's list, he did profess concern for American personnel lost in Laos, at least on paper.

Even at this late date Sullivan was worried about Hanoi's ability to hold up American prisoners as evidence of U.S. involvement in the supposedly "neutral" country. He even allowed a change in SAR procedures in order to facilitate the location and rescue of 0-1 "Raven" FACs who flew unmarked aircraft (and had Laotians as backseaters) in support of Laotian forces. The logic was that American crews flying from Thailand could be explained away, while Americans flying Laotian aircraft from Laotian bases could not.

On 17 April Army specialist Thomas Van Putten escaped from an NLF prison camp in the Ba Thu area of South Vietnam. He managed to slip away and evaded for twenty-one days before he was spotted and recovered by an observation helicopter. During debriefing he provided information on the four camps in which he had been held, but an attempt to launch a recovery operation was stymied by the movement of a division-size PAVN unit into the area. On 23 March ten ARVNs were freed in a raid by elements of the U.S. 9th Infantry Division and forty-eight more were liberated in separate operations conducted by the ARVN.[42]

Operation Monroe Bay began on 3 April when an 0-1 Bird Dog went down in the Central Highlands. The two-man crew, Arthur G. Ecklund and Perry H. Jefferson, managed to make radio contact, but then disappeared. A three-day search failed to locate even the aircraft. On 17 April a 25-man MACSOG Bright Light team (Monroe Bay) moved into the area, but there was still no sign of the crew. On 1 July a Chieu Hoi rallied at an ARVN outpost in Quang Tin Province. He had seen an American POW in a hospital at his former camp only a few days before. A force from the 5th Regiment of the 2nd ARVN Division and the provincial PRU quickly launched a raid on the camp. Because of the rough terrain, an ARVN soldier was lowered by a rope from a helicopter to reach the American, Larry D. Aikin, who was found suffering from a machete slash across his head inflicted by his captors in order to prevent his escaping.[43] With the aid of an American, the ARVN carried Aikin three hundred yards down a streambed to a waiting helicopter. The American was rushed to a military hospital in a coma from which he did not recover. He died on 25 July.

His death provided grist for the mill of those who frowned on POW rescue attempts. The war was winding down and a prisoner exchange was inevitable. Why risk the lives of Americans in vain attempts at rescue? Little did these civilian and military personnel know of the atrocious conditions in the camps, the torture inflicted on prisoners, and the massive casualty rate among Free World Military Forces POWs. Shortly after the announcement of Larry Aikin's death, Lt. Col. George R. Reinker took over the Recovery Studies Division.

MONTEREY ANGLER

At this point Colonel Cavanaugh and his deputy, Air Force colonel Robert Gleason, believed that the JPRC should have been turned over to SAR units.[44] They even went so far as to discuss the matter with MACV, but were turned down. The chief obstacle to a turnover was the continued necessity for security. SAR missions launched into Laos, Cambodia, and possibly North Vietnam had to remain covert. Only MACSOG retained men trained for extensive ground operations in denied territory, and only they had permission to carry them out. That MACV did not reconsider its position after three years of what it must have considered mediocre results for a mission of such importance was problematic to say the least.

Colonel Reinker attempted to spread tasking and improve response times to viable intelligence by having JPRC liaison officers appointed at the Field Forces down to divisional level, and local commanders were strongly encouraged to initiate operations on their own. One solution was the distribution of pre-approved blank operations plans. The blanks gave authorization for local commanders to launch prisoner recovery operations with any forces available. This concept was known as Monterey Angler.[45] If possible, however, MACSOG forces were still to be given first crack at the operations. General Abrams also granted permission for the use of battalion-size reaction forces in these operations (the only authorization ever given for the use of MACSOG Haymaker forces). During the year MACSOG also continued to provide information via MACV J-5 to the chief military negotiator at the Paris peace conference. The JPRC continued this input even after MACSOG's contribution ended.

Air Operations: Shedder (Op-75)
During the year, MACSOG decided that the paint schemes and lack of serial numbers on its aircraft were posing too many blatant questions and raising security issues. The all-Chinese or mixed crews of the aircraft also needed more cover. This problem was partially solved by having the aircraft exhibit standard camouflage paint schemes. The end was nigh for the "Blackbirds." Heavy Hook and Combat Spear aircraft flew a combined total of 6,706 hours while transporting 7,681,450 pounds of cargo and 42,590 passengers.[46]

1ST FLIGHT DETACHMENT
Heavy Hook C-123K missions were now limited to Laos, South Vietnam, and Cambodia. During the year unit aircraft flew 2,546 sorties (team insertions, resupply, and propaganda leaflet drops) including ten combat missions.[47] Administrative support for the detachment was provided by the 14th Special Operations Wing (SOW) located at Nha Trang Air Base, until 15 October when that installation was turned over to the VNAF. At that point the 14th SOW moved to Phan Rang. Although 1st Flight

remained at Nha Trang and remained under the control of the 14th SOW, its administrative functions became the responsibility of the 12th Tactical Fighter Wing at Cam Ranh Bay.

15TH SOS

Due to move of 14th SOW to Phan Rang, 63 maintenance specialists were transferred to the 15th SOS at Nha Trang. As with 1st Flight, all administrative functions were then taken over by the 12th Tactical Fighter Wing. Combat Spear aircraft flew 3,117 sorties during 1969, including 12 combat missions.[48] All of the unit's combat missions were flown in either Laos or South Vietnam. The four MC-130E Combat Spear aircraft of the 15th SOS were scheduled to undergo K-mod jet modifications in the United States and the aircraft were to be rotated out of Vietnam one at a time until the work was completed in March 1971.

20TH SOS

Originally, the twenty-two aircraft of the squadron were stationed at Nha Trang to support CCS activities at Ban Me Thuot, Duc Co, Ban Don, and Duc Lap. Four other aircraft were stationed at Udorn RTAFB, Thailand, to support MACSOG team operations when weather prevented mission launches from South Vietnam. Engine malfunctions caused by foreign object damage in the T-58-3 engines (which had begun in 1968) were continuing to have a detrimental effect on squadron operational readiness. On 31 August the mission tasking of the 20th was suspended due to lack of sufficient aircraft to carry out operations, and the slack was picked up by Army aviation units. On 5 September the 20th SOS was moved from Nha Trang to Tuy Hoa where a team was assembled to investigate the mechanical problems and find a solution.

To replace the 20th, two Army aviation units were tasked to support CCS. These were the 155th AHC "Stagecoaches" and the 195th AHC "Sky Chiefs" and their attached gunship platoons ("Falcons" and "Thunder Chickens"). By 1 December the 20th managed to get enough aircraft aloft to pick up the gunship portion of its MACSOG mission, but it is revealing that only four aircraft were available for operations. MACSOG also continued to utilize a leased China Air Lines Tradewind as a personal mode of transport for the commander of the unit and for VIP transportation. Transportation for other MACSOG assigned personnel came from a C-47 aircraft leased from the same company.

HELICOPTERS

As the war heated up and MACSOG programs increased in scale and scope, it became necessary to draw upon more air assets. Luckily, more

U.S. Army aviation units had arrived in-country and helicopter support for MACSOG operations came from a plethora of units. The great difficulty in acknowledging the contribution of these units lies in the fact that they were usually rotated on a sixty-day schedule by the 52nd Army Aviation Battalion, to which a majority of them were assigned. The expansion of cross-border operations and especially the opening of CCC meant that more helicopters were needed. They were provided by the Army's 119th AHC "Alligators," the 57th AHC "Gladiators," 170th AHC "Bikinis," and the 189th AHC "Ghost Riders." Fire support was provided by their attached gunship platoons: the "Crocodiles," "Buccaneers," "Cougars," and "Avengers," respectively.

In the spring of 1969 the AH-1G Cobra gunships of the 361st Armed Helicopter Escort Company (AHEC), "Pink Panthers," arrived to assist CCC. In May the unit requested an extension of its sixty-day assignment to provide support for the recon teams. The Pink Panthers continued to extend this assignment to MACSOG missions until April of 1972, earning the respect and admiration of MACSOG recon personnel. During 1969 increased communist reaction to helicopter-infiltrated reconnaissance teams led to increased experimentation in insertion techniques. Night helicopter paradrops were one method that looked promising. The first operational helicopter paradrop took place in December.

MODERNIZATION

Dedicated FACs in the form of U-17 aircraft had been assigned to MACSOG from the VNAF 83rd Group (later designated the 110th Liaison Squadron) at the inception of the cross-border effort. But, since the early days, these eyes and ears of the recon teams had been replaced by Cessna 0-1 Bird Dog observation aircraft of USAF and Army forward air controllers. By 1967 the 0-1s had been supplemented by the arrival of the twin-engine Cessna 0-2A Skymasters that were to replace them. These propeller-driven light aircraft reconned target areas, coordinated air support during insertions and extractions, and stayed in direct contact with the teams. USAF FAC units that often worked with SOG included the Da Nang–based 20th TASS "Coveys," the Ban Me Thuot–based 21st TASS "Mikes," and the Nakhon Phanom–based 23rd TASS "Nails." With the arrival of permission for the use of FACs over Cambodia, MACSOG utilized the services of the 0-1s of the U.S. Army's 219th Aviation Company, also known as the Sneaky Pete Air Force or SPAF in the Daniel Boone/ Salem House area of operations.

A new and valuable addition to the aerial campaign had been made during autumn of 1968 when the U.S. Army began fielding the new

Grumman OV-10 Bronco in-theater. The Bronco was the American military's first armed observation aircraft and was also the first to be specially designed for aerial reconnaissance work. It proved to be very effective. One PAVN defector confessed that his unit, after carelessly revealing itself to an OV-10, was devastated by F-4s directed by the Bronco. "After this strike we were afraid of the OV-10s" and they paid stricter attention to camouflage and concealment.[49]

From the early days of cross-border operations, former recon team members or men who were recovering from wounds or injuries began to fly as backseaters on FACs. Known as Covey Riders, these men had experience across the fence and knew the abilities and limitations of the recon teams. Riding shotgun on the FACs, they leant their expertise to the pilot and were a welcome voice to team members who were on the run or surrounded by communist troops.

Plans

Emphasis in planning was now concentrated on the possibility of a cease-fire, a reduction of U.S. forces in South Vietnam, and a post-hostilities environment. Vietnamization came to MACSOG in the form of plans centered on the improvement of South Vietnamese unconventional warfare capabilities, including the Navy and Air Force, in a post-U.S. Vietnam.

Maj. Gen. John Freund (SACSA) arrived for a three-day visit and was escorted by the Plans officer. The general also assigned an Army major to the Plans Division to go through the books for the proposed JCS *Documentation Study*. From 16 to 27 July the *Documentation Study* team (Special Studies Group, OJCS) arrived to reproduce documents for the project. There was a continued issuance of fact sheets to MACV J-5, which were then passed on to the senior military negotiator in Paris. The last of these fact sheets was issued on 14 June, but coordination between the negotiators and the Recovery Studies Division continued.

Logistics

The elements of the division were reorganized during the year, chief among which the transfer of the Research and Development officer to the position of chief, Operations Support Branch (R&D). The year 1969 saw a new record for the division: 2.5 million pounds of equipment and supplies were received and 3.4 million pounds were shipped out. It seemed as if the bad old days were over. The mission of the Logistics Division had become aligning and meshing with the conventional U.S. supply system in-country and tables of authorization were established for all three C&C Detachments. There was also a marked departure from the previous use of sterilized equipment by the recon teams and exploitation forces. The key reason for this change was that the prevalence of American weapons in Southeast Asia was so great that it was no longer felt necessary to attempt to disguise it. Another contributing factor may have been the lack of captured communist equipment and ammunition due to the drawdown of American forces and reduction in operations by conventional units. MACSOG still had to provide communist-produced hardware for its STRATA and Earth Angel teams, but it seemed to be having difficulties obtaining it. Throughout the year MACSOG was on the lookout for new sources of captured equipment and ammunition. The adoption of one new item of equipment had literal life-and-death consequences for the recon teams. The Stabo extraction rig was chosen to replace its predecessor, the McGuire rig.[50]

As a result of the move to House-50 in 1968, an inventory was conducted and a new stock record system was implemented. In June the doors were closed and a 100 percent inventory was conducted. Construction during the year included the completion of the VOF transmitter site at Con Te Island. The transmitter equipment was installed and tested and broadcasts were scheduled to begin in early 1970.

Communications

From 2 to 28 February, a communications security review was conducted by the Army's 101st Radio Battalion, the results of which indicated that MACSOG needed to beef up its radio and telephone security.[51] The study of C&C radio operations, procedures, and maintenance was disheartening. Old and mixed equipment, lack of spare parts, improper usage, and poor maintenance procedures were noted.

Comptroller

This was the first full year of operations for the newly designated Comptroller Division since it had been separated from Logistics. The division was responsible for MACSOG's financial management, accounting, auditing, and disbursing. The division was divided into two sections—Fiscal and Finance. During the year MACSOG received $400,000 in unclassified funds from CINCPAC through MACV. It also received $21,737,900 in classified funds through the CNO. This was a savings of $4 million from the previous year's proposed budget. The Comptroller estimated the budget for 1970 at $25,778,400.[52]

Comment: Psychological Operations

Psychological operations were MACSOG's bread and butter and the organization expended a lot of effort over the years on its programs. It is interesting that SOG's predecessor, the CIA, abandoned its covert paramilitary campaign in order to conduct psychological operations in South Vietnam. It is also cogent that MACSOG's most promising psychological programs were initially designed and instituted by CIA personnel opconned to SOG. Unfortunately the keystone of the effort—a legitimate resistance operation within North Vietnam itself—was all but eliminated at the birth of MACSOG. Since the peripheral operations hinged on just such a resistance movement, the program was fatally flawed from the beginning. Washington was averse even to the creation of a southern front organization, possibly fearing that it might spark real resistance in the North.

The fears of Washington were well placed. Assuming for a moment that enough of the northern population would have supported such a movement, what could it possibly have accomplished? There was fear that if the United States was implicated in such a movement (once again overt and covert policies were at loggerheads), the possible fallout would be tangible and quite possibly violent. The memory of the Hungarian revolt— initiated partially as a response to American print and radio propaganda— which had been so brutally crushed by the Soviets and during which the United States and its allies were powerless to intervene, was still fresh in the minds of politicians, the State Department, and the CIA.

As far as the programs themselves were concerned, they were pure genius. The SSPL and Red Flag (and the leaflet and radio operations that supported them) were fine examples of "black" operations. Although they may not have fooled the Hanoi authorities, they did make them nervous enough to react harshly to them. There were also plenty of examples to support the belief that the citizens and soldiers of North Vietnam were convinced of the "reality" of both organizations. As with MAROPS, the viability of these missions was destroyed by the 1968 stand-down. The announced cessation of overt U.S. operations and the sudden disappearance of SSPL craft were bound to have been noticed and linked by both the authorities and citizens of the North. It is seemingly beyond comprehension that the authorities in Washington would have been unable to separate covert and overt actions against North Vietnam and throw away such operations on a whim, but that is exactly what they did.

The diversionary operations later conducted under Forae were simply a knee jerk reaction to the final comprehension that Timberwork was completely blown. Why MACSOG had not conducted such operations during the operational heyday of Timberwork is a mystery. They were indeed devious and ingenious, but they were also too little, too late. Other psychological warfare projects like Eldest Son and Benson Silk truly exhibited the nature of tactical PSYOPS and were classics of their kind.

NORTH VIETNAM
The Vietnam War, like any conflict, was political in nature, and regardless
of what the West thought of the "true" motives of the Lao Dong Party,
the people of North Vietnam considered the conflict to be a struggle for
the reunification of their homeland. The propaganda machine of North
Vietnam, therefore, had little trouble cranking up to both further the
cause and to insulate the population from outside influences.

The Propaganda Ministry had no problem in remaining the sole public voice delivering news and opinion to the people. Television ownership
was unknown in North Vietnam, and Hanoi heavily regulated the private
ownership of radios. Only one of every thirty-two North Vietnamese
families owned one, since only a limited number were made available for
purchase and this required Party approval. The general public received its
radio programming through a system of 225,000 loudspeakers emplaced
throughout the nation.[53]

MACSOG's radios and gift kits were simply dismissed by Hanoi as
the insidious ploys of its enemies. The North Vietnamese countered them
by having the Ministry of Public Health warn the public that they had
been infected by the Americans with smallpox and tetanus germs. To further neutralize the propaganda value of "Peanuts" radios, Hanoi simply
banned the sale of batteries to anyone whose radio was not registered
with the police. U.S. propaganda efforts were decried as a poor attempt
to "bomb the brains" of the people. Another northern response to MAC-
SOG's efforts was to constantly warn the population of infiltration by
American and South Vietnamese commandos, spies, and saboteurs. Besides,
Operation Rolling Thunder provided Hanoi's propagandists with all
of the ammunition that they needed. The limited nature of the bombing campaign, designed to reduce civilian casualties, worked against the
Americans. The bombing "killed just enough people to instill a desire for
vengeance, but not enough to incite panic or defeatism."[54]

In most of the historical literature (and in the minds of the American
people) released since the end of the conflict, a set of general assumptions
have became historical truth. It became a given that, early in the conflict,
American political and military strategists made the mistake of believing
that airpower alone would be enough to convince Hanoi to end its support of the southern insurgency. Second, most military writers believed
that the gradualist approach followed by the Johnson administration
crippled the American military effort (especially the air effort) by allowing the North Vietnamese too much time to adapt. Third, some have
observed that the American military had obviously forgotten the results
of post–Second World War *Strategic Bombing Survey*, which had con-

cluded that strategic bombing of civilians was counterproductive. This viewpoint was given credence by the bombing that was supposed to drive the North Vietnamese to capitulation but which simply "rekindled their nationalistic zeal, so that many who may have disliked communist rule joined the resistance to alien attack."[55]

In terms of choking off the Trail by aerial interdiction, it was once again assumed by public opinion and some historians that American policymakers had fumbled the ball. The campaign forced Hanoi to pay a price, but it was a price that they were willing to meet. As Secretary McNamara numbly put it, the infiltration routes "seem to be one-way trails to death for the North Vietnamese—yet there is no sign of an impending break in enemy morale—nor has Rolling Thunder either significantly affected infiltration or cracked the morale of Hanoi."[56]

Yet, these historical assumptions were (and are) wrong. The Washington politicos and the strategists at the Pentagon knew full well before the first bomb was dropped on either North Vietnam or the Trail and before the first combat boot came ashore at Da Nang that it was not going to work. They already knew that bombing alone (regardless of its scope or scale) might not force Hanoi to the negotiating table. They already knew that bombing alone was not going to halt the flow of men and supplies, or even slow them enough to tip the military balance. But they did it anyway. Why? Because, in their view, they had no alternative. At most they assumed that once the bombing and the ground fighting had commenced, either the political constraints would be removed or they would simply outlast their enemy.[57]

Ironically troubles did not appear for the Hanoi government until the bombing halt of 1968. Evacuees from the cities returned to find insufficient food, a paucity of consumer goods, and no housing. Production quotas in northern factories fell and the Communist Party began to exhibit signs of frustration over developing public laxity. The government's response was to blame these problems on internal spies and counter-revolutionaries bent on sabotaging the war effort. Regardless of public ranting about "elements of the former exploiting classes, reactionary elements under the cover of religion, and armed bandits who refuse to be reeducated," the Hanoi government remained in firm control.[58] This alarming period for the communists was ended when American bombers returned to the skies of North Vietnam in 1970. Hanoi's public relations problems, quite literally, disappeared overnight.

Chapter Seven

1970: THE SECOND INDOCHINA WAR

Headquarters

Col. Steven "Rusty" Cavanaugh remained in command of MACSOG until 8 July when he was replaced by Col. John F. "Skip" Sadler. Sadler had been a paratrooper during the Second World War and had made combat jumps into New Guinea and Luzon in the same 11th Airborne Division as his friend Rusty Cavanaugh. After the war he became a para-troop instructor at Fort Benning, Georgia, and one of the Army's leading parachute experts. As a captain during the Korean Conflict, Sadler had served as John Singlaub's airborne specialist in the CIA-affiliated Joint Advisory Commission (JACK). He then returned to Fort Bragg, North Carolina, before serving a tour with the CIA in Operation White Star in Laos. He was serving as chief of staff with the 8th Infantry Division in Germany when he received the call from Rusty Cavanaugh to command MACSOG.

The organization's headquarters strength decreased from that of 1969. It began the year with 394 authorized personnel and ended with 383.[1] It is useful, however, to compare these numbers with a breakdown of the unit's operational strength by military branch provided by the unit's yearly Command History. The U.S. Army contributed 1,041 men, the Air Force 476, the Marines 17, and the CIA 7. South Vietnamese employees included 3,068 mercenaries and 5,402 civilians. There were also 125 third-country civilians on the payroll. This totaled out to 10,210 personnel assigned to or working for MACSOG.[2]

Intelligence

Regardless of the bombing campaigns, the North Vietnamese were still pumping enough supplies and manpower down the Trail to maintain their effort. From November 1969 through June 1970, MACV estimated that PAVN had put more than 63,000 tons of materiel in at the top of the pipeline and gotten about 20,000 out at the bottom.[3] And this effort was continued without the use of the Cambodian ports or infiltration by sea.

One of the results of the Lon Nol coup in Cambodia was the revelation of the extent of North Vietnamese supply infiltration through the port of Sihanoukville. The Lon Nol government presented the United States with documents and bills of lading disclosing that between December 1966 and April 1969 PAVN Unit K-20 had facilitated the movement of more than 25 tons of cargo per day into Cambodia and had then transported it to the border sanctuaries, including 100–300 tons of ammunition.[4] The unit had also purchased 55,000 tons of rice annually from Sihanouk and another 100,000 tons directly from Cambodian farmers.

To facilitate the collection of more accurate aerial intelligence, especially for the Menu and Freedom Deal campaigns, a low-level handheld photography program had been initiated in July 1969. Known as Ford Drum, the program utilized low-level FACs for reconnaissance and had initially collected photo intelligence in eastern Cambodia. MACSOG formalized Ford Drum on 21 October and the intelligence collected went to MACV J-2, the Regional Assistance Commands, and 7th/13th Air Force. During 1970, operations in the Prairie Fire area generated 558 intelligence reports on enemy activities while Salem House produced 477 for the division.[5]

How did MACV appreciate and utilize MACSOG intelligence collected in Cambodia, especially in light of the May incursion? General Abrams thought highly of the intelligence collected by the Salem House teams. He credited Operation Menu's success on intelligence collected on the ground and on the 70 percent of post-strike assessments that came from SOG's Ford Drum pilots and photographers.[6] As far as the American commanders in the field were concerned, however, something was lacking. Neither Gen. Phillip Davidson nor Col. Don Starry (commanders of the 1st Air Cavalry Division and the 11th Armored Cavalry Regiment, respectively, and both having participated in the Cambodian Incursion) had been made privy to MACV's most sensitive intelligence information. Both found out about the Menu bombings only by actually flying over Cambodia and seeing the bomb craters. As for SOG's contribution to tactical intelligence during the run-up to the incursion, Davidson responded by stating that he "often wondered about the accuracy of the reports made by these patrols."[7] The more-opinionated Don Starry considered SOG's tactical intelligence "worthless."[8]

This criticism may have been a bit extreme; recon teams had avoided Base Areas 352 and 353 since October 1969. By that time U.S. aircraft had been scattering antipersonnel mines on the South Vietnamese side of the border, thus impeding not only communist infiltrators, but the teams themselves. Moreover, the defenses within the Fishhook region of Cambodia had grown so strong that casualties inflicted had become unacceptable. Indeed, without air and artillery support the recon teams could not have approached the heart of the Base Areas.[9]

Operations and Training

During the year the Operations and Training Division (equivalent to a G-3 section) controlled the staff branches responsible for the Maritime Studies, Air Studies, Psychological Studies, and the Ground Studies Groups. On 23 October the Training Studies Group was also brought under the control of the division. A Statistics and Analysis Section was organized and put into operation during the year. Created under the direction of chief, SOG, this section streamlined the storage, retrieval, and presentation of intelligence information utilizing the IDHS system. It then collated the information and presented it in briefings to chief, SOG, and other highly cleared personnel.

The Ground Studies Branch was subdivided into three organic sections: the Special Studies Section administered the Timberwork program (and all the Forae sub-programs); the Field Studies Section administered the Prairie Fire/Nickel Steel and Salem House programs; while the Training Studies Section administered the training programs for Timberwork, Prairie Fire, and Salem House.[10]

Ground Studies Group (Op-35)

THE TRAIL

MACSOG cross-border operations in Laos continued in support of the 7th/13th Air Force's Operation Commando Hunt III through 30 April when Commando Hunt IV began. U.S. and South Vietnamese aircraft were then averaging 14,000 sorties per month over the Trail.[11] The Air Force estimated that 3,375 trucks were working the communist logistics system in southern Laos, yet the total number of trucks estimated destroyed by aerial interdiction rose from 9,012 in 1969 to 12,368 in 1970.[12] This number vastly exceeded the 6,000 trucks estimated by the CIA to comprise the entire North Vietnamese inventory.[13] The North Vietnamese had also beefed up their anti-aircraft artillery defenses on the Trail. 7th/13th Air Force believed that 700 23-mm and 37-mm anti-aircraft weapons guarded the logistical system during the year.[14]

The PAVN 559th Transportation Group was made the equivalent of a military region during the year and placed under the direct control of the Central Military Party Command. General Dong Sy Nguyen returned to assume command of the unit and he reorganized the 559th into five divisional headquarters, the 470th, 471st, 472nd, 473rd, and 571st. The group consisted of four truck transportation regiments, two petroleum pipeline regiments, three anti-aircraft regiments, eight engineer regiments, and the 968th Infantry Division. By the end of the year, the 559th was running twenty-seven *binh trams* that transported or stored 40,000 tons of supplies with a 3.4 percent loss rate during the year.[15]

The supplies were transported from North Vietnam in relays, with the trucks shuttling from one way station to the next. The materiel was then unloaded and reloaded onto "fresh" trucks at each subsequent station. If a truck was disabled or destroyed, it was replaced from the assets of the next northern way station, and so on until the truck was replaced by a new one in North Vietnam itself. Eventually the last commo-liaison station in Laos or Cambodia was reached and the trucks were unloaded. The supplies were then either cached, loaded onto watercraft, or man-portered to their destination.

During Commando Hunt IV (30 April through 9 October) allied forces began to feel the results of communist reaction to the Lon Nol coup. As early as October 1969 the North Vietnamese, possibly anticipating the loss of their Cambodian supply routes, began what Air Force historian Herman Gilster called "their largest and most intense logistical effort of the whole war" by constructing and expanding their routes into northwestern Cambodia.[16] Attopeu and Saravane had fallen to PAVN, opening the length of the Kong River transportation system into Cambodia to help replace the loss of Sihanoukville. During Commando Hunt V, the number of trucks claimed to have been destroyed rose to 16,266 vehicles with 4,700 damaged, but the numbers simply did not tally.[17] If only 6,000 trucks (by the U.S. estimate) were operating how could 20,966 have been destroyed or damaged? Air Force analysts, reviewing these figures, simply lowered the estimate to 11,000 destroyed and 8,000 damaged during Commando Hunt V alone.[18]

PAVN responded to Commando Hunt by observing the aerial effort and adapting to it. According to Air Force historian Bernard Nalty, the communists simply got inside the Air Force's "managerial loop." PAVN transportation units on the Trail took to the roads at dusk, with the peak of traffic coming in the early morning. As the fixed-wing gunships and B-57s arrived on station, traffic would subside until just before dawn, when the gunships and night bombers returned to their bases. The trucks then began rolling again, reaching another peak in traffic at around 0600 hours as drivers hurried to get into truck parks before sunrise and the arrival of the morning wave of fighter-bombers.[19]

PRAIRIE FIRE

Missions were launched into the northern portion of the Prairie Fire area and Nickel Steel from CCN, located at Camp Villarosa, Da Nang. The Mobile Launch Teams (MLTs) for the recon teams were still located at Phu Bai (Camp Eagle), Quang Tri, and the Heavy Hook site at Nakhon Phanom.[20] These teams consisted mainly of Vietnamese and Bru Montagnards while the exploitation force companies were evenly split among Cambodians, Brus, and Vietnamese. The total personnel assigned to CCN consisted of 244 Americans and 780 SCUs. The Phu Bai teams maintained personnel at, and were supported by, a radio relay site located at Fire Support Base Berchtesgaden in the Ashau Valley, while the Quang Tri teams were supported by the Hickory site, located on Hill 950, near the old Khe Sanh Combat Base. On 11 June the Sugarloaf radio relay site was established and manned by a platoon from CCN. Sugarloaf was located in Laos southwest of Base Area 607 and assisted radio communications in the central Prairie Fire area of operations. The site was abandoned on 4 October due to the onset of the northwest monsoon, but it was scheduled for reopening when the weather improved in 1971.

There was a concerted effort by Op-35 during 1970 to convert the leadership of the exploitation forces at all three C&Cs to South Vietnamese personnel. Previously SOG had depended on TDY personnel in the form of Snakebite teams to assume NCO and officer positions in its exploitation/reaction forces. It had been decided that South Vietnamese should assume these positions, both as a manpower-saving measure and as part of the Vietnamization process.

Back in November 1968 General Westmoreland had proposed that CCN Prairie Fire teams be sent to the Nape, Mu Gia, and Ban Karai Passes (the main northern access points of PAVN infiltration across the border with Laos) to gather intelligence on infiltration. At the time Ambassador Sullivan nixed the idea, claiming that "availability of aircraft, perishability of targets, (and) weather . . . had reduced the effectiveness of CIA roadwatch teams." Surely, these factors would hamper MACSOG as well.[21]

Sullivan had reconsidered the matter in January 1969. He finally gave his consent and MACSOG decided on an operation into the Mu Gia Pass area that was given the title Shiloh II. The probe was scheduled for launch in March 1970. Bad weather and further reviews by higher authority (both at the State Department and DOD) put the mission on hold until the 1970–71 dry season. The Joint Chiefs then indefinitely postponed the concept in October.

CCC was located at Camp Reno, Kontum, and launched missions into the southern Prairie Fire area and in the Zone Alpha portion of Salem House. Its MLTs were located at Dak To and Dak Pek, and on occasion teams were launched from the Duck Hook facility at Ubon, Thailand. The personnel assigned to CCC consisted of 244 Americans and 780 SCU mercenaries. The detachment's recon team members consisted of Nungs and members of various Montagnard tribes, while the exploitation forces consisted of Nungs and Vietnamese. CCC still maintained and was supported by the Golf-5 radio relay site, located above Highway 110 in Laos and by the Klondike site near Kontum.

On 1 April the North Vietnamese struck directly at MACSOG in South Vietnam. During the early morning hours, six PAVN sappers supported by a mortar barrage breached the north wall of the CCC compound at Kontum. They then proceeded to destroy the tactical operations center and the commanding officer's billet. No MACSOG personnel were killed, but sixteen SCUs were wounded. The sappers managed to escape without loss.

Between CCN and CCC, there were 422 recon missions launched into the Prairie Fire area of operations and 50 in-country missions.[22] During the year there were also 40 platoon and 4 multiplatoon-size exploitation force operations. The missions were supported by 1,439 tactical air and 1,180 helicopter gunship sorties. Three communist soldiers were captured on operations and 277 intelligence reports were generated. MACSOG suffered 14 killed, 99 wounded, and 6 men missing in action. Indigenous casualties included 54 dead, 176 wounded, and 6 missing.[23]

OPERATION HALFBACK

With traffic on the Trail reaching its peak during the dry season, MACSOG was determined to repeat the success of the previous year's Operation Spindown. The commander of Kontum's Hatchet Company B was so determined to repeat the success of the previous operation that he proposed that the company occupy the very same hill overlooking Highway 110 as had Spindown.[24] The 110 men of the force (two platoons) were landed on 23 February and, just as in the previous year, began to dig in to await the inevitable PAVN reaction. Once again the communists did not disappoint them. The hill was soon pounded by mortar and recoilless rifle fire, and ground probes were constant. That night PAVN troops launched a full-scale ground assault during which MACSOG got to try out one of its newest gadgets, the Miniponder. This was an electronic transponder for directing the 20-mm and 40-mm cannons of an orbiting AC-130 Spectre gunship. The device worked well and the assault was broken.

It did not take the North Vietnamese long to begin moving in heavy anti-aircraft weapons and using them. This new concentration of flak soon drove off allied aircraft. The company was then informed that radio intelligence indicated that the entire PAVN 27th Regiment was being prepared to overrun the roadblock. As a result of this intelligence, the decision was made to evacuate the position, but anti-aircraft fire made a direct extraction from the hill impossible. The only alternative was to ring the company with air support, gunships, and artillery and march off the hill to an LZ. In order to do that, the wounded would have to be evacuated first.

The first medevac Kingbee over the hilltop was riddled by fire and crashed and burned. The second managed to get in, but was so damaged that it could not lift off again. A third Kingbee came in, but it too was damaged and then crashed into the disabled chopper, detonating both in a ball of fire. The extraction was then called off. The march was still going to have to take place, but the wounded were going to have to be carried out. Thanks to Sfc. Lloyd O'Daniels, the orbiting Covey rider, the attempt was going to have plenty of air support. A-1s, F-4s, and Cobra gunships provided a screen of smoke and explosives while the company marched the kilometer to the LZ. The thirty-two F-4 Phantoms that supported the extraction expended two hundred tons of ordnance just by themselves.

The captain who led the company, however, was having difficulties. Leading the first platoon off the hilltop, he soon outpaced the second, which was carrying the dead and wounded. O'Daniels was having fits trying to get the captain to slow down the pace for the rest of the company. Finally, the men made it to the LZ and began to load for the extraction. When the final Huey came in, only three men were left: the captain, Sgt. Eulis Presley, and the last of the wounded SCUs.

The captain jumped aboard while Presley attempted to load the badly wounded Montagnard. As Presley laid his CAR-15 and radio on the floor of the chopper to make it easier to heave the Yard aboard, ground fire forced the chopper to lift off, leaving Presley and the wounded man unarmed on the LZ. When a Cobra rolled in to make a gun run, Presley thought the end had arrived. At the last moment, the Cobra screamed by without firing, turned, and led another Huey into the LZ for the pickup. Although mistakes were made and the commander almost lost control of the situation, the mission was counted as a success. The only American fatality was medic Bill Boyle. Vietnamese losses included the crews of two of the Kingbees and ten Montagnards.[25]

DAK SEANG

During mid-April PAVN continued its border-clearing operations by lay-ing siege to the Special Forces camp at Dak Seang with a battalion of ground troops. The personnel in the surrounded camp were not too wor-ried, since they had been scheduled for reinforcement by a larger ARVN force on the 15th. On that morning slicks and gunships of the 170th AHC began lifting an ARVN company to a hilltop overlooking the camp named LZ Orange. The first ship into the landing zone had no trouble, but as the second came in it was riddled by communist small arms fire and crashed on its side. Most of the crew and passengers were killed or wounded within minutes. Orbiting gunships laid down suppressive fire for two Air Force Jolly Green Giants that came in for the pickup, but they too were badly shot up and aborted the extraction. Both ships crashed while returning to their base.

April 15 was also a busy day for MACSOG Recon Team Montana, working out the fifth day of Bright Light duty from Dak To.[26] During the morning the team had already recovered the body of Sgt. Michel Kuropas, killed on a mission with RT Vermont. The crews of the two lift ships and two Cobras of the Bright Light mission, listening to the radio traffic from LZ Orange, requested permission from the recon team for release so that they could assist. Three staff sergeants, Dennis Neal, Joe Sample, and Michael Shepard, and their Montagnards consented and volunteered to go along.

As the Cobras provided cover on one side of the hill and A-1 Spads did the same on the other, the slicks roared in for a quick extraction. Withering ground fire greeted the command ship, wounding the copilot, Neal, and Sample, and killing several SCUs. While the ship leaked fuel and an unexploded B-40 rocket hung in the tail boom, the Huey powered up, lifted off, and headed for Dak Seang. The other Huey also managed to pick up some of the men at LZ Orange.

Not all of the Americans, however, had managed to get on board the lift ships. One of the two Pathfinders on the first chopper into the LZ, Cpl. Herndon Bivens, had covered the extraction with an M-60 machine gun (the other Pathfinder, Sgt. Rosaldo Montana, had already been killed). Also remaining were two warrant officers, David Barthelme and Roger Miller, the pilots of the downed Huey. Barthelme died of his wounds; Bivens and Miller were soon captured by the North Vietnamese, who promptly killed Bivens. Warrant Officer Miller would remain in captivity until the exchange of prisoners during Operation Homecoming. SOG recon man Dennis Neal died of his wounds in the compound at Dak Seang.

OPERATION TAILWIND

The CIA in Laos was desperate. Operation Gauntlet, a multibattalion Laotian offensive that was to determine the fate of the strategic Bolovens Plateau, was failing. The Laotians, under pressure from the agency, had launched a four-pronged offensive toward Chavane, Muong Phine, and Tchepone. Could MACSOG insert a Hatchet Force on the PAVN line of communication near Chavane and possibly disrupt their defense? Colonel Sadler had no hesitation in answering in the affirmative, even though no MACSOG team had ever operated so deep in Laos. As a matter of fact, the target area was twenty miles beyond MACSOG's authorized area of operations. Permission would have to be gotten from Ambassador Godley in Vientiane. It was given in record time.

On 11 September Operation Tailwind was launched by three platoons of CCC's Hatchet Company B backed up by two Pathfinder teams. The 16 Americans and 110 Montagnards, under the command of Cpt. Eugene McCarley, were lifted from Dak To into a valley about sixty miles to the west, near the town of Chavane. The distance to the target was so great that the force had to be infiltrated by three Marine Corps CH-53D helicopters (HMH-463 "Heavy Haulers") escorted by twelve Marine Cobra gunships.

McCarley knew that the only way the Hatchet Force could accomplish its mission was to keep moving and never become fixed in any one position. As long as they kept moving they would keep the initiative. Humping off to the northeast, the unit had not gone far when it overran a bunker complex stocked with thousands of 122-mm and 140-mm rockets. Quickly wiring up the cache for delayed demolition, the men moved off and heard the gratifying sounds of detonation and secondary explosions that could be heard for the next twelve hours.

The force began what rapidly became a routine: meet a PAVN delaying force, hit it with airstrikes, then bypass it and keep moving. That night McCarley decided that the company would not settle into a defensive position, since that was what the communists expected them to do. By dawn the next day, nine of the Americans and even more of the SCUs had been wounded. That morning, from a concealed ridgeline position, McCarley called in A-1 strikes on truck and troop columns sighted in the open in the valley below. By that time two attempts had been made to extract the wounded and both had failed. One Sikorsky came in to retrieve wounded, was badly shot up (and struck through and through by a B-40 rocket), and had to make a forced landing. The next HH-33 was also badly damaged by ground fire, lifted off, and was also forced down five minutes later. Both crews, however, were later recovered by SAR personnel.

On the second evening McCarley got his men into a perimeter to get some rest. Few men got any sleep, however, since they had been surrounded by probing PAVN troops. At 0400 hours McCarley got his men up and moving again, pushing through PAVN forces, and sidestepping. They marched west until they met another delaying action in a bunker complex. Fifty-four PAVN soldiers were killed in the area, but it looked like an empty hole until his men discovered a bunker that was dug in twelve feet below the ground.

Inside were wall maps and documents, lots of documents. Two footlockers full of them were finally collected. This was not the battalion base camp the Green Berets first believed it to be, but the *binh tram* headquarters that controlled all of Highway 165. The troops were not happy about hauling the extra weight of the paperwork, especially since half of them had been wounded at least once already, but they did it.

The North Vietnamese were closing in from all sides, the Hatchet Force had been on the ground for four days, and it was time to get them out. McCarley decided to avoid any LZ large enough to extract his entire force at one time since that would draw the attention of PAVN. Instead, three smaller LZs would be utilized, one platoon being dropped off and extracted at each as it was passed. Although the withdrawal of the force required the assistance of seventy-two U.S. fighters and a lot of bombs, it went off without a hitch.

Casualties amounted to 3 Montagnards killed and 33 wounded, while all 16 Americans were wounded. They had killed 144 North Vietnamese troops, wounded 50, and it was estimated that another 288 had been killed by air strikes.[27] The real reward was the treasure trove of logistical documents that immediately went to MACV J-2: Maps, codebooks, schedules, supply accounts; a detailed description of the operations of the 559th Group was accessible for study and exploitation. PAVN reacted harshly to these incursions. As a result, the North Vietnamese went on the offensive, seizing not only Attopeu, but Saravane as well. Unlike PAVN offensives of previous years, these gains were not going to be given up during the next monsoon season. The North Vietnamese were there to stay.

OPERATION SMEAR

On 7 June 1998 MACSOG popped into the public spotlight in a big way when an eighteen-minute segment ran on the premier broadcast of the Cable News Network's *NewsStand: CNN & Time*. The segment concerned Operation Tailwind. The broadcast, however, presented a totally different version of the events surrounding the mission than those described above. According to the report, the sole purpose of the operation was the elimination of a group of American soldiers, holed up in a Laotian village, who had defected to the communists. As if that were not enough, it went on to claim that nerve gas in the form of Sarin (GB in U.S. nomenclature) had been utilized twice during the operation, once to prep the village and once again during the extraction. The news segment claimed that over one hundred people, including women and children, had been killed in the chemical attack on the village.

The broadcast and a subsequent article in the 15 June issue of *Time* magazine seemed to have reasonable credentials. Adm. Thomas Moorer (chairman of the Joint Chiefs at the time of the action) stated that nerve agents had indeed been used, and not just during Tailwind. Several American members of the Hatchet Force, including MACSOG lieutenant Robert Van Buskirk (one of the platoon leaders) and sergeants Jay Graves, Mike Hagen, and Craig Schmidt lent testimony to support the allegations. Van Buskirk stated that he himself had killed two of the defectors by dropping a white phosphorus grenade down a spider hole that the men refused to evacuate. These were serious charges, since the killing of an unarmed enemy (and an American at that) and the first use of chemical weapons would have amounted to war crimes.

It did not take long, however, for the story to unravel. Anyone who had any knowledge of MACSOG knew that the stories were full of inaccuracies. The *Time* article stated that MACSOG operated without any rules of engagement and that "anything was permissible as long as it was deniable."[28] Even in 1998 statements like that aroused the suspicions of those who had not even been members of the organization.

The Hatchet Force was supposedly exposed on the LZ when the nerve agent was deployed to drive North Vietnamese back.[29] Van Buskirk stated that he had seen men convulsing after the wind blew the agent in their direction. They would not have been convulsing, they would have been dying, and yet all of the Americans made it out and only three SCUs were killed on the operation. The most telling fact from the story, however, was the one that was not there: PAVN had chemical warfare units deployed in the Laotian panhandle during Tailwind, yet Hanoi had never made any claim that the Americans deployed any antipersonnel agents other than CS tear gas.

On 22 June *Newsweek* ran an article that punched the *NewsStand* broadcast and *Time* article full of holes. Van Buskirk, it seemed, had forgotten the episode for nearly twenty-four years. He had only recently recalled his "repressed memory of the incident."[30] He also had psychological problems. Admiral Moorer (who had not appeared on camera) was eighty-six years old and under "assisted-care" retirement. He claimed that he had been pressured by the reporters to state that the gas used was not CS, but Sarin. The statements by the other participants had been selectively edited and distorted to fit the "facts" of the story.[31]

Just three and one-half weeks after the initial broadcast, on 3 July, CNN had issued a mea culpa and retracted the entire story. When the axe came down, it came down just as swiftly. CNN fired the producers of the show, April Oliver and Jack Smith, and issued a stern reprimand to international correspondent Peter Arnett. The network stated that the evidence was faulty and that the system of checks and balances within the system had failed.

The producers, although chastised, were not repentant. April Oliver believed that she and Smith had been abandoned by CNN, still believed in the story, and even considered that the change in the participants' statements were due to possible death threats.[32] Jack Smith believed that pressure applied by the Pentagon was responsible for the collapse of the story and considered CNN's retraction to be a corporate whitewash. It was rather apparent that both had firmly entrenched opinions on the Vietnam War and MACSOG's role in it, and no facts, no matter how many, were going to change them.

SALEM HOUSE

Early in the year MACSOG had requested that General Abrams seek approval for authorization to launch tactical airstrikes in Cambodia as an adjunct to the Menu bombings and, on 20 April, the JCS granted a thirty-day authorization for the strikes.[33] Six F-100s from Phan Rang and four F-4s from Phu Cat were dedicated to the missions, code-named "Patio," which were to be conducted in the strictest secrecy. The first strike went in on 24 April in the Wasteland area of Cambodia. For the first time in the history of Daniel Boone/Salem House, the utilization of platoon-size exploitation forces, tactical airstrikes, and FAC coverage were authorized in all of the SOG operational zones.[34] What was interesting about this series of strikes was the fact that the authorized Patio bombings did not begin until 29 April, making these first tactical airstrikes in Cambodia as controversial as the Menu bombings that had preceded them.

Due to the Cambodian Incursion of 24 May and the Freedom Deal bombing campaign that accompanied and followed it, MACSOG sought and received permission to extend its Salem House missions into the newly created Air Interdiction Zone (AIZ).[35] On 2 June permission was granted, and 113 recon missions were carried out in the AIZ during the remainder of the year.[36] This authorization was, however, to last only until 1 May 1971. Congressional response to the Cambodian Incursion included the passage of the Cooper-Church Amendment on 29 December. This legislation effectively forbade the use of U.S. ground forces in Cambodia, Laos, and North Vietnam.

By 27 May the Joint Chiefs had already decreed an end to American-led recon teams in the Salem House area. All participation by American forces was to be ended no later than 1 July.[37] Thereafter no more U.S. transport or gunship helicopters were to be allowed in the area. The Joint Chiefs later amended this operations order to allow the utilization of gunship support for all-indigenous teams. Luckily MACSOG was already in the process of handing over the operations to its South Vietnamese assets. In December 1969, 20 percent of the operations in Salem House were ARVN-led. By March 1970 that figure had risen to 65 percent. Realignment of the recon teams previously assigned to CCS and Salem House was complete by 1 July. Ten ARVN-led teams were transferred from Da Nang to Ban Me Thuot. Ten U.S.-led teams previously stationed at CCS went to CCN, five to CCC, and five were kept on hand at Ban Me Thuot for training and in-country missions. In December three of these teams went to Kontum and two to Da Nang.

CCS was headquartered at Camp Torres, near Ban Me Thuot. Its MLTs were located at Duc Lap, Duc Co, and Quan Loi. Recon team missions were also initiated from the detachment's launch sites at Dak To and Dak Pek. There were 244 American and 780 SCU personnel stationed at CCS; the indigenous recon team and exploitation force troops consisted of men from various Montagnard tribes. Cross-border operations in the Salem House area were supported by a new radio relay site known as "the Hill," located on a six-hundred-meter rise approximately eight road miles south of Ban Me Thuot. The Hill was continuously manned by two Special Forces communications personnel and thirteen Montagnards.

During the year 558 reconnaissance missions were launched into Cambodia, along with 19 in-country operations; 16 platoon-size and 3 multiplatoon operations were launched into the Salem House area.[38] These missions were supported by 1,239 tactical air and 1,548 helicopter gunship sorties. Nine prisoners were captured and 558 intelligence reports were generated by the program.

HALO

In July Colonel Sadler authorized the selection and training of the world's first combat high-altitude, low-opening (HALO) parachute team. HALO looked like a possible method of avoiding communist LZ watchers and was a reasonably silent method of insertion. In its search for alternatives to daylight helicopter insertions, MACSOG had already conducted the first static-line combat jump from a helicopter in 1969.

On 21 November CCS launched a night drop consisting of Sgt. David "Babysan" Davidson, Sgt. James Acre, and two Nungs. The men leapt from a helicopter of the 155th AHC into east-central Cambodia. The team was split when it landed, but, with the coming of daylight, the men managed to regroup (one Nung had broken both legs during his landing). The team was then extracted with no difficulty.

On 28 November Spike Team Virginia, consisting of three Americans (SSgt. Cliff Newman, Sfc. Sammy Hernandez, and Sfc. Melvin Hill) and three Montagnard SCUs, performed the first combat HALO jump on a Circus Act wiretap mission in the Prairie Fire area. Jumping from 14,000 feet, all of the team members were scattered six miles from their intended drop zone. After five days on the ground undetected, the men were picked up on 2 December from four separate locations.

Airborne Studies Group: Timberwork (Op-36)

The year 1970 saw the South Vietnamese taking responsibility for and control of the Timberwork program. STRATA was made the responsibility of Alpha Detachment, Group 68 of the STD, and relocated to Tan Son Nhut Air Base. By the end of 1970 STRATA had eliminated or absorbed all of its previously civilian employees and became an all-ARVN affair. The number of teams had been expanded from three to nine and they carried out missions in the Prairie Fire area. Bravo Detachment, 11th Task Force Group (MMFOB), Da Nang, was made responsible for Singleton, Forae, Borden, Earth Angel, Pike Hill, and the new Cedar Walk programs.

Borden, a diversionary program utilizing PAVN POWs for "special missions," deployed forty-seven men into communist-controlled areas during the year, fully expecting them to be caught or to turn themselves in and divulge "secret" information on MACSOG operations.[39] Unexpectedly, four of the men actually returned to ARVN control, and each was rigorously debriefed because there were suspicions that they could have been sent back as double agents. Three of the men were returned to POW camps, but one was transferred to the Earth Angel program.

Earth Angel, a low-level intelligence collection effort manned by ethnic Cambodians, was run in the Salem House area of operations. It was made up of PAVN ralliers who had agreed to return to their old areas of operations dressed and equipped as North Vietnamese troops. The program launched forty missions throughout the year.[40] Planning and training for Cedar Walk, a joint SOG/Cambodian government counterintelligence effort in the western Salem House area, was planned and developed during the year. Operations were set to begin in 1971.

Training began in June for Pike Hill operations, which were to consist of three-man teams of ethnic Cambodians that were to be inserted into non-communist–controlled villages in the Salem House area in order to recruit sympathizers and establish intelligence nets. The first mission was launched on 25 June and eleven additional operations were launched during the year.[41]

With the lifting of geographic restrictions and the exclusion of U.S. personnel from Cambodia, the Airborne Operations Group began to shift its forces southward to the Cambodian border to meet the demand. STRATA teams, which had been operating in the southern Prairie Fire area, were moved south to Salem House in June. The Joint Chiefs also authorized MACSOG to utilize cross-border artillery strikes from South Vietnam into Alpha and Charlie Zones as well as mines in those areas plus the new Air Interdiction Zone.

Maritime Studies Group: Plowman (Op-37)

The NAD and CSS had not run any northern operations in more than a year, but the Joint Chiefs still demanded that the group maintain itself in readiness to pick up its old operations. Since Parboil operations were forbidden, Dodge Mark operations in the I, II, and IV Corps Tactical Zones and the DMZ area were continued. These operations were shifted when high-surf conditions prevented them to IV Corps under the name Ivy Cover. Located at SEAFLOAT (a floating mobile advanced tactical support base) on the Son Cai Lon River, the operations supported U.S. Naval Forces, Vietnam.

The annual MACSOG Command History was quick to point out that four PTFs and two Sea Commando teams had participated in a successful joint mission in the DMZ. This was as close as they were going to get to North Vietnam. Seventy-three successful maritime operations missions were conducted during the year. CSS casualties for the year were one killed and one wounded.[42] During 1970 (as part of an overall STD reorganization) the CSS phased out all of its ARVN and civilian personnel (40 percent) to become an all-Vietnamese navy operation.

Training Studies Group (Op-38)

Training at Camp Long Thanh for the Ground Studies and Airborne Operations Groups continued apace. On 28 May MACSOG received authorization for the creation of Pike Hill agent teams. This meant more trainees at Long Thanh would be joining the Borden and Earth Angel teams already in residence and training there. After the fall of Kham Duc in 1968, Op-35 also dispatched men from the recon teams and exploitation forces to Long Thanh for initial and refresher training. As part of the SOG staff reorganization, supervision of Camp Long Thanh was taken over by the Operations and Training Division as of 23 October.

Psychological Studies Group: Humidor (Op-39)

The group continued to produce and broadcast Radio Red Flag and Voice of the Sacred Sword of the Patriot League programming into North Vietnam and the border areas. It had been two full years since the operational stand-down had denuded the group of its most productive programs, but the group soldiered on. Meanwhile, printed media had become the group's most lucrative operation. The effort included the design and production of propaganda leaflets for distribution in communist-controlled areas (including JPRC leaflet drops in support of the rewards program) of South Vietnam, Laos, and Cambodia. Project Pollack, the poison-pen letter campaign, also continued apace. Pole Bean (previously known as Eldest Son and Italian Green), the insertion of contaminated and booby-trapped ammunition into enemy caches, was ended in February.

Air Studies Group: Shedder (Op-75)

AIRLIFT SECTION

In 1970 MACSOG had to fight to justify the retention of the assets of the Air Studies Group. Several requests (from CINCPAC and 7thAir Force) for the transfer of those assets due to underutilization were countered by SOG with the Joint Chiefs' "Maintain in Readiness" policy for the group. Other issues discussed concerned possible security breaches that were possible if SOG had to utilize a common military carrier for logistics and passenger airlift. During the year there was an increasing use of group assets for HALO delivery of agent and recon team personnel. This tended to lend ammunition to the MACSOG side of the argument. A sign of the changing times, however, was the termination on 30 June of Project Jenny, MACSOG's Navy EC-121 orbiting radio propaganda platform.[43]

The position of director, Air Studies Group, was altered by a Memorandum of Agreement issued on 12 December. The DCSO was made directly responsible to the commander, 7th Air Force. Only U.S. crews were then allowed to fly the four Heavy Hook C-123s of the 1st Flight Detachment into Laotian airspace. Mixed crews were, however, allowed over Cambodia.

During the year 1st Flight conducted twenty-seven combat missions.[44] With the departure of the 12th Tactical Fighter Wing from South Vietnam in March, administrative duties for 1st Flight were picked up by the 483 Tactical Airlift Wing at Cam Ranh Bay Air Base. In June MACSOG aircraft took part in Operation Stick, the relief of Ba Kev and Labang Siek, Cambodia. In Ratanikiri Province 7,500 Cambodian troops and their dependents had been surrounded by PAVN forces and cut off from reinforcement and resupply.[45] MACSOG Heavy Hook aircraft were called upon to maintain the besieged garrison. A small SOG ground detachment was also dispatched, mainly to supervise the aerial resupply effort.

The 15th SOS was redesignated the 90th SOS on 31 October. Based at Nha Trang, the squadron consisted of four MC-130E(I) Combat Spear aircraft. All 21 of the squadron's combat missions (team insertions, resupply, and propaganda leaflet drops) during the year were flown over Laos. The squadron also conducted 432 in-country logistical missions. [46]

HELICOPTER SECTION

The twenty-five H-34 Kingbee aircraft of the 219th VNAF Helicopter Squadron continued to provide support for MACSOG reconnaissance operations. As of 1 July (resulting from the fallout from the Cambodian Incursion), use of U.S. helicopter assets in or over Cambodia was terminated.[47] The 219th was then transferred from Da Nang to Ban Me Thuot, Kontum, and Quan Loi to take over the mission of supporting recon efforts in the CCS area of operations. The 20th SOS Green Hornets, recovering slowly from the mechanical difficulties that had kept them sidelined for more than a year, were moved from Tuy Hoa to Cam Ranh Bay. The squadron also began converting from UH-1P to UH-1N model aircraft. For the first time in several years no aircraft losses were attributed to maintenance or mechanical failures.

MACSOG had been utilizing the Heavy Hook facility at Nakhon Phanom as an alternate launch site for the northern Prairie Fire area when weather precluded launching from South Vietnam. Thanks to continued agreement with the Thai government, SOG was also able to launch missions into the tri-border region and Zone Alpha of Cambodia utilizing the Duck Hook facility at Udorn RTAFB. In May MACSOG began using the PS-2 site (a CIA staging area on the Bolovens Plateau) for the refueling the USAF HH-3 and HH-53 Super Jolly Green Giant helicopters making the flights. PS-2 was closed in August, however, due to communist activity. To make up for the loss, MACSOG signed an agreement with the Thais to utilize the airbase at Ubon, as a substitute. Utilizing Ubon posed its own problems, however.

The HH-3s stationed there had to carry out the insertions and then fly to Quang Tri City, crossing the most heavily defended portions of the Trail. At Quang Tri the aircraft would refuel and then return to Ubon, usually following the same route. When the 21st SOS detachment stationed at Udorn was re-equipped with HH-53 Super Jolly Green Giant helicopters (which had an extended range capability) on 19 August, the facility at Ubon was made redundant.

Recovery Studies (Op-80)

On 3 July Colonel Reinker rotated out as commander of the division. Colonel Sadler wanted his replacement to be a Special Forces, not an Air Force, officer, which ran counter to the interservice agreement made at the inception of the JPRC. Instead Sadler installed Army lieutenant colonel Robert L. Morrissey in the position. The originally nominated man, Air Force lieutenant colonel Gerald E. McImoyle, served as operations officer. By October Morrissey's medical and personal problems led him to be replaced by McImoyle.

McImoyle immediately instituted changes in the E&E code system. This was necessitated by ambiguities in the system and by possible compromise by the communists. He also supervised the creation of E&E "Expedite Kits," smaller units that could be immediately dropped from a FAC. Monterey Angler, the blank Operations Order program initialized in 1969 was formalized into MACV OPLAN J201 Bright Light.[48]

The Recovery Studies Division was also made responsible for collecting and collating information on the number of bodies recovered, military personnel and civilians rescued, and the amount of reward money awarded for information or remains. This information went, via MACV, to the military negotiators at the Paris peace talks. During the year twenty-four prisoner recovery operations were launched and six of them freed one hundred South Vietnamese military personnel or civilians.[49] The remains of fifteen American personnel were recovered by Bright Light teams, one evadee was recovered, and one prisoner was released by North Vietnam.

A series of rescue operations were launched during the year in the IV Corps Tactical Zone by U.S. Navy SEAL teams. Their purpose was to attempt to locate and free Lt. Richard Bowers, SSgt. Gerrasimo Arroyo-Baez, and Lt. John Graff, all of whom had been captured in 1969 and all of whom were reportedly being held in the Mekong Delta. In July a Hoi Chanh led SEAL Team Juliet to the precise location of a communist POW camp only to find that the occupants had just been vacated from it. At the end of the month the SEALs tried again about thirty kilometers away.

This mission was a dry hole, but interrogation of locals revealed that the prisoners had been moved only days before.

OPERATION STORY BOOK

On 21 August a Vietnamese escaped from a prison camp near Vi Thanh, in Chuong Thien Province, and volunteered to lead a rescue force to the location.[50] At 0918 hours the following morning a SEAL team and a South Vietnamese Regional Forces platoon landed on the beach about six kilometers from the suspected camp location. The plan was for naval surface gunfire and air support to box the area in on three sides, leaving open only the side from which the SEAL assault would be launched. It was hoped that the camp guards would abandon their charges in order to escape from the cordon.

The escapee led the SEALs directly into the camp, where they discovered that the guards had decided to brave the naval gunfire in an attempt to escape, taking their prisoners with them. The SEALs took up the chase for two hours before they discovered twenty-eight Vietnamese prisoners, abandoned by their guards in a swamp. Quick reaction to intelligence was considered to be the key to the successful outcome of the operation.

On 22 November, the day after the raid on Son Tay, two captured NLF guerrillas provided information on a POW camp in the Ca Mau Peninsula area of An Xuyen Province. Once again a SEAL team responded quickly to the information. The team found and liberated the camp, which contained another nineteen South Vietnamese prisoners. Three more attempts by the SEALs, acting on information provided by ralliers, all ended up as dry holes. Although the two units were unaffiliated, the SEALs had done yeoman service for the JPRC during the last two years and they liked the work. When the commander of Operation Story Book returned to the United States, he drew up a game plan for the use of SEALs as a quick reaction force for JPRC operations.[51] The Navy was not in the least interested so he went to the CIA, who looked more favorably on the concept. Since the personnel were from the Navy, however, SACSA would have to make the call. The answer was, once again, no.

During the last six months of 1970 the SEALs had liberated forty-eight Vietnamese from the communists. Author George Veith considered that the JPRC's "failure to allow the SEALS free reign in the Delta and to coordinate their efforts in advance [was] the most serious policy mistake the JPRC made."[52] Meanwhile Monterey Angler seemed to be paying off. On 17 December, acting on local intelligence, the Vinh Binh Province Popular Forces conducted their own Bright Light raid. Overrunning an

NLF prison camp, the Popular Force troops liberated forty-nine individuals including thirty-one civilians, eight ARVN, and ten NLF members who were being punished by their fellows.[53]

Plans

The Plans Division generally concentrated on preparing for the takeover of MACSOG operations by the STD, with a target date for the completed program set in mid-1973. Toward the end of the year, however, CINCPAC and MACV once again took up the cudgel of northern operations. The Paris peace talks were at a standstill, so why not give Hanoi a nudge? In a series of messages in December, CINCPAC and General Abrams proposed and discussed with the JCS a range of maritime and sabotage missions for MACSOG that were remarkably similar to those that had preceded the bombing halt. One of their most audacious (and least thought out) plans was Perry Run, a proposed STRATA demolition raid into Dong Hoi, North Vietnam. The team was to be inserted by parachute from a MC-130 and spend nine days on the ground in the North.[54] Luckily, it was never carried out. A throwback to more interesting times was Annex N to MACV OPLAN 5J22 "Support of Internal Uprisings and Revolutions" within North Vietnam.

A SEACORD conference was convened in Bangkok from 29 June to 2 July. CINCPAC had mandated the conference for the purpose of discussing aid to the Lon Nol government of Cambodia. MACV, MACSOG, COMUSMACTHAI, and American embassies in Saigon, Bangkok, Vientiane, and Phanom Penh all sent representatives. On 19 October a "UW Planning Conference" was held in Bangkok with representation from the same organizations. It was at this conference that the Cedar Walk program was conceived. Curiously, and ominously, at both conferences the participants discussed PAVN/NLF threats to the Cambodian government and armed forces, yet no mention was made of the threat posed by the indigenous Khmer Rouge.

An Aerial Surveillance Section was added to the intelligence staff to provide supervision and support to the Ford Drum photographic intelligence program during the year. The initial draft of the JCS MACSOG Documentation Study was completed on 10 July and forwarded to MACSOG for review, and Annex F to the 1969 MACV Command History was completed by the division.

Logistics

The division continued it efforts in the procurement, storage, transportation, and allocation of a wide variety of supplies for SOG's operations and personnel. Three major logistical efforts made during the year were the creation of HALO packages, pre-packaged air drop supplies for Operation Tailwind, and palletized supplies for Operation Stick in Cambodia. During the year the Air Delivery Branch packaged parachutes and supplies for thirty-two missions, including eighteen personnel and fourteen cargo drops.[55] Much of the division's effort during the year concerned planning for the inevitable Vietnamization of MACSOG's logistics system. It was interesting to note, however, that as other American forces were being withdrawn from the conflict, the number and frequency of SOG's missions continued to increase.

Comptroller

The Comptroller Division provided financial guidance to chief, SOG, and furnished the financial planning and auditing that were its principal functions. One must, however, remember that MACSOG was a classified project, the largest of its kind ever run by the U.S. military. The disbursement of the money was also one of the division's responsibilities, and in a unit like MACSOG, such mundane matters as pay and allowances could be quite interesting.

The American military components of SOG were paid in Military Payment Certificates (standard operating procedure in the days before payroll automation), not by check. Like all the personnel assigned to MACV components, the men reported to a military paymaster, presented their identification, and were paid. This process usually necessitated false identification cards, with the designation of their "cover" units inscribed. If the men were in "civilian clothing" assignments, they donned sterile uniforms and went to collect their pay.

MACSOG's mercenaries and civilian employees (more than eight thousand of them) were paid by the Comptroller Division once a month in South Vietnamese piasters. In some cases (as with some Montagnard elements) where money was not desired, rice and fish of equal value had to be substituted. There was also a lump sum death gratuity, equal in value to one month's wages, which had to be paid to the deceased's next of kin. Cash payments also had to be arranged for rents on the civilian properties (MACV 2, supply facilities, transient barracks, safe houses, etc.) occupied by MACSOG operations. The division also handled large cash disbursements to the Recovery Studies Division in the form of payments for the recovery and return of U.S. personnel or their remains to friendly control.

MACSOG-authorized funding (unclassified and handled through CINCPAC) for 1971 was $160,000.[56] As for classified funds (handled through CNO), budget revisions lowered the original 1970 budget from $25,778,400 to $18,611,900. The 1971 budget was approved at $22,466,500.[57]

Communications

1970 was not a good year for communications security either in the field or at MACSOG's headquarters. On 15 February a survey of communications security was conducted by the U.S. Army's 101st Radio Research Company, which uncovered "disastrously dangerous" signals emanations from the communications center.[58] From 22 February to 4 March the Army Security Agency ran a series of signals radiation tests at the communications center. Deficiencies in the equipment led to a $400,000 refurbishment of the MACSOG communications center.

On 6 August the 525th Military Intelligence Group ran a COMSEC survey of the intercommunications system at MACSOG's headquarters and found more deficiencies.[59] This initiated an inspection of the site by the Communications Engineering and Installation Agency (CEIA) on 23 September, which led to recommended solutions to the problem. From 18 August to 22 October the 101st Radio Research Company ran a COMSEC survey of all MACSOG operations. Once again, deficiencies were noted.

Strategic Technical Directorate

A reorganization of South Vietnamese unconventional warfare assets took place during the year. The STD became a joint unconventional warfare task force under the control of the Vietnamese Joint General Staff. Planning began in January and by 1 November the reorganization was complete. The major change was that the 1,450-man Vietnamese Special Forces (LLDB) would be transferred into the STD. The effective date of this incorporation was put back to 1 January 1971 so as not to interfere with recruiting.[60]

The LLDB was redesignated the Special Mission Service (SMS). The old STD Special Task Force was incorporated as Detachments 11 and 68. The SMS (under command of Lieutenant Colonel Ngo The Linh) was ostensibly created for unconventional contingencies in North Vietnam. It would be trained at Nha Trang by the U.S. Special Mission Advisory Group (SMAG) composed of advisors from the 5th Special Forces Group.

There was also to be an expansion of exploitation assets. Six exploitation companies commanded by ARVN were already running during the year and eight more were to be created. But although troops were available to man five companies, a dearth of trained ARVN officers led to a reduction to only three companies. From this point forward, the STD was expected carry out the cross-border forays on its own.[61]

Kingpin

Unknown to all but those concerned, some MACSOG personnel had a rendezvous with history on 21 November when Operation Kingpin, the Son Tay POW camp raid, was carried out. The camp, located twenty-three miles west of Hanoi, was surrounded by PAVN installations and no Americans had been north of the 17th parallel for two years. Air Force general Leroy Manor was overall commander while "Bull" Simons served as his deputy. The strike force was made up of fifty-six Special Forces volunteers, some of them MACSOG alumni. The fourteen-man assault team that was to free the prisoners from their cells was led by SOG legend Cpt. Dick Meadows.

Despite last-minute intelligence (derived from aerial surveillance and from SOG) that the camp was abandoned, the raid proceeded anyway. Dozens of PAVN troops were killed during the operation, but not a single American. Although the camp was indeed empty and no Americans had been freed, it was still considered a success. As a direct result of the raid, all U.S. prisoners held in outlying camps were consolidated in Hanoi and all torture and solitary confinement were terminated. The real payoff, however, was the boost to prisoner morale, which was immeasurable.

A sign of the times was MACSOG's lack of direct participation in the raid. Beyond being queried about photo intelligence of the target area, SOG was never consulted or brought into the picture. This is surprising considering that Don Blackburn, serving as SACSA at the time, was Kingpin's guiding light. MACSOG was supposed to be the only U.S. military organization that had the authority—it certainly had the means—to carry out such an operation. The key issue that probably prevented the unit from more direct participation was strictly one of (perceived) operational security.

Comment: Cross-Border Ground Operations

Without doubt, the cross-border ground reconnaissance operations of MACSOG contributed most to the American effort in Southeast Asia. They were also the most avidly supported of SOG's operations by their superiors. The reasoning behind this was not difficult to determine, since they were also the most conventional operations carried out by SOG. In the rugged terrain traversed by the Ho Chi Minh Trail, neither aircraft nor sensors could provide enough detailed intelligence information for the bombing of specific targets during the interdiction campaign. Nor could they provide information on communist buildups or intentions. Only boots on the ground could do so.

There was also no doubt that the recon teams carried out their missions with intense courage and fortitude. It was bad enough to cross the border in the early days of the program, when communist reactions were slow and uncoordinated; it was quite another thing to jump the fence, knowing with certitude that the communists were working hard every day to improve their defenses. What can one say about men who not only conducted one of the most skilled and dangerous combat missions of the war, but who also then volunteered for tour after tour with MACSOG? These were fighting men who were proud of their abilities, who faced extreme danger in their enemy's backyard, knowing that capture meant certain death, and who were thus determined to hone their skills and go down fighting. Any nation would be proud to claim such men.

Most histories of MACSOG assert that the men of the C&C detachments tied down thousands (or tens of thousands) of communist troops in static security roles on the Trail system. This is a hard claim to prove. It was also a strange one to make when any comparison was made between the logistical structures of the Americans and the North Vietnamese. At least one-half of all U.S. personnel deployed in Vietnam served in logistical capacities (or in their defense), not in the combat arms; yet the Americans did not consider this as a deficiency nor did the North Vietnamese consider it a "victory." Granted, the North Vietnamese did deploy security forces (and specialized units) to defend their lines of communication. But the sanctuaries were also the location of many main force units resting, resupplying, or recuperating from action in South Vietnam. To separate one from another is difficult, so a cost/benefit ratio between communists killed or the divergence of their resources is very difficult to determine.

How did PAVN/NLF personnel feel about MACSOG interdiction operations in their rear areas? According to Nguyen Tuong Lai, a NLF regimental commander who fought in Tay Ninh Province, they worked very well: "They effectively attacked and captured our soldiers and disrupted our supply lines. This weakened our forces and hurt our morale, because we could not stop these attacks. We understood that these American soldiers were very skillful and very brave in their tactics to disrupt infiltration from the north."[62] There was no doubt that PAVN took the threat posed by the recon teams very seriously, and their reaction to the threat over time was obvious. The Trail was a logistical jugular vein that the North Vietnamese could not afford to have constricted or stopped. But neither the teams nor the aerial interdiction effort that they supported ever posed a serious threat to it. Proof positive was given during the

Cambodian Incursion, when huge stockpiles of communist materiel were overrun and captured. These supplies had been successfully transported down the system almost two years into the Commando Hunt aerial interdiction campaign, three years into Operations Daniel Boone/Salem House, and one year into Operation Menu.

The main drawback faced by MACSOG cross-border operations was the same one faced by MACV: limited ability to launch larger operations that would have threatened to cut the Trail itself. By the time the only operation that really threatened the logistical system, Lam Son 719, was launched, MACSOG could not even directly participate in it. By then it was too late anyway. The North Vietnamese had been ensconced far too long in strength and they faced only American airpower and South Vietnamese troops.

From the inception of cross-border operations the missions were severely restricted in the direction of approach, depth of penetration, locales of launch sites, and the limited number of usable LZs. These restrictions eventually made the teams predictable, let the communists key in their reaction forces, and led to higher American and South Vietnamese casualties. Attempts to overcome these limitations—the use of Thai launch sites, the mobile launch site concept, and parachute insertions—never really replaced the standard helicopter insertion from the east.

There were those within MACSOG, indeed within Op-35 itself, who opposed what came to be the standard mission profile of the recon teams. Lt. Col. Raymond Call, deputy chief of Op-35 at its inception, believed that the program had quickly become stale. He was convinced that SOG should have "stopped running so many missions . . . that the program should have been de-escalated and turned into a PSYOPS program. It became redundant and a waste of assets. If you double the size of something like Op-35 it doesn't mean its going to be twice as good."[63] By the colonel's second tour with Op-35 in 1970, Call's opinion had not changed. "I don't think we accomplished anything my second year . . . but the issue then was to put numbers on the board . . . never mind if you didn't get any intelligence."[64]

Chapter Eight

JANUARY 1971–30 APRIL 1972: DRAWDOWN

Headquarters

Col. John F. Sadler remained in the position of chief, MACSOG, until 30 April 1972, when he was relieved by Col. David R. Presson. The new commander held the position for only one month, until May 1972, when MACSOG was dissolved. Vietnamization had finally caught up with the unit. The headquarters' administrative JTD at the beginning of 1971 totaled 383 Americans, but this was reduced to 340 by December.[1] The overall command itself consisted of 8,487 men in October 1971 and was reduced to 7,787 by January 1972.[2] By mid-February, operations were being conducted only on a case-by-case basis as requested by MACV operations and intelligence. March 1972 saw the stand-down of MAC-SOG's dedicated air support and the dissolution of the task forces. By the end of March the unit was no longer capable of conducting operations and so indicated this to higher authority.

Operations and Training

On 30 April 1972 the division was consolidated with the Training Studies Group to form the Plans, Operations, and Training Advisory Division of Strategic Technical Directorate Assistance (STDAT-158).[3] The division then had responsibility for allocating and training American and South Vietnamese personnel for the various operations.

Ground Studies Group (Op-35)

THE TRAIL

The Commando Hunt series continued with Commando Hunt V, begun on 10 October 1970 and continuing until 30 April 1971. During the campaign 16,266 PAVN trucks were reported destroyed and another 4,700 were damaged.[4] These numbers were very high, especially when considering that the aerial effort had been thrown off balance during the year by Operation Lam Son 719. During the South Vietnamese thrust into Laos, fully 80 percent of all Commando Hunt sorties were shifted to support of the ARVN offensive.[5] The chief problem for Air Force intelligence analysts was rectifying the 6,000 trucks estimated at entering or operating within Laos with 20,966 reported destroyed or damaged. Reviewing these figures, analysts in Saigon lowered the estimate to 11,000 destroyed and 8,000 damaged.[6] The lack of physical and photographic evidence of truck kills that should have been accumulating in the Laotian landscape (at least ten carcasses per mile of road and trail) gave rise to the legend of the "Great Laotian Truck Eater."[7]

Evidently the Truck Eater was living high on the hog. The 7th/13th Air Force continued its interdiction in Commando Hunt VI (15 May 1971–31 October 1971) and VII (1 November 1971–29 March 1972). During the dry season portion of Commando Hunt VII, the Air Force fielded an average of 182 attack fighters, 13 fixed-wing gunships, and 21 B-52 sorties per day.[8] As a result of this all-out effort, intelligence analysts claimed that 10,689 PAVN trucks were destroyed and credited AC-130E Spectres with 7,335 of these kills.[9] The Air Force then claimed that the cumulative totals indicated that 51,500 trucks and 3,400 anti-aircraft weapons had been destroyed or damaged in the seven campaigns.[10]

U.S. intelligence sources reported that Hanoi had ordered as many trucks from the Soviet Union as it had from all other sources in 1970.[11] This seemed to indicate that PAVN was really hurting for transportation, but the Nguyen Hue offensive planned for early 1972 could just as easily have accounted for it. Since 80 percent of the vehicles arrived in North Vietnam at least six weeks before the offensive, they more likely reflected replacements for anticipated losses. Air Force historian Col. Herman Gilster finally burst the bubble of the Air Force's claims for truck destruction by working out total North Vietnamese logistical needs and comparing them with the available transportation (from the total of imported vehicles) and the figures for transport units in the official North Vietnamese history. In his estimation, during 1971–72 a maximum of only 2,500–3,000 PAVN trucks (each of which carried approximately four tons of materiel) were working the entire Trail system at any one time.[12]

MACV estimated that the North Vietnamese and NLF forces in South Vietnam required 1,220 tons of all categories of supplies each month in order to maintain a normal pace of operations.[13] The 559th transported or stored 60,000 tons of supplies in 1971 with a net loss rate of 2.07 percent.[14] During 1970–71, 195,000 PAVN replacements infiltrated to the

South.[15] Of the 800 tons of food necessary, 480 to 640 tons had come from direct purchases from the government of Cambodia or from communist sympathizers in eastern Cambodia. The Lon Nol coup and the incursion of 1970 had closed down these supply routes. Hanoi then had to provide, via the Ho Chi Minh Trail, between 580 and 740 extra tons of supplies per month, or 6,960 to 8,880 tons per year.[16]

To make up for this shortfall in the COSVN/B-3 Front area, PAVN continued its repair and expansion of the Trail network and the development of the Kaman River for water transport. The North Vietnamese also constructed the one-thousand-kilometer-long Road-K or the "Green Road" from north of Lum Bum to lower Laos. By the end of May 1971 North Vietnamese and Pathet Lao forces had occupied Muong Phalane, Ban Houi Sane, and Paksong while reoccupying Attopeu, Saravane, and Ban Thatang, cementing their hold on the strategic Bolovens Plateau. U.S. intelligence sources revealed that the North Vietnamese had also established a new logistical command to manage the flow of supplies and troops to the new battlefields in Cambodia.

In April 1970 the 470th Transportation Group supplemented the efforts of the 559th and completed the new "Liberation Route," which turned west from the Trail near Muong May at the southern end of Laos and paralleled the Kong River into Cambodia.[17] Eventually, this route extended past Siem Prang and reached the Mekong near Stung Treng.[18] The next step was the seizure of the town of Kratie in east central Cambodia, on 5 May. The 470th cleared the population out of the Mekong River town and turned it into its administrative headquarters. PAVN base areas to the east were fed by Kratie while men and supplies headed for the Mekong Delta region of South Vietnam were circled westward, around Phanom Penh, through the foothills of the Cardamom Mountains, and then east again to cross the border.[19]

The 559th and 470th groups functioned similarly, but the 470th had no integral anti-aircraft artillery units. By the end of the year an estimated 3,300 miles of road were being utilized by the communists in Laos and Cambodia, and construction and repair were now being conducted year-round. PAVN also increased its anti-aircraft defenses. The number of weapons defending the Trail in southeastern Laos reached approximately 1,500 guns.[20] On 10 January 1972 an American observation aircraft successfully dodged the first SAM-2 launched from Laotian soil. It also became common for North Vietnamese Air Force MiG fighters to cross into Laotian airspace, thereby forcing off B-52 strikes. PAVN took advantage of the American reluctance to incur losses to its bomber fleet and moved its SAM sites deeper into Laos.

ISLAND TREE

Since the inception of Commando Hunt in 1968, there had been no effort on the part of the 7th/13th Air Force to interdict PAVN troop infiltration on the Trail system. Originally this was due to the lack of an adequate system for alerting sensors to the presence of ground forces. This lack was institutionalized as the Air Force concentrated on the "war against trucks." This state of affairs reflected the absurdity of the interdiction strategy. If the purpose of the interdiction effort was to inflict so much pain on Hanoi that it would abandon its effort (Commando Hunt's stated strategy), how did the destruction of imported trucks and supplies contribute to it? During Commando Hunt VI both military planners and politicians finally concentrated their efforts on coming up with a solution that would cost the communists in blood as well as supplies and equipment.

From late spring through the summer of 1971, CINCPAC, MACV, CIA, MACSOG, and staff members from the various embassies began to work on an integrated, multinational (U.S./South Vietnamese/Cambodian/Laotian) plan to halt or retard communist troop infiltration. It was titled Project Island Tree.[21] Intelligence was culled from the files of those concerned to try to determine the geographic location of the troop infiltration routes. The key problem for any such operation was an almost total lack of knowledge concerning PAVN troop infiltration. All that was really known was that the routes taken by ground forces were separate from, but parallel to, the supply network. A survey of PAVN troops captured in 1967 (before Commando Hunt began) revealed that only one man in ten had so much as seen an air strike during the trip south. These disclosures were unusual (intelligence personnel were rather shocked to discover) since only about one prisoner in ten had undergone any previous interrogation concerning their infiltration.

Task Force Alpha then went to work analyzing old and new data in an effort to find locations for sensor strings that would pinpoint targets for the aerial effort. Ground interdiction of the Trail fell through (once again) due to political constraints. It is interesting to note that only in the waning years of the conflict did serious multi-institutional consideration take place for an anti-infiltration effort. It was too little and far too late. After PAVN launched the Nguyen Hue Offensive at the end of March, the number of Island Tree missions declined abruptly as aircraft were diverted to South Vietnam. The project was officially terminated on 9 May.[22]

Reorganization

On 8 February 1971 the JCS ordered the end of American participation in ground actions in the Prairie Fire area of operations, with the exception of the maintenance of a security force for the Golf-5 radio relay site, POW rescue operations, and aircraft crash site inspections (nicknamed Waco City).[23] MACSOG's role also included the training of ARVN officers and NCOs to take over the exploitation companies.

In the Salem House area U.S.-led teams had been forbidden on 1 July 1970 with the exception of POW rescue missions or crash site inspections. The use of American tactical air support (fixed and rotary wing) was permitted in Cambodia only when mission requirements were clearly beyond the abilities of the VNAF. Due to an article in the *Washington Post* compromising the old nicknames, Prairie Fire/Nickel Steel was redesignated Phu Dung (pronounced foo young—Vietnamese for an opium pipedream) and Salem House became Thot Not (pronounced tote note—a tree indigenous to Cambodia) on 8 April 1971. On 1 September the group's staff elements were relocated to Camp Nguyen Cao Vi, home of the STD Liaison Bureau, in order to provide closer counterpart coordination. On 30 April 1972 MACSOG Op-35 was disestablished and phased into the Plans, Operations, and Training Section of STDAT-158. It was then renamed the Liaison Service Advisory Detachment (LSAD).[24]

Due to redeployment of the 5th SFG in March 1971, CCN, CCC, and CCS were redesignated Task Force Advisory Elements (TF1AE, TF2AE, and TF3AE, respectively). Each of the TFAEs was maintained by 244 MACSOG and 780 indigenous personnel.[25] TF1AE (Da Nang), consisted of Mobile Launch Site 1 (MLS-1) at Phu Bai, MLS-2 at Quang Tri, and MLS-3 at Nakhon Phanom. On 30 March 1972 the Heavy Hook support facility at Nakhon Phanom was disbanded. TF2AE at Kontum maintained launch sites at Dak To, Ubon RTAFB, Thailand, and Plei Djereng (when Dak To was closed out). TF3AE at Ban Me Thuot maintained launch sites at Du Co, Quan Loi, and Song Be. During the spring TF3AE established an unmanned radio relay transmitter site to support Salem House/Thot Not operations. This facility was located on Nui Ba Rah, near Song Be.

PHU DUNG/THOT NOT

In January 1971 MACSOG dispatched recon teams into Laos to support actions by CIA-backed Laotian forces committed to Operation Silver Buckle. During the period 1 January 1971–31 March 1972, U.S.-led teams conducted 50 recon missions into Laos and 242 in South Vietnam.[26] During the same time period ARVN-led teams conducted 108 missions in Laos and 7 in South Vietnam. There were also 13 platoon-size and 3 multiplatoon operations in Laos and 26 in South Vietnam. These operations were supported by 1,025 tactical air and 2,540 helicopter gunship sorties, and the program generated 175 intelligence reports. Casualties were 12 SOG recon men killed, 56 wounded, and 10 missing in action. SCU casualties amounted to 45 killed, 142 wounded, and 30 missing.[27]

During the same time frame in the Thot Not area of operations, ARVN-led recon operations totaled 364 in Cambodia and 8 in South Vietnam while 73 STRATA missions were launched. These forces also carried out 26 platoon-size and 13 multiplatoon operations. U.S.-led teams conducted 8 recon missions and 7 multiplatoon operations within South Vietnam.[28] These operations were supported by 1,055 tactical air and 906 helicopter gunship sorties.[29] Communist prisoners taken numbered 6 and 396 intelligence reports were generated. American casualties in the Thot Not area came to 4 killed, 12 wounded, and 1 missing. SCU casualties were 28 killed, 113 wounded, and 44 missing.[30]

On 27 December 1971 Earth Angel team Beaver Scrap parachuted seventy-six kilometers inside Laos (forty-three kilometers outside SOG's authorized area), near the abandoned CIA airstrip PS 26. The four-man team was equipped with a TEMIG (tactical electromagnetic impulse generator) beacon used for transmitting encoded target information to orbiting AC-130s. The team was resupplied by napalm canisters dropped from F-4s and reported intelligence gathered on boat and truck traffic moving down the Se Krong River valley until the team was exfiltrated by the 21st SOS on 29 January 1972, after having spent an astounding thirty-three days behind North Vietnamese lines.[31]

On 7 May 1971, an all-American recon team made a high-altitude jump between the Ashau Valley and Khe Sanh. Two men were injured in the jump itself and were then extracted. The remainder of the team stayed in the target area undetected for five days before they too were extracted. A second jump conducted on 22 June resulted in one man MIA and three recovered. On 22 September a team jumped into the Plei Trap Valley to search for communist roads and trails coming across the border from Cambodia. All of the team members landed together and remained uninjured. They reconned the area undetected for four days and were then safely extracted. Later in the year, ten-man RT Wisconsin jumped twenty-five miles southwest of Pleiku into the Ia Drang Valley on 11 October. They were initially scattered during the drop, but managed to regroup and completed their mission.

LAM SON 719

Although there were urgent requests from MACSOG and CINCPAC for the unleashing of the recon teams for the proposed ARVN offensive, two dilemmas worked against the organization's participation in the mission that the Ground Studies Branch had essentially been created for. First was the Cooper-Church Amendment, which prohibited U.S. ground forces from participating in the operation. Even though MACSOG was a deniable covert organization, the JCS extended the prohibition to include it; second, and even more problematic: all available American and ARVN helicopter assets were soaked up by the invasion.

According to Colonel Sadler, he was a party to three planning sessions attended by General Abrams, the MACV J-2, and the commander of the 24th Corps, Gen. Jock Sutherland. When queried as to communist strength in the proposed area of the incursion, Sadler told them that they were headed into "a hornet's nest."[32] When Sutherland stated that his biggest worry was how to get into the Trail complex, Sadler warned him that "your biggest worry should be how to get out."[33]

MACSOG's participation in Operation Lam Son 719 came in the form of recon missions into the operational area prior to the incursion and diversionary efforts and road interdiction once it was under way. During the week before the launch of the offensive, SOG Blackbirds dropped dummy parachutists loaded with Nightingale noisemaking devices in seven locations west of Khe Sanh.[34] U.S.-led teams then carried out fake insertions at four locations in the same area. Three recon teams and two Hatchet Forces landed atop Co Roc Mountain during the week before the invasion, but were forced to withdraw due to the 7 February restriction on U.S. personnel in Laos.

On the following day, 8 February, ARVN forces rolled over the border in the long-anticipated attempt to cut the Ho Chi Minh Trail. When things began to fall apart and the ARVN began their withdrawal, MACSOG participated in roadwatch and interdiction missions meant to occupy and slow down PAVN forces. Six recon teams were sent into the Ashau Valley beginning on 18 February.[35] Their mission was to carry out reconnaissance for ARVN units withdrawing from Laos along Route 922. While participating in these operations, RT Intruder was being extracted from an LZ on Stabo rigs; at that time the extraction helicopter took hits and began to go down. Cpt. Ronald Watson and Sgt. Allen Lloyd were dragged into trees and killed as the chopper went over the edge of a cliff and crashed at its base. Sfc. Sammy Hernandez was lucky in that his rope either broke or was shot through; he plummeted through the canopy—banged up, but alive.

RT Habu was sent in to retrieve the bodies and had to rappel down the cliff to reach the chopper. After returning to the top, the team was attacked by a reinforced PAVN platoon. With half of the team wounded and pinned against the cliff top with nowhere else to go, the team members abandoned the bodies of their comrades and leapt over the edge of the cliff. Miraculously all of the men survived. Three more teams were sent into the dreaded Ashau to interdict Highway 548. This road had become the main line of advance for PAVN forces, which were closing up behind retreating ARVN elements. For twenty-one days these teams called in air and artillery support. Most teams had a hard time staying on the ground for up to twenty-four hours, one team that attempted insertion having been driven off by ground fire from twelve separate LZs before they called it a day.[36]

During these covering operations, RT Python occupied abandoned Firebase Thor in order to block PAVN access to Highway 548. During the night the team was surrounded by North Vietnamese troops who were so brazen that they utilized their flashlights and truck headlights with impunity. The team directed airstrikes against these targets and was probed continuously. On the following day the team received a mortar attack and at the end of the second day of its mission, the team was extracted. For his role during the action, SSgt. Leslie Chapman received the Distinguished Service Cross.

BATTLE OF HICKORY HILL

By the summer of 1971 CCN's radio relay site Hickory was the only American or South Vietnamese presence in northwestern I Corps. Located on a pinnacle about four miles north of the abandoned Khe Sanh Combat Base, Hickory had become a tiny island in a sea of communist forces. On the morning of 5 June the North Vietnamese launched an attack that promised to rid them of the troublesome outpost.[37] Defending the hilltop were SOG sergeant Jon Cavaiani and sergeant John Jones, who commanded sixty-seven SCUs and twenty-seven U.S. military personnel, including technical specialists, and a squad from L Company, 75th ARVN Rangers. As dawn broke PAVN troops, who had scaled the peak unnoticed, launched a vigorous attack supported by machine guns and B-40 rockets. The Americans were caught by surprise and many were wounded early in the action, including Sergeant Jones.

What the North Vietnamese had not expected, however, was the ferocious resistance of U.S. Army sensor reader Walter Millsap. Courage and desperate heroism could come at inexplicable times and in strange packages, and certainly none of his compatriots expected it to come that morning to the unobtrusive, bespectacled Millsap. Taking charge of a .50-caliber machine gun, he laid down heavy suppressive fire so that Cavaiani could distribute ammo and aid the wounded. When a communist rocket hit the bunker atop which he was fighting (knocking the .50 off of it), Millsap, despite being badly wounded, dragged the gun back up and carried on.

Cavaiani had called for evacuation, but was informed that the extraction would have to be done in relays. He put Millsap and most of the wounded on the first lift ship, but the sensor reader just got off and continued to fight. Around 1630 hours Cavaiani was informed that only one more lift ship was inbound but there were still thirty-one men on Hickory. By that time Millsap had been wounded two more times. Cavaiani forced him and six Montagnards onto the Huey, leaving twenty-three Montagnards and ARVN Rangers, John Jones, and himself to face the North Vietnamese. Beginning at 1030 hours the following morning, the North Vietnamese began to probe the small perimeter left to Cavaiani and his men. Eventually they launched a massed attack that threatened to overrun the outpost. Cavaiani was badly wounded during the assault and crawled into a bunker with Jones. Two North Vietnamese entered the bunker only to be dispatched by Jones and Cavaiani, who killed his opponent with a combat knife. When a grenade was tossed into the bunker, wounding both men, Jones attempted to surrender, only to be killed.

Cavaiani was knocked out by the grenade blast and awoke to find himself in a burning bunker surrounded by the North Vietnamese. He crawled out and managed to gain some distance before a bullet grazed his head, knocking him unconscious again. When he awoke his clothing was being rummaged through by a PAVN soldier. Cavaiani promptly killed the man with his knife and then managed to walk, stumble, and crawl for ten days toward Firebase Fuller, only to be captured within sight of the base. He was released from captivity in 1973. For his defense of Hickory, he was awarded the Medal of Honor.[38] The intrepid sensor reader, Walter Millsap, was awarded the Distinguished Service Cross.

RECON TEAM KANSAS

With the fall of Hickory and signs of a large PAVN buildup in western I Corps, the Field Force commander needed intelligence and MACSOG was going to provide it. On 7 August 1971 Recon Team Kansas was inserted onto a deserted hilltop firebase near Khe Sanh. The plan was to spend one night at the position and then extract half of the team. The other half would wait for the inevitable PAVN squad to arrive to check out the area. The recon team would then spring an ambush and possibly grab a prisoner.

The reinforced team consisted of six SOG recon men and eight Montagnards under the command of 1st Lt. Lauren Hagen. The men deployed on the hilltop and waited for daylight and the arrival of two "extraction" helicopters. What the team did not realize was that they had inserted within sight of a new six-inch fuel pipeline that ran from the DMZ and down the Cam Lo River Valley. Also located nearby was the headquarters of the 304th PAVN Division.

The morning was shrouded in fog, but the team members could hear the nearby arrival of trucks and the dropping of tailgates. It was later estimated that five battalions of North Vietnamese troops, a reinforced regiment, were massing to assault the hill. Then they came on. A tremendous blast of small arms fire swept up the slopes as the North Vietnamese advanced. Lieutenant Hagen was the first to die as he advanced to aid wounded SCUs. He was followed by SSgt. Oran Bingham and two more of the SCUs. Four of the defenders had been killed in less than four minutes. A Covey FAC soon arrived, saw the action, and called off the planned extraction. It called for fighters instead, but that was going to take time. Command on the hilltop had fallen to SSgt. Tony Anderson, who consolidated the men for a last stand. By that time the communists had advanced to the crest and the fighting took place at not much more distance than the end of a rifle barrel.

Cobra gunships then arrived and rolled in to strafe the North Vietnamese with Vulcan miniguns and grenade launchers. They were soon followed by fighters that splashed the hillsides with napalm. Even with their dead stacking up around them, the PAVN troops came on. Eventually, however, they lost heart and broke, streaming down the hill to safety. At that moment the extraction Hueys arrived. Anderson loaded his wounded comrades onto the choppers and they lifted out. Three hours later he was back, taking part in a Bright Light mission to recover the remains of his comrades. Lieutenant Hagen, Staff Sergeant Bingham, and 3 of the Yards were dead while Sgt. Bruce Berg was missing and presumed dead. All of the other members of the team, including Anderson, had been wounded multiple times. It was estimated that at least 185 of the North Vietnamese had been killed. First Lieutenant Hagen was posthumously awarded the U.S. Army's last Vietnam Medal of Honor.[39] Sgt. Tony Anderson was awarded the Distinguished Service Cross and the 4 other American defenders were given Silver Stars.

QUAN LOI

On 30 March 1972 PAVN launched its Nguyen Hue Offensive. Originally falling like a thunderbolt upon the ARVN in I Corps, this was no repeat of Tet. The communists utilized infantry/armor attacks supported by massed artillery fire, employing conventional tactics. On 5 April the relative quiet in III Corps was shattered when the 5th NLF/PAVN Division moved out of Cambodia and down Route 13 to attack the district town of Loc Ninh. After rolling over the 9th ARVN Regiment and a Ranger battalion, the communists proceeded twenty-five kilometers south to An Loc, capital of Binh Long Province and last stop on Route 13 before Saigon.

Several miles to the east of An Loc was Quan Loi, long utilized by SOG as a launch site for recon teams into the Salem House and southern Prairie Fire areas.[40] By 1972 TF1AE was planning a move from Da Nang to Quan Loi, but the process had just begun when the offensive was launched. Only three recon teams, seven American advisors, a small force of SCU from TF3AE's exploitation company, and some technicians were on site. Early on 5 April the North Vietnamese launched a sapper attack on Quan Loi that was repulsed, but they then continued to attack the launch site throughout the night and into the following day. Heavy PAVN anti-aircraft fire prevented aerial resupply or reinforcement, so it was decided to abandon the site. A total of 157 personnel were helilifted out without any casualties incurred. Only 1 SCU had been wounded during the battle. To the west, the epic struggle for An Loc was just beginning.

CIRCUS ACT

When it came to intelligence collection, MACSOG ran on all cylinders. Aerial reconnaissance operations like Ford Drum collected photographic evidence of communist movements and positions, while recon teams eyeballed the North Vietnamese and collected documents during their operations. Nothing, however, spoke louder than the voice of the communists themselves, and when it came to eavesdropping on enemy communications, MACSOG utilized what was, at the time, state-of-the-art surveillance equipment. From the origination of cross-border operations, wiretapping missions were conducted whenever possible on communist communications lines located along the Trail.[41]

These missions were extremely dangerous due to the nature of early taping equipment, which, according to recon team member John Plaster, "begged to be discovered."[42] Battery-powered portable reel-to-reel tape decks were emplaced next to a discovered communications line and then hard-spliced into the line itself. This usually caused a decibel line loss, a drop in audio strength that was easily detectable by the telephone system operator. The communists would then send teams of men to trace the line and either discover the team or the taping equipment. The equipment was heavy, bulky, and difficult to work with under combat conditions. Complicating matters were short battery life and the time limitations of the tape itself.

By late 1966 SOG teams were issued cassette tape recorders (then not even available on the civilian market) and, with CIA guidance, began to utilize more advanced forms of bugging. The agency advised against hard splicing and advocated the use of electromagnetic couplers that utilized the principle of induction, usually in the form of probes or spring-loaded clips that simply touched the line and did not cause signal loss. The decks were voice-activated, equipped to record only when actual signals were emanating, thus extending battery life and the time length of the tape. Working under the tutelage of Bull Simons, Shining Brass launched its first wiretap mission from 3 to 7 October 1966. The operation was carried out in Target Area MA-10, in the tri-border region, by Spike Team Colorado. The mission was successful and, after several more insertions, yielded seven cassette tapes of PAVN tactical communications. The intelligence collected on this mission had led to the launching of the first SLAM operation.

The wiretap operations were as fraught with peril as any of SOG's other missions. On 28 March 1968 the three Americans and six indigs of RT Asp were sent into the Se Samou Valley, northeast of Tchepone, to emplace a tap on a discovered PAVN commo line. This was to be the first mission of the newly titled Circus Act program. After launch from Nakhon Phanom, the mission went well and the tap was emplaced. When the extraction helicopter appeared, however, things went terribly wrong. All of the indigs made it into the CH-53 up an extraction ladder extended from the ramp of the chopper while the team leader, Alan Boyer, was still climbing aboard. Intense communist ground fire then erupted from the jungle.

The helicopter then lifted off with Boyer still hanging on the rungs of the ladder. At 1,500 feet, the rung to which he clung broke and Boyer plunged to his death. The two other Americans, George Brown and Charles Huston, were left on the ground. Bad weather postponed any rescue attempt until 1 April, when FOB-4's RT Boa was inserted to locate them. After six hours on the ground and the loss of one indig, the team was extracted. Brown and Huston were listed as missing in action.

During 1970 one of the most successful wiretapping operations of the program was carried out. MACSOG was notified of a PAVN corps-level communications establishment in front of Kontum in the tri-border area, and the CIA requested that MACSOG tap into nearby communications lines and provided it with the required capability. The mission included firing a rocket with an attached line (which had some attached electronic components) that would hang over the four-wire communications cables.

The message traffic was then picked off by induction and recorded. The recordings were retrieved by simply flying over the cables and electronically transferring the information. By late 1970 MACSOG was utilizing the Left Twist device, which consisted of a ten-foot-long spiked tube with a three-inch diameter that was air dropped or hand-inserted near a communication line disguised as a small tree. The device pulled signals by induction, compressed the recordings, and then had the ability to burst-transmit the messages upon request to a passing aircraft.

Airborne Studies Group: Timberwork (Op-36)

The Airborne Studies Group ceased to exist on 1 October 1971, when its two subsidiary programs were placed under the control of the Ground Studies Group. Detachment A was redesignated Special Operations Detachment (Earth Angel, Pike Hill, Cedar Walk) and Detachment B (STRATA) at the Monkey Mountain Forward Operating Base, Da Nang, retained its title. During the time frame covered by the 1971–72 Command History, there were twenty-four STRATA missions launched into Laos before the shift south to Cambodia.[43] Only one Earth Angel mission was launched into Laos before that program's personnel were also shifted to Cambodia, where they conducted forty-one more missions.[44] Pike Hill teams conducted fifteen missions in Cambodia while Cedar Walk teams carried out five operations.[45]

Maritime Studies Group: Plowman (Op-37)

MACSOG was given permission to carry out a series of maritime interdiction raids against the North Vietnamese coast (code-named "Newport Casino") as another diversionary operation in support of Lam Son 719.[46] The NAD launched two missions to support the operation. On the afternoon of 10 February 1971, three Nasty-class PTFs set out on their first mission north of the DMZ in twenty-seven months. The first raid was a great success. During its course the PTFs ran one junk aground, then boarded another and sank it with a demolition charge after taking off its six-man crew.

While the second junk was being searched, a larger prize was sighted by the PTFs. An 85-foot TL-15 cargo vessel was chased and shelled by one of the PTFs before it was halted and boarded by the NAD crew. Once again explosive charges were placed and the 100-ton steamer went to the bottom. At 0500 hours the three PTFs sighted a North Vietnamese SL-4 trawler and gave chase. Gunfire was exchanged, but the trawler managed to make it into the mouth of the Cua Giang River and to safety.

The climax of the operation came on 19–20 February, when the most successful naval engagement in NAD history took place. Four PTFs discovered and were photographing two Chinese freighters and a tanker off the North Vietnamese coast when they were attacked by a P-4 torpedo boat. The vessel was quickly sunk by gunfire. One hour later, as the PTFs were leaving the area, they were again attacked, this time by a Chinese-built 130-foot Shanghai II attack craft and a *Swatow* gunboat, both of which were badly damaged and left behind.

Later, as the PTFs were passing between Hon Gio Island and the coast, they were beset by another Shanghai II and another P-4. As the Nastys attempted to disengage and withdraw, the North Vietnamese vessels followed, only to get a bloody nose for their trouble when the PTFs damaged both the PT boat and the Shanghai II. Only one Vietnamese crewman was killed during the action. Two more missions were launched at the end of the year, coinciding with the return of U.S. bombing of North Vietnam (Operation Linebacker II). At the end of December 1971 the PTFs were again sent north to participate in Operation Hai Cang Tudo II. On the 23rd, 24th, 26th, and 27th, multiboat operations were launched with the mission of interdicting transhipment points along the North Vietnamese coast. All of the operations, however, were unsuccessful.

During the year ninety-seven Dodge Mark cross-beach missions were conducted in South Vietnam, fifty-six from Da Nang and forty-one from the five FOBs. Twenty communist troops were killed in action and forty-two prisoners were taken.[47] The seven Nastys and Ospreys and related equipment were returned to U.S. control. On 31 March the NAD was disestablished and all properties and materials not going to the CSS were turned over to the U.S. Navy.[48]

Training Studies Group (Op-38)

Due to the redeployment of the 5th SFG from Vietnam, Detachment B-53, Special Forces Augmentation, was redesignated Training Center Advisory Element (TCAE) on 4 March 1971.[49] Although administratively attached to Training Support Headquarters, U.S. Army, Vietnam (USARV), the TCAE operationally belonged to MACSOG. The ARVN Airborne Training Center (Camp Quyet Thang) at Long Thanh was renamed Camp Yen The on 1 August 1971, after a South Vietnamese newspaper disclosed its name and operations in an article. On 15 April 1972, the TCAE was consolidated with the Plans Division and the Operations and Training Division to form the Plans, Operations, and Training Advisory Division of STDAT-158.[50]

Psychological Studies Group: Humidor (Op-39)

The group continued its operations in support of the Psychological Warfare Service of the STD and continued to advise the Psychological Warfare Division of the ARVN General Political Warfare Department. The Psychological Studies Group severed its relationship with MACSOG on 31 December 1971. The Radio Studies Group (Op-70) continued its operations under the joint direction of MACSOG and JUSPAO until 30 April 1972, when its operations were also transferred to the ARVN General Political Warfare Department.

Air Studies Group: Shedder (Op-75)

The mission of the Air Studies Branch was still to obtain and coordinate air support for MACSOG operational activities and to coordinate logistical air support. The year 1971 saw a continuation by the Airlift Section of the fight to justify retention of Combat Spear and Heavy Hook assets. On 4 March 1971 authorization came down from the JCS for the utilization of Combat Spear and Heavy Hook aircraft in Cambodia for support of indigenous efforts.[51] Twenty-seven combat missions were flown and completed by 1st Flight Detachment Heavy Hook C-123K aircraft in 1971.[52] Combat Spear MC-130Es flew and completed 226 combat missions during the same period.[53] Only 1 mission was flown in 1972 and that was by a Combat Spear aircraft. In September 1971 SOG's VIP aircraft (a China Air Lines C-45 Tradewind) was upgraded. The aircraft was replaced by a C-46 and a C-47 aircraft, both leased from the same company.

Operational assets for the reconnaissance effort were now run through the Combat Support Section (a change from previous year's Helicopter Section). The VNAF 219th Helicopter Squadron spent the year finally converting from H-34s to UH-1H model aircraft. From June 1971 through March 1972 the 219th was augmented by the VNAF 235th Helicopter Squadron, which helped take up the slack during the conversion process. The 20th SOS was also still converting its aircraft complement to the UH-1N model. The N model had a Bell twin-engine configuration, carried a heavier payload (ten thousand pounds), chin armor, and self-sealing fuel tanks. The aircraft's only fault was that it had a shorter range and loitering duration. All of this, however, became moot on 15 March 1972 when the 20th SOS stood down for withdrawal.[54] It was quickly followed by the 90th SOS and 1st Flight Detachment, which stood down for redeployment on 31 March. All units had departed South Vietnam by 30 April. On that date all functions ceased and Op-32 was disbanded.[55]

Recovery Studies (Op-80)

Twenty-four JPRC prisoner recovery missions were launched during 1971 and one in 1972. Nine South Vietnamese prisoners were recovered during one operation conducted by elements of the 23rd Infantry Division on 12 February 1971.[56] Thirteen personnel were rescued by Waco City recovery teams.[57] In March Lieutenant Colonel McImoyle departed Vietnam and was replaced by Air Force lieutenant colonel James A. Black. When Black rotated out on 2 September, he was replaced by Marine Corps lieutenant colonel Andrew Anderson.

The drawdown of American forces and the necessity to maintain some form of prisoner recovery reaction force caused a flurry of communications among MACSOG, CINCPAC, and the JCS during the first half of 1971. Although SOG requested that two companies of personnel for Bright Light missions be retained, this was reduced to two platoons by MACV and approved by the JCS in June.[58] These Combat Recon Platoons (CRPs) at Task Force 1 (Da Nang) and Task Force 2 (Kontum) combined a command and control element with three U.S.-led recon teams. Each task force had three elements divided into three teams each. In February 1972, however, MACV was in a rush to eliminate twenty-five personnel positions, so both CRPs were disbanded. As a result, no Bright Light teams were available when, on 30 March, PAVN launched its largest offensive thus far in the war.

The Screeching Owl

On 24 March 1971 an Air Force OV-10 Bronco flown by 1st Lt. Jack Butcher was shot down over the Trail in Laos.[59] After landing, Butcher was captured by a North Vietnamese patrol and his wounds were treated. He was then taken to the headquarters of Binh Tram 34 for interrogation. After five days in captivity, Butcher managed to escape, but he was recaptured within a few hours. On 4 May Butcher and two guards began the trip up the Trail to North Vietnam. Five days later he took advantage of the laxity of his guards and once again bolted into the bush. In Saigon MACSOG received Songbird signals intelligence from the NSA that indicated that an American was evading the North Vietnamese in Laos. PAVN communications circuits were abuzz with the news and the communists were trying to coordinate a search.

The JPRC quickly gained the assistance of the 7th/13th Air Force. The brass was initially skeptical, but since the communists were obviously looking for an evadee that they were having some difficulty finding, the Air Force decided to contribute whatever was necessary to get Butcher back. On 16 May a Bright Light team was sent in to investigate an E&E code symbol, but it turned out to be too old. North Vietnamese radio communications showed that PAVN was just as desperate to get to Butcher as the JPRC was. He had specific information on the location of the *binh tram*, and the North Vietnamese were puzzled as to why they had not been able to recapture him in their own backyard. They suspected that Butcher (given the nickname "Screeching Owl" by the North Vietnamese) was receiving help from the local civilian population.

On 19 May, Butcher, suffering from malaria and lack of food, unknowingly approached the outskirts of Tchepone. After walking nonchalantly for a time through the base area, he was recaptured by rather startled PAVN troops. He was then tied up, thrown into a bunker, and told that if he tried to escape again, he would be shot out of hand. Jack Butcher returned to the United States during Operation Homecoming in 1973.

SEBASTIAN DELUCA

1st Sgt. Sebastian Deluca, a three-tour MACSOG man, was serving as top sergeant at the JPRC. He had grown increasingly frustrated by failed rescue missions and especially with the situation in Laos, where he felt the U.S. Embassy was needlessly restraining the JPRC's efforts.[60] He had also grown to believe that he knew the location of fifty American POWs being held near Tchepone. He then decided to take action on his own. He requested and was granted a seven-day leave to Bangkok and left on 6 June. When his leave time was up he asked for and was granted a two-day extension. When he did not return on 15 June he was declared AWOL.

MACSOG immediately notified Thai officials and American military authorities that Deluca was missing and that he had detailed knowledge of classified operations, but by that time Deluca was already in Vientiane, attempting to recruit other Americans for a rescue mission. He and a bar girl rented a motorized sampan and headed down the Mekong to southern Laos. The pair was eventually stopped at a checkpoint by a Royal Lao Army patrol, and since Deluca did not have a passport, the pair was detained. The next series of events was (and is) shrouded in mystery. The girl later reported that Deluca told her that he was going outside to urinate, but that he did not return. Later the guards showed the girl Deluca's blood-covered wallet and then turned her loose. Lao military officials reported to the American Embassy that he had been killed by another RLA patrol on the night of 26 June.

Deluca's body was recovered on 13 July and taken to Nakhon Phanom. From there it was brought to Saigon and positively identified. He had been shot in the back of the head twice and once in the left leg. Deluca's co-workers at Recovery Studies were stunned by the news. They believed that he had been murdered by the patrol simply to relieve him of a quantity of jewels and gold that he had taken on his one-man Bright Light mission. Deluca's death, following hard on the failure to rescue Butcher, was a severe blow to the morale of the JPRC and a sad end for a courageous soldier.

JCRC

Sergeant Deluca was not the only American dissatisfied with the obfuscation and foot-dragging by various U.S. agencies in Southeast Asia. The American military (the JPRC and CINCPAC in particular) had never been satisfied with the information it was getting from other American agencies concerning captured and missing personnel. It seemed that although many agencies had POW and MIA information (the military, CIA, DIA, NSA, the State Department, etc.) and although there had been several interagency meetings among them to coordinate their efforts, information was still scattered and disconnected.[61] The war was winding down and the American people wanted either their POWs back or at least some closure on the fates of those who were classed as MIA.

The final, and longest-lived, creation of SOG took place in November 1971. With the blessing of Secretary of Defense Melvin Laird, CINCPAC issued OPLAN 5100, which created the Joint Casualty Resolution Center (JCRC), a clearinghouse for POW/MIA information from the American military, the CIA, and the State Department.[62] Upon the disestablishment of the JPRC, the JCRC would take over its functions of data coordination and consolidation. The JCRC would continue in its efforts to discover the fate of America's missing servicemen (and civilians) in Southeast Asia for more than twenty years.

BAT-21

On 2 April 1972, during the opening phase of PAVN's Nguyen Hue Offensive, a USAF RB-66 electronic countermeasures aircraft, call sign Bat-21, was shot down near the DMZ by a surface-to-air missile. Of the six-man crew, only one, Col. Iceal Hambleton, made it out of the aircraft alive. Breaking a wrist and finger, Hambleton landed near the Mien Giang River near Cam Lo, far behind the advancing North Vietnamese. He contacted a FAC, who then vectored in A-1s and some U.S. Army helicopters that were in the area. Heavy North Vietnamese anti-aircraft fire shot down two of the choppers and drove the others off. One of the crews was extracted, but of the other four-man crew, three were killed and one was captured. The next morning an OV-10 FAC arrived, only to be shot down by another SAM. The pilot was killed but the backseater, Lt. Mark

Clark (son of Gen. Mark Clark of Second World War fame), landed and evaded. There were then two Americans on the ground and on the run.

FACs then called in up to ninety air strikes per day to protect the two men. After two days an HH-53 Jolly Green Giant was dispatched to pick up Hambleton. It got within one hundred yards before it too was destroyed by anti-aircraft fire and all six crewmen aboard were killed. The 7th Air Force, unwilling to lose another HH-53, asked MACSOG if one of its Combat Spear Blackbirds, equipped with the Fulton Recovery System, could not extract Hambleton. The answer was no. The long, slow, straight approach that was necessary, flown through that kind of anti-aircraft environment, was tantamount to suicide.

On 7 April communist flak claimed more victims. An OV-10 looking for the two missing officers was shot down, but both of its crew made it to the ground alive. USMC first lieutenant Larry Potts reportedly died in communist captivity and USAF first lieutenant Bruce Walker made several transmissions warning others not to come to get him. Both men remain MIA. The Air Force had had enough. Five aircraft had been destroyed, eleven airmen were either killed or missing, and two men had been captured. It was now up to SOG. The commander of the JPRC, Andy Anderson, went to Cam Lo, the nearest ARVN outpost to the evadee's location, to direct the effort. He then sent for a five-man SOG Sea Commando Team and their advisor, SEAL lieutenant Tom Norris, from the NAD at Da Nang.

Lieutenant Clark was told by radio to inflate his life vest and float down the Cam Lo to where the Sea Commandos would be waiting. A passing PAVN patrol forced the team to stand fast as Clark floated by. They found him at dawn, however, exhausted but alive. Hambleton was supposed to do the same thing, but the fifty-three-year-old was totally exhausted after ten days on the run without food. Norris and the Sea Commandos would have to go get him. Only one of the Vietnamese, Petty Officer Nguyen Van Kiet, was willing to make the attempt. He and Norris boarded a sampan disguised as fishermen, paddled upriver, and accidentally passed Hambleton's hiding place. Finally they found him hiding in the brush by the riverbank, delirious. The three men coasted downstream past PAVN sentinels until dawn, when a machine gun opened up on them. Calling on A-1s and a pair of F-4s to give them cover, the trio landed safely. For his effort Lt. Tom Norris received MACSOG's only SEAL Medal of Honor while his teammate, Nguyen Van Kiet, was awarded the Navy Cross, the only South Vietnamese to receive so high a U.S. award for heroism.[63]

ALL GOOD THINGS . . .

By 1972 the mission of the JPRC had been downgraded to performing crash site inspections and preparing for the post-hostilities period. On 15 March the JPRC became a staff element of MACV J-2 and ended its long association with MACSOG.[64] On 3 April Andy Anderson was replaced as commander by Maj. D. E. Lunday. The organization's last days were sluggish. Due to lack of rescue forces, Bright Light missions could no longer be launched, and besides, a prisoner exchange was sure to take place that would preclude any benefit that might be gained. Why mar Henry Kissinger's negotiations with a possible failure when all the POWs would be returning and there would be a final reckoning on the issue of MIAs? On 23 January 1973 the JPRC was disbanded by CINCPAC and, on the same day, its replacement, the Joint Casualty Resolution Center, took over the mission.[65]

Logistics

The last fifteen months of MACSOG's operations must have been harried ones for the Logistics Division, as it reoriented its mission to support the Vietnamese takeover of operations. Plans for the transfer of mission-essential equipment had to be submitted and instituted. Equipment was retrograded, and excess and unserviceable items eliminated and replaced. The Logistics Division had to consider the future needs of the STD and close coordination with it, and the ARVN logistics apparatus had to be carried out while items of equipment that were not going to be available through proposed ARVN stockpiles had to be provided for. This the division handled through Project Tango, a proposed two-year stockpile of equipment that was not going to be available through ARVN logistics channels.[66]

It was as if a film of the American commitment to South Vietnam was being run backward to its beginning. With increasing withdrawals by U.S. forces, the interservice support agreements that had provided MACSOG with common items were closing down and the division scrambled to take up the slack. By 1972 MACSOG began the transfer of its camps to the STD. This entailed documentation, thorough inventories of equipment, and power surveys before the changeovers could take place. The first camps handed over were the first that MACSOG itself had occupied—the Da Nang bases of the CSS.

Comptroller

As with all of SOG's other elements, the Comptroller Division was winding up its commitments and obligations. MACSOG's 1971 budget amounted to $21,080,000, a savings of $1,386,000.[67] Planned force reductions lowered the projected FY 1972 budget to$12,561,000.[68] With MACSOG's reduction to the level of an advisory group, the projected 1973 budget was estimated at$8,265,000.[69]

Plans

One can only imagine the exertions that the division must have been making during MACSOG's last year and a half of operations as Vietnamization caught up with it. The unit would have been laboring under mandatory force and mission reductions imposed by MACV's Vietnam-wide Improvement and Modernization Plan. It replied by proposing its own responses under the MACSOG Reduction Plan, which sought to transfer SOG's responsibilities, missions, and assets to the STD.[70] In February 1971 it submitted Appendix C to COMUSMACV OPLAN J203, which postulated the creation of a staff assistance element to the STD known as the Strategic Technical Directorate Assistance Team, or STDAT. The division also scrambled to face reductions and mission changes in the JPRC. On 30 April 1972 the Plans Division was consolidated with the Operations and Training Division to form the Plans, Operations, and Training Advisory Division of STDAT-158.

Communications

The Communications Division worked hard during 1971 and the first three months of 1972 to prepare for the handover of operations to the STD. Communications equipment was updated and repaired and STD communications circuits were hooked up and running. Communication security tests were passed without much of a problem and the division managed to beat every step of the phased schedule of the Improvement and Modernization Plan.[71]

Strategic Technical Directorate
SPECIAL MISSION SERVICE (SO CONG TAC)

The Vietnamization of MACSOG's operations that had begun in 1970 accelerated during 1971 as the STD picked up the slack. In January the 5th SFG redeployed from South Vietnam. The Special Mission Service (SMS) was created from the disbanded South Vietnamese Special Forces on 1 January and was authorized to retain 990 of the 1,450 former LLDB personnel to make up 45 unconventional warfare teams (Hac Long, or Black Dragon, commandos) of 12 men each.[72] The organization was advised and assisted by the Special Mission Advisory Group (SMAG), created in February from residual U.S. Special Forces personnel within South Vietnam and opconned to MACSOG.[73]

The organization originally consisted of groups 71, 72, and 75, for a total of 27 teams. In September, before the SMS had a chance to test out its capabilities, the Vietnamese Joint General Staff altered its mission from the conduct of unconventional warfare to strategic reconnaissance in Laos. On 18 October Group 71 was returned to Long Thanh for reconnaissance training. It was joined there by groups 72 and 75 in the spring of 1972. After retraining, Group 72 was deployed along with SMAG Advisory Element One (AE1) to Camp Fay at Da Nang on 4 January 1972. Following it from Long Thanh, Group 75 was deployed to Kontum along with SMAG AE2. The last of the retrained South Vietnamese, Group 71, and AE3 arrived at Da Nang on 1 February and were co-located with Special Operations Detachment (SOD) Group 11 of the Liaison Service at Camp Black Rock. The SMS elements assumed the Phu Dung mission on 1 April 1972. On the same day SMAG was redesignated the Special Mission Service Advisory Detachment (SMSAD).[74]

On 30 April STDAT-158's Special Operations Detachment and Detachment B were ordered to focus their resources toward in-country efforts to halt the Easter Offensive. On 23 May Detachment B placed its STRA-TA assets under control of the SMS, which had shifted its staff to Hue. On the 25th members of the SOD, twelve Vietnamese counterparts, and twelve Earth Angel agents departed for Hue to link up with them.

LIAISON SERVICE (SO LIEN LAC)
The STD Liaison Service consisted of thirty ARVN-led reconnaissance teams that were already responsible for the Thot Not operational area. There were ten recon teams (Loi Ho, or Thunder Tiger, commandos) each in Da Nang (relocated to Quan Loi in April 1972), Kontum, and Ban Me Thuot. The nine exploitation companies were deployed, two at Task Force 1, four at Task Force 2, and three at Task Force 3. These nine companies were, however, disbanded when MACSOG stood down on 30 April 1972.[75]

Opconned from the Liaison Service to the Special Mission Service were the SOD, which became SMS Group 11 (formerly Earth Angel, Pike Hill, and Cedar Walk), and Monkey Mountain Forward Operations Base (formerly STRATA), which became SMS Group 68.[76]

COASTAL SECURITY SERVICE (SO PHONG VE DUYEN HAI)
The Coastal Security Service became a 412-man all-Vietnamese navy organization on 1 January 1971.[77] All civilian personnel had been discharged and members of other services were returned to their parent organizations.

The unit's inventory consisted of seven PTFs and three PCFs. All of the PTFs, however, were returned to the U.S. Navy and the CSS was restricted to operations below the 17th parallel.[78]

Comment: Aerial Interdiction

By late 1967 it had become evident that SOG recon activities were not going to be utilized as a precursor to more conventional ground operations against the Trail system. The nails were driven into the coffin by Washington's refusal to allow COMUSMACV to launch a counteroffensive in the post-Tet period. From that point onward, SOG elements were relegated to intelligence collection for MACV and the bombing campaigns carried out by the U.S. Air Force. The goal of these programs was not to halt infiltration (it was never assumed that they could), but to make Hanoi pay too heavy a price for its effort. Corollary to this was the destruction of as much of the logistical system as was practicable and the occupation of as many North Vietnamese troops as possible in static security roles. Aerial interdiction could not succeed unless the North Vietnamese felt the pressure and relented. Despite an enormous expenditure in ordnance, however, the level of violence was never going to be sufficient to deter Hanoi. The bombing campaigns, in the long run, achieved little.

This failure had three sources. The political constraints imposed from Washington that limited the entire effort in Southeast Asia did the same for the efforts of MACSOG and the 7th/13th Air Force. Although Laotian and Cambodian "neutrality" was violated every day, airpower alone could do little more than slow the infiltration of North Vietnamese troops and supplies. Another source of failure was that the Air Force utilized what Col. Charles Morrison has called "oversophisticated methods" against "elemental systems."[79] The communists' primitive logistical needs and methods (at least until the latter stages of the conflict) allowed them to slip under the radar of their more technologically advanced enemy. This was exacerbated by the doctrinal dilemma confronting the U.S. Air Force both before and during the conflict. For more than a decade the Air Force had been institutionally and technologically geared to fight a nuclear war, not a brushfire conflict against such an unsophisticated enemy.

Finally, all of the above were compounded by the PAVN and the NLF's enviable ability to adapt their doctrine and tactics and to turn weaknesses into strengths. Between 1967 and 1971, the CIA estimated, North Vietnam had sent over 630,000 soldiers, 100,000 tons of food, 400,000 weapons, and 50,000 tons of ammunition via the Ho Chi Minh Trail.[80] The number of soldiers, engineers, and civilian laborers who perished in its construction and operation is unknown, but after the war a forty-acre memorial cemetery was constructed in their honor. At the head of the Mu Gia pass stands a huge statue of a woman operating a gas pump, a symbol of the people's will to maintain what the NSA's history of the war called "one of the greatest achievements in military engineering of the twentieth century."[81]

As was the case with other contemporary conflicts, the one in Southeast Asia was fought at the advent of a new age in military technology. Some of the advanced systems that would have aided the interdiction effort were still in their infancy (widespread use of infrared vision devices, precision-guided munitions, reconnaissance drones, satellite imaging, interpersonal communications, etc.). It was due to technological limitations that the aerial campaigns did not even make a serious attempt to halt personnel infiltration until Island Tree, late in the effort. As a result Commando Hunt turned into an effort to destroy North Vietnamese trucks and materiel, which worked against the grain of the effort, since both were provided from outside sources that could not themselves be attacked.

The interdiction effort (like the entire American effort) became focused on statistics as the measure of success and, according to Air Force historian Bernard Nalty, it "devolved from considered tactics to meaningless ritual."[82] After Commando Hunt VII, the Air Force Intelligence Service claimed that 51,000 trucks and 3,400 anti-aircraft guns had been destroyed or damaged in all seven campaigns.[83] Statistics, however, proved no substitute for strategy, and "for all the *perceived* success in that numbers game, the Air Force succeeded *only* in fooling itself into believing *Commando Hunt* was working."[84]

By the end of the conflict American aircraft had dropped 2.75 million tons of bombs on Laos (the majority of them on the panhandle), but they never seriously impeded the flow of men or materiel to the southern battlefront.[85] The North Vietnamese maintained their logistical flow to combat units in the field and managed to launch major offensives in 1968 and 1972 and a counteroffensive in 1971. PAVN had constructed and maintained, under this massive rain of ordnance, over three thousand kilometers of roads and paths through the mountains and jungle while only 2 percent of Hanoi's troops sent south had been killed by the American effort to halt their infiltration.[86]

After five years of operations in the Prairie Fire area and two years in Daniel Boone, what did the Air Force think of MACSOG's contribution to its interdiction effort? Evidently not very much. According to the conclusions of a December 1969 7th/13th Air Force Ad Hoc Evaluation Group, "SOG-produced intelligence has been of minor value to the development of tactical air and *Arc Light* targets."[87] This finding was rather astonishing. Either the Air Force was so dependent on its sensor-oriented program that it considered human intelligence negligible, or it considered MACSOG's intelligence as limited, faulty, and/or unreliable.

Regardless of one's stance, pro or con, the interdiction effort (on the ground and in the air) did provide the shield for Vietnamization and withdrawal. As American ground units returned from Southeast Asia, MACSOG and the Air Force maintained steady pressure on the communists. By 1970 the conflict had become predominantly a conventional effort by the North Vietnamese, one that demanded a significant and substantial logistical effort to sustain. When this occurred, the interdiction effort was more successful, but it was also too late. The United States was steadily pulling out of its commitment, and any response that it made was bound to grow weaker or be preempted (as it was in the end) by political constraints.

The U.S. Air Force was a long time in admitting its failure. Its official analysis of the interdiction campaigns (five years later) postulated that the North Vietnamese had invaded South Vietnam in 1972 because aerial interdiction had so denuded logistical stockpiles that it forced Hanoi's hand in launching the offensive. It was not until the release of Maj. Mark Clodfelter's *The Limits of Air Power* in 1989 that the Air Force began to face the realization that it had not been nearly as effective during the conflict as it thought it had been. As Earl Tilford (author of another revisionist Air Force history) put it, "the fact that it took nearly two decades for an Air Force officer to write a book critical of the way the Air Force fought the war is indicative of a larger problem endemic to the service."[88]

For some of the participants in the conflict, these realizations had come somewhat earlier. Cpt. Jerome Brown, the chief Air Force targeting officer for Project 404 in Vientiane during 1967–68, had been startled by a reconnaissance photograph taken over the Trail. After the photo was further analyzed, it did indeed turn out to be what Brown thought it was: a sixty-foot yacht, loaded on a trailer, making its way south. The NSA confirmed through radio intercepts that the Chinese government was sending the yacht as a gift to Prince Sihanouk. "You've got to think of it now . . . through bombing missions and the whole works. It blew our minds."[89] As well it should have.

Chapter Nine

MAY 1972–MARCH 1973: STDAT-158

Headquarters

Activated on 1 May 1972, Strategic Technical Directorate Assistance Team 158 (STDAT-158) was tasked with lending advice, assistance, and limited material support to the STD; developing combined plans; and maintaining direct liaison between the STD and MACV agencies concerned with intelligence collection and unconventional warfare.[1] Another mission of the assistance team was "to exert all possible efforts to insure that STD operations best served the objectives of MACV."[2] A tight rein was to be kept on South Vietnamese special operations, especially during the final phases of the Paris negotiations.

MACSOG's last commander, Col. David R. Presson, became the senior advisor at the unit's creation and held the position until his tour of duty ended in November 1972. He was then replaced by his executive officer, Col. Robert W. Hill, who became the commanding officer through March 1973 when STDAT-158 was disbanded.[3] At its inception, the team consisted of 152 U.S. Army, 6 Navy, and 2 Air Force personnel.[4] By December those numbers had been reduced by the MACV Increment 14 drawdown to 42 Army, 1 Navy, and 1 from the Air Force.[5] The Personnel and Administration Division consisted of the Personnel and Administrative Branch and the Classified Control and Records Branches. On 1 December 1972 control of that division was transferred to the STDAT executive officer. It was at this point that tens of thousands of pages of documents pertaining to SOG operations and the unit's entire photographic collection were destroyed, making life more difficult for future historians of the organization.

A curious reflection of the changeover of operations to STD control was a directive from the JCS tasking MACSOG to "keep MACV J-2 and MACV J-3 fully informed as to the activities of the STD . . . and as to the location of all operational elements."[6] One had to keep in mind that the Saigon government was being pressured into negotiating for peace terms in Paris by its American allies. Through the STD Saigon had the capability of launching operations into North Vietnam unilaterally. The reduction of CSS assets (see below) by the removal of the only craft in its inventory that had the capability of reaching North Vietnam must be seen in this context. The Nixon administration wanted no surprises from Saigon.

Intelligence Advisory Division

The division continued its close liaison with the STD intelligence personnel and consisted of the Current Indications, Photo Interpretation, and Intelligence Data Handling System Branches. The senior advisor was responsible for advising the STD on all intelligence matters, including targeting, management of resources, and reporting procedures.

In May 1972, due to the promulgation of JCS/CINCPAC Contingency Plan (Conplan) 158 (see below), the division faced a targeting mission that was far beyond its capabilities to meet. On 1 June assistance was formally requested from MACV and the Combined Intelligence Center, Vietnam. Eventually thirty-two target packages were put together for STD/STDAT use. At the height of the process, work on this project accounted for half of the division's output and was related to photo interpretation, target and area analysis, operational concepts, and mission feasibility studies.[7] In November 1972 the Intelligence and Operations Divisions were consolidated and the Intelligence Division was deactivated on 1 December 1972.

Plans, Operations, and Training

The communist Nguyen Hue Offensive (known in the West as the Easter Offensive) threw a monkey wrench into STDAT-158 plans for cross-border strategic reconnaissance operations during most of 1972. All STD recon elements were thrown into action in South Vietnam, where they were tasked by the military regions (which replaced the corps tactical zones during the year) with gathering tactical intelligence. The STD launched more than two hundred in-country recon- and intelligence-collection missions during the year.[8] Out-of-country operations were a moot point anyway, since all helicopter and fixed-wing aircraft assets were dedicated to the in-country effort (including the 219th Squadron, which was detached from the STD in May).

Evidently due to President Nixon's dusting off of the old Duck Hook concepts, a serious expansion of operations inside North Vietnam was contemplated. On 25 May the Plans, Operations, and Training Division was advised to begin planning in conjunction with JCS and CINCPAC Conplan 158, a series of diversionary operations in communist-occupied areas of Quang Tri Province and commando operations and naval forays in North Vietnam, that was so classified that operations went beyond the Top Secret/NOFORN security classification of the annual MACSOG Command History.[9]

During the post-offensive period the military regions continued to retain their STD recon units rather than returning them for strategic missions. The STD itself was stuck, since it had become totally dependent upon the military region commanders for air assets. This situation was only alleviated in mid-November, when, under a Vietnamese Joint General Staff directive, the regional commanders began to make more air assets available. The STD managed to launch ten cross-border missions before the end of the year.

On 9 February 1973 a meeting was held between Colonel Hill, Gen. Frederick C. Weyand (COMUSMACV as of June 1972), and the Vietnamese Joint General Staff. Topics under discussion included the lack of funding for some STD programs and the termination of special logistical support from STDAT. It was estimated that, at the then-current level of operations, the STD had a one-year supply of mission-specific equipment. As a result of this meeting, the Earth Angel program was shut down and Pike Hill personnel were drafted into the ARVN and then reassigned to the STD.

As part of MACV's Increment 14 reduction schedule, the Plans, Operations, and Training Division was reduced from fifteen men to seven and reorganized into the Operations and Intelligence Division. Unit deactivation was scheduled to take place forty-five days after the signing of a cease-fire agreement in Paris. On 12 March 1973, the division was deactivated.

Special Mission Service Advisory Detachment

The purpose of the Special Mission Service Advisory Detachment (SMSAD) was to provide support and coordination for SMS (formerly the Vietnamese Special Forces) unconventional warfare and strategic reconnaissance operations in the Phu Dung area of operations.[10] The SMS was organized into only three of its five assigned groups (71, 72, and 75). On 23 May 1972 Group 11 (STRATA) of the Liaison Service was opconned to SMS to support its operations in Military Region (MR) I, and on 1 October the group was formally assigned to the SMS. It was believed that eventually Group 68 (Earth Angel/Pike Hill) would be reassigned from the Liaison Service to the SMS as well.

On 19 May, due to the North Vietnamese offensive, SMS was tasked to support ARVN operations in the MR I. On 22 May SMS headquarters and Groups 11 and 71 moved from Da Nang to Hue to conduct area reconnaissance operations. Groups 72 and 75 remained at Da Nang (at separate bases) to conduct training, camp defense, and local security operations. In June Groups 71 and 72 swapped locations. On 11 July Group 75 took over security for the Leghorn radio relay site. Eight days later Group 72, its Advisory Element, and most of the headquarters moved from Hue to Chu Lai to conduct area recon operations west of the ARVN 2nd Division's area of operations. During the last week of the month, Groups 71 and 72 again swapped tactical areas of responsibility.

In September a request came down from the ARVN Joint General Staff and the commander of MR II for the SMS and SMSAD to help conduct a training program for ARVN conventional reconnaissance and Ranger companies. As a result of this request, a Special Training Team (STT) was created at Pleiku and the team conducted training operations between 11 September and 15 November.[11] It was then decided to close down the Golf-5 site and, after all equipment had been removed, Group 75 returned to training and security operations at Kontum.

On 1 October Group 11 was formally assigned to the SMS. One week later SMSAD received notification of its phasedown and closeout. During the month, the SMS assumed responsibility for the tactical area of the ARVN 81st Airborne Battalion. By 25 October 1972 all advisory elements had been deactivated and this was followed on 15 November by the formal stand-down of SMSAD.[12]

Liaison Service Advisory Detachment

The mission of the Liaison Service Advisory Detachment (LSAD) was to support Liaison Service operations in the Thot Not area of operations. The LSAD concentrated on communications, operations, medical, supply, and intelligence support of its South Vietnamese counterparts. Located at the Liaison Service compound at Camp Nguyen Cao Vi, Saigon, the detachment consisted of fifteen (later thirteen) U.S. Special Forces personnel.[13] The LSAD supervised the operations of the seven-man (later four-man) U.S. Task Force Advisory Elements (TFAEs), which were located at Camp Yen The, Kontum, and Ban Me Thuot.[14] The LSAD was also responsible for the Group 68 Advisory Element (AE), located at Camp Nguyen Cao Vi, the Group 11 AE at Camp Black Rock, Da Nang, and the Golf-5 Security Element initially located at Kontum.

By mid-May North Vietnamese pressure had forced the evacuation of Kontum and the Golf-5 Security Company was relocated to the Group 66 compound at Pleiku. It was then redesignated the Special Mission Force (SMF) and tasked with in-country crash site inspections (Waco City) and Bright Light missions.[15] On 1 August 1972 the SMF was removed from the operational control of LSAD and made a separate command under STDAT. During the Easter Offensive, the separate task forces (TFs) supported ARVN operations in-country. TF1 operated within the Capital Military District while TF2 and TF3 carried out missions in MR I.

Only two cross-border missions were launched by TF1 during the year.[16] During the first, a team was parachuted on 25 August into Base Areas 701/702. The second mission went into Base Area 354 on 2 September. TF1 was further tasked with providing a platoon to guard the ARVN Joint General Staff compound in Saigon, further reducing its cross-border capabilities. TF2 cross-border operations were curbed by the overrunning of the Plei Djering Forward Launch Site on 4 September and by the necessity of manning the Klondike radio relay site. TF3 was even more limited in its operations due to the size of its security commitment in defending its compound at Ban Me Thuot. The task force was moved across town to Camp Coryell on 15 November, but the camp was so dilapidated that all of the task force's efforts went into its rehabilitation.

On 5 June 1972 a C-46 contract aircraft (EM-2) enroute from Ban Me Thuot to Pleiku crashed, killing all thirty-two passengers. On board were the LSAD senior advisor, assistant operations advisor, and the intelligence and communications NCOs. Other casualties included the senior advisor of Group 11, the intelligence/operations officer of the Golf-5 Security Company, the chief surgeon, and two communications personnel from AE2.[17] A scratch task force was deployed for a crash site inspection/body recovery mission consisting of LSAD personnel and troops from the Golf-5 Security Company. TF1AE was deactivated on 16 October 1972. It was quickly followed by TF2AE on the 18th and TF3AE on the 20th.[18] The LSAD itself was deactivated on 3 November 1972.[19]

Training Center Advisory Detachment

Not much changed over the years for the advisors at Camp Yen The (formerly Camp Long Thanh). Their mission still consisted of training STD personnel and evaluation of concepts and equipment. The advisors also put together mobile training teams of STDAT personnel. From 1 May to 1 July 1972 the unit consisted of 3 U.S. officers and 5 enlisted men.[20] On 1 August 1972 there was a reduction of personnel due to tasking for the Special Training Team in MR II. This left 2 American officers and 4 enlisted men at Yen The. During the period covered by the annual Command History, 226 ARVN personnel entered the training programs at Yen The, and 179 completed their training.[21] The Training Center Advisory Detachment was deactivated on 10 November 1972.

Group 68 Advisory Element

AE 68 advised and assisted the Earth Angel and Pike Hill agent operations (Group 11) of the Liaison Service. Pike Hill teams consisted of PAVN ralliers who volunteered to reenter their old areas of operations for intelligence collection. Pike Hill teams were made up of ethnic Khmers and South Vietnamese of Cambodian extraction who were infiltrated into Cambodia for the same purpose. Both units operated out of the isolation compound at Camp Yen The. Two Earth Angel and nine Pike Hill missions were conducted in Cambodia during the period covered.[22]

THE MAN WHO NEVER WAS

On 11 June 1972, during the period before the beginning of the ARVN's counteroffensive in Quang Tri Province, four hidden parachutes and a dead body were discovered by PAVN troops along Route 548 in the heart of the Ashau Valley. On the body was a radio codebook that allowed communist communications specialists to listen in on two other teams— one on Route 9 west of Khe Sanh and the other west of Dong Ha, far behind PAVN lines. On 19 June, utilizing information gleaned from the broadcasts to these teams, PAVN troops intercepted two South Vietnamese agents who had dropped into the Ashau Valley. The two men were defectors to the STD from the PAVN 304th Division.

Two days later the team west of Dong Ha was ordered by radio to cooperate with a combined airborne and amphibious landing that was to begin on 27 June. The lead element of the air assault (Operation Lam Thuyen) took off for the LZ northwest of Dong Ha, but was forced to abort due to bad weather. Meanwhile an ARVN Marine Corps company and a battalion of Regional Forces, the spearhead of the much larger Operation Ngoc Thuyen, landed near the mouth of the Cua Viet River on the same day. This element too was forced to retire due to bad weather. The teams were real, but the corpse, codebook, and radio messages were a ruse, an STD Borden deception operation launched to cover the real counteroffensive, Operation Lam Son 72.[23]

CONPLAN 158

When word came down the pipe from the JCS and CINCPAC for the launching of a series of deception and harassment raids behind communist lines, Group 11 was immediately brought into the planning process for Conplan 158. The operations were to include notional teams, Earth Angels, Borden, and airdrops of counterfeit currency into communist-controlled areas. Also envisioned was the use of a company-size airborne raider force specializing in demolition work for long-term missions (of up to sixty-days' duration). All STD assets, however, were being utilized in recon operations in Quang Tri and Thua Thien Provinces. Since all STD assets were tied up in the counteroffensive, it was decided to create a new unit to execute operations under Conplan 158 from scratch. Thang Long was the title given to the all-volunteer force that was thrown together in the isolation compound at Camp Yen The by Lieutenant Colonel Nguyen Van Hy, the camp commander.[24] Three targets in the North were chosen for the operation, including a petroleum pipeline near the Laotian border.[25]

The operations, however, never took place, President Nixon preferring instead to utilize the aerial mining of North Vietnamese ports and bombing by B-52s. In October the Thang Long unit was disbanded (approximately thirty of the sixty-nine men were retained within the STD). Detachment B was dissolved and the SOD was reduced to two men on 25 November. On 9 February 1973, due to a lack of funding for their operations, the Earth Angel program was disbanded. The Pike Hill agents were discharged from the STD, drafted into the ARVN, and then reassigned to the STD.

Coastal Recovery Force

STDAT continued to assist the South Vietnamese Coastal Security Service and provided cadre for the Coastal Recovery Force (CRF), which was created to provide ground and maritime support for search and rescue missions. Impetus for the creation of the CRF came from CSS assistance in the recovery of Hambleton and Clark in April 1972. The CRF consisted of two operational teams of five men each, led by two Navy SEALs on temporary assignment from the NAD.[26] The teams were to be deployed upon request from the 37th Aerospace Rescue and Recovery Squadron, USAF, Da Nang, and were to be utilized in support of tactical air operations against North Vietnamese forces. The creation of the CRF points out the winding down of U.S. commitments in South Vietnam. Personnel recovery and post-SAR missions had, in the past, been handled by conventional forces under the direction of the Field Forces. STDAT-158 itself did not have the capability to launch such missions. As a result, the unit was tasked by CINCPAC to develop plans to establish a permanent force for crash site inspections and personnel recovery in addition to the SAR mission. COMUSMACV approved a permanent JTD on 25 July 1972 and the four SEALs were assigned on 1 August.[27]

The naval portion of JCS/CINCPAC Conplan 158 was to be assembled by the CSS at Da Nang, but all of the unit's Nasty boats had been returned to U.S. control in April, leaving only two Swift boats and a pair of action teams that had not seen any action in North Vietnam since 1968. As a result, thirty-four action team members were dispatched to Subic Bay between 10 January and 13 August for a nine-week course in diving and underwater demolitions.[28] All of this hectic scrambling with too few resources went nowhere. On 2 September the Sea Commando teams were detached from the CSS and opconned to the commander of MR 1 for two months of cross-beach recon operations between Quang Tri and the DMZ. On 31 October all American support of the CSS came to an end.

MICHAEL THONTON

The war had not ended for Medal of Honor recipient Lt. Tom Norris. On 31 October he and E2C Michael Thornton, along with three South Vietnamese, were on a CRF prisoner snatch and intelligence-gathering mission against a communist river base on the Cua Viet River. Launched from a junk on a rubber boat, the team made it ashore and moved inland, where they discovered that they had been inserted eight miles north of their target area and were actually in North Vietnam. While trying to extract through an area of sand dunes to the beach, the team triggered an ambush and called in naval gunfire support. Communist pressure forced the firefight back to the waterline, where Thornton was informed by one of his teammates that Norris had been shot through the left forehead and left behind for dead in the dunes. With only five minutes remaining before an American cruiser obliterated the area with heavy shells and although already wounded by grenade fragments, Thornton ran through intense enemy fire, killed two North Vietnamese, and carried the unconscious lieutenant across four hundred yards of bullet-swept beach. He inflated Norris' life vest and led the Vietnamese (one of whom had been wounded by the same grenade that had wounded Thornton) into the water. Thornton towed the two men seaward for two hours before the team was picked up by the junk that had inserted them. Tom Norris survived his ordeal. For this exploit, Thornton was awarded the Medal of Honor, the only serviceman in the history of the medal to receive that honor while saving the life of another recipient.

Special Mission Force

The security company attached to the Golf-5 radio relay site consisted of 219 indigenous personnel, including 140 combat troops, while the U.S. complement consisted of 21 Special Forces personnel.[30] On 11 July 1972 the company was relieved of its security mission by Group 75 of the SMS. The company was then transferred from Ban Me Thuot to Pleiku, and on 1 August it was removed from the LSAD and made a separate command under STDAT. It was then redesignated the Special Mission Force (SMF). The unit performed as a jack-of-all-trades, but its main responsibility was the conduct of Bright Light missions and crash site inspections. Once again, this was a reflection of the lack of such a force in South Vietnam during the latter stages of the conflict.

The U.S. contingent was increased to 21 men and, at this stage of the game, they were an oddity. They were not advisors, but actually commanded and led their troops in the field.[31] The 140 indigenous personnel of the force were the cream of the crop, some of them were ex-recon team or exploitation force personnel with years of experience in special operations. Commanded by a major, the SMF had three platoons, a force headquarters, and an administrative section. Key operations for the unit were the crash site inspections and body recovery missions launched on a China Airlines C-46 (see above) and a Cathay Pacific airliner.

Logistics

The Logistics Division spent the last thirteen months of its operations preparing the STD to assume its own logistics responsibilities and preparing for the eventual termination of its activities. The division was originally divided into a Supply Branch and a Support Branch, both of which were consolidated in November 1972. The division consisted of two officers, one warrant officer, and seven NCOs. With the November drawdown, five NCO positions were eliminated, but they were soon taken up by an equal number of Filipino contract employees. These personnel were assisted by between seventy-seven and eighty South Vietnamese civilian employees.[32]

Tragedy struck the division on 5 June 1972 when the surgeon advisor and his STD counterpart were killed in a plane crash near Pleiku while en route to Kontum. On 6 March 1973 the supply facility at House 50 was handed over to the STD (House 10 had already been closed out) and the Logistics Division was deactivated.

Comptroller

The comptroller scrambled like everyone else in the organization at the end of STDAT-158 operations. The unit's budget for FY 1972 amounted to $12,664,000 while total obligations for the year came to $12,444,532.[33] During 1972 the division still directly financed the STRATA, Earth Angel, and Pike Hill programs. When funding was no longer possible, they were cut off. This prompted the shutdown of the Earth Angel program and the discharge of the Pike Hill team members. Discussions had already taken place between CNO, CINCPAC, and the division concerning final close-out. With the signing of the 28 January cease-fire, formal auditing began immediately and the division was deactivated in March 1973.

Communications Advisory Division

The division prepared for final closeout of operations by advising and assisting the STD in communications electronics matters. It had already been decided that the main method of communications for the STD would be the existing single-side band radio network. As a result of this decision, the preexisting teletype and secure voice communications accounts were eliminated. The division was itself deactivated on 17 November 1972 and its residual functions were absorbed by the Operations and Intelligence Division.

Comment: JPRC

The JPRC was established with the best of intentions, that of conducting search and rescue operations after all other allied attempts had failed. There has never been a definitive disclosure of how many American soldiers and aviators were rescued by Bright Light missions. Recon man and historian John Plaster's best estimate was several dozen and "double that if you add aircrew who were downed and rescued while supporting SOG operations." He believed that there were an equal number of body recoveries.[34]

Regardless, most members of the organization considered it to be a failure. The tragic fate of Sebastian Deluca was testimony to that. Yet, it was hard to understand why this attitude prevailed within the organization. Hundreds of ARVN prisoners, and a like number of South Vietnamese civilians, were freed by JPRC-sponsored or approved missions. Perhaps that in itself was the answer—the vast majority of those liberated from communist captivity were Vietnamese, not Americans.

Once again suspicions were aroused and blame was cast upon possible communist agents who had infiltrated the organization. Or was it simply that NLF and PAVN forces took extra precautions when dealing with American POWs as opposed to those who were members of the South Vietnamese military or civilians? The American prisoners, although horribly treated, tortured, and tormented, could serve purposes for the communists that the South Vietnamese could not. American POWs served as propaganda weapons, both at the local and international levels. They became examples of the superiority of the "Liberation Forces" to the villagers they were paraded before, and they might possibly have served as converted "friends" of the movement. As a last resort, the prisoners could also serve as bargaining chips in any future negotiations.

During its operational life the JPRC always labored to collect and collate as much information on prisoners as possible, and this effort did not end until the final days of the conflict. Simultaneously, the unit had to struggle with almost every other U.S. agency to gain cooperation, since the competing entities involved seemed loath to divulge whatever information that they separately held.

In retrospect, the division was saddled with too many requirements for its size, and those requirements took up valuable time considering the perishability of any viable intelligence that could be obtained. This burden was initially exacerbated by granting the division sole responsibility for coordinating and launching POW rescue operations. This turned out to be too great a responsibility for the JPRC, and thankfully the mission was later facilitated by the granting of operational authority to local area commanders and units.

The long-term benefits of the JPRC were in its collation of POW-MIA information (which was rather late in coming) and in the creation of the JCRC. Although the United States and Socialist Vietnam did a lot of posturing toward one another throughout the late 1970s and early 1980s, the two nations finally came to a diplomatic understanding and this, in turn, allowed the creation of a continuing process of searching for the remains of missing American personnel. The information collected by the JPRC/JCRC then proved instrumental in the recovery of remains and final closure for many American families. Thanks to advances in DNA identification and collection practices within the U.S. military, the Vietnam War would probably be the last military conflict engaged in by American forces in which the physical remains of servicemen could not be identified.

Chapter Ten

CONCLUSION

MACSOG was without doubt the most unique American unit to participate in the Vietnam War. Its operational mandate allowed its varied operations, on land, sea, and in the air, to take place in North Vietnam, Laos,
and Cambodia where most other American units were forbidden to go.
It also managed to participate, even if only on the periphery, in most of
the significant operations and incidents of the conflict. MACSOG was
there in the Gulf of Tonkin, during air operations over North Vietnam,
during the Tet Offensive, the secret bombing of and ground incursion
into Cambodia, Lam Son 719, the Green Beret murder case, the Easter
Invasion, the Phoenix Program, and the Son Tay Raid. During nine years
of operations, 163 MACSOG personnel were killed in action and an additional 80 were listed as missing.[1] Only two SOG recon men (SSgt. Car-
roll Flora, captured in the Ashau Valley in 1968, and Sgt. John Cavaiani)
were released from North Vietnamese captivity in 1973.

SOG was also unique in that its operations served as a counterpoint
to those of more conventional U.S. units during the conflict. Its Spike/
Recon Teams, Sea Commandos, aircraft, and agents almost always operated deep in what was known as Indian Country, and they were always
heavily outnumbered by their opponents, with only air support (when it
was available) as an equalizing factor. The irony of this position was that
although MACSOG was freed from some of the operational limitations
of more conventional units, it was itself handcuffed by other proscrip-
tions imposed by higher authority.

In retrospect, MACSOG and its operations failed to achieve the goals
that its masters set for it. This occurred not because of a lack of effort
or initiative on the part of the unit or its personnel, but because of the
inherent flaws in U.S. political/military strategy during the conflict. Other
problems, which were evident from SOG's inception, were exemplified by

MACV's and SACSA's inability to adapt MACSOG to fit their strategy. Or was it that the lack of a strategy (outside of search and destroy) precluded any more successful utilization of MACSOG? The unit was also caught on the horns of the very dilemma faced by the American government and MACV—it did not control or completely dominate its counterpart. It could suggest, but it could not command. Only SOG's cross-border ground operations seemed to fit into the American command structure's view of operational utility. This was a reasonable enough assumption on MACV's part, since SOG could have served as both pathfinder and spearhead for an attack on the Trail system by larger conventional forces. Thanks to unchanging political restrictions, however, that was never going to happen.

If there was ever a conflict that demonstrated von Clausewitz's dictum that war was politics by other means, it was this peculiar struggle in Southeast Asia. By supporting (at least in public) the neutrality of Laos and Cambodia, the United States forfeited any real chance of throttling the communists in South Vietnam. The continuous functioning of Hanoi's logistical system and border sanctuaries (regardless of the interdiction campaigns) allowed the North Vietnamese to retain the strategic and tactical initiative, which they utilized very effectively. The bizarre ritual dance performed by the United States, Cambodia, Laos, and North Vietnam was necessitated by Cold War presumptions and the perceived dangers of spiraling escalation. Those presumptions and perceptions have been proven to be correct. The possibility of escalation by the Chinese, derided both then and now by many as illusory, was very tangible. It has since become known that China was going through its largest rearmament and military buildup since the creation of the People's Republic of China and that Beijing fully expected to enter the war against the Americans.[2]

The limitations and restrictions imposed on MACSOG—indeed, on the entire American military effort—precluded victory as it was understood by both the Pentagon and the American public. The only alternative was to simply outlast the communists, but time proved to be on the side of the North Vietnamese. Whether there would ever have been a breaking point for Hanoi, what strategy could possibly have been adopted to reach it, and what length of time would have been necessary to achieve it are matters that have produced endless debate among historians and that will probably never be fully resolved.

What was not open to question or debate by the end of the conflict (and what had been so underestimated by the Americans at its advent) was the commitment and dedication of the Hanoi government to the unification of the two Vietnams. There have been few examples in history in which the concept of nationalism was carried to such an extreme and required so much sacrifice against so superior an enemy. It was the supreme irony that it was the United States, with its revolutionary origins and the sacrifices made by both sides during its own Civil War (both of which were enshrined in its national mythology), which failed to comprehend the dedication of the Vietnamese people to the creation of a unified state. So bound up was the United States in Cold War ideology and the gestalt of the times that it failed to see its own values, determination, or history reflected in those of its enemy.

Legacy

During the post-Vietnam force reductions and retrenchment in the American military, Special Forces paid the price. By the early 1980s, only the Army's 5th, 7th, and 10th Special Forces Groups had survived (by the skin of their teeth) and only about three thousand Green Berets remained within the ranks. This process of reduction (historically typical of post-war U.S. military practice) was arrested only by the rise of worldwide terrorism and by the spectacular success of elite foreign anti-terrorist units (e.g., the Israelis at Entebbe and the Germans at Mogadishu) in the late 1970s. These developments spurred President Jimmy Carter to authorize the Army to form the Delta Force in 1977. Modeled on the British Special Air Service, Delta was established by many personnel who had made their bones in MACSOG. The methods and techniques developed and utilized by SOG in Southeast Asia (search and rescue, strategic reconnaissance, air operations, HALO, etc.) were adopted by Delta and have become standard operational practices.

From the mid-1980s until the turn of the century, U.S. special operations forces underwent a renaissance. The end of the Cold War and the necessity of facing new and unconventional challenges throughout the world provided the incentive for this sea change. Less than stellar performances by special operations forces during Operation Eagle Claw (the Iran hostage rescue attempt) and Operation Urgent Fury (the invasion of Grenada) led to a lot of interservice finger-pointing and bickering over future special forces missions and coordination. Although the individual services fought the prospect vociferously, on 13 April 1987, the U.S. Congress took a firm hand and demanded that the Department of Defense establish a Joint Special Operations Command (SOCOM). By the onset of the 1989 invasion of Panama during Operation Just Cause, most of the wrinkles had been ironed out of the system, and U.S. special operations forces have performed their missions in an exemplary manner ever since.

Although still relatively unknown to the American public, MACSOG had carved out a legend for itself in Southeast Asia among the special operations community and among those whose interest in the conflict went beyond the superficial. Ironically, the conflict itself having gone badly for the United States only seemed to add luster to the dedication and operational fortitude of the personnel who continuously risked everything in the mountains and jungles of Southeast Asia. It was not the fault of those courageous men that their country had entered a conflict that it little understood and could not, given the geopolitical situation and the restrictions that it imposed upon itself, win.

The Presidential Unit Citation (Army)

for Extraordinary Heroism to the Studies and Observations Group, Military Assistance Command, Vietnam

AWARDED ON APRIL 4, 2001

The Studies and Observations Group is cited for extraordinary heroism, great combat achievement and unwavering fidelity while executing unheralded top secret missions deep behind enemy lines across Southeast Asia. Incorporating volunteers from all branches of the Armed Forces, and especially, US Army Special Forces, SOG's ground, air, and sea units fought officially denied actions, which contributed immeasurably to the American war effort in Vietnam.

MACV-SOG reconnaissance teams composed of Special Forces soldiers and indigenous personnel penetrated the enemy's most dangerous redoubts in the Laotian jungle wilderness and the sanctuaries of eastern Cambodia. Pursued by human trackers and even bloodhounds, these small teams outmaneuvered, outfought, and outran their numerically superior foe to uncover key enemy facilities, rescue downed pilots, plant wiretaps, mines and electronic sensors, capture valuable enemy prisoners, ambush convoys, discovered and assessed targets for B-52 strikes, and inflicted casualties out of all proportion to their own losses. When enemy counter-measures became dangerously effective, SOG operators innovated their own counters, from high altitude parachuting and unusual explosive devices, to tactics as old as the French and Indian War.

Fighting alongside their Montagnard, Chinese Nung, Cambodian, and Vietnamese allies, Special Forces-led Hatchet Force companies and platoons staged daring raids against key enemy facilities in Laos and Cambodia, overran major munitions and supply stockpiles, and blocked enemy highways to choke off the flow of supplies to South Vietnam. SOG'S cross-border operations proved an effective economy-of-force, compelling the North Vietnamese Army to divert 50,000 soldiers to rear area security duties, far from the battlefields of South Vietnam.

Supporting these hazardous missions were SOG'S own US and South Vietnam's Air Force transport and helicopter squadrons, along with USAF Forward Air Controllers and helicopter units of the US Army and US Marine Corps. These courageous aviators often flew through heavy fire to extract SOG operators from seemingly hopeless situations, saving lives by selflessly risking their own. SOG's Vietnamese naval surface forces - instructed and advised by US Navy SEALs - boldly raided North Vietnam's coast and won surface victories against the North Vietnamese Navy, while indigenous agent teams penetrated the very heartland of North Vietnam.

Despite casualties that sometimes became universal, SOG's operators never wavered, but fought throughout the war with the same flair, fidelity, and intrepidity that distinguished SOG from its beginning. The Studies and Observation Group's combat prowess, martial skills and unacknowledged sacrifices saved many American lives, and provided a paragon for American's future special operations forces.

Notes

ANTECEDENTS
1. Neil Sheehan et al., eds., *The Pentagon Papers as Published by the New York Times* (New York: Bantam Books, 1971), 131.
2. For a detailed account of the evolution of SOG's Vietnamese counterpart organizations see Joint Chiefs of Staff, U.S. Military Assistance Command, Vietnam, Studies and Observations Group, *Documentation Study* (July 1970); (hereafter cited as MACSOG, *Documentation Study*), Annex F, Appendix x.
3. For a description of the Joint Chiefs' attitudes and responses see Richard H. Shultz, *The Secret War against Hanoi* (New York: Harper Collins, 1999), 281–87. See also Rufus Phillips, *Why Vietnam Matters* (Annapolis, MD: Naval Institute Press, 2008), 103–5.
4. U.S. House of Representatives, Records of the House Committee on Armed Services, *United States–Vietnam Relations, 1945–1967: A Study Prepared by the Department of Defense* (Washington, DC: Government Printing Office, 1971), IV.C.2.(a):2.
5. MACSOG, *Documentation Study*, Appendix C, 1.
6. Ibid., 2.
7. Ibid., 3. The Military Assistance Advisory Group, Vietnam (MAAGV) was redesignated the Military Assistance Command, Vietnam (MACV) on 18 February 1962.
8. Ibid.
9. Ibid., Appendix C, Annex A, 1, Appendix B, 1, Appendix C, 5.
10. Ibid., Appendix B, B-184.
11. Ibid., Appendix C, C-4.
12. Ibid., 11.
13. Ibid.
14. Ibid.

CHAPTER 1. 1964: OPLAN 34A

1. U.S. Military Assistance Command, Vietnam, Studies and Observations Group, Annex A, *Command History, 1964* (Saigon: MACVSOG, 1965), A-1-1. Individual command histories hereafter cited as, for example, *Command History, 1964*, Annex A.
2. MACSOG, *Documentation Study*, Appendix C, 5.
3. Ibid., Appendix B, 343.
4. *Command History, 1964*, Annex A, A-1–3.
5. MACSOG, *Documentation Study*, Appendix C, 14.
6. Sedgwick Tourison, *Secret Army, Secret War* (Annapolis: Naval Institute Press, 1995), Appendix 1.
7. Robert McNamara today shrugs off responsibility for 34A by stating that the missions amounted to little more than pinpricks. Why were they continued? "The South Vietnamese government saw them as a relatively low cost means of harassing North Vietnam." Robert McNamara with Brian VanDeMark, *In Retrospect* (New York: Times Books, 1995), 130.
8. *MACSOG Documentation Study*, Appendix B, Annex U, 2. Colonel Ho and his subordinates had a good relationship with the commanders of MACSOG. Their apolitical nature allowed them to retain their positions when many ARVN Special Forces officers were sacked because of their political allegiances.
9. Interview with Quach Rang in Tourison, *Secret Army*, 99.
10. MACSOG, *Documentation Study*, Appendix B, Annex N, 4.
11. Ibid.
12. Ibid., Appendix C, 60; and Tourison, *Secret Army*, Appendix 1.
13. Michael E. Haas, *Apollo's Warriors* (Maxwell Air Force Base, AL: Air University Press, 1997), 40.
14. MACSOG, *Documentation Study*, Appendix B, 94.
15. Ibid., Appendix C, 58–63.
16. *Command History, 1964*, Annex A, A-IV-2–8.
17. For the most detailed and accurate description of the Gulf of Tonkin incidents see Edwin Moise, *Tonkin Gulf and the Escalation of the Vietnam War* (Chapel Hill: University of North Carolina Press, 1996); Robert J. Hanyok, *Spartans in Darkness* (Washington, DC: Center for Cryptologic History, National Security Agency, 2002), 184.
18. Marshall Green, "Immediate Actions in the Period Prior to Decision," in Mike Gravel, ed., *The Pentagon Papers*, vol. 3 (Boston: Beacon Press, 1971), 609.
19. McNamara with VanDeMark, *In Retrospect*, 141.
20. Moise, *Tonkin Gulf*, 68.

21. Conflicting communications from the land-based command, the naval headquarters at Haiphong, and the ignoring of conflicting orders by boat commanders have yet to be straightened out. Hanyok, *Spartans in Darkness*, 189–90.
22. Ibid., 191, 192.
23. Ibid., 192.
24. All questions pertaining to whether the North Vietnamese attacked on the night of 4 August were conclusively answered in the negative by the release of Hanyok's *Spartans in Darkness*, 195–223.
25. McNamara with VanDeMark, *In Retrospect*, 133.
26. 88th Congress, Joint Resolution 1145, 10 August 1964.
27. Moise, *Tonkin Gulf*, 86.
28. Ibid., 162. See also Stanley Karnow, *Vietnam: A History* (New York: Viking Books, 1983), 361.
29. MACSOG, *Documentation Study*, Annex A-IV-2–8.
30. Ibid., Appendix C, 60.
31. Ibid., Appendix C, Annex A, 3.
32. Ibid.
33. Kenneth Conboy and Dale Andrade, *Spies and Commandos* (Lawrence: University of Kansas Press, 2000) 77–80.
34. MACSOG, *Documentation Study*, Appendix B, 85–86.
35. John Prados, *The Blood Road* (New York: John Wiley and Sons, 1998), 108–9. See also Harve Saal, *SOG, MACV Studies and Observations Group: Behind Enemy Lines*, vol. III, *Legends* (Ann Arbor: Edwards Brothers, 1990), 80–81.
36. MACSOG, *Documentation Study*, Appendix J, 26.
37. Charles M. Simpson III, *Inside the Green Berets* (Novato, CA: Presidio Press, 1983), 1.
38. Interviews by Dr. Richard Shultz in Steve Sherman, ed., *MACV Studies and Observations Group Documentation Study and Command Histories* (CD-ROM) (Houston, TX: Radix Press, 2002), 52; hereafter cited as Interviews.
39. Shultz, *The Secret War*, 79.
40. Interviews, 30–31.
41. On a trip to Vietnam in 1964 Army chief of staff Harold Johnson disparaged the Special Forces as simply "a new gimmick" and the men who served in it as "primarily fugitives from responsibility." The Harold K. Johnson Papers, U.S. Army Center of Military History, Carlisle Barracks, PA, 3:12:7–10.
42. Benjamin F. Schemmer, *The Raid* (New York: Harper and Row, 1976), 47–48.

43. Ibid, 287.
44. MACSOG, *Documentation Study*, Appendix A, 26.

CHAPTER 2. 1965: SHINING BRASS
 1. *Command History, 1965*, Annex N, N-1.
 2. Ibid., N-3.
 3. Jacob Van Staaveren, *Interdiction in Southern Laos* (Washington, DC: Center for Air Force History, 1993), 29.
 4. *Command History, 1965*, Annex N, N-VIII-4.
 5. Prados, *The Blood Road*, 103.
 6. Only forty members of PAVN left the country, leaving around six thousand others in the eastern border regions of Laos. The United States continued to support Vang Pao's guerrilla army, also in violation of the agreement.
 7. MACSOG, *Documentation Study*, Appendix C, Annex A, 4.
 8. Ibid., 12.
 9. Ibid., 14.
10. Ibid., Appendix B, 126.
11. Shultz, *The Secret War*, 101.
12. *Command History, 1968*, Annex F, F-III-4-C-1–14.
13. In 1964 Transportation Group 125 was created and equipped with twenty steel-hulled vessels with which it delivered eighty-eight shiploads of materiel (equaling four thousand tons) to the south. By 1965 the eight ships of the group managed to transport just fifty tons of supplies.
14. Military Institute of Vietnam, *Victory in Vietnam*, trans. by Merle Pribbenow (Lawrence: University of Kansas Press, 2002), 88.
15. Ibid.
16. Van Staaveren, *Interdiction*, Appendix 5. Actual figures from Prados, *The Blood Road*, 45.
17. Military Institute of Vietnam, *Victory in Vietnam*, 88.
18. Ibid., 127.
19. Van Staaveren, *Interdiction*, 97.
20. Ibid., 262.
21. Edward Doyle, Samuel Lipsman, and Terrence Maitland, *The North* (Boston: Boston Publishing, 1986), 46.
22. Military Institute of Vietnam, *Victory in Vietnam*, 170.
23. John Prados, "The Road South," in Andrew Wiest, ed., *Rolling Thunder in a Gentle Land* (Oxford, UK: Osprey Publishing, 2006) 83.
24. Military Institute of Vietnam, *Victory in Vietnam*, 170.

25. Prados, *The Blood Road*, 111.
26. In its initial phase, Barrel Roll was allowed only two strikes per week of no more than four aircraft per mission.
27. John Morocco, *Rain of Fire* (Boston: Boston Publishing, 1985) 27–28.
28. MACSOG, *Documentation Study*, Appendix D, 4.
29. Ibid., 16–17.
30. Schemmer, *The Raid*, 79.
31. Terrence Maitland and Peter McInerney, *A Contagion of War* (Boston: Boston Publishing, 1983), 123–24.
32. *Command History, 1965*, Annex N, N-VIII-10–11.B.
33. Kenneth Conboy with James Morrison, *Shadow War* (Boulder, CO: Paladin Press, 1995), 118, 120.
34. Ibid., 144.
35. *Command History, 1965*, Annex N, N-2.
36. MACSOG, *Documentation Study*, Appendix C, 67.
37. Ibid., 66.
38. Ibid., 67.
39. Ibid.
40. Ibid., Appendix J, 34, 37.
41. Shultz, *The Secret War*, 274.
42. For an in-depth examination of this topic, see Andrew F. Krepinevich, *The Army and Vietnam* (Baltimore: The Johns Hopkins University Press, 1986) 27–55. The author's arguments, two decades after his work became the bible of the "never again" set of military officers, later had an eerie resonance in light of events in Afghanistan and Iraq.
43. Ibid., 69–75.
44. Shultz, *The Secret War*, 53
45. Interviews, 11.
46. Shultz, *The Secret War*, 273.
47. Interviews, 57–63.
48. John K. Singlaub and Malcolm McConnell, *Hazardous Duty* (New York: Summit Books, 1991), 253.
49. Shultz, *The Secret War*, 276.
50. Ibid., 277.
51. Ibid.
52. Interviews, 8.

CHAPTER 3. 1966: MISSION EXPANSION
1. Arnold Isaacs, Gordon Hardy, and McAlister Brown, *Pawns of War* (Boston: Boston Publishing, 1987), 81.
2. Footboy was the cover name given during the year to designate all

MACSOG operations carried out in North Vietnam, its territorial waters, or in its air space.

3. *Command History, 1966*, Annex M, M-3.
4. Ibid., M-III-I-2, 3.
5. Ibid.
6. MACSOG, *Documentation Study*, Appendix C, 72.
7. The Skyhook system consisted of a ground-launched balloon that towed a cable to which the individual to be extracted was attached. The aircraft, equipped with a V-shaped yoke at its nose, snagged the line and drew the individual into the air, where he was then drawn into the rear cargo area.
8. Van Staaveren, *Interdiction*, 107.
9. It was later estimated that the kill ratio for B-52 interdiction operations was one infiltrator killed for every three hundred bombs at a cost of $140,000. Morocco, *Rain of Fire*, 33.
10. Van Staaveren, *Interdiction*, 191.
11. Thanks to interservice rivalries, Westmoreland had extreme difficulties even coordinating the air assets within his purview. See John Prados and Ray W. Stubbe, *Valley of Decision* (Annapolis: Naval Institute Press, 1991), 295–97.
12. MACSOG, *Documentation Study*, Appendix C, 70.
13. Ibid.
14. Tourison, *Secret Army*, 174.
15. John L. Plaster, *SOG: The Secret Wars of America's Commandos in Vietnam* (New York: Simon and Schuster, 1997), 60–62.
16. Doyle, Lipsman, and Maitland, *The North*, 46.
17. Ibid.
18. Ibid.
19. Van Staaveren, *Interdiction*, 147–48.
20. Military Institute of Vietnam, *Victory in Vietnam*, 182.
21. Jason Hardy and Michael Tucker, *SOG: Team History and Insignia of a Clandestine Army* (Port St. Lucie, FL: MilSpec Publishing, 2008).
22. Van Staaveren, *Interdiction*, 122.
23. *Command History, 1966*, Annex M, M-IV-1.
24. MACSOG, *Documentation Study*, Appendix D, 27.
25. *Command History, 1966*, Annex M, M-IV-A-1–8.
26. Ibid., M-IV-3.
27. Van Staaveren, *Interdiction*, 159–60.
28. *Command History, 1966*, Annex M, M-V-1.
29. George J. Veith, *Code-Name Brightlight* (New York: Dell Publishing, 1998), 114–20.

30. Lt. Walter Meinzen, "Raid on Little Dachau," in Albert N. Garland, ed., *Infantry in Vietnam* (Nashville: The Battery Press, 1967), 62–67.
31. Plaster, *SOG: The Secret Wars*, 65.
32. Veith, *Code-Name*, 137.
33. Ibid., 135–36.
34. MACSOG, *Documentation Study*, Appendix J, 59.
35. Shultz, *The Secret War*, 300.
36. Ibid., 298.
37. Ibid., 303.
38. Interviews, 37.
39. Ibid., 40.
40. MACSOG, *Documentation Study*, Appendix B/Pt 5, 10.
41. Shultz, *The Secret War*, 274.

CHAPTER 4. 1967: DANIEL BOONE
1. *Command History, 1967*, Annex G, 1.
2. *Command History, 1967*, Appendix A, A-27.
3. MACSOG, *Documentation Study*, Appendix C to Annex B, C-b-166–70.
4. *Command History, 1967*, Annex G, G-II-4–10.
5. Ibid., Appendix B, 79–80.
6. By 1969 two CIA analysts, Sam Adams and Robert Klein, compiled a report that concluded that the number of NLF agents within the South Vietnamese government and military totaled around 30,000. Needless to say, the agency was not happy with the report. Ralph W. McGehee, *Deadly Deceits* (New York: Sheridan Square Press, 1983), 156–57.
7. Conboy and Andrade, *Spies and Commandos*, 268.
8. Shultz, *The Secret War*, 246–47.
9. Joseph A. McChristian, *The Role of Military Intelligence* (Washington, DC: Department of the Army, 1974), 142–43.
10. Singlaub and McConnell, *Hazardous Duty*, 303. This was Vu Ngoc Nha, a Catholic intellectual and close personal friend of Thieu's. Nha's spy ring was rolled up by the CIA during Operation Projectile in 1970. Eventually forty-one NLF agents were convicted, including Huynh Van Trong, special assistant to Thieu. Shortly thereafter, Van Khien, another communist agent with close ties to the command elements of ARVN, was accidentally arrested. Eventually, ten members of his net were also rounded up. See also John Prados, "Dawn of the War," in Samuel Lipsman, ed., *War in the Shadows* (Boston: Boston Publishing, 1988), 12–20, and McGehee, *Deadly Deceits*, 150–57.

11. Plaster, *SOG: The Secret Wars*, 464.
12. Conboy and Andrade, *Spies and Commandos*, 274–75.
13. MACSOG, *Documentation Study*, Appendix B, Annex I, 12.
14. *Command History, 1967*, Annex G, G-III-1-2, 1-3.
15. Ibid., G-III-2–6.
16. Plaster, *SOG: The Secret Wars*, 50–51.
17. Ibid., 83–84.
18. It must not be forgotten (as it often was by American troops in Vietnam) that members of the South Vietnamese Armed Forces did not rotate home after one year, or after a decade for that matter. They were in it for the duration. Technically, barring death or serious wounds, an ARVN soldier could have been participating in combat operations for ten to fifteen years.
19. MACSOG, *Documentation Study*, Appendix D, 84.
20. *Command History, 1967*, Annex G, G-III-2–3.
21. Van Staaveren, *Interdiction*, 226–28.
22. Ibid., 236–39.
23. MACSOG, *Documentation Study*, Appendix C, 21.
24. Ibid., 20–21.
25. Plaster, *SOG: The Secret Wars*, 121.
26. MACSOG, *Documentation Study*, Appendix B, Annex I, 13.
27. Ibid., 13–15.
28. As late as 10 May the FY 1967 Timberwork/STRATA mission statement for 1968 read that one of the operations of the teams was to establish resistance organizations and "to contact vulnerable groups, e.g., Catholics." MACSOG, *Documentation Study*, Annex B to Appendix C, 11.
29. Ibid., Appendix C, 29.
30. Ibid., 74.
31. *Command History, 1967*, Annex G, 4.
32. Ibid., 24.
33. The two HH-3 aircraft commanders were decorated for their exploit. Maj. Alton Deviney was awarded the Silver Star while Maj. James Villoti received the Distinguished Flying Cross.
34. MACSOG, *Documentation Study*, Appendix B, Annex N, 49.
35. Ibid., Appendix D, 52.
36. Plaster, *SOG: The Secret Wars*, 160.
37. MACSOG, *Documentation Study*, Appendix D, 293–94.
38. Military Institute of Vietnam, *Victory in Vietnam*, 208.
39. For the first time in the war, NSA cryptographers were able to penetrate PAVN voice communications from the Trail system, providing

better detail in estimating communist infiltration. The information provided by the "Vinh Window," however, quickly swamped the available translators and analysts. Hanyok, *Spartans in Darkness*, 110–16.

40. Van Staaveren, *Interdiction*, 244.
41. Ibid., 247.
42. Ibid., 244.
43. Military Institute of Vietnam, *Victory in Vietnam*, 208.
44. *Command History, 1967*, Annex G, G-IV-A-1, 2.
45. Van Staaveren, *Interdiction*, 197–202.
46. MACSOG, *Documentation Study*, Appendix C, and Van Staaveren, *Interdiction*, 198–99.
47. Van Staaveren, *Interdiction*, 199.
48. MACSOG, *Documentation Study*, Appendix D, 50.
49. *Command History, 1967*, Annex G, G-IV-3.
50. Conboy and Andrade, *Spies and Commandos*, 239.
51. Ibid., 239.
52. Singlaub and McConnell, *Hazardous Duty*, 311.
53. Saal, Vol. I, *Historical Evolution*, 132.
54. Plaster, *SOG: The Secret Wars*, 90–94.
55. Committee on Veteran's Affairs, U.S. Senate, *Medal of Honor Recipients, 1863–1978* (Washington, DC: Government Printing Office, 1979), 924; hereafter cited as *Medal of Honor Recipients*.
56. John Plaster, *SOG: A Photo History of the Secret Wars* (Boulder, CO: Paladin Press, 2000), 108.
57. *Medal of Honor Recipients*, 948.
58. MACSOG, *Documentation Study*, Appendix C, and Van Staaveren, *Interdiction*, 230.
59. Prados, *The Blood Road*, 264.
60. Military Institute of Vietnam, *Victory in Vietnam*, 465, fn 24. By 1966 PAVN was buying 100,000 tons of rice directly from Cambodian peasants, paying the world price in U.S. dollars. The Cambodian government, which paid a fixed price and pocketed the difference, thereby suffered export losses and spiraling inflation. Issacs, Hardy, and Brown, *Pawns of War*, 85.
61. MACSOG, *Documentation Study*, Appendix E, 14.
62. Ibid.
63. Ibid., 12.
64. Ibid., 66.
65. "MACSOG Position Paper," *Project Omega Sampler* in Steve Sherman, ed., *MACV Studies and Observations Group Documentation Study and Command Histories* (Houston: Radix Press, 2002).

66. MACSOG, *Documentation Study*, Appendix E, 17.
67. Sherman, *Project Omega Sampler*.
68. *Command History, 1967*, Annex G, G-IV-6.
69. Van Staaveren, *Interdiction*, 255–92. See also Paul Dickson, *The Electronic Battlefield* (Bloomington, IN: University of Indiana Press, 1976).
70. Ibid., 257.
71. The facility was also known as Dutch Mill, due to the size and shape of an antenna array.
72. The title of the site was changed regularly during its five-year occupation. It included Eagle's Nest, Gibraltar, Diamond Head, Leghorn, and Golf-5. For the sake of consistency and clarity, the term "Golf-5" will be used throughout the text.
73. Veith, *Code-Name*, 175–76.
74. Interviews, 4.
75. MACSOG, *Documentation Study*, Appendix J, 70.
76. Sheehan, *The Pentagon Papers*, 521.

CHAPTER 5. 1968: SUSPICIONS AND STAND-DOWN
1. *Command History, 1968*, Annex F, F-1–2.
2. Lewis Sorley, *A Better War* (New York: Harvest Books, 1999), 86–87.
3. MACSOG, *Documentation Study*, Appendix C, 128.
4. Ibid., 239.
5. *Command History, 1968*, Annex F, F-II-1–10, 14.
6. William Shawcross, *Sideshow* (New York: Washington Square Press, 1979), 68.
7. *Command History, 1968*, Annex F, F-II-1-17, 18.
8. Ibid., F-III-1-1–3.
9. Ibid., F-III-2-1-1.
10. Ibid., F-V-1–4.
11. Shawcross, *Sideshow*, 93.
12. Tourison, *Secret Army*, 167.
13. *Command History 1968*, Annex F, F-III-C-1-1–14.
14. Tourison, *Secret Army*, 65–66.
15. *Command History, 1968*, Annex F, 167–68.
16. Ibid., F-III-IV-1–6.
17. Ibid., F-IX-2.
18. Prados, *The Blood Road*, 193.
19. Ibid., 238.
20. Military Institute of Vietnam, *Victory in Vietnam*, 257.
21. *Command History, 1968*, Annex F, F-IV-1–8.

22. Ibid., F-III-A-1–2.
23. MACSOG, *Documentation Study*, Appendix D, 87.
24. Clark Dougan and Stephen Weiss, *Nineteen Sixty-Eight* (Boston: Boston Publishing, 1983), 47.
25. Saal, Vol. III, *Legends*, 231.
26. Prados, *The Blood Road*, 258.
27. Jack Schulimson et al. *U.S. Marines in Vietnam, The Defining Year, 1968* (Washington, DC: History and Museums Division, Headquarters, U.S. Marine Corps, 1997), 277.
28. Ibid., 278.
29. *Medal of Honor Recipients*, 949.
30. Plaster, *SOG: The Secret Wars*, 183–90.
31. Ronald H. Spector, *After Tet* (New York: Free Press, 1993), 169, and Alan Gropman, *Air Power and the Airlift Evacuation of Kham Duc* (Maxwell Air Force Base, AL: Air University Press, 1979).
32. Spector, *After Tet*, 169–70.
33. Shelby L. Stanton, *Green Berets at War* (Novato, CA: Presidio Press, 1985), 161–65.
34. The McGuire rig, designed by a Project Delta NCO, was a rope system deployed from a helicopter when no suitable LZ was available. Personnel snapped onto the rope and were lifted "on strings" without being hoisted aboard the aircraft.
35. *Medal of Honor Recipients*, 867.
36. Plaster, *SOG: A Photo History*, 414.
37. *Medal of Honor Recipients*, 856–57.
38. Howard was awarded the Medal of Honor, the Distinguished Service Cross, the Silver Star, three Bronze Stars for Valor (all awarded for separate actions), and eight Purple Hearts (for being wounded fourteen times) during his fifty-four-month stint in Vietnam. Murphy and York received more foreign decorations, but they were mainly awarded for the same combat actions.
39. MACSOG, *Documentation Study*, Appendix E, 37.
40. Ibid., 33.
41. Conboy and Andrade, *Spies and Commandos*, 233–34.
42. *Command History, 1968*, Annex F, F-IV-1–11.
43. *The Congressional Medal of Honor* (Forest Ranch, CA: Sharp & Dunnigan, 1984), 28–29.
44. Bernard C. Nalty, *The War against Trucks* (Washington, DC: Air Force History and Museums Program, 2005) 48.
45. Morocco, *Rain of Fire*, 33.
46. Van Staaveren, *Interdiction*, 290.

47. Morocco, *Rain of Fire*, 178. U.S. aircraft flew 22,126 sorties and dropped 39,179 tons of ordnance in the Khe Sanh area. Prados and Stubbe, *Valley of Decision*, 297.
48. Earl H. Tilford, *Setup* (Maxwell Air Force Base, AL: Air University Press, 1991) 173.
49. Nalty, *The War against Trucks*, 111. One should take these figures with a large grain of salt. The CIA estimated that only 872 trucks were working the Trail in late 1968.
50. *Medal of Honor Recipients*, 838–39.
51. *Command History, 1968*, Annex F, 1968, F-XI-1–4.
52. Veith, *Code-Name*, 187.
53. Ibid., 188–89.
54. Ibid., 193–95.
55. Ibid., 236–37.
56. Ibid., 230.
57. Ibid., 240–43.
58. *Command History, 1968*, Annex F, F-III-1–10.
59. Ibid, F-IV-1–3.
60. Herbert Weisshart quoted in Shultz, *The Secret War*, 15–16.
61. *Foreign Relations of the United States, 1961–1963: Vietnam*, vol. 1, 1961 (Washington, DC: Government Printing Office, 1990), 421–22.

CHAPTER 6. 1969: COMMANDO HUNT

1. Roger Warner, *Shooting at the Moon* (South Royalton, VT: Steerforth Press, 1996), 389.
2. Veith, *Code-Name*, 278.
3. Stanton, *Green Berets*, 168.
4. Ibid, 169.
5. *Command History, 1969*, Annex F, F-II-8–11.
6. Prados, *The Blood Road*, 303.
7. Tilford, *Setup*, 173.
8. Nalty, *The War against Trucks*, 129–30.
9. Ibid.
10. Prados, *The Blood Road*, 304.
11. Nalty, *The War against Trucks*, 111.
12. Military Institute of Vietnam, *Victory in Vietnam*, 499, fn 4.
13. Ibid., 37.
14. Nalty, *The War against Trucks*, 167–69. Within one two-and-one-half-month period in 1970, over ten thousand POL barrels were spotted in the water in the northern Prairie Fire area.
15. Ibid., 172.
16. Ibid., 175.

17. Plaster, *SOG: A Photo History*, 187.
18. *Command History, 1969*, Annex F, F-III-4–12.
19. MACSOG, *Documentation Study*, Appendix D, 94.
20. *Command History, 1969*, Annex F, F-III-4-A-2.
21. Plaster, *SOG: The Secret Wars*, 253–54.
22. Shelby L. Stanton, *The Rise and Fall of an American Army* (New York: Dell Publishing, 1985), 283.
23. Prados, *The Blood Road*, 268.
24. Menu was the code name given to a series of covert B-52 strikes conducted in Cambodia between 18 March 1968 and 26 May 1970.
25. John Morocco, "Operation Menu," in Samuel Lipsman, ed., *War in the Shadows* (Boston: Boston Publishing Company, 1988), 140.
26. *Command History, 1969*, Annex F, F-III-4-B-1.
27. *Medal of Honor Recipients*, 893.
28. Doug Miller was a fine example of the men working in Op-35 by 1969. His first two tours in-country were with a recon company of the 1st Air Cavalry Division (March 1966–68). After extending his tour, he had gone to Nha Trang to volunteer for SOG. For a fascinating firsthand account of his experiences in SEA, see Franklin D. Miller with Elwood J. C. Kureth, *Reflections of a Warrior* (Novato, CA: Presidio Press), 1991.
29. Plaster, *SOG: The Secret Wars*, 234–39.
30. Ibid., 234.
31. Jeff Stein, *A Murder in Wartime* (New York: St. Martin's, 1992), 84.
32. This was done on COMUSMACV's order. It was unusual in that it was customary for officers to retain their liberty until a verdict was rendered in their court martial. General Abrams did not like the Special Forces, especially when they were embarrassing him.
33. *Command History, 1969*, Annex F, F-IX-10.
34. Hoi Chanhs were NLF/PAVN troops who had voluntarily rallied to the Saigon government under the Chieu Hoi (open arms) program.
35. MACSOG, *Documentation Study*, Appendix D, 93.
36. *Command History, 1969*, Annex F, F-IX-7–9.
37. Interviews, 37.
38. Ibid., 38.
39. Saal, Vol. I, *Historical Evolution*, 138.
40. Interviews, 10.
41. Veith, *Code-Name*, 246–47.
42. Ibid., 263.
43. Ibid, 263–64. It was a standing order among the NLF and PAVN that American prisoners be killed by their captors rather than letting them be recovered.

44. Ibid., 265.
45. Ibid., 266–67.
46. *Command History, 1969*, Annex F, F-III-2–4.
47. Ibid., F-III-2–3.
48. Ibid.
49. Nalty, *The War against Trucks*, 40.
50. The Stabo rig (utilized for helicopter extractions) consisted of a nylon harness with two snap rings at the shoulders. The line from the helicopter was snapped into the rings, freeing the individuals to utilize their weapons. It was also much safer for the extraction of wounded personnel, who might not be able to use their hands as in the McGuire rig.
51. *Command History, 1969*, Annex F, F-VI-5.
52. Ibid., F-VII-1–2.
53. Doyle, Lipsman, and Maitland, *The North*, 106.
54. Ibid., 107.
55. Karnow, *Vietnam: A History*, 458.
56. McNamara with VanDeMark, *In Retrospect*, 66.
57. See Robert M. Gillespie, "The Joint Chiefs of Staff and the Escalation of the Vietnam Conflict, 1964–1965" (master's thesis, Clemson University, 1994).
58. Doyle, Lipsman, and Maitland, *The North*, 116.

CHAPTER 7. 1970: THE SECOND INDOCHINA WAR
1. *Command History, 1970*, Annex B, B-1-4.
2. Ibid., B-16.
3. Prados, *The Blood Road*, 316. The actual loss rate was about 3.9 percent.
4. Ibid., 296–99.
5. *Command History, 1970*, Annex B, B-II-7, 9.
6. John M. Shaw, *The Cambodian Campaign* (Lawrence: University of Kansas Press, 2005), 37.
7. Ibid., 61.
8. Ibid., 182 fn 81.
9. Bernard C. Nalty, *The Air War over South Vietnam, 1968–1975* (Washington, DC: Air Force History and Museums Program, 2000), 184.
10. *Command History, 1970*, Annex B, B-III-31.
11. Morocco, *Rain of Fire*, 40.
12. Tilford, *Setup*, 183.
13. Nalty, *The War against Trucks*, 183.
14. Ibid., 228.
15. Military Institute of Vietnam, *Victory in Vietnam*, 261.

16. Herman L. Gilster, *The War in Southeast Asia* (Maxwell Air Force Base, AL: Air University Press, 1993), 20.
17. Tilford, *Setup*, 183.
18. Nalty, *The War against Trucks*, 184.
19. Ibid., 218.
20. With the advent of General Abrams as COMUSMACV, the title Spike Team was replaced by Recon Team. The Spike Team moniker had been initiated by Westmoreland, but the men on the teams never really took to it. The two terms were, in fact, interchangeable.
21. Nalty, *The War against Trucks*, 244. The pass areas were routinely under surveillance by CIA roadwatch teams.
22. *Command History, 1970*, Annex B, B-III-48.
23. Ibid., B-III-49.
24. Ibid., B-50.
25. Ibid., B-51.
26. Frank Greco, *Running Recon* (Boulder, CO: Paladin Press, 2004), 210–12.
27. *Command History, 1970*, Annex B, B-VIII-8–10.
28. April Oliver and Peter Arnett, "Did the U.S. Drop Nerve Gas?" *Time Magazine*, 15 June 1998, p. 38.
29. Ibid., 37.
30. Evan Thomas and Gregory L. Vistica, "What's the Truth about Tailwind?" *Newsweek*, 22 June 1998, pp. 32–33.
31. Howard Kurtz, "CNN, Time Retract Report on U.S. Use of Nerve Gas in Laos," *Washington Post*, 3 July 1998, pp. A1, A14.
32. Ibid.
33. *Command History, 1970*, Annex B, B-VIII-7–8.
34. Ibid., B-21.
35. Ibid., B-22. This effectively extended Zone Alpha all the way to the Mekong River.
36. Ibid., B-III-55.
37. Ibid., B-22.
38. Ibid., B-III-61.
39. Ibid., B-IX-4.
40. Ibid., B-IX-5.
41. Ibid., B-IX-5–6.
42. Ibid., B-III-8.
43. Ibid., B-III-18.
44. Ibid., B-XIV-5–6.
45. Isaacs, Hardy, and Brown, *Pawns of War*, 98.
46. *Command History, 1970*, Annex B, B-XIV-13.

47. Ibid., B-XIV-24.
48. Ibid., B-XII-3.
49. Ibid., B-XII-2.
50. Veith, *Code-Name*, 294.
51. Ibid., 295.
52. Ibid., 297.
53. *Command History, 1970*, Annex B, B-XII-7.
54. Conboy and Andrade, *Spies and Commandos*, 246–47.
55. *Command History, 1970*, Annex B, B-IV-14.
56. Ibid., B-VII-1.
57. Ibid., B-VII-2.
58. Ibid., B-VI-6.
59. Ibid., B-VI-9.
60. Ibid., B-XVI-9.
61. Ibid., B-V-6, 11.
62. Al Santoli, *To Bear Any Burden* (New York: E. P. Dutton, 1985), 149.
63. Interviews, 61–64.
64. Ibid., 41.

CHAPTER 8. JANUARY 1971–30 APRIL 1972: DRAWDOWN
 1. *Command History, 1971–1972*, Annex B, B-1-5.
 2. Ibid.
 3. Ibid, B-3-1.
 4. Tilford, *Setup*, 184.
 5. There were also fewer and fewer aircraft to conduct the missions. During Commando Hunt, for example, there had been 1,777 aircraft utilized. By the opening of Commando Hunt VI, that figure had decreased to 1,199 and this figure further decreased to 953 before the end of 1971. This state of affairs was exacerbated by the withdrawal of sorties to conduct missions for Freedom Deal in Cambodia. Nalty, *The War against Trucks*, 155.
 6. Tilford, *Setup*, 184. The North Vietnamese placed orders for 5,600 trucks during 1971. They had received this number annually since the beginning of Commando Hunt in 1968.
 7. Ibid., 212, fn 47.
 8. Gilster, *War in Southeast Asia*, 21.
 9. Nalty, *The War against Trucks*, 232.
10. Tilford, *Setup*, 220.
11. Ibid., 184.
12. Gilster, *War in Southeast Asia*, 21.
13. Shaw, *The Cambodian Campaign*, 163.

14. Ibid., 352.
15. Ibid.
16. Ibid.
17. Prados, *The Blood Road*, 191.
18. Military Institute of Vietnam, *Victory in Vietnam*, 382.
19. Shawcross, *Sideshow*, 247.
20. Nalty, *The War against Trucks*, 215.
21. Ibid., 197.
22. Nalty, *The War against Trucks*, 202.
23. Ibid., 42.
24. *Command History, 1971–1972*, Annex B, B-9-1.
25. Ibid., B-18.
26. Ibid., B-3-50.
27. Ibid., B-3-51.
28. Ibid., B-3-57.
29. Ibid., B-3-58.
30. Ibid., B-3-59.
31. Conboy with Morrison, *Shadow War*, 378.
32. Interviews, 23.
33. Ibid., 24.
34. This device was a 2 x 3-foot wire mesh screen with 115 M-80 and cherry bomb fireworks attached. Ignited by a time pencil, the device simulated the sounds of a firefight.
35. Plaster, *SOG: The Secret Wars*, 320–32.
36. *Command History, 1971–1972*, Annex B, B-39.
37. Ibid., B-158–159. Plaster, *SOG: The Secret Wars*, 325–30.
38. *Medal of Honor Recipients*, 819–20.
39. Ibid., 850–51.
40. *Command History, 1971–1972*, B-IX-14–16.
41. Plaster, *SOG: A Photo History*, 168–70.
42. Ibid.
43. *Command History, 1971–1972*, Annex B, B-3-50.
44. Ibid., B-3-57.
45. Ibid., B-3-57.
46. Ibid., B-3-101–2.
47. Ibid., B-3-9.
48. Ibid.
49. Ibid., B-12-4.
50. Ibid., B-5-2.
51. Ibid., B-5-38.
52. Ibid., B-15-5.
53. Ibid., B-15-11.

54. Ibid., B-15-2.
55. Ibid.
56. Ibid., B-7-22.
57. Ibid., B-7-4.
58. Ibid., B-9-10.
59. Veith, *Code-Name*, 327–36. See also Plaster, *SOG: The Secret Wars*, 282–84.
60. Veith, *Code-Name*, 345–48. See also Plaster, *SOG: The Secret Wars*, 272–78.
61. Veith, *Code-Name*, 284–85.
62. Ibid., 315–16.
63. *Medal of Honor Recipients*, 899–900.
64. *Command History, 1971–1972*, Annex B, B-7-2.
65. Veith, *Code-Name*, 396.
66. *Command History 1971-1972*, Annex B, B-4-3.
67. Ibid., B-8-2.
68. Ibid., B-8-2.
69. Ibid., B-8-3.
70. Ibid., B-5-11.
71. Ibid., B-6-1.
72. Ibid., B-16-12.
73. Ibid., B-21.
74. Ibid., B-16-3.
75. Ibid., B-9-1.
76. Ibid., B-17-16.
77. Ibid., B-17-12.
78. Ibid., B-17-18.
79. Nalty, *The War against Trucks*, 175.
80. Hanyok, *Spartans in Darkness*, 94.
81. Ibid.
82. Nalty, *The War against Trucks*, 294
83. Ibid., 220.
84. Tilford, *Setup*, 185.
85. Morocco, *Rain of Fire*, 76.
86. Ibid., 78.
87. MACSOG, *Documentation Study*, Appendix I, 27.
88. Tilford, *Setup*, 295.
89. Morocco, *Rain of Fire*, 33–34.

CHAPTER 9. MAY 1972–MARCH 1973: STDAT-158

1. STDAT-158, *Command History, 1 May 1972–1973*, 3.
2. Ibid.

3. Ibid., 10.
4. Ibid.
5. Ibid., 4.
6. Ibid., 6.
7. Ibid., 26–27.
8. Ibid., 5.
9. Ibid., 9, 35–36.
10. Ibid., 73.
11. Ibid., 76.
12. Ibid., 74.
13. Ibid., 62.
14. Ibid.
15. Ibid., 63.
16. Ibid., 65.
17. Ibid., 65–66.
18. Ibid., 67–68.
19. Ibid., 62.
20. Ibid., 82.
21. Ibid., 86.
22. Ibid., 88.
23. Dale Andrade, *Trial by Fire: The 1972 Easter Offensive, America's Last Vietnam Battle* (New York: Hippocrene Books, 1995), 207–9. The idea for the operation had come from Ewen Montagu's classic account of Second World War counterintelligence, *The Man Who Never Was* (Philadelphia: Lippencott, 1954).
24. STDAT-158, *Command History, 1 May 1972–1973*, 87.
25. Conboy and Andrade, *Spies and Commandos*, 265.
26. STDAT-158, *Command History, 1 May 1972–1973*, 92.
27. Ibid., 92.
28. Ibid., 93.
29. *Medal of Honor Recipients*, 933–34.
30. STDAT-158, *Command History, 1 May 1972–1973*, 95.
31. Ibid., 97.
32. Ibid., 41.
33. Ibid., 59.
34. Plaster, *SOG: The Secret Wars*, 67.

CHAPTER 10. CONCLUSION

1. Plaster, *SOG: The Secret Wars*, 466.
2. Following their experiences during the Korean Conflict, the Chinese utilized Vietnam as a training ground. Between July 1965 and Decem-

ber 1968, the PRC rotated 320,000 troops (most of whom served in 23 anti-aircraft divisions) for eight-month tours in North Vietnam. There is no evidence, however, that any unit served south of Hanoi or on the Ho Chi Minh Trail. Xiobang Li, *A History of the Modern Chinese Army* (Lexington: University of Kentucky Press, 2007), 217–19.

Bibliography

UNPUBLISHED GOVERNMENT DOCUMENTS

Joint Chiefs of Staff. Military Assistance Command, Vietnam Studies and Observations Group. *Documentation Study* (July 1970). [A study compiled by the SACSA staff in 1970 for future utilization of lessons learned. An absolute necessity for the researcher.]

U.S. Military Assistance Command, Vietnam, Strategic Technical Directorate Assistance Team-158. *Command History, 1 May 1972–March 1973*. Saigon: STDAT-158, 1973.

U.S. Military Assistance Command, Vietnam, Studies and Observations Group, Annex A. *Command History, 1964*. Saigon: MACVSOG, 1965.

———. Annex B. *Command History, 1970*. Saigon: MACVSOG, 1971.

———. Annex B. *Command History, 1971–72*. Saigon: MACVSOG, 1972.

———. Annex F. *Command History, 1968*. Saigon: MACVSOG, 1969.

———. Annex F. *Command History, 1969*. Saigon: MACVSOG, 1970.

———. Annex G. *Command History, 1967*. Saigon: MACVSOG, 1968.

———. Annex M. *Command History, 1966*. Saigon: MACVSOG, 1967.

———. Annex N. *Command History, 1965*. Saigon: MACVSOG, 1966.

[These annual annexes to the MACV Command Histories are useful, depending upon their level of sanitization. It goes without saying that any information concerning the CIA, the State Department, or descriptions of operational methods that were thought to have any future utility (especially psychological operations) has been deleted.]

U.S. Senate. Records of Senate Subcommittee on POW/MIA Affairs. Working Papers of Sedgwick Tourison. 102nd Congress, last revision March 15, 1993. Charles E. Schamel Center for Legislative Archives, National Archives and Records Administration, Washington, DC. [Besides Reske's annotated annexes, these records were the first direct source of the SOG Command Histories and the Documentation Study.]

PUBLISHED GOVERNMENT DOCUMENTS

Gropman, Alan. *Air Power and the Airlift Evacuation of Kham Duc.* Maxwell Air Force Base, AL: Air University Press, 1979. [Best description of the fall of one of SOG's FOBs even though the organization is not mentioned in the text at all.]

Haas, Michael E. *Apollo's Warriors: U.S. Air Force Special Operations During the Cold War.* Maxwell Air Force Base, AL: Air University Press, 1997. [A thorough (though at times inaccurate) account of SOG air operations.]

Hanyok, Robert J. *Spartans in Darkness: American SIGINT and the Indochina War, 1945–1975.* Washington, DC: Center for Cryptologic History, National Security Agency, 2002. [Highly sanitized NSA history of the agency's activities in SEA. Has definitive information on the Gulf of Tonkin, some material on the Trail and on snooping on communist communications.]

McChristian, Joseph A. *The Role of Military Intelligence: 1965–1967.* Washington, DC: Department of the Army, 1974. [A work of self-congratulation. Its description of multilateral declassification and intelligence sharing with the South Vietnamese is rather frightening in retrospect.]

Military History Institute of Vietnam. *Victory in Vietnam: The Official History of the People's Army of Vietnam, 1954–1975.* Trans. Merle L. Pribbenow. Lawrence: University of Kansas Press, 2002. [This heavily biased official history of PAVN does provide many useful details on the Ho Chi Minh Trail and the logistical effort in the Laotian panhandle.]

Nalty, Bernard C. *The Air War over South Vietnam, 1968–1975.* Washington, DC: Air Force History and Museums Program, 2000. [The official Air Force history of in-country operations, which also includes the only official description of Operation Menu and Operation Freedom Deal. It also describes the horrendous political ramifications of both.]

———. *The War against Trucks, Aerial Interdiction in Southern Laos, 1968–1972.* Washington, DC: Air Force History and Museums Program, 2005. [The official Air Force history of the Commando Hunt interdiction campaigns. Highly critical of the claims made by the 7th/13th Air Force.]

Schulimson, Jack, et al. *U.S. Marines in Vietnam, The Defining Year, 1968,* Washington, DC: History and Museums Division, Headquarters, U.S. Marine Corps, 1997. [Official history of Marine Corps operations. Coverage of Khe Sanh has some SOG material in reference to the fall of Lang Vei.]

Tilford, Earl H., Jr. *Setup: What the Air Force Did in Vietnam and Why.* Maxwell Air Force Base, AL: Air University Press, 1991. [One of the earliest voices of dissatisfaction with the official history of his service branch, Colonel Tilford went beyond Vietnam to criticize the Air Force for both the lack of a coherent strategy and the "our hands were tied" excuse in Laos and Cambodia as well.]

U.S. House of Representatives. Records of the House Committee on Armed Services. *United States–Vietnam Relations, 1945–1967: A Study Prepared for the Department of Defense.* Washington: Government Printing Office, 1971–1972. [The Ur-documents of MACSOG. Prepared by RAND at the request of Robert McNamara, this study covers the period from the Truman administration until 1968. The first official description of the establishment of MACSOG and its early operations.]

U.S. Senate. Hearings before the Committee on United States Security Agreements and Commitments Abroad of the Committee on Foreign Relations. *United States Security Agreements and Commitments Abroad, Kingdom of Laos.* 91st Cong, 1st sess. Washington, DC: U.S. Government Printing Office, 1970. [This first public revelation of America's secret war in Laos blew the cover on the bombing campaign and on CIA and MACSOG operations there.]

———. Hearings before the Senate Armed Services Committee. *Bombing in Cambodia.* 93rd Cong., 1st sess. Washington, DC: U.S. Government Printing Office, 1973. [These sessions not only revealed Nixon's secret Menu bombings, but MACSOG's recon role in them as well.]

Van Staaveren, Jacob. *Interdiction in Southern Laos, 1964–1968.* Washington, DC: Center for Air Force History, 1993. [This volume deals with Steel Tiger and Tiger Hound interdiction campaigns on the Ho Chi Minh Trail. Also describes Shining Brass, Prairie Fire, and the inception of Muscle Shoals operations. Accurate and critical.]

DOCUMENT COLLECTIONS

Gravel, Mike, ed. *The Pentagon Papers: The Defense Department History of United States Decision-making on Vietnam.* 5 vols. Boston: Beacon Press, 1971–72. [A condensed version of the much longer *U.S.–Vietnam Relations.*

Sheehan, Neil et al., eds. *The Pentagon Papers as Published by the New York Times.* New York: Bantam Books, 1971. [A condensed version of *U.S.–Vietnam Relations,* with excellent annotations by the NYT staff.]

Sherman, Steve, ed. *MACV Studies and Observations Group Documentation Study and Command Histories.* Houston, TX: Radix Press,

2002. CD-ROM. Steve Sherman can be reached at 11715 Bandlon Dr., Houston, TX 77072. Tel. 281-879-5688 or email at sherman1@ flash.net. [This collection contains as much of the Documentation Study and Command Histories as has been declassified to date. It also includes much information on Projects Sigma and Omega and oral history interviews conducted by Dr. Richard Shultz. All in all, this is a researcher's delight.]

MEMOIRS AND AUTOBIOGRAPHIES

Acre, James. *Project Omega: Eye of the Beast*. Central Point, OR: Hellgate Press, 1999. [Acre spent 1969–70 running recon at CCS. This is an excellent and unvarnished memoir of the tour of a recon man. It is also unusual in its outlook on the war itself.]

Colby, William. *Honorable Men: My Life in the CIA*. New York: Simon and Schuster, 1978. [Part memoir, part apologia for some of the activities of one of the agency's top guns.]

Greco, Frank. *Running Recon*. Boulder, CO: Paladin Press, 2004. [Greco ran recon at CCC in 1969–70 and was later assigned to the camp photo shop. Thanks to a propitious fire, he managed to save and bring home many of these photos. A good complement to Plaster's photo history. Unfortunately, as a historical work, it is highly inaccurate.]

McGehee, Ralph W. *Deadly Deceits: My 25 Years in the CIA*. New York: Sheridan Square Press, 1983. [CIA paramilitary/counterintelligence operative McGehee spent a lot of time in Thailand, Laos, and South Vietnam and was not happy with the results of the covert war he spent his time fighting.]

McNamara, Robert S., with Brian VanDeMark. *In Retrospect: The Tragedy and Lessons of Vietnam*. New York: Times Books, 1995. [The former secretary of defense waxes apologetic on the mistakes made during his tenure. His memory, however, tends to be rather selective.]

Meyer, John S. *Across the Fence*. St. Ann, MO: Real War Stories, 2004. [This account was written by a recon man who served first at FOB-1 and later at CCN from 1968 to 1970.]

Miller, Franklin D., with Elwood N. C. Kureth. *Reflections of a Warrior*. Novato, CA: Presidio Press, 1991. [Unabashed and unrepentant autobiography by Medal of Honor recipient Miller, who spent an amazing six years in Vietnam, four of them with MACSOG, mostly running with RT Vermont at CCC.]

Nicholson, Thom. *15 Months in SOG: A Warrior's Tour*. New York: Random House, 1999. [Captain Nicholson was a Hatchet Force commander at CCN in 1969–70. An excellent description of how difficult SOG operations had become later in the war. Nicholson has been accused of condensing and rearranging the chronology, and of fictionalizing the text.]

Plaster, John L. *Secret Commandos: Behind Enemy Lines with the Elite Warriors of SOG*. New York: Simon and Schuster, 2004. [A personal memoir of Plaster's three-year tour with CCC. Harrowing and engrossing.]

Singlaub, John K., with Malcolm McConnell. *Hazardous Duty: An American Soldier in the Twentieth Century*. New York: Summit Books, 1991. [The only biography of or by a chief of MACSOG. Unfortunately, it does not contain much material that cannot be found elsewhere.]

Westmoreland, William C. *A Soldier Reports*. New York: Dell Publishing, 1980. [COMUSMACV tells all, and according to him, he got along with his special operations personnel very well. This is not borne out by the remarks of either SOG personnel or their commanders.]

SECONDARY SOURCES

Conboy, Kenneth, and Dale Andrade. *Spies and Commandos*. Lawrence: University of Kansas Press, 2000. [The second general history of MACSOG. The authors work hard to debunk the idea of "the inside man" theory of the failure of SOG's effort, especially in agent team operations.]

Conboy, Kenneth, with James Morrison. *Shadow War: The CIA's Secret War in Laos*. Boulder CO: Paladin Press, 1995. [Highly detailed history of the "other war" in Laos. This volume serves as a useful adjunct to study of Shining Brass/Prairie Fire operations in the panhandle.]

Doyle, Edward, Samuel Lipsman, and Terrence Maitland. *The North*. Boston: Boston Publishing, 1986. [This volume of the Vietnam Experience series covers North Vietnamese political and military decision making and has some material in reference to the Trail system.]

Hardy, Jason, and Michael Tucker. *SOG: Team History and Insignia of a Clandestine Army*. Port St. Lucie, FL: MilSpec Publishing, 2008. [The first of a projected seven-volume series covering recon team histories and the development of SOG insignia. Seven recon teams from CCN and CCC are covered in this heavily illustrated work.]

Isaacs, Arnold R., Gordon Hardy, and McAlister Brown. *Pawns of War: Cambodia and Laos*. Boston: Boston Publishing, 1987. [This volume of Boston Publishing's Vietnam Experience series deals solely with Laos and Cambodia. Excellent analysis of their politics and history.]

Lipsman, Samuel, ed. *War in the Shadows*. Boston: Boston Publishing, 1988. [This volume of the Vietnam Experience series deals with covert warfare. Contains a chapter on Operation Menu by John Morocco. The chapter dealing with MACSOG was written by Shelby Stanton and is dated and inaccurate.]

Maitland, Terrence, and Peter McInerney. *A Contagion of War*. Boston: Boston Publishing, 1983. This fifth volume of the Vietnam Experience series contains a chapter on SOG operations, especially the launching of the first Shining Brass missions.

Maitland, Terrence, and Stephen Weiss, eds. *Raising the Stakes*. Boston: Boston Publishing, 1983. [This third volume of the Vietnam Experience deals with the takeover of the conflict by the United States. It also has one of the first published descriptions of MACSOG's organization and activities.]

Moise, Edwin. *Tonkin Gulf and the Escalation of the Vietnam War*. Chapel Hill: University of North Carolina Press, 1996. [Much more accurate than Marolda's work. Dr. Moise makes the direct connections between SOG and the Desoto patrols that led to the Tonkin Gulf incidents.]

Morocco, John. "Operation Menu." In *War in the Shadows*, edited by Samuel Lipsman. Boston: Boston Publishing, 1988. Describes Nixon's covert aerial campaign and SOG's recon role in it.

———. *Rain of Fire: 1969–1973*. Boston: Boston Publishing, 1985. [Succinct coverage of the interdiction campaigns in Laos and Operations Linebacker/Linebacker II.]

Plaster, John L. *SOG: A Photo History of the Secret Wars*. Boulder, CO: Paladin Press, 2000. [A beautiful and historically important piece of work. Hundreds of never-before-seen photos of SOG teams, weapons, and operations. Most of the text, however, is a rehash of his previous work.]

———. *SOG: The Secret Wars of America's Commandos in Vietnam*. New York: Simon and Schuster, 1997. [This was the first general history of SOG, by an author who served from 1968 to 71 with CCC. Outside of the context of Op-35, however, there are inaccuracies.]

Prados, John. *The Blood Road: The Ho Chi Minh Trail and the Vietnam War*. New York: John Wiley and Sons, 1998. [The only conflict-length, detailed study of the Trail system. MACSOG information is well integrated into this fascinating story and places it within a larger context.]

———. *Vietnam: The History of an Unwinnable War, 1945–1975*. Lawrence: University of Kansas Press, 2009. [Replaces Stanley Karnow's *Vietnam: A History* as the most comprehensive and up-to-date single-volume history of the war. This tome incorporates most of the information gleaned since the 1980s, including declassified documents (from several nations) and presidential tape recordings.]

Prados, John, and Ray W. Stubbe. *Valley of Decision: The Siege of Khe Sanh*. Annapolis: Naval Institute Press, 1991. [Best volume on the battle in Quang Tri Province and describes SOG's operations from the FOB and its involvement in the relief of Lang Vei.]

Reske, Charles F. *MACV-SOG Command History: Annex B 1971–1972*. Sharon Center, OH: Alpha Press, 1990. [Reske did a better job with this work than his 1992 publication, or is it that the annexes themselves are just less sanitized than the previous ones?]

———. *MACV-SOG Command History: Annexes A, N, & M (1964–1966)*. Sharon Center, OH: Alpha Press, 1992. [The first release of the (highly sanitized) early SOG Command History annexes. The commentary is dated and highly inaccurate.]

Saal, Harve. *SOG-MACV Studies and Observations Group: Behind Enemy Lines*. 4 vols. Vol. I, *Historical Evolution*; Vol. II, *Locations*; Vol. III, *Legends*; Vol. IV, *Appendices*. Ann Arbor: Edwards Brothers, 1990. [Recon veteran Saal's (CCN's ill-fated RT Idaho) four volumes are disorganized, repetitive, highly biased, and heavily concentrated on Op-35. That said, they also contain nuggets of information not available elsewhere.]

Santoli, Al. *To Bear Any Burden: The Vietnam War and its Aftermath in the Words of Americans and Southeast Asians*. New York: E. P. Dutton, 1985. [First of the "oral histories" of the Vietnam War. Has some SOG information.]

Schemmer, Benjamin F. *The Raid*. New York: Harper and Row, 1976. [Highly readable and accurate description of Operation Kingpin.]

Shaw, John M. *The Cambodian Campaign: The 1970 Offensive and America's Vietnam War*. Lawrence: University of Kansas Press, 2005. [An operational analysis of the incursion that somehow fails to mention its long-term effects on Cambodia; it claims that an American military defeat was precluded and that an "indecent interval" was guaranteed by the operation.]

Shawcross, William. *Sideshow: Nixon, Kissinger, and the Destruction of Cambodia*. New York: Washington Square Press, 1979. [The harrowing account of Cambodia's descent into mass murder and auto-genocide. Decried at the time of its publication, this account of Operation Menu, the Cambodian Incursion, the role played by the Nixon administration in the destruction of a nation and its people, and the victory of the Khmer Rouge has held up well over time.]

Shultz, Richard H., *The Secret War against Hanoi*. New York: Harper Collins, 1999. [The first analytic (and critical) look at the history of SOG. Shultz had access to many classified documents that were previously unavailable. It does, however, contain some minor inaccuracies.]

Simpson, Charles M., III. *Inside the Green Berets*. Novato, CA: Presidio Press, 1983. [The first good postconflict history of Special Forces. Simpson spent nine years inside the organization in unconventional warfare and counter-insurgency fields.]

Spector, Ronald H. *After Tet: The Bloodiest Year in Vietnam*. New York: The Free Press, 1993. [Contains a good description of the fall of SOG's Kham Duc operations base.]

Stanton, Shelby L. *Green Berets at War: U.S. Army Special Forces in Southeast Asia, 1956–1975*. Novato, CA: Presidio Press, 1985. [This is a more detailed version of Simpson's work and describes more operational history. The chapter dealing with special reconnaissance (Sigma, Omega, Delta, and SOG) is generalized and has many inaccuracies.]

———. *Vietnam Order of Battle*. New York: Galahad Books, 1986. [A brilliant piece of organizational history that contained the first description of SOG. The dates of the creation and organization of the C&Cs are the same as in the work above, are inaccurate, and were copied by almost every author that followed.]

Stein, Jeff. *A Murder in Wartime*. New York: St. Martin's, 1992. [A thorough description of the "Green Beret Murder Case" and SOG's involvement in exonerating the defendants.]

Tourison, Sedgwick. *Secret Army, Secret War: Washington's Tragic Spy Operation in North Vietnam*. Annapolis: Naval Institute Press, 1995. [The only work dealing solely with the disastrous Operation Timberwork. Research for this work coincided with the release from prison of the last of the agents inserted into North Vietnam. Tourison blamed the failure on possible communist infiltration of SOG and the STD rather than on operational ineptitude à la Shultz.]

Veith, George J. *Code-Name Brightlight*. New York: Dell Publishing, 1998. [The only work dealing solely with the JPRC, POW rescue attempts, negotiations, and escapes. It describes SOG's role well, but contains many mistakes and omissions.]

Warner, Roger. *Shooting at the Moon: The Story of America's Clandestine War in Laos*. South Royalton, VT: Steerforth Press, 1996. [A description of the CIA's covert war in northern and southern Laos. Best read in conjunction with Conboy's work on the same subject.]

JOURNAL ARTICLES

Andrade, Dale. "The Lost Commandos." *Soldier of Fortune,* September 1995. [A condensation of information that was coming out with the publication of Tourison's work. Andrade's work on MACSOG was five years from publication.]

Conby, Kenneth, and James Morrison. "The Rise and Fall of Recon Team Asp." *Vietnam Magazine,* August 2001. [A brief history of RT Asp by two of the premier authors of the clandestine war in Laos.]

Do Cam Tran, "The Gulf Raiders." *Florida Vie Bao Directory Yearbook, 2000.* Miramar: FL, 2000. [Article by a former PTF commander on MAROPS. He served for six years (1964–70) with the CSS and tells the story from a Vietnamese naval officer's point of view.]

Dwyer, John B. "Inside Story." *Vietnam,* December 1992. [Although more accurate than Jim Graves' work below, this article is still riddled with inaccuracies.]

Graves, Jim. "SLAM Mission into Laos." *Soldier of Fortune,* June 1981. [Describes the mission for which Fred Zabitosky received the Medal of Honor.]

———. "SOG's Secret War." *Soldier of Fortune,* June 1981. [As far as the author can deduce, this was the first detailed description (albeit murky) of the operations of MACSOG.]

FICTIONALIZED ACCOUNTS

Harris, Raymond D. *Break Contact, Continue Mission.* New York: Berkley, 1991. [This account was written by a former CCC RT Iowa member who served during 1969. After a tour extension he worked in the Earth Angel program in 1970.]

Maurer, David A. *The Dying Place.* New York: Dell Publishing, 1986. [This work was written by a recon man who served at CCN during 1968–69.]

White, Kent. *Prairie Fire.* St. Ann, MO: Real War Stories, 2004. [The original edition of this work, published in 1983, was the first fictionalized account by a former recon man. White served with MACSOG during 1968–69.]

Index

Abrams, Creighton, 62, 63, 89, 90, 132, 177, 182, 183, 198, 216, 277n32, 279n20

agent teams: capture of, 19, 43, 138–39; drop zones for, 19, 70; evaluation of program, 106; EWOTS, 41, 43, 106; financial contracts with agents, 74–75; isolation of, 108; mission of, 41, 43, 107, 163–64; North Vietnamese response to activities of, 104; opposition to, 103; outcome of program, 106, 137–39, 163–65, 184; phantom teams and psychological operations, 102–3, 107–8; recovery of, 107, 272n33; recruitment and training, 15–16, 43–44; resupply missions for, 98–99, 102–3, 107; teams and activities, 5–6, 14–18, 21, 24, 42–43, 57, 69, 70, 74, 105–6, 137–39, 184

Air Force, U.S., 11, 31, 59, 72–73, 81, 157–58, 214, 246

Air Force Cross, 156

air operations (Midriff/Shedder): aircraft for, 130, 136, 189, 191–92; airlift section, 154, 212–13; asset utilization, 212; Footboy operations, 97–102; funding for, 31; intelligence gathering operations, 19; mission of, 68–73, 154, 236; name change of, 93, 168; OPLAN 34A, 18–19; organization of, 154; pilots, skill of, 130; Shining Brass operation, 55–57; tactical air operations, 71. *See also* helicopters

airborne operations (Timberwork): control of, 210; cross-border ground operations, 108–25; dissolution of, 234; intelligence gathering and dissemination, 93, 134–35; mission of, 272n28; name change of, 93; OPLAN 34A, 14–18, 266n7; outcome of program, 164, 194; reorganization of, 184; STS/STD, dependence on, 105; training for, 18, 108, 199. *See also* agent teams; *specific operations*

Anthis, Rollen H. "Buck," 85–86, 89

Army, U.S., 11, 20, 21, 56, 72

Army of the Republic of Vietnam (ARVN), 16, 30, 49, 50–51, 241, 272n18

Ashau Valley, 113, 146–47, 177–78, 228–29, 252, 258

B-52 bombers and missions, 67, 72, 73, 112–14, 179, 253, 270n9, 277n24

Barrel Roll, Operation, 47, 269n26

Benevidez, Roy, 152–53

Benson Silk program, 103, 194

Bifrost/Dodge Mark, Operation, 135, 161, 169, 211, 235

Blackbirds, 68–69, 98–99, 189, 270n7

Blackburn, Donald D. "Don": agents, financial contracts with, 74; experience of, 36, 87–88; infiltration program and resistance movement, 41–42; Kingpin operation, 51, 219; MACVSOG command

Shriver, Jerry "Mad Dog," 181–82
Sigma, Project, 122–23, 128, 151, 176
Silver Buckle, Operation, 226–27
Silver Star, 120, 231, 275n38
Simons, Arthur D. "Bull," 34, 50–51, 53, 65, 84–85, 219, 233
Singlaub, John: agent team program, 137, 165; covert operations and overt policy, 42, 105; cross-border operations in Laos, 113; driver for, 95; experience of, 64; intelligence sharing, 96; MACVSOG command by, 62–63, 64, 91–92; personnel, training of, 34; replacement of, 131; rice stockpiles, contamination of, 109; Sullivan's control of Laotian operations, 66–67, 114; tranquilizer dart use, 109; Westmoreland, relationship with, 62–63
Sisler, George K., 118, 120, 125
SLAM (Search, Locate, Annihilate, Monitor) concept and missions, 80–81, 112–14, 121, 144
Soap Chips program, 103
Son Tay raid (Operation Kingpin), 34, 50, 88, 215, 219
South Vietnam: anticommunist and pro-American groups, funding for, 104; border of, moving on map, 50; communist agents in government, 95, 271n6, 271n10; cooperation between U.S. and, 9; coup in, 9, 10; fall of, prevention of, 1–3, 4–5; infiltration program, opinion about, 15, 266n7; insurgency in, 3–4, 7, 11; intelligence sharing with, 95–96, 271n10; invasion of, 11; psychological and propaganda efforts in, 2, 6
South Vietnamese armed forces, 7, 8–9, 20
South Vietnamese Navy, 21
Southpaw project, 121
Soviet Union, 1, 10, 11, 25, 39–40
Special Assistant for Counterinsurgency and Special Activities (SACSA), 6–7, 85–90, 259
Special Forces, U.S., 5, 6, 12, 13, 32–35, 36–37, 39, 61–62, 63, 90, 267n41
Special Forces Command, 7–8, 186
Special Forces Group (SFG), 12, 48–49, 51, 64, 91–92, 108, 111, 260

Special Mission Service (SMS), 218, 242–43, 249–50. *See also* Luc Luong Duc Biet (LLDB)
Special Operations Division, 6–7, 89
Special Operations Group (SOG), 8, 11. *See also* Military Assistance Command, Vietnam, Studies and Observations Group (MACVSOG)
Special Operations Squadrons (SOSs), 71, 98, 154–55, 190, 213, 214, 236
Special Topographical Exploitation Service (TES), 5, 7–8
Spike Teams (STs). *See* Recon Teams (RTs)/Spike Teams (STs)
Spindown, Operation, 176–77, 202
Stabo rig, 193, 278n50
Star, Project, 54, 115
Steel Tiger, Operation, 47, 101–2, 110, 153
Stick, Operation, 213, 217
Story Book, Operation, 215–16
Strategic Exploitation Service (SES), 13, 20–21, 37
Strategic Technical Directorate Assistance (STDAT-158): activation of, 247; Coastal Recovery Force, 253–54; communications, 256; comptroller, 256; creation of, 242; headquarters, 247–48; intelligence operations, 248; Liaison Service Advisory Detachment, 226, 250–51, 255; Logistics Division, 255; Plans, Operations, and Training Advisory Division, 222, 226, 235, 242, 248–49; Special Mission Force, 255; Special Mission Service Advisory Detachment (SMSAD), 243, 249–50; Training Center Advisory Detachment, 251–52
Strategic Technical Service/Strategic Technical Directorate (STS/STD): agents, payments to dependents of, 74–75; base transfers, 241; communist agents in, 106, 186; coordination with, 161, 186; creation and mission of, 37; exploitation assets, 218–19; funding for, 249; name change of, 93; personnel from, 105, 185; recon operations, 249; reorganization of, 93, 218; takeover of MACVSOG operation, 216; U.S. withdrawal and, 185–86

About the Author

Coming from an extended family of military veterans, it was no surprise to them that Bob Gillespie became a lifelong student of military affairs and history. He holds a BA and an MA in history from Clemson University, where he studied under the tutelage of Edwin Moise. He lives in the place where his heart has always been—the upstate of South Carolina—with his wife Yvonne and a cat named Bubba.

The **Naval Institute Press** is the book-publishing arm of the U.S. Naval Institute, a private, nonprofit, membership society for sea service professionals and others who share an interest in naval and maritime affairs. Established in 1873 at the U.S. Naval Academy in Annapolis, Maryland, where its offices remain today, the Naval Institute has members worldwide.

Members of the Naval Institute support the education programs of the society and receive the influential monthly magazine *Proceedings* or the colorful bimonthly magazine *Naval History* and discounts on fine nautical prints and on ship and aircraft photos. They also have access to the transcripts of the Institute's Oral History Program and get discounted admission to any of the Institute-sponsored seminars offered around the country.

The Naval Institute's book-publishing program, begun in 1898 with basic guides to naval practices, has broadened its scope to include books of more general interest. Now the Naval Institute Press publishes about seventy titles each year, ranging from how-to books on boating and navigation to battle histories, biographies, ship and aircraft guides, and novels. Institute members receive significant discounts on the more than eight hundred Press books in print.

Full-time students are eligible for special half-price membership rates. Life memberships are also available.

For a free catalog describing Naval Institute Press books currently available, and for further information about joining the U.S. Naval Institute, please write to:

Member Services
U.S. NAVAL INSTITUTE
291 Wood Road
Annapolis, MD 21402-5034
Telephone: (800) 233-8764
Fax: (410) 571-1703
Web address: www.usni.org